Let Us
Build Us
a City

Let Us
Build Us
a City

Eleven Lost Towns

Donald Harington
Photographs by the Author

A Harvest Book
A Helen and Kurt Wolff Book
Harcourt Brace & Company
San Diego New York London

Library of Congress Cataloging-in-Publication Data
Harington, Donald.
Let us build us a city.
"A Helen and Kurt Wolff book."
1. City and town life—Arkansas. 2. Cities and towns—Arkansas—History.
3. Arkansas—Social life and customs. I. Title.
F415.H37   1986   976.7   86-3136
ISBN 0-15-150100-9
ISBN 0-15-650530-4 (pbk.)

Designed by Dalia Hartman
Printed in the United States of America

First Harvest edition 1994

A B C D E

CONTENTS

And the whole earth was of one language, and of one speech.

And it came to pass, as they journeyed from the east, that they found a plain in the land of Shinar; and they dwelt there.

And they said one to another, Go to, let us make brick, and burn them throughly. And they had brick for stone, and slime had they for mortar.

And they said, Go to, let us build us a city and a tower, whose top may reach unto heaven; and let us make us a name, lest we be scattered abroad upon the face of the whole earth.

—Genesis 11:1–4

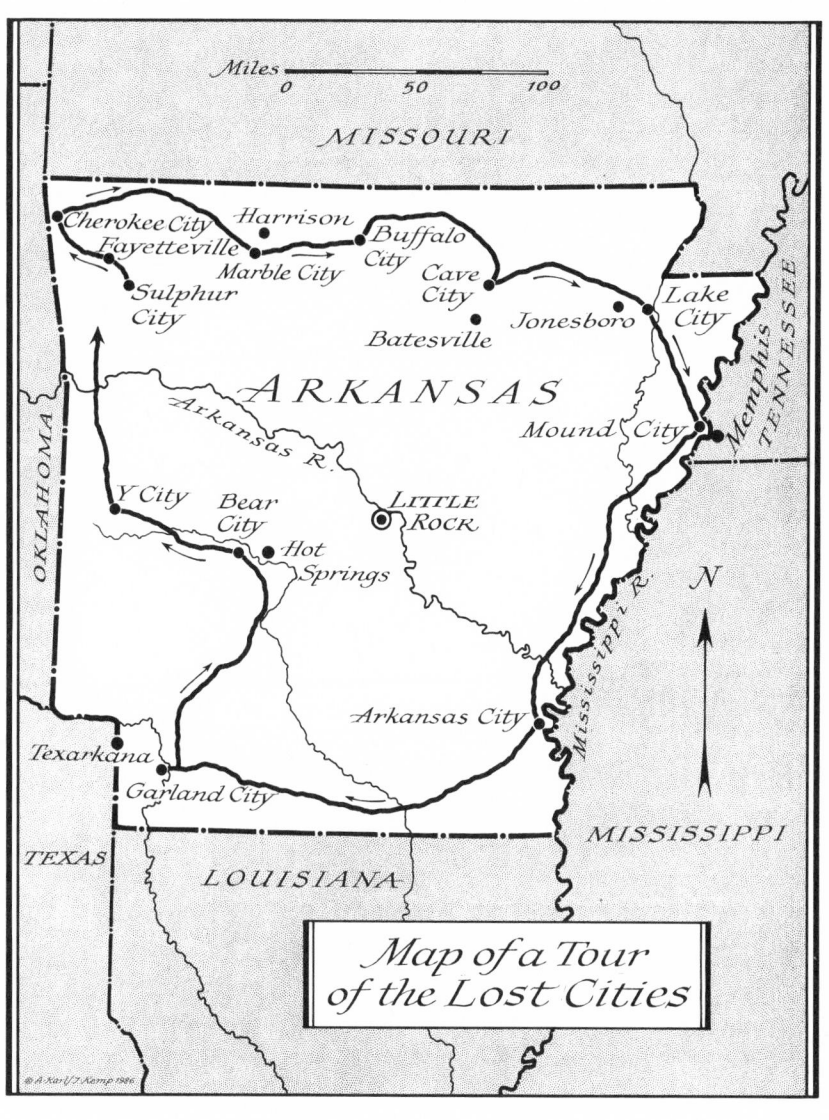

Miles
0   50   100

MISSOURI

Cherokee City
Harrison
Buffalo City
Fayetteville
Marble City
Cave City
Sulphur City
Jonesboro
Lake City
Batesville
Memphis
TENNESSEE

ARKANSAS

Arkansas R.

Mound City

OKLAHOMA

Y City
Bear City
LITTLE ROCK
Hot Springs

N

Arkansas City

Texarkana
Garland City

MISSISSIPPI

TEXAS
LOUISIANA

Map of a Tour of the Lost Cities

© A. Karl / J. Kemp 1986

Prologue: Let Us Build Us a Book. . . .

OUR STORY begins at a two-room walk-up apartment over a furniture store in far-off Brookings, South Dakota, on Main Avenue—not Street, which would be commonplace, but Avenue, with a hint of aspiration and vainglory comparable to naming an ambitious hamlet "city" out of pure hope and dreaming.

For the length of a school year a man was the sole renter of that apartment. It wasn't conveniently close to the state university where he was teaching, but he had always wanted, for a few months at least, to dwell in a Main Street walk-up, over a store, to see what such urban living was like; most of his life he had lived in the country on the edge of a village, in the green hills of New England.

The two rooms consisted of a kitchenette with a refrigerator so small it wouldn't make ice, requiring trips to the little store on the corner for ice cubes for his regular drinks, and a living-sleeping area with newspapers and magazines scattered and piled, an unmade cot, and a lone window covered with his grandmother's Ozark crazy quilt to blot out the harsh rising eastern sun. A long flight of stairs led from Main Avenue's sidewalk up to the level of his apartment; at the top of the landing lived the woman super, who never spoke to him but sometimes taped a note to his door: "Mr Harrigan—The Next Time You get Drunk— You just Don't Pisse All over the Foot of the Stairs—Or Clean it

Up Yourself." (She never got his name right, but we may as well use her error as a handy disguise.) Since the foot of the stairs was frequented at night by dancers from the Go-Go Lounge next door, transient cowboys, the town bum, the village idiot, as well as reveling college students and an occasional dog, Professor Harrigan could never be sure if it had indeed been himself who had committed the offense.

Main Avenue changed character after dark; during the daytime it was a respectable street of shops, cafés, the post office, drugstore, barbers, the dentist, a florist, and even a bookshop (used); by night it became a drag strip and cruising strip for whatever cars could roar or glide down its three-block length, turn around, and come back. From the west, farmers and teenaged farm boys swept in off the plains like drifting snow and settled in the beer joints and went to the Go-Go Lounge to watch the naked girls. From the east, students from the state university, who never seemed to have any reason to open books at night, pub-crawled the college hangouts in cellars and side streets. But after dark the professor changed character, too.

Harrigan spent the early hours of each evening assembling his lecture and color slides for the next day's class in the history of art. Then, when the noise on the street grew too oppressive, he would check to see if he had enough ice cubes and cigarettes to get him through the night, refill his tumbler of bourbon, hook up the safety latch on the door, sprawl into the lone easy chair, overstuffed and threadbare or overthreaded and stuffingbare, and begin his nightly Meditation Upon Ruins. He could have shut out the noise on the street by the simple expedient of turning off his hearing aid, but then he would not have heard the knock at the door—even though, in all the months he lived there, the knock never came. But the sounds of the imagined musical instruments playing the Theme of the Meditation Upon Ruins, along with his usual tinnitus, an auditory phenomenon of the hearing-impaired, were enough to obscure the street's constant honks and yelps and clatters.

* * *

One day, toward the end of the calendar year, when the students were all gone home for the holidays to their sunflower farms and their jerkwater towns with names like Crook City and Hub City and Junction City, and the poinsettia the department's secretary had given him as his only Christmas present had begun to droop, and the blizzards had not yet blown in off the plains, he got away for the first time since coming to Brookings, and headed his four-wheel-drive Blazer northeastward toward Sauk Centre, taking back roads and blue highways snowplowed and accessible but leisurely, wandering through tiny hamlets with names like Clara City and Big Bend City and Holmes City. Slowing down just enough to pass through, he wondered, How did they dare name such places "City"? When he got to Sauk Centre he discovered that it looked exactly like Brookings. There were even walk-ups over the Main Street furniture store, and he almost knocked at the door of one that looked like his own. Instead he drank a half-pint at the grave of Sinclair Lewis and returned the way he had come. Driving back to South Dakota, he felt a pang of conscience for not having knocked at that door, behind which someone was probably waiting for a knock.

Back in Brookings he found a substitute for the knock that never came at his door: a letter in his mailbox. Apart from his monthly bank statement and the usual offers of instant riches if he would but subscribe, there were not even bills. He had no memberships and he had escaped from Visa. He had also escaped from the few living friends of his past and from all but his wife, who did not write. He had given his Main Avenue address to only a few, including his publisher, who had not published him for years but needed to send semiannual computerized royalty statements attesting to the absence of sales, and, less than semi-annually, a forwarded fan letter. This appeared to be one of those, its return address in Minnesota, whence he had just come. One of those little sad accidents of destiny: had its gushing author written a few days earlier, he might have gone to visit him (or her) during this recent trip.

The writer had carefully typewritten the letter and thus could not be easily sex-checked; he (or she) had recently read an old

Harrigan novel about a young couple's exploration of Eastern ghost towns. "Never has a story so totally captured my interest and attention. . . ." ". . . I reacted with varied emotions—curiosity, uneasiness, fascination, sadness, and finally, awe. . . ." Before he could get a word in edgewise, the reader continued this prefatory flourish. ". . . captivating . . . such suspense and romance . . . portrayed beautifully . . ." Harrigan realized why he had been so reluctant to open this letter: he did not need such praise at a time when he had almost convinced himself that he was not worthy of it. He did not want to be enticed into any more ambitions, to give up the mere teaching of art history and turn his hand again to fiction. "STOP!" he nearly yelled, but waited until the enthusiastic fan paused for breath and asked Harrigan an abrupt question:

"Have you ever lived in Arkansas? How did you know so much about it?"

Before answering, he stole a quick glance again at the return address. His mistake: Minnesota was the name of the street, not the state, a certain Minnesota *Street* in a certain Beebe, Arkansas. He remembered, vaguely, Beebe (pronounced identically with the projectile of the airgun manufactured by Daisy of Arkansas), and he mentally changed his reply from "You'll be surprised I drove through your town just the other day" to "You'll be surprised to know I've driven through Beebe a thousand times, but never stopped. Maybe next time I'll stop."

"Yes, as a matter of fact," he said to—what's the name? the signature at the bottom, Kim, was bold and boyish; Kipling's Kim was very much a boy—"I was born in Arkansas, and grew to manhood there. I've been through Beebe many times."

The New Year's Eve party of the Brookings Singles Club went on without him. The students returned from Mound City, Lake City, Rapid City, Silver City. The blizzards blew in and his Blazer's engine block froze and cracked, making him walk to the university each day, better than coffee for sobering up. One evening he came back with both arms full of groceries, necessities, half-gallon of bourbon, bag of ice cubes, carton of cigarettes, and just enough fingers to pluck the letter out of the mailbox.

"How interesting you've traveled through Beebe so many times. It's a small and comfortable little town. The library has your other novels, and now I've read them all! Yesterday I hopped into my Z and drove off to Newton County and tried to find 'Stay More.' I didn't; I found Jasper, though, and Parthenon, and some other places. Being there gave me a sense of history, of serenity, and"—she paused, seemed to be groping for words—"and a longing for something I am not even sure of."

A longing for the author, perhaps? Every writer writes, one of them once said, in expectation of love. Suddenly the music of the Theme of the Meditation Upon Ruins began playing in his tinnitus as she went on: "It is as you wrote, in that most haunting of passages, interrupting your own narrative of the love story to interject: 'Oh, this is the story of—you know it, don't you?—a story not of ghost towns but of lost places in the heart, of vanished life in the hidden places of the soul, oh, this is not a story of actual places where actual people lived and dreamed and died but a story of lost lives and abandoned dreams and the dying of childhood, oh, a story of the ghost villages of the mind. . . .' "

He wished she had not quoted back his words to him. Of all the words he had written, those were the ones he could not bear to hear.

"You say that Stay More does not exist," she continued. "Maybe not. But while driving around Newton County in search of it, I came upon a place that is called, or used to be called, Marble City. It isn't Stay More by a long shot, although the people who once lived there must have been the same kind of folks who populate your books. I couldn't help wondering, Did they really expect it to become a *city*? It could have been one, if all their dreams had come true. But it never even came close to being a city. And now there's nothing there."

He wanted to tell her that Minnesota and, yes, South Dakota, too, are full of places that had once aspired to be cities, and had called themselves Illgen City and Canyon City and Grove City and Trail City in anticipation of becoming metropolises, but had long since abandoned the dream. For all he knew, all over America there were such "cities." Newton County, the actual place in Arkansas, was literally the back yard of his novels, the palm of his own hand, and yet he had never mentioned, or known about, Marble City.

"Yes, I'm going to find out what I can about Marble City," she continued. "As a first step, I've gone to the larger libraries in Little Rock, and the historical associations, and I've written a few letters. Should I keep you informed?"

Oh, by all means, Kim, keep me informed. South Dakota is still in the grips of winter. Daffodils will soon be blooming in Arkansas, will they not?

"For one thing, I've found that Marble City is only one of thirty or forty places in Arkansas that called themselves 'City,' and not one of them made it."

He told Kim that he had not exactly been transfixed with immobility at his end of the correspondence. In the library of South Dakota State University, he had looked at atlases and totaled up these figures: the state of Missouri had seventy-six "cities," California had twenty-nine "cities" that were ghost towns as well as fifty-six populated "cities," Pennsylvania had sixty-six populated and unpopulated "cities." Even tiny Rhode Island had one inhabited city, Garden City, and one ghost town, Rice City. Every state in the Union, including Hawaii and Alaska, had "cities."

"Let's just stick to Arkansas," Kim replied.

Let's, he agreed. He suggested that she ought to try to find a plat map, if one was ever drawn, for each city, by writing to the county clerk or circuit clerk of the county in which the city was located. A plat map, with streets named, would give some idea of how much ambition each "city" had had in the beginning. Also, maybe you could write a letter to the editors of all the county newspapers, trying to locate residents of those "cities" or former residents.

"I've bought a tape recorder," she informed him, "and tomorrow I'm taking off for the mountains to talk to some of the old-timers."

Wait for me! he nearly implored. Seriously he considered chucking his job and going to join her in the quest for those places. The semester had three more months to run. If he simply quit, he would never find academic employment elsewhere again. But, for that matter, since his contract was only for one year, he might never get a college teaching job after this year anyway. Even apart from the excruciating homesickness that he often felt for Arkansas, now he was feeling a kind of future-sickness for this kindred spirit, seeker of lost places in the heart and in the landscape.

Only a sequence of fortuities kept him from rushing to join Kim at once. He had his Blazer towed into the shop and its cracked engine removed and replaced. But the replacement turned out to be defective. The people at the shop searched for two more weeks, and again a replacement was found that turned out, maddeningly, to be defective. He had no way of getting himself and his modest personal effects down the eight hundred miles of interstate highway to Arkansas. Or maybe he was simply a coward. If he really had had the nerve to quit his job, he could have taken a bus, or bought a cheap secondhand car.

In the weeks ahead, a postcard or a longer note would come from Kim, occasionally written on the stationery of some motel in some out-of-the-way Arkansas town.

On her way back to Marble City, Kim had decided to detour through a place called Sulphur City, just to look around, but had stopped to talk to a sweet old couple who lived in a little white cottage beside the road there, and that interview had led her to talk to the local pastor, and to some other people, and before she knew it . . .

"Be sure," he wrote to her, "to ask them who was the most colorful or interesting individual who ever lived, or who still lives, in the town. Also find out if the city was founded as a resort, trading center, mining town, or what."

"Our book will have to have lots of hermits. And suicides. The village idiot. The town bully. The town drunk."

"*Our book?*" he asked her.

"Our book," she answered. "Well, I can just help find the raw material, and do the interviews, because you can't hear, but you will have to do the writing and handle the illustrations."

"Be sure," he suggested, "to ask each person, 'Did you have any hopes or dreams that never came true?' "

He promised her that when the semester was over, the very day it ended and the grades had been handed in to the dean, he would come and join her. She did not know whether to believe him or not. In the weeks ahead, she would sometimes encounter a person in some "city," a village idiot or a town drunk, and wonder if it was Harrigan in disguise, playing a joke, planning to surprise her. Once she met an idiot who was also drunk and was so convinced it was Harrigan that she addressed him as such, to his genuine bafflement. Then she gave up, and began to wait patiently for the day when he might actually come. It was something to look forward to, for her, for him, both of them who, like these lost cities, had abandoned all ambition.

Sulphur City,
Arkansas

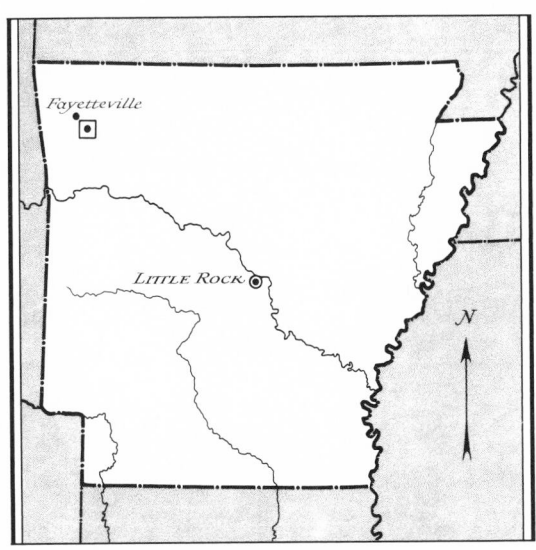

Fayetteville

LITTLE ROCK

N

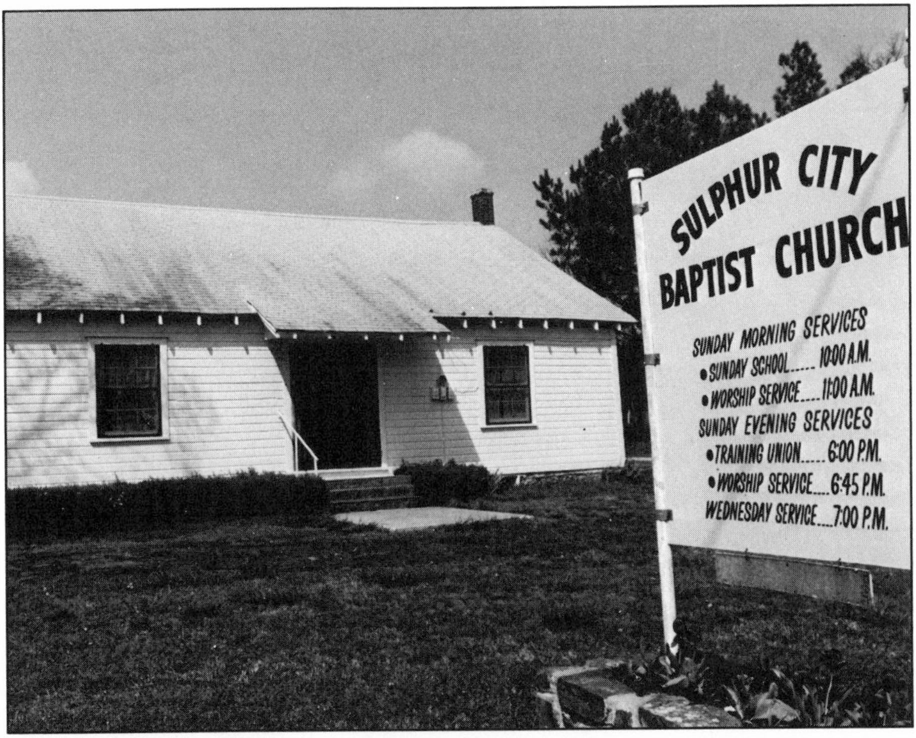
SULPHUR CITY
BAPTIST CHURCH
SUNDAY MORNING SERVICES
• SUNDAY SCHOOL...... 10:00 A.M.
• WORSHIP SERVICE..... 11:00 A.M.
SUNDAY EVENING SERVICES
• TRAINING UNION...... 6:00 P.M.
• WORSHIP SERVICE.... 6:45 P.M.
WEDNESDAY SERVICE.... 7:00 P.M.

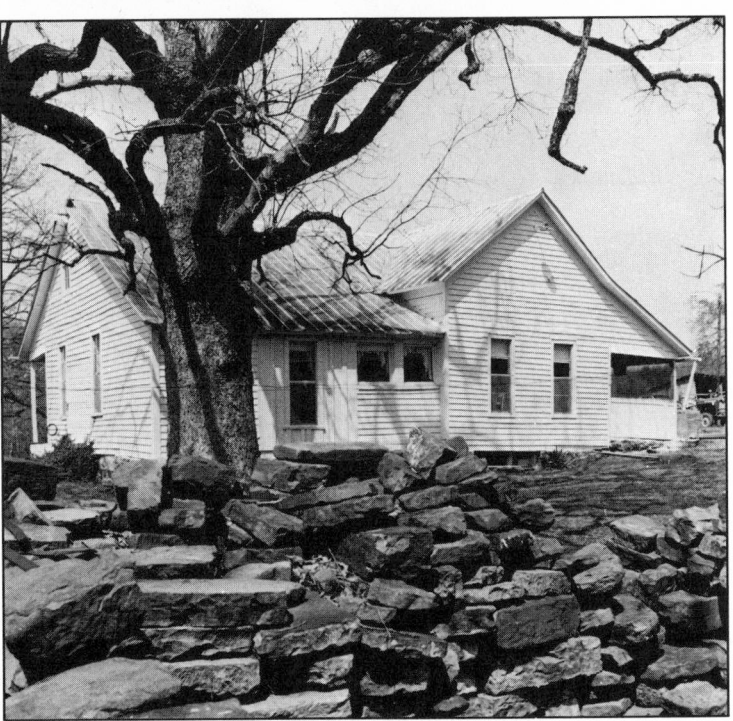

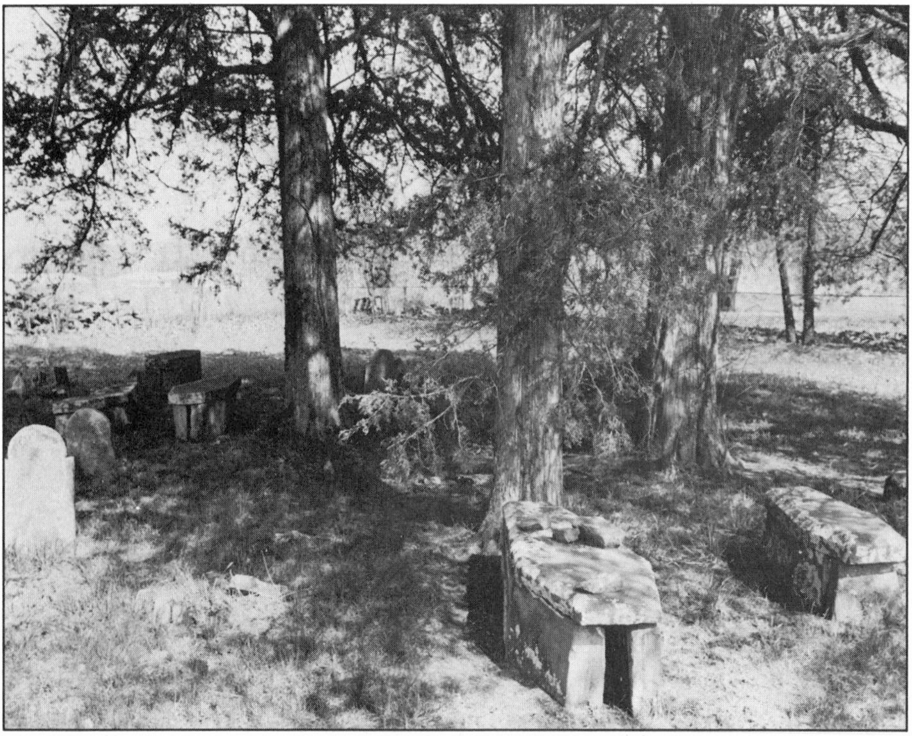

IN
MEMORY OF
NARCISUS MAN
KINS WIFE
PETER MANKINS
DAUGHTER OF
DIED

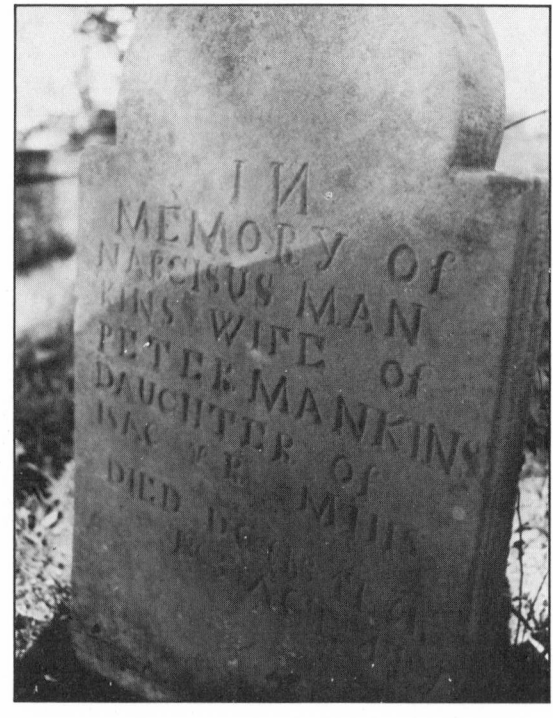

Mankind Dies at Sulphur City
   —typographical error in newspaper obituary, 1899

IT IS NOT ON THE ROAD to anywhere. The closest it comes, shy and lonely, is two miles to the highway, a little highway, State 16, used by farmers mostly, and seasonally by Razorback fans and students who call it the "Pig Trail" and use it to avoid the traffic from Fayetteville to Little Rock and back but get stuck behind farmers' pickups moving sanely around the treacherous curves. Fans and students never detour to Sulphur City.

The landscape comes as a sudden delight, something Constable would have painted, or perhaps Inness, gentle pastoral downs, undulant as a massage. These are Ozark hills, but not the crewcut tables found elsewhere around, no flatwoods, as the natives call the plateaued vistas. "New Prospect" was the first name of the place (almost all of these cities have had more than one name) and that is what it was, and remains: a river valley rimmed by hills, no two alike; a new view, a new chance for success, a new present to the eye.

New Prospect was settled in 1833 by a youth named Peter Mankins, a name whose metaphorical connotations are to prove inestimable: little man, mankind, everyman, or a Möbius strip of "kinsman." As in the medieval moralities, Everymankins progresses from sin to a kind of salvation of his own, not on the scale of John Bunyan but, rather, that of Paul Bunyan: Peter Mankins comes closest to being the only authentic folk hero that Arkansas ever had, and yet almost no one has ever heard of him.

He left behind him Paintsville, Kentucky, itself a frontier town with no aspirations to become a city, since "-ville" always implies a perpetual village (although Louisville became the biggest city in Kentucky, and Fayetteville, Arkansas, is at least a city of the second class). Paintsville was a pleasant enough place, unpainted, carved out of the dark forests and cane thickets in the mountains of eastern Kentucky around the Big Sandy River, which surges into the Ohio and thence westward, always westward. Although the Indians and the first white settlers in Dan Boone's wake had depleted the elk and driven the buffalo westward, Paintsville was still hinterland, but not virgin enough for Peter Mankins, who had the moving-on itch that infects all young folk: the pack-up, get-out, keep-going, don't-look-back blues, the relocation yearning, exact opposite of homesickness: craving passage, deliverance, transmigration. "Wanderlust" is such an arty and effete word. So many of us leave our fathers behind.

Paintsville got its name from the first white settlers' discovery, not too long before, that the Indians or somebody had stripped the bark off large trees and painted the smooth undertrunks with representations of birds, elk, and buffalo, in red colors and black. This artwork, along with captions in indecipherable hieroglyphs, was also found all over the sandstone slabs of the creeksides and any other smooth surface: paint everywhere, not splashed but carefully brushed, as if the Indian or somebody in his departure before moving had to graffitize the landscape with a valedictory to old happy hunting grounds. As a child Peter Mankins asked his father about these paint jobs, which, in all modesty, he thought he could outdecorate, if only there were a buffalo standing still long enough to model. There were no buffalo any more. His father (hereinafter called "Old Pete" or "Mankins the Elder" or some such distinguisher) asked him, "Son, is what's drawn from memory better'n what's drawn from 'magination?" Mankins the Younger thought about this often, and wondered if he could learn to answer it.

Peter Mankins left Paintsville, his father making bereft faces while his mother and three brothers and five sisters cried and cried, to find a new country, a new prospect in which to locate a buffalo or two, which is what he told his weeping sisters and his sniveling brothers, who assumed, wrongly, that they would never see him again. Nowadays when we leave home we do it subtly by going off to college or going off to the big city to work and never coming back, or coming back only to visit when it is demanded or begged, but in those days a man of twenty did not have a big city to go off to, let alone a college, and he simply jumped on the next boat heading down the Ohio and disappeared forever and didn't even have to write home, most of the time, because he was illiterate. Mankins the Elder watched his namesake son hopping on the raft and thought he was as good as dead already because Mankins the Younger would never write the old man and tell him how much he missed him and how obliged he felt for his upbringing.

How do founders find the places they are looking for? New Prospect, later called Mankins, later still called Sulphur City, straddles a pretty stream of water, which is the Middle Fork of the White River in Arkansas but was then known as Buffalo Fork, and maybe the name alone attracted Peter Mankins, although he was already well settled or well squatted and into the third month of clearing his 160-acre pre-emption of good alluvial bottom land before he actually saw a buffalo or two come moseying down the banks of Buffalo Fork. In squatting on bottom land, he could not have known that year after year the river would flood his fields and ruin his crops or/and deposit more rich silt, like the Nile; or perhaps he did remember a previous incarnation alongside the Nile. When his bottom was all cleared and planted or grazed, Peter Mankins hiked up to the heights east of it and looked down on it, not with fear of the floods to come, but with pride and probably with a vision of a city rising there, and here on the heights, safe from any flood. Try as he would, he could not avoid imagining that city.

Today, the seeker who comes for the first time upon Sulphur City expecting to find even the ghost of a town will be utterly dashed. People live roundabouts, yes, maybe sixty of them, but there is not one business, no store selling gas or candy or cigarettes, no store selling anything, no sign of anything (the last post office closed thirty years ago) except a white sign in front of a forties-built white house that somehow looks less like a home than what the sign claims it is: "Sulphur City Baptist Church." But the Reverend J. B. Kyger, age fifty, pastor for seven years, does not even know that once a fledgling city tried to take off from here. "City?" he says. "Why, that's just the name of the church. That's what folks around here call the church, its name, like the sign says, 'Sulphur City Baptist Church.' That's just the church, there's not any city." Reverend Kyger knows nothing of the history of the place. He has never heard of Peter Mankins. But Peter Mankins never lived his life hoping to be remembered by J. B. Kyger, or even by Kyger's God, although late in life Mankins professed to be a Baptist himself, because late in life, when most things are done, there isn't much left to be done except profess. Peter Mankins, late in life, also sat down, whereas most of his life he had remained standing, or running, except for that once when he climbed the heights east of New Prospect to sit and rest from clearing bottom land and to speculate about what the neighborhood would look like if it ever became a city. This effort for Peter Mankins must have been baroque and whimsical, for he had never seen a city.

Although ringed by hills, his land was as flat as he could find it. No doubt this was deliberate: his graduation from mountaineer to valleyer. The farm back in eastern Kentucky had been steep, not a flat patch in it, not even one approaching flat, some approaching vertical. It has been described after a recent visit by one of the Mankins descendants, Louisa L. Personkins (a genealogist who, despite her pride in her family name, had it legally changed in 1972 at the height of the women's movement), as "so hard to reach that nobody could go up the mountain at the same time that anybody was trying to come down the mountain. Some guy in his pickup had to pull over smack against the side of the mountain to let us go by."

Why did the mountaineers pick mountains? For many reasons. Mountain land is infertile and therefore cheap at half the price. Being so steep, it takes twice as much exercise, for man and beast, to cultivate, and this builds bodies and character. It offers good views but, paradoxically, limited views, only as far as the next range. The air is said to be superior, and mountain spring water has no equal in the bottoms. There is more variety in the topography, and this range of highs and lows, peaks and depths, ins and outs, becomes a metaphorscape for achievement and disappointment. Flatlands have little mystery, less visual stimulation, and less challenge.

But mountains restrict. They enclose and contain and limit, and, though lifting a man high, leave him there, stranded, aloof. He wants a new prospect and he goes looking for one, one that combines the elbow room of the valley meadows with the hugs of the embosoming hills. Keeping the mountains at arm's length, always handy, there to see, there to climb, but not there to plant, any more. Peter Mankins fashioned a bull-tongue plow from local oak and an heirloom steel point, drove it behind a yoke of oxen, and converted his Buffalo Fork river bottom into the finest pasture in Arkansas, helped by the sulphur branch that meandered through it. He did not know of the sulphur; the water tasted "off," but he had no inkling of what it did for the grass and the cows and the people.

What does sulphur do? Everette William "Buster" Price, a farmer of seventy-five who owns the Mankins spread today, isn't sure himself what sulphur does. Like most people, he hasn't thought about it too much. Born in Sulphur City and having lived all his life there, he used to take a drink from the sulphur spring now and again, especially when he felt ill. Today the spring is virtually dried up. Margaret, Buster's lovely wife two years his senior, says, "I never took a drink of it in my life, never did, it smelled so bad." Reverend Kyger admits he has tasted it: "It just tastes like bad water with a real salty taste to it."

Buster admits it smells like rotten eggs. "But it really has a better taste to it than it smells," he declares. "If I really got real thirsty, it'd satisfy my thirst when other water wouldn't do it." Cows' thirst, too? "Why, cattle used to come to this sulphur branch for miles and miles. There was somethin about it that did 'em good and they knew it."

There is something about Sulphur City that does one good,

and one knows it. Buster and Margaret have heard about Peter
Mankins; though they are leading members in Reverend Kyger's
church, they haven't told their minister anything about Peter
Mankins. They live in a very pleasant old white cottage at one
end of "Main Street" in Sulphur City, not far from the Baptist
church, not far from the sulphur spring, a little farther from the
old general store, which Buster's father operated from 1907 to
1970, when the last business left town—or stayed there but closed
and became a rental dwelling, paneled and carpeted. A little
farther down the road is the stone foundation of the two-story
schoolhouse where both Buster and Margaret were once school-
teachers, until the school closed, too, and was consolidated with
that of Elkins, a larger town three miles east (and, like Atkins,
Gaskins, Watkins, and Perkins, one of several "-kins" towns of
Arkansas, as Mankins once was). Until it fell, Buster used the
schoolhouse to store hay for his cattle.

In the Prices' back yard are neatly stacked the hewn stones
that once made up the tall chimney of Peter Mankins's two-story
log mansion. The stones are just waiting there until Buster can
use them to build a patio. What would Peter Mankins have thought,
laboriously dragging those rocks from the creek bed on a "stone-
boat," or sled, if he had known they would one day be used to
pave a patio? Would his wife, who did the harder work of trimming the stones into even rectangular blocks, have minded? Her
name was Narcissa (variously misspelled Narcissus, Narsissia,
Narcissis, or, on her tombstone, Narcisus) and she would bear
Peter ten children, as well as do the hard work, like trimming
chimney stones.

Where did he find his daffodil, Narcissa? We know so very
little of the origins, let alone the appearance and demeanor, of
the wives of all our frontiersmen, founding fathers, or settlers.
Her tombstone says that she was the daughter of "Isac ʋ R Mills,"
who was, we gather, an Indianian, but did Peter find her in
Indiana or was she waiting for him in Arkansas? If the former,
did he bring her with him (unlikely)? If the latter, how did he
meet her, woo her, and wed her? We will never know. We can
only visualize her, one day, sitting in the broad meadow anent

Buffalo Fork, hacking away at slabs of sandstone to square them off into building blocks for a chimney. Although Buster Price could not leave that chimney standing alone in the meadow and had to take it down, there are enough similar chimneys still standing all over the Ozarks to give an idea of its texture, its height, and its shaftiness. Narcissa cooked on the hearth of that chimney's fireplace and warmed ten babies beside it, and at the age of forty-seven, at the height of the Civil War, sat alone beside it, ill, while her husband was off whacking the bushes for Yankees, and died. Her grave in the old Baptist cemetery at Sulphur City is clearly marked, which is more than can be said for her husband's.

Whereas Narcissa had ten babies, one each year for a decade, Margaret Price had only two, both girls. Peter and Narcissa and everybody else in the nineteenth century had so many babies not because methods of birth control were unknown but because a couple had to have so many to guarantee that a few would survive. Even in the twentieth century, only one of Buster and Margaret's daughters survived. Narcissa Mankins's best friend, Sara Long, is buried in the old Baptist cemetery beneath one of several curious coffin-shaped cenotaphs (strugglingly described by other writers as "mummy-type tomb," "box-grave cover," "sarcopha-gus-like crypt": an irregularly hexagonal slab of sandstone making the capstone of a dolmen, an empty chamber, symbolizing the long-rotted pine coffin in the earth beneath it; "cenotaph" comes from the Greek meaning "empty," an empty tomb, hence a monument erected in honor of a dead person buried elsewhere, the elsewhere being in this case the earth directly below it; there are some of these coffin-shaped cenotaphs in other cemeteries in the valley of the Middle Fork, and the name of the stonecarver, Nathan Tharp, is known, although Tharp himself did not get a coffin-shaped cenotaph when he died). Sara Long's five children, who died before her or, in the case of the last one, *with* her, are buried in smaller coffin-shaped cenotaphs of diminishing size on either side of hers, a tragic sight in this or any cemetery, reflecting the high child-mortality rates of a time when diseases as simple as worms, rickets, or mumps, or as complicated as typhoid fever, whooping cough, or diphtheria, could be expected to snuff out a lot of good kids.

We are all descendants of Peter Mankins. But he was a descendant of Old Peter Mankins himself. Question: what is better than a Peter Mankins? Answer: *two* Peter Mankinses. Even with newfound Narcissa to pleasure him in his new days and novel nights in New Prospect, he missed his father. Peter Mankins the Elder was already a legend in his own time, in all the places he had lived—Maryland, North Carolina, Kentucky, Illinois, a travelogue of America's westward movement. Born near Annapolis the year of the Boston Massacre, 1770, the same year frontiersman Mike Fink was born, he drew from memory rather than imagination to tell his son about standing, at the age of eleven, on the parade route of Washington's march to Yorktown to defeat Cornwallis, and about remembering, not the military pomp of the spectacle but his own question, simple but puzzling: Why do women wave their handkerchiefs? To dry them when they are soaked with tears? To flag their surrender to the brave warriors? Or to stir a little air to speed them on? Such basic but inconsequential questions would occupy his thoughts all of his life. He told, too, of working as an apprentice baker at Mount Vernon; he never saw Washington, but he often wondered if the bread he kneaded helped sustain the general.

Peter Mankins the Elder was himself the son of a John Mankins and a Delaware Indian maiden named Masa, called Macy. The first of the Elder's three marriages, in North Carolina, was to a young widow, Rachel, with three children, destined to have nine more, among them Peter the Younger. In Kentucky he planted all of his steep acreage in corn, made bourbon whiskey from it, and sold all that he could not drink. There is a well-documented legend that the senior Mankins once fought and whipped Mike Fink, the fighting king of the keelboatmen. Mike Fink actually did engage in so many brawls—gouging out eyeballs, tearing off ears, and biting off noses while living a lifetime free from mutilation himself—that any man who would challenge him and not only survive unscathed but actually reduce Fink to

begging for mercy was guaranteed instant and perpetual noto-
riety. There were a number of such men, but Peter Mankins the
Elder was one, and he never let his son forget it.

Surely among the many reasons young Peter ran away to
Arkansas was the hope of escaping his father's shadow and cast-
ing his own. But after a time, the son wished his father and his
mother and sisters and brothers and half-brothers all lived in
Arkansas, too, instead of Kentucky. There was plenty of room
for them on his 160 acres, and he decided to send for them. How
does a frontiersman send for the kinfolks he left behind? In the
Johnson County, Kentucky, Historical Museum is a letter dated
October 13, 1833: "Dear Pappy & All. Well, here I be, safe in
the Territory, and aint dropped off the far side of the airth yit.
I aint writ you before count of no news. Have been monstrous
busy clearin land & haulin rock & shootin elk & buffalo & bar &
sech. Methodists are sceerce. It is fair land, O, fair like you never
seed. You would be alive here. It is country like you aint never
hearn tell of. Please come, all, soon. I will look for you. Well my
paper has gin out. Your son, His ✕ Mark." There is no proof
that this letter was addressed to Peter Mankins, Sr., or written
by Peter Mankins, Jr. But, whatever, a short time later the Elder
Mankins sold his distillery and removed his family down the Ohio
and the Mississippi and up the Arkansas in the wake of his son.
To the confusion of neighbors and historians, the future Sulphur
City would have *two* Peter Mankinses in its population.

But both would find themselves nonplussed not so much by
the confusion of names as by the indelicacy of the given name
itself. Throughout the Ozarks, "Peter" is a common byword for
the male "family organ" and therefore indecent, unmentionable
in mixed company. Respectable parents never name a boy "Peter,"
and they even avoid "Richard" because "Dick" is pretty bad, too.
In the old days, "Peter" simply would not do, at all. Once a Baptist
circuit rider visited New Prospect and preached before a large
gathering, including all the Mankinses, on the subject of the
Apostle Peter's denial of Christ, at the conclusion of which he
demanded grandiloquently and rhetorically, "How many *Peters*
are they here?" Nobody laughed or tittered; the congregation

was simply shocked into silence. When the preacher realized what he had said, he flushed scarlet and withdrew.

Everybody called the elder Mankins "Ole Pete" and his son "Young Pete." The latter was sixty-eight years old before they stopped calling him "Young Pete," following the death of his father, who was then 111 years old. Then the elderly son was called "Ole Pete" for the rest of his life, another eighteen years.

One of Young Pete Mankins's first paid labors after getting settled in the bright new land of Arkansas, perhaps even before finding and wedding and bedding Narcissa, was to ride his horse a dozen miles each day into the little county seat village, Fayetteville, and lay it out, or help lay it out. He was only the chain carrier in the survey crew; his task was to stretch the chain out from the surveyor's leveled telescope, attach the chain to the rod, or pole, and plant the pole. The historical record says only that "A. Mankins bore the chain" when Fayetteville was surveyed into lots in 1835. Since there was no Archibald Mankins or even Albert Mankins, we can only assume that there was *a* Mankins, and that was Pete. His work was confined to laying out the twenty-four blocks of "downtown" Fayetteville around the square, which is still there. These twenty-four blocks of Fayetteville are all irregular rectangles, suggesting that Mankins and the rest of the crew may have been drunk, but twenty-four became a magic number for Peter Mankins: a double dozen divisible by three or six; a half-century later he would use the same number in laying out the blocks of Sulphur City, all perfectly even, all stone sober, each divisible into twelve lots separated six to a side by an alley. This is a perfect, orderly mathematical grid: man's—or Mankins's—imposition of logic, harmony, and convenience upon nature. Almost all of the thousand cities of the American West are grids: right-angled intersections, a plexure of streets, monotonous in their network but handy and rational, *manlike*; no animal, not even the busy ant (or the octagonalizing bee), duplicates it in making a place out of places.

"Stick!" the surveyor hollers, commands. The rodman or

chain carrier, Peter Mankins, holds the pole with both hands and jabs it down into the earth and replies, "Stuck!" Surveying, like garbage collecting, is a conspicuous public profession: all over the landscape or all along the road from time to time, we see the man with the telescope or transit mounted on a tripod, peering through his instrument and waving his arms overhead to signal the other man holding the pole way off out yonder, who answers, loudly, "STUCK!" Every time he yelled it, Peter Mankins couldn't help thinking of a bawdy ejaculation that rhymes with "stuck," and each time he yelled it and thought of such, he daydreamed of women or perhaps already Narcissa in particular, and he thought of the planting of seeds in the earth and the planting of cities and the rising of cities and perhaps his mind already entertained visions of the Fayetteville Hilton, a modest skyscraper where a lot of that sort of planting and sticking or stucking still goes on.

Peter Mankins the Younger became the first American cowboy. Although he never wore chaps or a ten-gallon hat, didn't carry a lasso or know how to rope, and his footwear bore no resemblance to cowboy boots, he fits, by any definition, the idea of the archetypal working hero of the American West. It wasn't really west, except that in those days Sulphur City was about as far west as you could go without getting scalped. There were scarcely any fences; barbed wire hadn't been invented; it wasn't necessary for him to brand his cattle, because he knew them by sight; and his chief cowboy-function wasn't to round up the cattle and drive them into the ranch but, rather, to drive them away from the ranch once they became addicted to sulphur water. If one word were required as a job placement category for everything that Peter Mankins ever did, it would be "drover." Years before he became a far-reaching drover of cattle and thus the first cowboy (although he never heard the word until late in life, when he watched his first Wild West Show), he was a far-reaching drover of swine and thus the first hogboy. He drove huge herds of hogs on the hoof as far north as Chicago and as far south as New Orleans. There is nothing romantic about a hogboy. For one thing, hogs cannot move nearly as fast for sustained distances as cows can. Hogs *can* stampede, but, compared with a stampede of cattle, a hog stampede is about as dramatic as a rush of shoppers getting into a department store at opening time on sale day. Hogs are far more intelligent than cattle and like to take their time and enjoy the scenery, and they are in no hurry to go all the way from Sulphur City to Chicago on foot. We do not visualize Peter Mankins attempting to hurry them.

The trail over the mountains from New Prospect to the Arkansas River landing at Ozark, where the hogs would embark on large rafts for New Orleans, followed almost exactly the route of what would become the crooked highway that today is called the "Pig Trail" not in memorial to Mankins's swine but because the road is used, as previously mentioned, as a convenient shortcut for fans of the Razorback football team to go to and from games at Fayetteville or games at Little Rock. The Razorback is of course purely a creature of legend and tall tale, although Peter Mankins did not believe that, because all of the hogs driven to New Orleans were mixed-breed razorbacks of the unmistakable spiny-bristled backbones that give the animal its name.

Surely in his drovings Peter Mankins had helpers other than his trusty horse and his trusty dogs, but he may not have needed human helpers, because he was very strong. His strength should be part of his legend. In his prime he measured six feet four inches, and cleared 275 pounds on the scales! In those days there were no standards such as "bench press," "snatch," or "clean and jerk" for weightlifting, but the main test of physical prowess was to stand in a bushel basket with the feet close together (no flexing of the knees) and to reach forward and try to lift a hundred-pound sack of flour or a hundred-pound pig with arm strength alone. Peter Mankins could lift and shoulder a two-hundred-pound pig with eyewitnesses and a three-hundred-pound hog without eyewitnesses.

Without eyewitnesses Peter Mankins killed a panther by forcing its jaws open and breaking its neck. With eyewitnesses he killed a bear with a bear hug.

He was an expert marksman with musket, rifle, or knife, but

his favorite weapon, because it was most handy, was the rock, especially for deer. Forcing open the jaws of a deer, or giving a deer a bear hug, is not quite seemly or manly, but from a distance of twenty paces or more, with eyewitnesses, Peter Mankins could throw a rock and hit a buck deer, in the side if not the head, stunning if not killing it. There was never any lack of game on the Mankins table, although all of them preferred pork.

He was never, like Roy Rogers, called "King of the Cowboys," but at the stations en route to New Orleans where hog drovers congregated, the early equivalent of today's truck stops, he became the equivalent of what his fellow drovers might have called "King of the Hogboys." One eyewitnessed story of the early 1840s from a Louisiana drover stop was that, in his haste to get his rig of hogs parked for the night and fed, he carried to them in one load on his back fourteen bushels of corn wrapped in a bed tick, and then, throwing aside the cloth after feeding them, ran and jumped over a five-foot gate. "What's the hurry, Pete?" he was asked as he settled onto his usual stool at Mrs. Turner's Tavern. He replied that he had heard there was only one piece left of Mrs. Turner's persimmon pie.

The most eyewitnessed event demonstrating his strength occurred in the autumn of 1845 at Marshall's Prairie, as Elkins was known then, just over the mountain east of New Prospect. One Stephen Enyart, considering himself the strongest man in Arkansas, challenged Mankins on his own turf, as it were. Captain Enyart would later organize and command a company of Arkansas volunteers in the Mexican War; he had worn the belt of the greatest wrestler in Arkansas for several years and could stand in a bushel basket and reach out and lift Antaeus off the earth. On a bitterly cold day, in a snowfall that did not deter hundreds of paid and wagering spectators, Enyart met Mankins in the field of Marshall's Prairie. They stripped down, not to their shorts, which were not known in those days, but to their long drawers, which were, and they wrestled and scuffled for three hours. For three solid hours, they grappled and tussled, boxing a little but mostly mauling the grass with each other, cracking necks, getting hitches and holds and hanks, body-slamming and backfalling, trading throttles and grunts, bending bones, outgrowling, and rubbing bruises upon each other. The three judges declared it even-Stephen, but since Enyart was Stephen, he took the stakes. He had abundant time to count his money, however: for three days afterward he couldn't leave his bed, whereas Mankins went about his work as usual and, consulting his calendar, discovered he was scheduled to meet a challenge to run a sixty-yard foot race the next morning with William Fine, champion sprinter. This time Mankins won, although there were hardly any spectators, because nobody watches track meets; the Razorback track team, walking off with the National Championship, is met at the Fayetteville airport by no bands and no fans crying "Wooo-pig, sooie!"

All this activity did not distract Peter Mankins from observing that the pace of life quickens steadily as civilization progresses, and that it behooved him to give up hog droving and concentrate on cattle droving. But he did not realize that in order to become a successful cowboy he would have to establish an adversary relationship with the Indians. The cowboy-and-Indian difference of opinion was destined to become a central issue in American history and westering imperialism, as well as an essential fund for legends, dime novels, campfire songs, and grade-C Hollywood motion pictures. A cowboy without an Indian was like salt without pepper, or oil without vinegar. Peter Mankins had nothing personal against Indians. He had never seen the Kentucky Indians during his boyhood but had admired their paintings. The Indians he had seen in Arkansas were mostly Cherokee and just as civilized as anybody. He had never seen a savage or hostile Indian. But he had seen hungry Indians, and was destined to see many more of them, and there is something about hunger that puts a person on his very worst behavior.

The Great California Gold Rush of 1849 sometimes put Peter Mankins on his worst behavior. He should have stuck to cows, but the get-rich-quick fever was too much for him. A group of "vigorous, enterprising and substantial citizens" who called them-

selves the Fayetteville Argonauts decided that no expedition could
succeed without Peter, and they appointed him second lieutenant, to serve as guide far in advance of the company on its long
crossing of the plains. For two thousand miles the wagon train
crept westward, and the Mankins legends grew right and left.
There was, for instance, the story of his catching buffalo by the
tail, throwing them off their feet, and dispatching them with his
Bowie knife. The Cherokee were recruited to go along on the
expedition, because, according to the advance advertisements,
they "are on the most friendly terms with all the Indian tribes of
the prairie; consequently there will be no danger of attacks from
our red brethren." But many of our red brethren were not in a
brotherly mood.

The eighty Argonauts had provisioned themselves with 175
pounds of bacon per person, and it required a great prairie
schooner drawn by four yoke of oxen to haul such a load of salted
side meat. Oxen are not well suited for movement across dry,
sandy desert, or for steep mountains, as the Argonauts discovered, and they decided they could not transport so much bacon
to California.

Jettisoning it was easy. A band of eight hundred hungry
Plains Indians had been following the expedition, begging for
table scraps. Now they could get the trimmings of the bacon,
which were mostly rank and salty. Peter Mankins, put in charge
of distributing the bacon trimmings, came face to face with mass
ravenous hunger for the first time—and, because the meat was
so salty, mass unquenchable thirst. The Indians ate all they could
hold and drank whatever water they could find, and Peter watched
two hundred of them die from the effects of this gorging. It
seemed to convince him that life is cheap, especially for an Indian.
He wished the six hundred survivors would quit following the
Argonauts, but the Indians, like dogs blessed with benefaction
from new masters, attached themselves more firmly to the wagon
train, and nothing would get rid of them.

The Argonauts came to a river that required them to build
rafts for crossing. Since the Indians had nothing with which to

build rafts and could only swim, hundreds more might have drowned trying to follow the wagon train; as a more charitable but rude alternative, Peter Mankins decided to scare them off. He discovered in the ruins of an old fort a still-workable cannon, which he loaded with a charge of a quarter of gunpowder tamped full to the muzzle with dirt and gravel. According to an eyewitness, Mankins trained the cannon "on the dusty tents of the dusky hangers-on, and touched off this ludicrous load. The old thing reared up like a snake-bitten cayuse and belched forth what looked like an avalanche over the camp to the wild consternation of the Indians." And, no doubt, to the great laughter of everybody else, including Mankins himself, no miser with a guffaw. But after recovering from their fright and stilling the cries of their little ones, the Indians were merely saddened to discover that the man who had touched off the cannon was the same big man who had given them all the bacon trimmings. Their hunger made them follow the train, like seagulls following a ship, but they kept Peter Mankins under surveillance and never trusted him.

At an oasis, where, according to Indian custom, the braves slaked their thirst before allowing their women and children any water, Mankins was so irritated by the cries of the children that he rashly decided to change Indian custom then and there; he strode to the center of the crowd brandishing his Bowie knife and threatened to hack up any brave who drank another drop before letting the children have their fill. One brave came at him with a tomahawk; he dodged and with one swing of his Bowie knife decapitated the Indian. Years later the same knife was used by child labor for cutting sorghum cane in Sulphur City, and many a boy remembered pretending the cane tops were Indians' heads as he cut them down. These boys grew up and had children who used wooden play-knives when playing cowboys-and-Indians, a game in which the Indian always lost.

The Indians always lost to Peter Mankins. Having killed one of them with his Bowie knife, he decided it would be just as easy to kill more of them. When the Indians realized that they would get no more handouts from the Fayetteville Argonauts, they began stealing and eating the remaining oxen. Mankins and the Argonauts shot or knifed these thieves, and the survivors decided to wait for the next passing wagon train and hope for better luck or charity.

Once arrived in California, Mankins saw his first city, which was called Sacramento City, a crowded, thoroughly platted city of ten thousand, which would retain "City" in its name long after it became the capital of California. From there, he and his fellow Fayettevillians fanned out into the gold fields, where they discovered that each man had a claim of only fifteen feet to dig in and it was every man for himself. There is nothing romantic about gold mining: the work is grueling and often futile.

Back home in New Prospect, Peter's family and friends could only wonder what he was doing and what luck he was having. One of Peter's friends, Hiram Davis, writing home to his wife at Fayetteville, reported that all of the Argonauts had been very sick and that Mankins was near death, and described further problems with the Indians, who were killing small parties of the Argonauts: "The large influx of whites has driven the Indians to the verge of perpetual snow where they can neither get game of any kind, nor can they with safety approach the rivers to fish, so they are quite in a starving condition and consequently desperate." Davis described the rugged country, the deep snows, the floods of the melting snows, and the grueling work, then grew eloquent: "This whole country is swarming with human beings. Every ravine and mountain is crowded and wherever level ground enough can be found it's certain to be covered with tents. And I learn there are still more coming from all points of the Union. In the name of heaven let no person that you can influence even come to this wretched country."

Some of the best Arkansawyers would come home poorer than they had left. One leading Fayettevillian, Isaac Murphy, a future governor of Arkansas, came home flat broke. According to Buster and Margaret Price, California is where most of the erstwhile residents of Sulphur City now live. Indeed, more of the former citizens of the lost cities of Arkansas live in California than in all other locations put together.

After recovering from the near death mentioned above, Peter Mankins, perhaps through dint of more elbow grease than any of the other Argonauts used, came home from California with, according to the best accounts, $3,750. The figure varies with the reporter. His descendant and chronicler, Louisa Personkins, insists that it was over $6,000; other stories put it at $4,500; whatever, it was more than most, better than average. He could afford to take the long but easy way home, a two-month sea voyage down to Panama and a crossing of the Isthmus, followed by another voyage across the Gulf to his old familiar stomping grounds at New Orleans; from there he went by steamboat to Ozark and thence home, where in a timeworn gesture he up-ended a bag and dumped all of his gold in a cascade of yellow by the glittering yellow light on the kitchen table, for everyone to see. Everyone except his mother, Rachel, who had died.

"During the nights, yellow was the prevailing color in my dreams," Peter told Narcissa, and he continued to dream yellow in other forms for the rest of his life, especially in autumns, when the trails of the Middle Fork would be lined with yellow weed flowers—black-eyed Susans, tickseeds and sneezeweed—and then again in the spring.

In the springtime yellow is the first to appear: jonquils and daffodils, crocuses and yellow tulips, forsythia and dandelion. Yellow is the easiest of all colors to detect from afar, and these early buds get the bee: the wakening worker bee herself, dressed in yellow pinafore, spots the yellow pollen and carries out the symbiotic flower-bee sex stroke, getting and giving, and going home to the hive with yellow buskins to make nectar into honey (yellow) and wax (yellow) and to feed the yellow queen.

One of the only colors of late evening and darkening night is yellow: the lightning bug's light. The peep of dawn is yellow, and so are the peeping canary, the goldfinch, and the school bus.

Yellow says, "It's coming!" Yellow warns that the red light is coming, the school bus is coming, the spring is coming. Yellow in the rainbow says fair weather is coming. Yellow is the middle, central color band of the rainbow's colors. Yellow is a coming color.

(Parenthesis: yellow is not only the color of the first light of sunrise, but also the color of dusk. One of the loveliest words of English, from Old English, is "gloaming," which comes from the same root, *ghel*, as yellow, and means literally "yellowtime." "Daybreak" is another lovely word, and a yellow one. As a word, "corn" looks like corn, and is yellow, like corn on the cob, and produces an abundance of good yellow things: bourbon whiskey, cornbread, cereal, syrup, tamales and tacos, cob pipes and feed for hogs and chickens, waffles with yellow butter, salad oil, and cornstarch. Many edibles are yellow: squash, lemons, grapefruit, bananas. Peter Mankins *père et fils* never had any of the latter three items; indeed, it is told of a hillman having his very first banana and asked what he thought of it that he replied: "Wal, when I got it shucked and threw away the cob, there weren't much left.")

According to Jungian psychology, among the various functions of the mind, yellow represents the function of intuition, the function that grasps as in a flash of illumination the origins and tendencies of happenings, hence also the intellect and magnanimity—Apollonian qualities, not by coincidence. Yellow is bright but also dignified and serene. This book is the story of communities that aspired to dignity and achieved serenity; thus this digression on the color yellow is necessary if prolix. It is leading up to something, or someone.

Sulphur is yellow. So, if Sulphur City had its own banner, a heraldic pennant to wave perhaps from the mast of the Prices' TV antenna, or from the tallest cedar in Reese Cemetery, the tinctures of the escutcheon's field would be yellow. All the blazonry would be yellow (or *or*, gold). All emblazoned and bespangled with timeless radiance, the flag would furl and billow over this little city that sought dignity and found serenity.

Something or someone led up to: blonde is yellow hair. See her riding in Buster Price's pickup truck, on a very cold winter's

day, riding down to the Great Meadow where the Mankins house
once stood, and the chimney stood longer, until Buster took it
down and stacked it in his back yard. Buster is a *stout* man in
both senses, strong and bulky; or in all three: add determined,
bold, or brave. Buster has shown her the pile of stones he hopes
to use for a patio one day. Now he intends to show her the lone
tree in the big pasture where his cows graze, the tree beneath
which lies buried the pet deer (according to some, merely a pet
goat) of Rachel, Old Pete's first wife, buried with Rachel, who
against all custom and reason was buried beside the house.
Throughout this book of lost cities, we will find that the graveyards were usually established a considerable distance from the
town, as if, far from *memento mori*, the citizens wanted to forget
death, or at least have no daily reminders of it. Reese Cemetery,
where so many of the Mankinses and their kin have moldered,
is a good country mile as the vulture flies from downtown Sulphur
City. Yet Rachel and her pet deer/goat turned to dust in a grave
excavated practically in the back yard of her home. Why? See
the girl with yellow hair looking down at the roots of the tree
that is the only, belated memorial or marker for Rachel's grave.
She is thinking about Rachel and wondering simply if it was a
goat or a deer, or perhaps wondering why Rachel was buried
here so close beside the site of the house.

The girl with yellow hair, to whom all this something has
led, is named Kim, who additionally has blue eyes and is very
tall and is a teacher of ninth-grade civics and tenth-grade English
in Beebe, Arkansas. She was married to a farmer eight years her
senior, and the civics textbook she is required to teach is so dull
that she would do anything to escape it. They have to study cities,
of course, because "civics" means pertaining to cities. They have
to study city government and city planning and the grid system
and all that. Beebe isn't much of a city, and some of the kids
haven't even seen Little Rock, thirty miles away. Kim once thought
of asking the kids to draw their ideal concept of a city, to plan
one on paper, an assignment not in the teachers' resource book.
The results were predictable. Kim knows enough of cities, Little
Rock and Memphis, to know what is ideal and what isn't. She is

urbane, in the sense of civil, polite, even elegant in her manners. But she speaks the language of Buster and Margaret Price, and is very good at asking them questions about Sulphur City.

When Peter Mankins was very old—Old Pete the Younger, Peter Junior the First American Cowboy, the Gold Rusher, and, as we shall see, the Civil War Hero—when, as the century ended, he was old and in the grip of grippe and dying, he sold all his land to Buster's grandfather, fellow native of Paintsville, Kentucky, who farmed it and then left it to Buster's mother, who farmed it and left it to Buster's brother, who left it to Buster, who farms it still.

Kim asks Buster, "What did the house look like?" Buster shows her the foundation stones, half buried in pasture sod and half obscured by weeds. Buster says the house had two stories, of hewed logs, with a T attached to the back containing the kitchen and dining room. This house plan, with living room or parlor in front and bedrooms upstairs, was very old, and can be traced readily not only to Kentucky and Tennessee, but also to North Carolina and Virginia and from there back to medieval England. Probably it was not a double pen, a "pair cottage," or a dogtrot, because of the T where the breezeway would be. Probably it was no more comfortable or presentable than any other log house; it was merely much larger. It was not a log cabin but a log castle, and few other comparable examples exist in the history of Arkansas architecture: the famous Wolf house of Norfork comes closest. Peter Mankins (the both of them) built it so large not simply because the family was populous but because they wanted to show off, which has been the motive during immemorial time of people who overdevelop their real estate. The Middle Fork valley was filling up with Lewises, Fines, Van Hooses, Dickersons, Carters, Ballards, and Crawfords, most of whom were Mankins kin by blood or marriage, and it was important for the Peters to maintain superiority. Old Peter could never forget the impression of Mount Vernon. Not many years after the Mankins mansion in its valley setting passed into desuetude and fell, some modern people with unlimited money built a castle, a fortress really, on a nearby hilltop, where they can lord it over all creation.

Several pages later on, Kim will take a look at "Raheen," which actually means "fortress" in Gaelic. The intentions of the Mankinses were not at all unlike the intentions of the Alexanders, who built the latter-day castle.

Most of that $3,750 from the California gold fields went into home improvement, or overdevelopment of the real estate, until there was no question that Peter Mankins was the boss squire of the White River, and it was about this time that people of the valley, which was filling up with people, forgot that the place had ever been designated as New Prospect and began referring to it simply as Mankins, in honor of the boss squire and his sire of the same name. Justifiably, Old and Young (now nearing forty) Pete could refer to their land, their town, their village, as "me." Throughout the Ozarks, in the mellifluous language endemic to the natives, "me" meant not simply the person in his awareness of himself but the person in his property, his whole habitat, as when he would say something like "That thar rail fence is right on me," or "The creek come down and throwed gravel all over me."

"Aint we a sight?" Boss Squire Pete asked his sire one day, apropos of nothing and without any reference to their physical persons but, rather, in observation of the land, the land itself. This was a rhetorical question, and the Elder Pete answered it with a question: "Aint we, though?"

Old Pete still plowed, and Young Pete plowed all the money he could find into the improvement of Mankins. During the Mormon War of 1857, when Federal troops were sent to Utah to put down the rebellion of the "state of Deseret," Peter Mankins sold $34,000 worth of beef cattle to the quartermaster supplying the soldiers' food, personally delivering the herds. He also drove herds to Chicago and to Westport, Missouri, the latter a small platted village that Mankins helped to transform into a city and rename Kansas City, which became the largest of all American places bearing the "City" name—next, of course, to New York City. The cattle trail from Texas to Kansas City remained known to drovers and insiders for the rest of the century as "the old Mankins trail." This never got into any history books, however, and there is no monument to Peter Mankins in any park or civic area in Kansas City, an oversight that ought to be remedied by the public officials of those double cities in Kansas and Missouri, perhaps by erecting a statue—which would have to be purely conjectural, since no image of Peter Mankins actually exists.

Year after year Peter Mankins was gone from Mankins for long stretches of time on these far-flung cowboying expeditions, which always resulted in a pouch of gold emptied and pyramided on the family dining table. When in due course he grew tired of cows and their dumb, questioning faces, he became interested in human chattels, whose faces might be dumb but never questioning, only compliant. There were a number of wealthy townspeople in Fayetteville who owned these pitchy-skinned persons for the purpose of toil, and some of the well-to-do Cherokee had taken slaves with them to the California gold fields, where nearly all of them died from shit work, but Peter Mankins knew only a few farmers hereabouts who used niggers in the field. Farther south, in flatland Arkansas, however, they were in great demand, in greater demand than the supply available, and Peter discovered after his cattle drives to Kansas City and Chicago that there was a surplus supply of these dark folks running around with nothing to do and on the market dirt cheap; he began buying them up in droves and driving them South. Dark-complexioned drudge-type people were a lot easier to drive than cows or hogs, and thus Peter Mankins, after years as a hogboy and many years as a cowboy, became a blackboy. Never questioning the philosophy of slavery, he thrived and prospered, and stocked the plantations of the South with all the blacks they could hold, although many were sold on a time-payment plan. There is a book waiting to be written about Peter Mankins in his most profitable career, which terminated one day when, stopping in Fayetteville with a wagonload of slaves, he discovered his little city occupied by dozens of United States soldiers. Some of these men were the same ones who had been sent to Utah to put down the rebellion of Mormons who wanted to be independent. Now they were putting down the rebellion of Arkansawyers who wanted to secede from the Union. Mankins couldn't unload his cargo of chattels, so he turned them loose in a wooded hollow just east of the town square, where they stayed and thrived and multiplied. They called their hollow Tin Cup, which it remains today, the only black ghetto in northwest Arkansas.

Northwest Arkansas was overwhelmingly pro-Union, and the nine thousand Arkansawyers who fought as Federals in the Civil War were all from this part of the state, but Peter Mankins knew that if the North won the war he could never hope to collect what was owed him for the slaves he had sold on credit to plantation owners. His kinsmen of the Middle Fork were indifferent and neutral but spoiling for excitement, and when he offered to outfit them for battle at his own expense, nearly a hundred of them agreed to wear the Confederate gray and follow Boss Reb Mankins into the carnival atmosphere of the summer of 1861.

Just why Captain P. M. Mankins, CSA, resigned his commission almost immediately is a great mystery. The various histories of the Civil War in Arkansas merely report that he "turned his company over to Colonel W. H. Brooks." His reasons must remain speculative, and the death in 1861 of his favorite daughter, Millie, at the age of fifteen had nothing to do with it; more probably Narcissa, pure Yankee by birth, was, despite his extensive involvement in the slave trade (which quite likely he kept secret from her), a staunch abolitionist and a loyal Unionist and was outraged by her husband's spending money to outfit a band of Rebels. Few women had any influence on their husbands in the Civil War, but somehow Narcissa may have swayed Pete. He could not stay in the background for long, however; probably all unbeknown to Narcissa, he sneaked off and raised a band of guerrillas—or bushwhackers, as they were called—who eschewed all standards of military conduct to harass and kill not only the Union troops but also the Union sympathizers in the civilian population of northwest Arkansas. In time, this population generally knew of Pete's involvement, and in their attempts to find him and stop him the Federals arrested his father and tortured the ninety-one-year-old Pete for three days in an attempt to get him to confess his son's whereabouts. "They would never've got a thing out of me," Old Pete told Narcissa, who nursed him back to a semblance of health, but then took sick herself and began dying. Of Young Pete's actual wartime activities, the usually invaluable mass publicist Goodspeed (1891) says only, "In 1863 he swam the Arkansas River with 300 soldiers shooting at him all the time." This has been fleshed out by various imaginations, including Peter's own, but let the Goodspeed line stand as it is, unembellished.

When Peter escaped and returned home, Narcissa was dead. He buried her in Reese Cemetery and was never quite the same man again.

The rest is not very exciting. The South lost the war. Peter lost almost all his money. Peter's only subsequent office was a stint as county coroner in 1866–68, to which he was elected without further qualification than his lack of squeamishness in the presence of dead bodies. Though he resumed raising sulphur-drinking cattle and hogs, he never drove them anywhere any more. He had nothing further to do with Negroes, and never stopped when he passed through Tin Cup on his way up to downtown Fayetteville. He took a second wife, a pretty woman eleven years his junior named Easter (or Esther) Hanna Gilliland, a widow. (Old Peter had also taken a widow as a second wife, and when she died he took another widow as his third wife, and when some customary reporter interviewing him customarily on his hundredth birthday asked him why he had married three widows, he was unable to give any satisfactory reason. He did, however, answer the customary question about how he had achieved such longevity: every morning he took a "tonic" of a dram of good whiskey mixed with yellow-root bitters and administered the same tonic to each member of his family.)

How does a legend live out his years? The one-time football hero, the fading movie star, the former president, the one-shot best-selling novelist—how do they face the endless empty denouement of their later lives? How does a once-flourishing town aspiring to call itself "City" endure the long days of its decline?

In 1876 the United States designated Mankins Post Office, and the Baptist Reverend Johnson Crawford in the same year established the first general-merchandise store. There were three churches in the village. Peter Mankins, always nominally a Baptist like his father, began to attend worship services at the church where his father was a deacon (despite his daily dose of whiskey, even on Sunday mornings), and read the Bible sometimes or suffered it to be read to him; he also took a great interest in politics, in which he was a Democrat. Devotion to the church had no more effect on his consumption of whiskey than it did on his father's, and his righteousness gave him no regret for his earlier treatment of Indians and Negroes. He had a few close friends, with whom he sat many hours on the porch of the general store, swapping yarns and wartime reminiscences and speculating about what the world was coming to. He resisted invitations to join the newly formed Masons, a dull, stodgy collection of brethren, and he resisted efforts to borrow his name for the membership rolls of the more rambunctious IOOF, or Odd Fellows (whose name, contrary to popular belief, comes not from their peculiarities or eccentricities but simply from their status as exceptions to the ordinary conventions of fraternalism). He was still boss squire of the Middle Fork valley, despite having lost most of his fortune in the war; in fact, because he was just as poor as everyone else, he seemed to be more popular than when he had been a rich man. James Mitchell, an editor of the *Arkansas Gazette* of Little Rock, then as now one of the most distinguished, literate, and intelligent newspapers in the country, and "the oldest newspaper west of the Mississippi," visited "the oldest man in Arkansas" as Peter Senior's 107th birthday was approaching, and sat on the porch and interviewed him, although he was quite deaf and the younger Pete had to serve more or less as an interpreter. "His memory, as would naturally be expected," Mitchell wrote, "is very defective, except as to the events of his early life, which he says are all clear and complete." Actually, nothing had happened to him since the war, so he had nothing to report. The editor stayed around for both dinner and supper and an all-afternoon interview in between, and reported that Old Pete had an excellent

appetite, had never had a decayed tooth in his life, ate heartily
of boiled cabbage and bacon at dinner, but had only bread and
milk at supper. Of the son Mitchell wrote, "Pete is not satisfied
with Arkansas, but says he feels it to be his duty to remain and
take care of his father as long as he lives."

His father lived for several more years; Old Pete's only disappointment in his very last years was that he had outlived all
of his enemies and had no one to argue with. Three months after
his 111th birthday, at the end of 1881, he took sick, and Peter
Junior attended him in his last hours, gave him his last cup of
water, and listened to his last breath. All of the dining tables of
Middle Fork were brought to the Great Meadow and set up,
reaching from the house all the way to the river, and covered
with new white cloths; seven hundred pounds of beef, mutton,
and pork were barbecued, along with hundreds of chickens. Nobody attempted to count the people who attended the funeral
feast, but of these, half a thousand attempted to crowd into Reese
Cemetery for the burial. Peter Senior lies buried beneath tall
stately cedars (parenthesis: he was born beneath cedars at Cedar
Point, Maryland) and one of those curious coffin-shaped cenotaphs, which is inscribed merely with his name and his astonishing
age at death.

There is an identical cenotaph adjoining it but without inscription. City and family historians, among them the opinion-
ated Louisa Personkins, insist that this unmarked cenotaph covers
the grave of Peter Junior, but Young Pete was not *that* devoted
to the old man, who probably contrived to have the remains of
his second and favorite widow/wife, Sabra, interred on his right
side. The male cedar tree blooms in January, Kim notices: when
it blooms, masses of yellow pollen produced in the small catkins
appear to turn the tree a golden-yellow color, emblematic of the
males buried beneath it (yes, Young Peter *is* in there somewhere).

What question editor Mitchell asked Young Pete that made
the editor conclude in public print that Young Pete was not
satisfied with Arkansas cannot be imagined; in any case, Old Pete,
as Young Pete was now known, showed no inclination to leave
Arkansas after his father's death. Rather, he became more and

more interested in the woolgatherings and castle buildings of the townsmen who wanted to turn the place into a booming resort or spa. The individual, like the nation as a whole, goes through periodic cycles of obsession and indifference toward health, and the gilded age of the 1880s saw a mass mania over magic water, or ablutomania, a bathing craze. Whereas our own gilded eighties, a hundred years later, are witnessing the apogee of the jogging craze, the people of a century ago, who wouldn't jog their way out of a burning building, eagerly subjected themselves to long hours of submersion in any water that looked, smelled, tasted, or felt funny. The entrepreneurs of the town of Mankins sought to capitalize upon the poorly kept secret that the town had *four* springs: a sulphur spring, a warm spring, an alkali or soda spring, and a limestone spring. None of these springs amounted to more than a trickle or percolation from the permeable rock strata of the village slopes, and there was only *one* sulphur spring, whose flow was scarcely enough to keep a few cows happy and the citizens without tooth decay, but the entrepreneurs, with or without permission from Peter, changed the town's name from Mankins to Sulphur Springs, in the plural, and began widely advertising the curative and restorative powers of their water, good for the treatment of rheumatism, gout, liver trouble, blood ailments, dyspepsia, and even cancer. They mailed a formal request to the Post Office Department concerning the name change. They painted signs pointing to Sulphur Springs and planted them all over the county. A bright yellow carriage inscribed "Sulphur Springs Transportation Company" was set up to bring passengers from the new train station at Elkins. A jerry-built bathhouse with adjoining guest cottages, ancestor of the motel, was erected over the sulphur spring, although there was scarcely enough flow of water to cover the whole body and the baths were limited to footbaths at one foot per half-hour. A third blacksmith shop opened to handle the traffic. Dr. John C. Carter (who deserves a whole book to himself) of the nearby community of Carter's Store, where he had his own post office, general store (still standing but fast falling; see illustration) and clinic (ditto, but not pictured), geared up the clinic to handle patients who needed not merely a bath but also blood-letting, leeching, or other medical attention. In due course, the Post Office Department replied with the information that there was already a Sulphur Springs post office in Benton County, to the north. Most of the Sulphurites were in favor of restoring the name Mankins, but Peter himself pointed out that such a name would draw no health seekers, and he proposed the name Sulphur City, which the Post Office Department accepted and designated. (Both the actual Sulphur Springs and especially Eureka Springs, founded in the magic year of 1886, were well on their way to becoming thriving resorts, and cities of sorts.)

Business at the Sulphur City springs was never brisk, and the bathhouse was used more frequently as a kind of community center or polling place for school elections, gubernatorial elections, the elections of Grover Cleveland (twice), and the defeats of William Jennings Bryan (twice). Since it took the one small bathtub, carved from rock, nearly an hour to fill with five gallons of sulphur water, only the cows seemed to have the patience to wait that long; for hour upon hour they would stand and sip the water as it came out.

A city founded upon such little expectation cannot flourish, but Peter Mankins remembered enough of the work of his youth to survey the place into twenty-four city blocks of twelve lots each, just as he had done to Fayetteville a half-century before, but this time hollering "Stick!" and letting others holler "Stuck!" (Years hence, movies will be made about the life of Peter Mankins, when the genre of the "Western" has died of atrophied realism and been replaced by a new genre called "Ozarkern"; climactic scenes will show Old Pete standing in the pastures above the village, peering through a surveyor's transit and waving his arms overhead.) Peter Mankins is not in any wise to be blamed for it, but there is something offensive and unnatural about the plat plan for Sulphur City, with its perfectly ordered rows of lots like barracks or tombstones in a military cemetery. All organic sense is lost, replaced by whatever sense of power the platter-planner feels. Fortunately, perhaps, there were no takers, no buyers of the lots. The city died in its cage of even streets and alleys. Even

Cherokee City, of our next chapter, which met a similar fate, at least had three hotels of sorts. Sulphur City never got its expected hotel. Year after year, the town's local correspondent to the Fayetteville newspaper, George Van Hoose, a Mankins nephew and as good a country reporter as ever mailed in his weekly observations of crop failures, funerals, visits, and permanent departures, would declare, "We haven't got our hotel built yet," and "The hotel has not yet been built," and "Our hotel remains built only in the air," and "The timbers of the hotel remain growing in the forest."

The people seemed to forget the outside world entirely and concentrated instead on their own, building a good large schoolhouse (which was never filled) with a fine Odd Fellows lodge on the second floor (sometimes filled). The stores did enough local business to support the storekeepers' families, and the blacksmiths continued to sweat until the motorcar arrived. Because Sulphur City was not ever really on the road *to* anywhere, few tourists or "furriners" ever passed through, and fewer still ever stopped. It would be wrong to call Sulphur City, as Louisa Personkins did in her article for *The Midwestern Roots-Rooter*, "The Town That Time Forgot." Time never forgot Sulphur City; Time never noticed it in the first place.

Doubtless, Peter Mankins wanted to see the century to its close, but he missed it by several months. In the eighty-sixth and last year of his life he was blind, lame, susceptible to pneumonia, influenza, and anything else microscopic and respiratory, and totally dependent on others, having lost the small pension the state of Arkansas had been paying him, a pittance in token remembrance of his wartime services. Strangely, the only friend, other than family, of Peter's last years was an old Federal veteran, Sam Dunlap, like Peter a kind of survivor but a survivor of a particular kind: the disastrous sinking of the steamer *Sultana* at the close of the war, which cost the lives of over fifteen hundred Federal prisoners on the verge of freedom (see the chapter on Mound City). Like Peter, he was totally blind, and the two vet-

erans of opposite sides would sit together for hours, Homer and
Milton, regaling each other with old war stories and with vale-
dictories for dreams that never came true. Sam Dunlap delivered
a kind of eulogy at Peter's funeral, attended by the survivors of
a blinding snowstorm that blew through Reese Cemetery and up
and down Middle Fork. Although the newspaper misspelled his
name in the headline, "Mankind Dies at Sulphur City," the rest
of the obituary got it correctly, and concluded, "This old path-
finder we feel sure sleeps well. Peace to his ashes."

The precise location of Peter's grave will remain ambiguous,
perhaps by his own design. But there *is* an unmarked grave
between that of his beloved first wife, Narcissa, and that of his
second wife, Easter, who survived him by one year; quite likely
he contrived to keep his resting place unmarked in order to spare
Easter's feelings and be hugged in the grave parenthetically by
both wives, as it were, and it was. Some Hollywood mogul will
erect an obelisk on the spot in a few more years, with an inscription, "Peter Mankins, the Archetypal Arkansawyer."

Kim conducts most of her interview in Buster and Margaret's
living room, a place of furnishings not exactly nondescript, and
certainly not shabby, but, rather, in a manner of zeal without
taste common to living rooms Kim is fated to see across the length
and breadth of Arkansas, and which probably can be found any
place in America where people with good intentions have assembled, without plan and without any semblance of art or elegance,
the objects of comfort pleasing to their untrained eyes. This
homely attempt to prettify one's surroundings deserves a word,
a name of its own, and we are about to find one: based upon the
typical contents of the Prices' living room. Nabokov's good word
poshlost will not quite do; although it conveys a hint of the corn-
iness and philistinism, it is too snobbishly critical. A catalogue of
the furnishings of this room: not one but four recliners (Bar-
caloungers? La-Z-Boys? of Naugahyde or artificial leather or just
plastic), two pole lamps, two reproductions of paintings (an old
man praying for *This Daily Bread* and a panorama of an autumn

forest stream, its colors matching the sofa pillows beneath it),
two frames filled with about fifty family snapshots, two Bibles on
the coffee table, and everywhere, on shelves, tables, and the man-
tel, decorative colored glassware: shell-shaped vases, etched glass
and frosted glass, Depression glass, Fostoria and Sandwich, saucers and bowls and compotes. "Compote": *there* is our word, the
long-stemmed dish for holding stewed fruit. Compote. Something about the word itself is fruity and stewed, suggesting a host
of affiliates: "effete," "compost," "camp," "Truman Capote,"
"compute" as in "It does not compute." In German it looks and
sounds even worse: *Kompott*. It is possible to identify an entire
stewed-fruit *Kompott Kultur*: not just the whatnots, gewgaws, and
gimcracks of living-room decoration, but also any home display
of taxidermist's art or gun racks is compote, anything plastic is
compote, any cheaply pictorial representation of Jesus Christ,
the Virgin Mary, or the Last Supper is compote, as are panoramic
overcolored scenes of waterfalls, snow-capped mountains, lakes,
and moonlight; Burt Reynolds and Dolly Parton are compote
movie stars; soap operas and game shows are compote entertainment; Harlequin romances are compote literature; the list is
endless, and the word will be found occasionally throughout this
book, not in censure but in description. Kim enjoys the Prices'
living room, and shall return.

"Why didn't you take over the general store from your father?" she asks Buster.

The last general store, abandoned though it is, is not particularly
old, as antiquities go: it was built around 1935, when another
store on the same site, built in 1908 in roughly the same dimensions, burned. Both stores were unashamedly plagiarized from
Carter's Store in their basic neat one-floor, gable-to-the-front,
white-temple style and plan. Kim notices that the deserted Price
store is just like the ruin of Carter's Store in that both have an
addition, a side room on the left with sloping shed roof. Throughout the Ozarks stores had these side rooms, which served several
functions: most commonly for holding sacks of feed and thus

separating the animal feed from human foodstuffs, but also for storage of items accepted in barter, such as live chickens, fresh eggs, berries, and other things to be shipped to Fayetteville for resale; some storekeepers used one of the side rooms for dispensing coal oil, vinegar, and other smelly liquids in quantity to keep their smells from the rest of the store, and the other side room as a combination office and storage shed for the wool that sheep-raising farmers bartered for groceries. Kim also notices one major difference between the two stores, Carter's and Price's, the first built around 1875, the second a modern (circa 1935) copy of it. The older store, even without its broken windowpanes and peeling-away clapboards, somehow looks older because of certain little details of construction: narrower clapboards, a double door paneled elegantly by some local millwright, the iron door latch, the six-over-six windows, and the six-paned transom light, the bargeboard in the gable's cornice. Carter's Store once had a porch and porch roof, as Price's store does, but porches are the first things to fall when a building decays. Still, Carter's Store has a character that Price's store lacks. It *invites*, Kim reflects: it makes her *wonder*.

When Price's store ceased to function as such and lost its gasoline pump out front, its shelves were already bare or becoming so, and an inch of bare shelf is anathema to any grocer, as all the manuals for supermarket operation insist and insist. At one time Buster's father carried and sold such things as women's house slippers, men's straw hats, socks, work gloves, yard goods, and hardware, as well as the usual staples. But he had refrigeration enough (iceboxes) only for soft drinks (sody pop) and not for milk, meats, the cool things that customers journeyed to Elkins or Fayetteville for.

Margaret loved to visit her father-in-law's store, sometimes just as a cure for the doldrums or the blues. "We'd see people we never did see any other time," Margaret tells Kim. "People would come out of these hills. They would come out of these hills just to trade at the store." It was Buster's father's dream, like many fathers' dreams, that his son would follow in his footsteps and keep the store going. Sometimes the elder Prices would go somewhere, into Fayetteville or to visit, and turn the keeping of the store over to Buster and Margaret. "They tried to get us to promise that we would take the store, and it was the heartbreak of their lives that we wouldn't."

"Why didn't you take the store?" Kim asks.

"Why, we'd be tied down, honey," Margaret says.

"Couldn't make a livin at it!" Buster says.

The last mail was delivered to the Sulphur City Post Office thirty years ago. When the office was forced to close, many stamp collectors ordered "last day of cancellation covers" or "final cancellation marks," but to the people of the community, says Margaret, "it was part of our lives that was taken away from us." Everyone was sad, even though the post office had been the main source of factions because the postmastership, Margaret explains, "was by appointment. His dad would have it for five or six years, and then we'd get a new congressman in or something, and the post office would cross the street to a different store."

Kim: "Did people take sides?"

Margaret: "Oh, *sides!* They'd carry guns!"

Buster: "And knives."

Today their mailing address is simply Rural Route 7, Fayetteville, even though Fayetteville seems a long way off.

But the Reverend J. B. Kyger commutes to the Sulphur City Baptist Church from Fayetteville, where he has a home and an air-conditioning contracting business, his source of livelihood.

Kim: "Have you ever heard of Peter Mankins?"

Reverend Kyger: "No, I have not."

In the Fayetteville telephone directory there are no Mankinses, but there are Manatts, Manaughs, Mandrells, Maneses, Mangans, Mangers, Mangolds, Manires, Mankers, Manleys, Manns, Mannens, Mannings, Mansells, Mansfields, Manskes, Mansours, Manteganis, Mantooths, and Manwarrens.

The Reverend Kyger does not know when the church was built, and when Kim asks him he is silent for a while before replying, "Our church does not have a complete set of records. I think it was in the early twenties, but I'm not for sure." The architecture and construction of the building suggest that it was built just before America entered World War II. One notices that the rafter ends in the cornices are deliberately exposed, in what was known as the "Craftsman" style through the thirties, and one wonders if this deliberate exposure of rafter ends is a kind of vernacular imitation of modillions in classical architecture, just as the modillions themselves were marble translations of original timber ends. Kim writes in her notebook, "Is there such a thing as vernacular classicism?"

As the sign says at the Sulphur City Baptist Church, there are Sunday-morning services, Sunday-evening services, and a Wednesday service; according to the Reverend Kyger, most of the fifty-odd faithful are so faithful that they go to all three. Kim asks him to explain the difference between the Primitive Baptists, which the Mankinses were, and the Missionary Baptists, which these present-day Sulphurites are. The only essential difference, Reverend Kyger explains, is that the former believe in foot washing and the latter in establishing missions. Thus, the one is inward, the other outward.

Kim dares a question: "Reverend, since sulphur is the brimstone of the Bible associated with hell, has anyone made cracks equating Sulphur City with hell?"

Kyger answers, "I did not know that sulphur had that definition. I always thought that brimstone was something different."

If Sulphur City enjoyed no boom whatever from its mineral water, it enjoyed twenty years of prosperity from its apples. Shortly after Peter Mankins brought his century to a close, orchards planted all across the Ozarks of northwest Arkansas began bearing in profusion. The Mankinses and other families of the Middle Fork had always had home orchards, with all the apples they could eat and a few to sell in Fayetteville and even, when the Frisco Railroad came in 1882, to ship to market in St. Louis, but it was not until early in our own century that apple production peaked and became the leading crop of the Middle Fork and elsewhere throughout the region. Buster's father built an apple dryer, or evaporator, on the banks of the Sulphur Branch, using sulphur to lighten the color of the dried apple slices, and hired forty local women to help during the picking, peeling, paring, and slicing season. Two other men opened competing apple evaporators, each with a dozen helpers. Local orchardists had an abundance of dryer apples, culls from the fruit sent to big city markets, the harvest of Winesaps, Grimes Golden, and Rome Beauties. Pests and diseases had not yet discovered the delicious apple; there was no spraying. When the pests came in the thirties and spraying began, the apple industry began to die out, year by year, and all the trees were cut for firewood. There are no great orchards left today, only a family tree or two. The air misses the smells of blossomtime and harvest.

Except for Carter's Store and his little clinic across the road, Sulphur City doesn't even have the picturesque but stereotyped "ghost-town" architecture. Among the few bona-fide ruins of Sulphur City are the remains of the Jones cabin east of town, just off the Mount Salem road, which the Prices live on. The traveler coming across such a log cabin with its notched corners usually assumes that this is a pioneer dwelling of early vintage, when in fact most such derelicts are of modern construction. The late Leon Jones's father did not build this cabin until 1930. Leon Jones, born in our key year of 1886, left Sulphur City in its heyday to find real cities, traveled around the world on tramp steamers, and came home in 1950 to live the rest of his life in the cabin as a hermit bachelor, Thoreau-like but apparently without any journals.

Was Leon Jones a "character"? Kim inquires of the Prices. "Yeah," Buster says, "quite a character." Margaret says, "If anybody needed a hundred-dollar loan or somethin, he'd always go to Leon Jones—if he liked ya." And where did he get the money? Margaret: "I don't know that." Buster: "Well, he just never did spend any! He kept all he got!" Kim: "He didn't have a family to spend it on?" Buster: "Not a family! And he wore dirty clothes all the time, made his own home brew, hunted a little bit, and tole big lies on himself." Leon Jones kept dogs; Margaret says,

"He'd let those dogs crawl up on the bed and have their babies!" He also had an old cat who liked to visit the neighbors. One time Leon Jones fell and broke his leg and hip; since he couldn't move or be heard if he yelled, he tied a message to the neck of his old cat. For two days the neighbors noticed the cat wandering around with the message hanging from its neck, and finally Buster got the message and loaded Leon Jones into his pickup and took him to the hospital in Fayetteville. Leon Jones slipped his wallet to Buster, saying, "I want you to take care of this." Buster tells Kim, "It had four hundred dollars in there, and he was afraid to take it to the hospital, because they'd get his money, you know, and he didn't want 'em to have it. Anyway, that ole billfold was . . . it just . . . the stink, you could hardly stand it, you know, it was molded, and he had it next to his ole body, you know, and I carried that thing around here for a while and then decided I'd hide it, and kept it till he got back out of the hospital."

In Elkins is a small café called Smitty's. Any town of any size has one of these, where the farmers come each morning, sometimes twice, to drink coffee or have a second breakfast or even a first breakfast to get away from their wives, to meet in fellowship and be good buddies for a moment, sitting under their two-color bill caps exchanging menfolks' gossip—how the sheriff's deppity screwed that gal before takin' her on in to the lockup, ha ha, wudn't that a good 'un?—and to discuss the weather and crops and to tease the waitress. Buster never goes to Smitty's, because he loves Margaret so much, but the other men of Middle Fork have helped make Smitty's into a fraternal temple, and strangers aren't welcome, although if the stranger is Kim they will ogle her appreciatively and wink and maybe even grunt and sigh. An occasional visitor, before he got the message that he wasn't welcome, was Robert Alexander, who, despite his faded blue jeans and old plaid shirt and sweat-stained cowboy hat, seemed just too good to be an authentic farmer, although he owned more

sheep than anybody in the county. Bob Alexander had worked
for twenty-five years as an executive of the Ford Motor Company,
and when he decided to retire early, he and his wife, Alice, who
breeds rare American domestic shorthair cats, searched the United
States for the ideal location for a home. After plotting all the
geographic data and running the information through a computer, they decided that Middle Fork had the prettiest scenery
and the best climate, and neither of them liked Florida or Arizona
as a retirement spot. They did not know that around .1907 the
Sulphur City dealer in hacks and buggies was one Grant Alexander, possibly but not likely a relation. For years Bob Alexander
had been head of Ford in Australia, and later in London, whence
they flew to Fayetteville one morning to buy their hilltop spread
near Sulphur City before noon and hire Euine Fay Jones, the
best architect in Arkansas, to spare no expense in designing their
dream home and building it of native stone. Jones, no relation
to Leon, had designed a scandal-ridden sprawling hilltop mansion for Governor Orval Faubus years before in a style and fashion really not comparable to what he did for the Alexanders;
Jones's recent Thorncrown Chapel in Eureka Springs is his mas-
terpiece and has won numerous awards.

Kim sits in the Alexanders' living room ("cathedral ceiling"
doesn't do justice to it, and there is not a trace of compote anywhere; a strange, monkeylike cat brushes against Kim's arm). She
asks, "Have you ever seen former Governor Faubus's house in
Huntsville? Did you visit it to get an idea about Fay Jones's
work?"

"No," Bob Alexander replies, "not till afterward. What we
actually did was buy this place, and see Fay, and tell him we were
going back to England, and generally describe to him what we
wanted in the way of a house, and tell him we'd be back in nine
months. Which we were, and he had it done! The house had to
be designed for the site. We had told him we wanted it low and
ground-hugging and we wanted to take advantage of the splendid
view."

Alexander takes Kim out onto a deck cantilevered over the

bluff; the view is excellent, all up and down the valley as far as Carter's Store, but Kim is terrified of heights and stays close to the door. Bob and Alice named their place Raheen after the bishop of Australia's estate, which adjoined their Melbourne house; they thought it was an Australian aborigine name, but later learned it was Gaelic for "ringed fortress."

Alice says, "The view, the lovely view."

But there are compote farmhouses visible down below, and Bob says, "I think the thing that bothers me most about the area is the poverty."

Alice agrees, "That's what I would've said next."

Kim asks, "Has no one ever mentioned to you the history of Sulphur City?"

Bob and Alice exchange glances and together say "No."

Kim asks, "Have you heard of the Mankins family?"

Alice says, "It sounds familiar, but no. . . ."

"No," says Bob.

Buster and Margaret Price are not impoverished, although their living room is pure compote. Kim has already asked them what they think of the Alexanders, whom they have never met. Buster has said, "Before they ever moved in, everybody around here flocked up there and looked the house over while it was being built. Everything in that house is custom-built, I mean, just built to the walls." Kim has asked Margaret, "How do people feel about that house? Does it cause a stir?" And Margaret has answered, "I don't think so. No envy."

Now, in this dream house, Kim thinks that sometimes dreams do not get broken, and she asks the Alexanders, "Is life here—the house, the land, the life style—is it a fulfillment of your aspirations? Is there everything here you need and want?"

They think a while about that. Alice says, "That's a heavy question. I think there's always *something* missing, but in general I'd say yes. . . ."

"I think we're happy here," Bob says. "I still feel vigorous enough that every once in a while I wonder if I should be doing something more constructive than I am. There's enough around here to keep us *physically* busy, but once in a while you miss the pace of the city."

Alice says, "We do find ourselves going often to Tulsa, for the operas, the museums, the art, you know."

"You do miss the pace of the city," Bob Alexander says.

Cherokee City, Arkansas

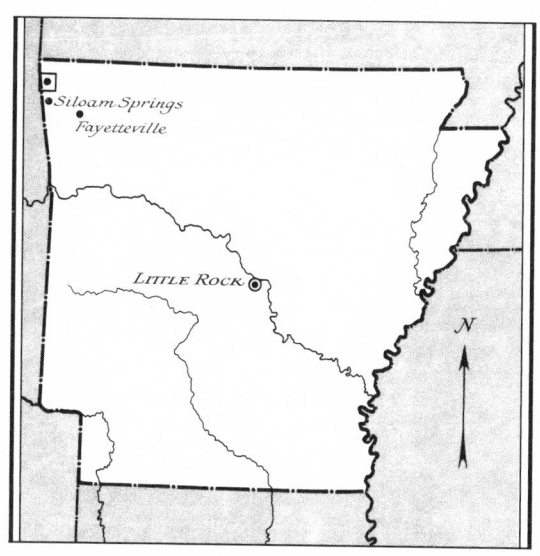

CAROL'S
COUNTRY
STORE
CHEROKEE
CITY
ARK.
CAROL'S COUNTRY STORE
CHEROKEE CITY ARK
500 FT
Pepsi
Taste that beats the others cold!

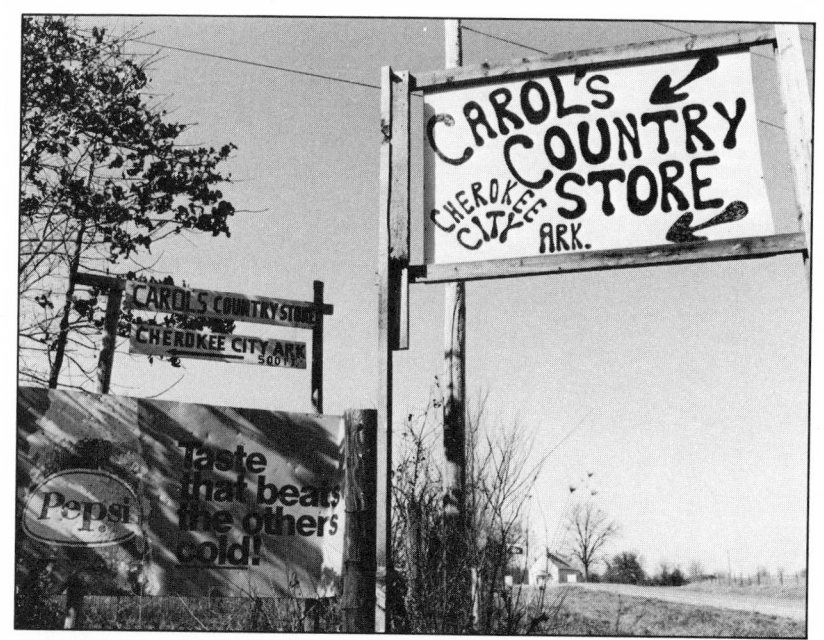

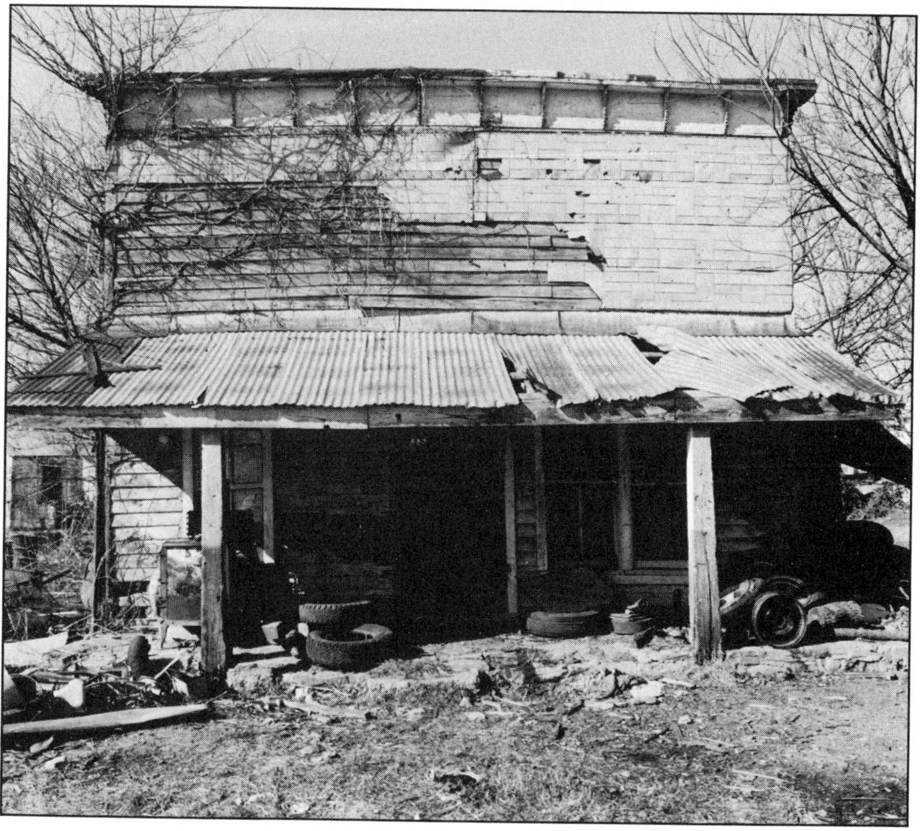

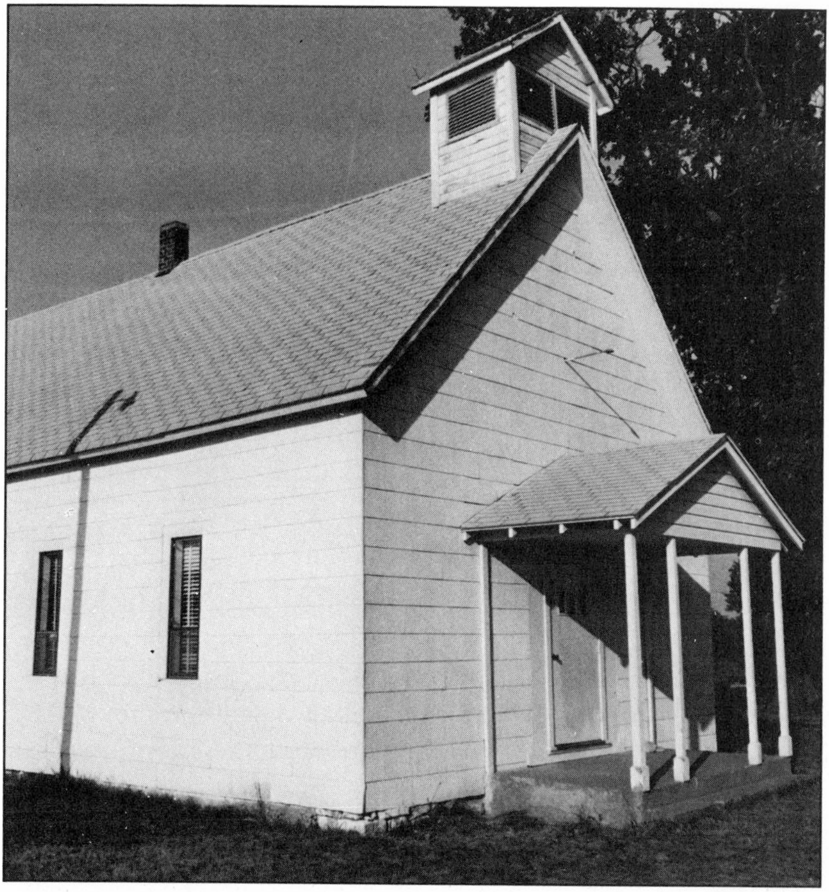

CHEROKEE KID GROC.
Dr Pepper

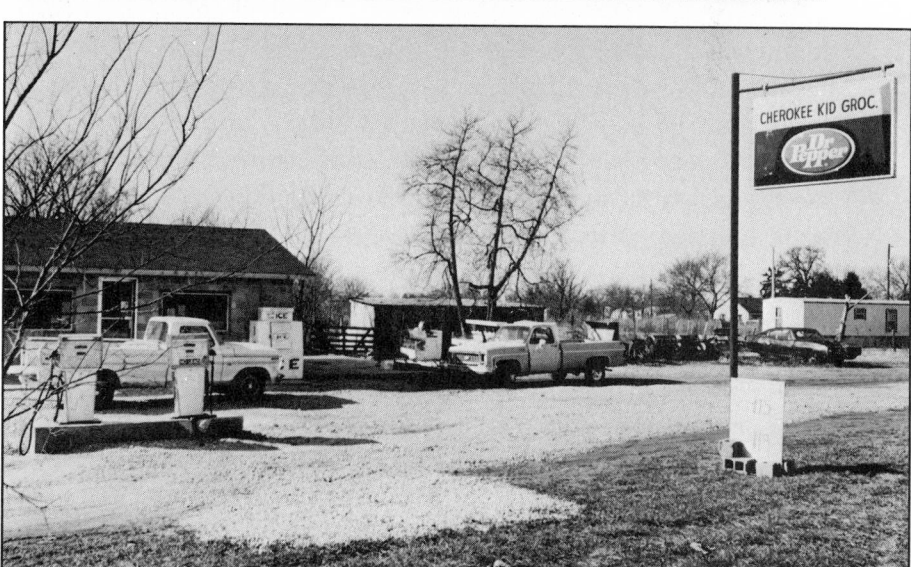

BUT THE ONE AGEE had just invented out of his own head was in Alabama, the county seat of his pseudonymous county of sharecroppers (in reality, Tuscaloosa) which he and Walker Evans visited and lived in one hot summer half a century ago, when Agee was just a kid of twenty-seven but wrote the finest prose in the American English language, a prose and a book which make one of the lasting volumes of American literature, attempting "a form and set of tones rather less like those of narrative than like those of music," as Agee within his art described his art, that rich Beethovenesque rhetoric, sonorous and orphic, that seems to find a song in the dirty fingernails of a sharecropper's child. Our Cherokee City is a "real" one of that "real" name, without any sharecroppers but with a poverty of architecture that makes Tuscaloosa look almost metropolitan. Poor Roethke in his last days wrote the poem "In Evening Air" with its single plaintive desperate and ambitious line, "I'll make a broken music, or I'll die." And then he died. Perhaps workmen of the word have no business approximating music.

There is no hotel to put up at in the "real" Cherokee City, not now, although once there was, which is its chief difference from Sulphur City, only thirty-eight miles away as the crow flies— but what self-respecting crow would fly from the upland pastoral tranquillity of Sulphur City to the flatland barren somnolence of Cherokee City? It is another world entirely, flat as the Great

Plains, a warning of Oklahoma, which it closely verges upon; indeed, its name comes from the people who dominate the eastern counties of Oklahoma, which was, as late as 1905, Indian Territory, and sometimes is still locally referred to as "The Nation" because for most of the years of Cherokee City's growing up that's what it was, the Cherokee Nation of the most advanced of the civilized tribes of redmen.

Whereas Sulphur City in both geography and history gives the impression of calm, Cherokee City was a wild, rowdy place. There were once half a thousand people, now fewer than twenty-five. The older people with whom Kim talks tell her that in their childhood they were forbidden to venture into downtown Cherokee City. At one time, downtown Cherokee City resembled Hollywood's conception of the Western town, with a Main Street in which the sheriff meets the villains at high noon . . . although Cherokee City never had a sheriff. At high noon Cherokee City is asleep and empty, deathly quiet. But it still looks as if a town might once have been there; Sulphur City doesn't even suggest a town. At the lone crossroads of Sulphur City is nothing but Price's neat but empty little white store. At the lone crossroads of Cherokee City are no fewer than three stores on three corners. One of them, with a false front of an elaborate cornice, has its door wide open and a single fluorescent light burning in the dark interior, although there is nobody around and it is obviously abandoned but not empty: an abundance of debris litters the interior, and the porch is a junkyard of old tires and wheels. Another store is breathtaking in its decay, if you find beauty in ruins: its show window has been covered with a handwritten sign in large letters, "WE ARE OPENED," turned upside down as if to signify that we are not opened. One corner of the building is shaved off at an angle, perhaps once to accommodate a porch for the gas pumps of a service station long gone; the building has a side room on the right instead of the left, a side room that not too long ago, in the Age of the Automobile, stocked tires, batteries, oil, and fan belts. Brick-patterned asphalt siding covers most of the old clapboards. *Tarpaper*, Kim jots in her notebook, but it is actually asbestos-permeated siding that comes (or came, in the forties and fifties) in rolls, with embossing imitating not only bricks but also stonemasonry and fish-scale shingles. This "tarpaper" is the most compote of all building materials, and it was used liberally to sheathe everything in Cherokee City.

In the absolute silence of high noon, Kim sits in her car, a sporty Datsun that she named Zephyra after the west wind; she ponders these tumbledown emporia and scarcely notices the third country store, which is not falling, and from which a woman emerges to ask Kim, "Can I help you?" This is the first time that a storekeeper has ever waited on Kim outside the building, except at service stations.

"I'm just prowling around the lost cities of Arkansas," Kim says.

"You've sure found a good one," the woman says, and offers, "Come inside."

Kim notices the small sign on the porch of the false front covered with fish-scale tarpaper: "Carol's Country Store." "Are you Carol?" she asks, following her into the store.

She is. Carol Trammell Medlam, forty-seven, an Arkansaw-yer who spent fifteen years carrying mail in Kansas City but came home every year to Huntsville, and whose uncle happened to own the "WE ARE OPENED" store across the road. If it is possible, as Kim has done, to fall in love with such a foundling store, then Carol has fallen in love with *this* store, which she has bought and operates. All of the stores were shut down when she reopened this one. The highway used to come through here, but then a new little paved bypass was built to the east, and there's a new "store" of sorts just opened over there. Carol has some signs on the new highway pointing out that her store is a detour of only five hundred feet, but few travelers notice or bother.

"Since you've been here," Kim asks, "has your business improved steadily, or stayed the same, or have you had declining periods?"

"All of the above!" Carol says. The old man who ran the store before her had let his stock run down and had given too much credit. Carol doesn't give credit and she has built up the stock, but the economy has fallen off and the competition from the new store—Cherokee Kid, actually just a gas stop—has hurt her. But people don't go to Cherokee Kid to socialize, let alone to sit down and loaf in the time-honored fashion of country stores. Carol's store is homier and cozier, Kim observes, and it even has a checkerboard ready if anyone wants to play.

Carol is interested in the history of Cherokee City, but she doesn't know very much about it. She shows Kim a photograph, blown up from an 1890s postcard, showing the broad Main Street lined with stores shoulder to shoulder on each side, wooden sidewalks connecting their porches, the John M. Norris Drug Store with an Odd Fellows Hall upstairs, a post office where John M. Norris is postmaster, and the balconied John M. Norris residence in the distance. There are general stores, a furniture store, an apple evaporator, a barber shop, a feed store, a blacksmith shop, a newspaper office, a saloon or two—all gone today. The dirt road is filled with wagons and buggies, and the wooden sidewalks are lined with men in beards and Stetson hats.

John M. Norris was the merchant prince and leading citizen of the little city in its golden age. Born in Audrain County, Missouri (Mark Twain country), in 1849, he learned the plasterer's trade to put himself through Warrenton College. This area of Missouri is littered with cities manqué: Benton City, Kingdom City, Montgomery City, Wright City, Cedar City, and even the capital, Jefferson City, one of the tiniest state capitals. After college, Norris searched for younger, fresher cities in Missouri, Indian Territory, Texas, and Kansas (he could have gone east to Norris City, Illinois, but had to go west), until in our key year of 1886 he discovered Cherokee City. There was already an empty building on Main Street, in which he unloaded his fixtures and drug supplies and remained for the rest of his life, expanding his store with the expansion of the town, serving as postmaster all through its boom years of 1888–97, contracting his store with the contraction of the town, and raising a family of seven sons. Although he wasn't even a registered or licensed pharmacist, he knew enough about the dysfunctions that befall humankind to serve as a kind of quasi-doctor to the town, particularly to the poor and to kids who couldn't afford the town's regular physician, who wasn't registered or licensed, either.

Doc Norris, as everyone called him, sold a cornucopia of pharmacopoeia that was a little heavy on the narcotic side. There were no federal or state regulations on drugs in those days, and even the nonprescription remedies, like Mother's Friend, Carter's Little Liver Pills, Thedford's Black Draught, and Dr. Pierce's Golden Medical Discovery, all contained a little dope or booze. Doc Norris had a genius for knowing how much cocaine to give a woman to help her out of her menopausal depression, or how much laudanum was needed to comfort a grieving widower. Even young people, for whom Doc Norris would rarely administer the comforts of whiskey, could get their aches and pains soothed with a little tincture of some opiate. In the days before Midol, nothing was better for menstrual cramps than morphine, and in the days before aspirin, a boy's cracked skull and wounded pride could be treated only with a smidgin of heroin. Even the forbidden whiskey could be given in a small one-time-only dose when Doc Norris was setting a broken bone.

A genial fixer like John Milton Norris was symbolically appropriate to a town whose very existence had been based upon the power of manufactured chemistry to alter consciousness. A sluggish little stream called Hog Eye Creek (identified as Cherokee Creek on modern maps) laps past the southern edge of the village, half a mile from the Indian Line, and the first white settlers there before the Civil War operated a distillery not only for their own use but also to slake the thirst of the Indians, who needed immoderate quantities of whiskey to palliate the real and imagined injustices done to them by the white man. Hog Eye served briefly as a way station, a kind of "Last Booze Before Oklahoma" on the infamous Trail of Tears, the long, long route of the displaced Cherokee in 1838–39, when, because gold had been discovered on their ancestral mountain lands in North and South Carolina, Georgia, Tennessee, and Alabama, they were forced to march beyond the Mississippi and across Arkansas into the flatlands of Indian Territory, where only the memory of mountains sustained them (aided by whiskey), and will go on sustaining them for the rest of their existence. The Trail of Tears got its name, naturally, from the fact that the Indians were inclined to weep along the way. Some of them discovered, on reaching Hog Eye and pausing for refreshment at the tavern there, that their tears dried up after three or four drinks, and they entered the Territory with happy smiles on their faces.

Because by law Indian Territory was "dry," for years the Indians kept coming back to Hog Eye (or to the saloons of other border towns like Tiff City and South West City, Missouri, which expected to achieve cityhood on the strength of their firewater trade with the Indians). Drunken Indians, like their white counterparts, tend to become mean and unruly, and Hog Eye very early acquired its reputation as a wild and woolly town. Since the word "woolly," so often used in combination with "wild," means precisely "having the characteristics of the rough, generally lawless atmosphere of frontier America," the saloonkeeper James Ingle, when informed by the Post Office Department that the name Hog Eye would have to be dropped because there was already a Hog Eye in Washington County, decided to call the place Woolly City as a kind of joke, and when his dubious colleagues wondered why, he would explain that it was in honor of his predecessor as saloonkeeper of Hog Eye—in fact the first white settler of Hog Eye Creek, in the 1830s—one Jeremiah Woolly.

If anyone asked, James Ingle could tell the entire biography of old Jeremiah Woolly, a yard wide, born on the Big Sandy River in Kentucky not far from Peter Mankins II, descended from illiterate Britishers who couldn't spell the family name, Wolsey, as in the cardinal of Henry VIII's time. This invented Jeremiah Woolly became so real to everyone that James Ingle had to establish a little cemetery east of town and erect a kind of gravestone for Woolly in it. The slab is crumbled and effaced today, but the little cemetery is still there and is shown on a government map, although scarcely anyone knows where it is.

The real origin of "woolly" is just as obscure as that of "hog eye." Anyone who has stared down a pig knows that the porcine

optic is so inscrutable as to be almost invisible. A bull's eye is a
good term for concentric circles, but "hog eye" can only suggest
the vacant, glazed look of a drunk staring upward and sideways
(a nearly obsolete Ozark adjective, "hog-eyed," referred to the
facial expression resulting from looking upward and sideways
without turning the head). Just as "wall-eyed" is another description for both divergent strabismus and drunkenness, we may
assume that "hog-eyed" likewise meant either condition, or both,
in the case of wall-eyed individuals who became intoxicated.
"Woolly" possibly derives from the fact that cowboys wore vests
and jackets made of sheepskin with the wool still on. James Ingle's
customers, Indians included, eventually suspected that he was
pulling the wool over their eyes with his plan for turning Hog
Eye into Woolly City. So he abandoned the memory of Jeremiah
Woolly to the valhalla of fictional heroes, and called the town
officially Cherokee City.

James Ingle plotted and platted the city along pretty much
the same lines the village has today; that is, the Main Street and
its principal intersector, named Spring Street (a little city that
names its streets intends to become a city), were in the same
location as they are today, and the rest of the "city" was divided
into twenty-four blocks, just like Sulphur City (but with fourteen
lots per block instead of the conventional twelve).

Cherokee City needed, in order to fulfill herself "as a bride
adorned for her husband" (Revelation 21:2), a hotel. Sulphur
City had desired a hotel, but never got one. Cherokee City got
one, very early, and, *mirabile dictu*, it is still standing, still inhabited—although, compared with, say, the Fayetteville Hilton, it is
but a tarpaper shack, or, properly speaking, a brick-patterned
asphalt roll-siding shack, composted like so many other buildings
in town. In 1876, on the country's Centennial, one Samuel Hoag,
born in France in 1811, built Cherokee House, sometimes called
simply Hoag Hotel, which he operated until he died of tuberculosis in 1892. It was hastily constructed out of the frantic
speculation in real estate characterizing "cities" sprouting like
mushrooms in the American West, the same atmosphere of impatient hope that nurtured, or precipitated, all these lost cities.

But the carpentry was unavoidably craftsmanlike and sound, with foot-square timbers dovetailed and joined with mortise and tenon and square nails, and the architecture was of a style we might call "hostelry vernacular." The present owners of the hotel, having finished raising their children, have moved into a small house they built next door. Carol Medlam tells Kim that she ought to talk to them, Elton and Dovey Yates, who are "descended from everybody" and "know everything" about Cherokee City.

Kim visits the Yateses in their living room, compotishly styled with scenic mural of sunset on water. Elton Yates, age seventy-five, coeval to stout Buster Price, is a small, frail man who smokes cigarettes constantly but asks Kim if she minds, and although she has never smoked she doesn't mind. Now retired, Elton was once a dairyman (like Kim's father) and has also worked as a tie hauler, service-station and ice-plant operator, and nurseryman, and in airplane factories for the air force. The stove in the living room is very hot. Dovey prepares and serves coffee, but Kim does not like caffeine. Many redbirds flock around the window, where seed has been left on the ground for them. A pet bird in a cage twitters and tweets and is heard in the background on the tape that Kim is recording. The Yateses, like the Prices of Sulphur City, have much respect and affection for each other, and, as long-married couples do, they often speak the same answers simultaneously, or repeat each other immediately, or finish each other's sentences.

Kim begins with a standard question: whether they have lived here all their lives. Never left? Elton says, "Oh, yeah, I've went off, then come back, then go off, come back." Just what is it about Cherokee City that keeps bringing him home? Elton chuckles and shakes his head. "There was plenty of meanness around here when I was a kid—drunks and fights. I've seen 'em ride up and down the streets and fire guns up in the air. And they used to come to the old hotel here to gamble. Fact, they's bullet holes up there in the ceilings of that old house yet."

Cherokee City was born as a drinking and gambling town, then. But did it have any other attractions? Elton says, "Yeah, they was several springs here people came for—had different kinds of water in it." What kind of water? "Well, I just really don't remember, only, the iron, and the . . . hell, I've forgotten now what the other ones . . ." Dovey puts in: "They've done away with all those springs." Elton: "Don't remember what was in the other ones, but they was two or three springs that had different types of water in it." Sulphur? "No, they were no sulphur here, that I know of."

Why did the town start dying? Well, it was surveyed for the Kansas City Southern Railroad track, but then they decided to put the track through the town of Gentry, six miles to the east. Did the bypassing of the railroad hurt the town? Killed it. And has the bypassing of the paved highway killed it a little deader? Yes, but Elton and Dovey like it better the way it is, and gladly gave the Highway Department the right-of-way, because vehicles used to go around the corner so fast they'd spray gravel all over the porch.

Did the highway shift affect "downtown" Cherokee City? Yes, two of the stores there—groceries, Dawson's and Gordon Evans's—went out of business. Where do you shop for groceries now? Gentry, six miles to the east. What happened to Dawson? Moved to Gentry. What happened to Gordon Evans when he closed his store and turned the "WE ARE OPENED" sign upside down? Moved to Gentry.

Kim drives to Gentry, six miles to the east. The railroad tracks still run through it, and sometimes a freight train runs through it, but downtown Gentry City, as it was known until recent times, is in pretty sorry shape itself, the shops lining Main Street turned mostly into secondhand-furniture stores. All over Arkansas, perhaps all over America, the deserted downtowns have shops that were once department stores or drugstores or hardware stores or firsthand-furniture stores but are now secondhand-furniture stores, some of them claiming to sell "antiques" but others publicly admitting that they sell only "junque." One Gentry store says, "Used and Abused Furniture." Kim reflects that cities are used and abused, that towns are secondhand. She pauses to watch the destruction of the Elberta Hotel, once a large white rambling hotel. Now there is only one small motel on the highway, whose proprietor is Gordon Evans. Signs on the door of the motel say, "We will charge you $10 if you knock to ask for directions or to borrow jumper cables" and other testy cautions directed at the various abuses of the motel business in a place like Gentry, Arkansas. Gordon Evans, however, is a gentleman, coeval to Elton and Buster, soft-spoken, cordial, unassuming, the model of the genial country storekeeper, and seems out of his element running a motel.

"Did you enjoy having that store?" Kim asks him.

"You had better believe I did!" Gordon Evans replies. "Had it for twenty-one years."

"What did you enjoy most?"

"Gettin acquainted with people," he says. Gordon's wife, who is Carol Medlam's aunt, remembers the old-timers who came to the store to sit around on nail kegs, or loafed on the benches of the porch. But Gordon remembers best the Indians. "I had a big Injun trade from over in Oklahoma, and they'd come for miles over to my store. I got along real good with 'em." Any trouble at all? No, and in the winter Evans would buy their fence posts, which they made and hauled to him by the thousands, and which he resold to customers from as far away as Texas and Kansas. He had a good business, as well as a DX service station connected.

"Do you miss it?" Kim asks.

"Yes," Evans admits. "I wouldn't go back to a country store now, but when I had it, it was good. I thought I could make a livin at it, and I did. I wouldn't be afraid to go out there and do it again, but I wouldn't!"

Robert Yates, Elton's dad, called Rob by everyone, died fifteen years ago at the age of ninety-two. John Milton Norris was his mother's kid brother; therefore Doc Norris was Rob Yates's uncle. Nancy Norris, Doc Norris's sister, had eloped at a young age with Billy Yates, a mule trader, a tall, tough man with red hair and red beard, who impregnated Nancy every two years until ten children were born biennially between 1863 and 1882. Rob was the eighth of these, born in Texas while Billy was driving a herd of mules to Dallas to sell. Billy usually took his mules to market in St. Louis, and spent much of what he got for them on whiskey. Nancy hoped they could get so rich in Texas that he couldn't spend it all on whiskey, and sure enough he made so much money he took the family back to Missouri and built a house with his Texas profits, which, however, were still enough for much more whiskey than he could safely consume. It wasn't his drinking itself that bothered Nancy so much, but when he drank he became mean to her, and abusive to her and the children, and the only thing good for him was to let him take her so many times that she would be with child again. After two more, when she learned that her dear brother John Milton was moving to a nice new town called Cherokee City down in Arkansas, she wrote to him and told him that she didn't know how much longer she could put up with Billy's drinking. John Milton wrote back and told her to leave Billy and come to Cherokee City. She didn't have any money for the trip, but the next time Billy drove a herd of mules to St. Louis, she sold their cows and their pigs and took her ten children to Cherokee City, and none of them ever laid eyes on Billy again. Rob was nine years old, and he missed his father although his father had beaten him; he kept asking his mother when Billy would come to Cherokee City. But Nancy never told her husband where she was, and Uncle John, who owned the drugstore and a big farm that Nancy and her children lived on, was very nice to Rob, treating him almost like his own son, whose name was Thomas Harvey. Cousin Harve was only two years older than Rob, and Harve and Rob grew up together like Tom Sawyer and Huck Finn, the adventures of the former published the year that Harve was born.

Harve Norris, John Milton's firstborn, missed having his birthday on the Centennial of the United States by only one day: he was born on July 5, 1876, which was just as well, because the celebration of the Fourth each year was such a big event that his birthday would have gone unnoticed. As it was, he got all the leftover pink lemonade and pies and cakes, if there were any. Some years he got leftover fireworks, if there were any, but there usually weren't. There were two events, contests, that he and Rob always entered during the big picnic on the Fourth: climbing the greased pole and catching the greased pig. Or trying to. The greased pole was a twenty-foot cedar trimmed of all its branches and sanded down to the slickness of a pencil, then coated with hog lard. You wrapped your legs and your arms around it and tried to shinny to the top, where a silver dollar was waiting for the winner. It was a rare Fourth that any of the kids could climb that high, but Rob Yates generally always could, and he always gave the silver dollar to Harve the next day as a birthday present. Shinnying the greased pole was terrible on your crotch and your nuts and peter, nearly raising blisters on the latter if it got stiff from all that rubbing. Catching the greased pig wasn't so hard on the privy parts, real soft by comparison with the pole. Harve could outrun Rob, and he usually got to the pig first and locked his legs and arms around it, but the way the pig squirmed and squealed always made his peter so thick he was afraid it would show through his pants, though only Rob seemed to notice and laugh behind his hand. One year, the year Harve turned thirteen, he got such a hard-on from wrestling the slick pig that anybody would have noticed, but the prize for winning was a cheap guitar, full-size enough to cover Harve's belly and haunches. He pretended to play it while letting his erection subside, and in fact began learning how to play it, picking out tunes by ear, discovering that strumming the strings was a pretty good public substitute for beating his meat.

In time Harve became an accomplished public guitarist as well as an accomplished private peter-player; his stringed instrument and his fleshed instrument became the same in his mind and in his fingers. The differences between Harve and Rob were as great as those between Tom and Huck: the one a town boy, the other a farm boy; Rob was tone-deaf and couldn't play a note and, being only eleven, didn't seem interested in masturbation yet, but he knew a whole bunch of cuss words and dirty words that Harve had never heard in town. In town, Harve didn't have the opportunities to watch farm animals copulating on a daily basis, and he didn't understand that the reason Rob didn't play with himself was that Rob had already found a country girl or

two, particularly half-breeds or purebloods, who kept him supplied with plenty of openings for his rising manhood. Harve liked
to boast to Rob of what he was going to do when the time came
for him to diddle a girl; Rob smiled and didn't tell Harve the
details of his steamy young life. Rob respected Harve, who was,
after all, the oldest son of Uncle Doc Norris, postmaster, druggist,
merchant, quack, shaman, and landlord of the farm where Rob's
mother raised her kids. All the girls in town and at school adored
Harve, and when he played his guitar at picnics and square dances
and play-parties, all the girls watched him with entranced faces
and came close to swooning. Of course, these were good girls
who never fornicated; half-breeds and purebloods didn't go to
the picnics and square dances and play-parties, but did go to the
Norris barn when they wanted Rob to mount them.

Harve was not popular with the other boys, except Cousin
Rob. The other boys envied and resented the girls' adoration of
him, his fancy clothes, his speed in catching the greased pig, and
above all his ability to play the guitar. Like him, they could pick
and fiddle their peters, but that was all, and their envy made
them shun him or goad him into fights. Every Saturday afternoon
all of the hot-blooded youths of Cherokee City and environs
would congregate at Big Rock on Hog Eye Creek in order to
swap gossip, tell dirty jokes, exchange taunts and teasing and
insults, create disputes, start fights, argue with their fists or by
wrestling in the dirt, throw rocks at one another, sometimes draw
knives and use them, sometimes even fire pistols. Someone or
two was always getting hurt, and would have to go to Doc Norris
for bandages and dope and Doc's own simple brand of psycho-
therapy, which Doc called simply "mendin feelins." Doc was very
good at mendin feelins, and always made a point of being available at his drugstore on Saturday afternoons when the fights
were over, though much of the rest of the time he was gone. In
a free-for-all fight, Harve could depend on his tough cousin Rob
to take his side. Harve wished he could sneak some of the dope
out of his dad's drugstore and distribute it among his fellows;
that would guarantee his popularity. But his father kept all of
his strong medicines, the ones with belladonna and laudanum

and cocaine, under lock and key. Even when, at fourteen, Harve went to work for his father as the main clerk in the drugstore, John Norris wouldn't trust him with the key to the dope cabinet. If a customer came in and wanted something that had belladonna or laudanum or cocaine in it, Harve had to go find his father. And often Doc Norris was hard to find. If he wasn't gone on business to some distant town, or overseeing one of his several farms, he would be paying a house call as a "physician." These house calls were mysterious to his wife, his son, and his customers who needed some dope but had to wait until Doc Norris returned, because sometimes he would be gone for two or three days. He never talked about just where, or how far, he had driven his buggy to the patient's house, but usually he had to stay with the patient overnight, or two nights, or three; sometimes the patient died anyway, and sometimes the patient lived, but always Doc Norris was gone away from home and from his drugstore and mercantile business and farms for days at a stretch. If a customer needed a fix of dope very badly and couldn't wait for Doc Norris to come home, he or she would just have to go away off to Bentonville for a drugstore.

Since Doc Norris lost some of his customers because of this, both he and Harve were glad when Harve achieved the age of sixteen; Doc Norris interrupted his healing of injuries sustained on the Fourth long enough to observe the Fifth and present Harve with a birthday present in the form of keys to the strong-dope cabinet. "You're a big and reliable young man, now," Doc Norris told Harve, showing him the various bottles. "Don't let anybody have more than an ounce of this one, four ounces of this one, a gram of this, or a pinch of this one." By this time, Harve was no longer interested in impressing his peers or ingratiating them with dope. All he wanted was girls, or *a* girl.

Tom Sawyer has his Becky Thatcher, whom he dearly loves and for whom he will do anything, risk anything, sacrifice anything. Harve Norris had his . . . we will have to call her, for want of her real name, Rebecca Scratcher of West Cherokee City, Arkansas. She was beautiful beyond description, sweet sixteen, and like Harve a virgin, which was rare for a mixed-blood, as she was. She herself did not know how much or how little Indian she had in her; not half, certainly, for neither her father nor her mother was an Indian or even half an Indian, but one or the other of them had one parent who had given or received Indian sperm, or half-Indian sperm, scant traces of which still were noticeable in Rebecca: her cheekbones, perhaps, or her dark eyes. There was not enough Indian in her to exclude her from the dances or play-parties, but there was enough Indian in her so that, when Harve informed his parents that he would do any-thing, risk anything, sacrifice anything for Rebecca Scratcher, they laughed at him and told him that she wasn't worth it because she was from a "no-account family." The other girls of Cherokee City also, the ones who worshipped Harve for his guitar and his looks and his clothes, but whom he spurned in favor of Becky Scratcher, spoke among themselves of how low-class Becky was. They envied her the beauty that had won Harve's heart, just as the boys had envied Harve his popularity. Both Harve and Becky were outcasts of a sort: pariahs to their peers, ostracized because of their superiority; at the dances and play-parties they were ignored, except by faithful Rob, always Harve's friend.

If Harve noticed this ostracism, it didn't seem to affect him, because he was too busy trying to think of some way to persuade Becky to let him do more to her than dance with her and hold her hand and steal a quick kiss now and then. To his loyal side-kick, Rob, Harve would complain, "I jist don't know how to git ole Beck to take down her bloomers." Rob, experienced as he was with Indian girls and half-breeds, didn't know what advice to give Harve on the seduction of octoroon Injuns. For Rob it had never been a matter of verbal suasion; he had never had to *ask* a Injun girl to take down her bloomers for him. Rob did not know how to explain to Harve his Theory of Apocrines and Pheromones. Of course he did not call them apocrines or pher-omones, which had not been discovered yet or given names. Both were simply a matter of different smells. Just as you could tell the difference between a honeysuckle and a rose from the way they smelled, you could tell the difference between an Indian girl and a white girl. But also, on account of the pheromones, you could also smell the difference between a girl who wasn't the least bit interested in having you fool around with her and a girl who would begin to feel like screaming if you didn't do something real quick to stop the itch in the place where babies come from. This, more or less, is the way Rob tried to explain apocrines and pheromones to Harve.

From then on, whenever Harve got the chance, he would lean over toward Becky and take a deep sniff. Sure enough, he could inhale some of the apocrine that clearly indicated that Becky was at least one-thirty-second and maybe even one-sixteenth Indian. But he couldn't detect any pheromone. He wasn't sure exactly what a pheromone would smell like. He asked Rob, "Jist what kinda stink is it?" Rob couldn't explain it or describe it, other than by comparing it to certain things like "your sister's breath when she's been eatin mud-turtle soup" or "a whiff of jimsonweed when the mornin dew's not yit offen it" or "a crawdad if you drop a rock on it." Harve's nose could not perceive any of these scents coming from Becky. Rob decided that the only way to help his friend learn how to detect the exact aroma of a pheromone would be to introduce him to it in the form of one of the Indian girls who came to the Norris barn when they wanted Rob to mount them. When Rob invited Harve to the Norris barn one evening, Harve was all excited, but he hoped his cousin was not just pulling a prank on him. "What do I do, what do I do?" he kept asking Rob. "You dont do nothin," Rob assured him; "you jist do what she shows ye she wants."

They did not have to wait long. An Indian maiden came into the gloom of the barn's interior. Rob gave Harve a little shove, and he went to meet her, and that was all. She took him down into the hay. There was a very clear and a very strange and sweet and exciting fragrance to her; she reeked of something that was not at all like crawdads or jimsonweed or turtle soup but much spicier and more penetrating, and it grew stronger the longer Harve penetrated her. He would never forget it as long as he lived.

But the Indian girl knew that he wasn't Rob; even if she hadn't recognized him in the half-light of the hayloft, he had his own apocrines and pheromones, which she identified, and these pheromones of his were still lingering upon her body later when she met that snooty Becky Scratcher and bragged that she had gotten a full load of jism from Harvey Norris. Becky knew the girl wasn't lying, because she could identify Harve's pheromones, too, and she pulled the girl's hair and scratched her face and would have scratched her eyes out if the girl hadn't broken loose and run away.

Now that Harve could easily recognize rutty pheromones, he couldn't wait to get another sniff of Becky, but when he did she sniffed back at him, and the two of them just stood there getting snootfuls of each other until Becky scratched at his nose and would have torn it off if her own nose hadn't started running so much because she was crying and angry. She ran away from him, and he was left holding his nose and wondering what had gotten into her. His nose hurt him so much that he had to go let himself into the drugstore, open up the dope cabinet, and take a pinch of something for the pain.

Maybe Becky never had pheromones, he decided, or maybe virgins don't produce pheromones. The next time he saw her again, at a square dance he was playing for, she was with H. T. Tucker, a big guy all of nineteen or twenty years old. Harve tried to get her for a dance, but she wouldn't, and ole H.T. was nasty about it. However, Harve got close enough to smell her, and there was no mistake about it: she was practically covered with pheromones big as cockroaches. Harve was crushed. He couldn't play any more. He wanted to break his guitar over H. T. Tucker's head. He stared at Becky as if his eyes could scrub her clean of all her scents, but his heart was breaking, and once, when she caught him staring at her, she grinned at him with such a self-satisfied look that he knew she was not a virgin any more and he could never marry her.

He dropped his guitar on the floor with a clatter and said to his fellows, "Eat, drink, and be merry, 'cause tonight I'm gonna die." Then he ran away from the square dance, and that was the last time that any of the young people of Cherokee City saw Harve Norris alive. Rob said he would have followed him, except he had no idee what frame of mind Harve was in, and figured Harve was just steppin out for a leak or somethin.

Of Rob's son Elton, Kim gently and hesitantly inquires, "Do you know anything about Harve Norris?"

Elton replies, "Well, I don't remember him myself, but I've heared the folks talk about him. The best I can remember, he got mad about some gal."

Dovey says, "His dad didn't want him going with this girl. He wanted to marry the girl."

"Do you know the girl?" Kim asks. "What her name would've been?"

Elton and Dovey together say, "No. Don't know."

"It's such a tragic story and very romantic!" Kim says. "Over a girl. He was just sixteen when he killed himself."

Dovey says, "I doubt there's anyone who could help. His nephew lives out here, but he's a cousin to us. I doubt if this nephew would know anything about it, or he might not want to talk about it."

Through Carol Medlam, Kim tries to set up an interview with the nephew, George Norris, but George tells Carol to tell Kim that he just isn't interested in talking about anything. This is a problem that Kim will encounter in a few of these lost cities: the respondent doesn't respond, because either (1) he has heard every conceivable sales gimmick or pretext for gaining admittance, and is convinced that Kim is peddling cosmetics or *Watchtowers*, or (2) he knows nothing and therefore has nothing to say.

Kim contacts Gordon Evans again in Gentry. Evans has heard of Harve Norris but knows nothing. "You might ask George Norris," he says, but adds, "No, George wouldn't tell you anything if he knew." Kim tries Fannie Baxley of Gentry, former postmaster of Cherokee City. Mrs. Baxley, age seventy-five, has only a vague memory of the story, but remembers the Norrises fondly and still hears from the ones in California; Brandt Norris was postmaster of Cherokee City throughout the Depression and until the war, when Fannie became postmaster. Brandt built Carol's Store in 1935, and is the son of Harve's kid brother, James Monroe (Uncle Jim) Norris, who was himself postmaster during

World War I. In fact, Uncle Jim had another son, Jewett, who ran a grocery store out there in California at one time, but came on back to Arkansas.

Simply by checking the local phone directory, Kim locates Jewett Norris and his wife, Seritha, living in a place called Rainbow Valley east of Siloam Springs. (This town was named for the pool outside Jerusalem mentioned in John 9:7, where the blind man was healed by Christ, who "said unto him, Go, wash in the pool of Siloam [which means "Sent"]. He went his way therefore, and washed, and came seeing." But Kim has never read the Bible.) Kim is enchanted with the name Rainbow Valley, because a few years before she had become so captivated by the image and meaning of the rainbow that she began to collect them, and among her possessions are rainbow pillows, rainbow stained glass, rainbow posters, a rainbow calendar, rainbow decals and towels and stickers and candles and badges and pendants and stationery; the rainbow could so easily be compote, but it is too metaphysical to be compote.

Rainbow Valley is scarcely a valley, just a hollow with small pastures and a man-made pond and Rainbow Valley Lodge, a pleasant but ostentatious brick ranch-style house with colonial iron gates bearing baronial lions rampant in bronze. Although Seritha Norris is wearing the same lavender slacks that so many of the other mature ladies wear, the interior of her house is not compote at all but tastefully decorated, and betrays no sign of religiosity. Jewett Norris is a white-haired man whose face suggests that at the age of sixteen he looked very much like his uncle Harve: a handsome dude, a stud, a man-about-town or, rather, boy-about-town.

"Do you remember being told about Harve?" Kim asks them.

Seritha answers for both: "I've heard Grandma—Jewett's grandmother, that's Harve's ma—tell about it. Harve went to this dance down on Hog Eye, and his girlfriend, some way or 'nother, was with another guy, and it made him real despondent."

"Do you know her name?" Kim asks.

"No," Seritha says, "but he went back to Jewett's grandfather's drugstore—that's John M. Norris's drugstore, you know—

and mixed this . . . laudanum, is it? Mixed this laudanum and drank it."

Jewett affirms, "Drank a full-ounce bottle of laudanum."

Seritha adds, "He was probably already drunk to begin with."

"No question about it," Jewett says. "There was a big distill in those days in Cherokee [like many others, he pronounces this "Cherry-kee"], and they only sixteen but drank the stuff, and that night I guess Harve just got drunk enough and said, 'That's it, I've had enough,' and headed for the drugstore. 'Course he had keys to the store and all, and went in, and took that bottle of laudanum, and started up and drank every bit of it, the whole bottle, he drank it all. That night, they walked him—my grandmother told—she and my grandfather, they walked him till after daylight. Back then I guess that was about the only thing they knew to do. And as long as they could keep 'im a-movin . . . They said finally he just went to sleep on their shoulder till they couldn't even walk him any more."

In their grief, John Milton Norris and his wife, Lidie, clung to each other for many days and nights. Later Lidie would become cold and harsh, never letting John forget that his carelessness with the keys to the drug cabinet had caused their son's death, but in the first days and nights of her grief she clung to him, so much that she immediately became pregnant again, and less than nine months after Harve's death she bore another son. She wanted to name him Thomas Harvey, in replacement of dead Harve, but John Milton Norris insisted that the boy be named John Milton Norris, without any "Jr.," in replacement for himself, for the self of him that he thought had died with his firstborn son. Lidie would have two more sons in the five years left of her twenty-two years of childbearing.

Harve was laid to rest in the Dickson Cemetery, north of Cherokee City, beside a spot reserved for and later filled by his father. Kim visits the two graves; the cemetery, like that of Sulphur City, is exactly a mile and a half away from the village, a convenient but not-too-convenient distance. Harve's stone notes that he lived sixteen years, seven months, and eleven days, and quotes a bit of stock poetastery: "A precious one from us is gone / A voice we loved is stilled / A place is vacant in our home / That never can be filled." The young John Milton Norris was expected to fill the place, but he filled it only in anticipation, as a town styled "city" is given its name only in anticipation, never fulfilled.

Anticipating other suicides or sensational news, a newspaper was founded and issued weekly, *The Cherokee City Advance.* But except for national and international news received by telegraph, the newspaper was thin and had little local news. "J. M. Norris sent a load of fat hogs to Siloam Springs last Monday." "Several of our people made the trip to Siloam Springs to see the elephant at the circus." "J. M. Norris is building a picket fence around his garden." "J. T. Quimby has enclosed his garden with a picket fence." "Dr. Norris has lost several head of shoats." "John Yates has erected a picket fence on each side of his garden." "John Norris went to Gentry." "Anderson Hood has set up a picket fence encircling his garden patch." "J. T. Quimby went to Gentry." "J. M. Norris has returned from The Nation." "John Yates went to Gentry." "Mrs. Gadberry has hired the Gildersleeve boy to build a picket fence bordering her garden." "Anderson Hood has returned from The Nation." "Try Taylor's Cherokee Remedy for your next cough, croup or consumption; made of sweet gum and mullein." One event of interest did occur: John Norris's sister Alice—sister also of Nancy Yates, Rob's mother—had a son named Jack, older than Harve. The girl he wanted to marry was a pure-blood white, but his mother, who worshipped him and wanted him always for her own, would not hear of the match. She became so furious when Jack told her of his plan to marry the girl that she pointed a pistol at her son and told him he was as good as dead to her if he left her to go ahead with it. Jack tried to take the pistol away from his mother, and in the scuffle she was shot and killed. When he saw that his mother was dead, Jack turned the gun on himself and committed suicide more quickly than his cousin Harve had done. But John Norris persuaded the editor to leave the story of the two deaths out of his newspaper, and shortly thereafter the editor left Cherokee City and took the *Advance* with him to another town, where picket fences bloomed like garden weeds.

There have been other suicides, down to the present day. The Cherokee House hotel, when Samuel Hoag died of tuberculosis in 1892, was bought by a Mrs. Haxon, who ran it for several years during the height of the city's prosperity in the 1890s. Her husband took several shots at himself before hitting and dying; the holes of the misses remained visible in the walls and ceiling of the lobby until recently, when Elton Yates covered them with sheetrock. Kim tries to locate another old-timer, named Bill Lamphear, son of the town marshal John Lamphear who investigated several of these suicides, only to learn that Bill Lamphear had done away with himself a few months before. "He had lost his wife," Carol Medlam tells Kim. "She was ill. I guess it was just too much for him. They found him with her picture in one hand and a gun in the other."

Kim decides to stop in at the "new store in town," the Cherokee Kid Groc., sign courtesy of Dr. Pepper soft drinks (called "sody pop" throughout the Ozarks), which are one of the few things it sells other than gasoline. A very small building of unpainted cement blocks, it seems even smaller because it contains so little merchandise: candy, cigarettes, cold drinks, the bare essentials. The woman running it, Dorothy Asher, is not the owner. Who owns it? Kim asks. "Linda," the woman says. Linda is the woman's daughter. Kim wishes Linda were available for questions. The woman is watching a soap opera on a very loud television set. How long has the store been in business? Kim tries to hear the answer: " 'Bout five months, something like that I guess."

Kim requests, "Could we turn down the TV? I can hardly hear you!" The woman makes a gesture of turning it down, but the volume is not reduced. "Who named the store Cherokee Kid?" Kim inquires.

"I guess *them*, own know," the woman says. "Own know" is the way she pronounces "I don't know" without enthusiasm.

"Was it named for Cherokee City?" Kim asks.

"Own know," the woman says. "I didn't ast no questions."

"Are you in competition with the other store, Carol's Store?"

"Own know. I 'magine. I haven't been down there in a long time."

Kim asks, "Would you say this is a gathering place? Do people come here and visit?"

"No. Just people come in and out."

Later Kim learns from others that the woman's husband, Jewell Asher, died under a bridge, in his car, over across the Oklahoma line. Asphyxiated. Not a suicide, apparently, just an accidental asphyxiation. The Ashers are one of the oldest families in Cherokee City.

Another old family, for whom the cemetery was named, is the Dicksons. Kim interviews Medea Dickson, age eighty-four, living in a mobile home (called, variously, "house trailer" or "trailer house"), spacious, tastefully decorated without compote, neat and clean. Mrs. Dickson taught school, first through eighth grades at the Cherokee City school, a two-room building no longer standing, just up the road from the present Cherokee Kid store. She has arranged for her son, Don, to visit and meet Kim. Don Dickson is a research archaeologist working professionally for the University of Arkansas. He has grown up in Cherokee City, explored it thoroughly as a boy and a man, and although his field of archaeology is the prehistoric Indian, not the modern Cherokee, he has made a hobby of local history, inventoried the Dickson cemetery, and, Kim is delighted to discover, interviewed Rob Yates before his death.

"I didn't use a tape recorder," Dickson says, noticing the silent whirring of Kim's Realistic CTR-55. "I took notes. At ninety-two, Rob Yates was as sharp as he could be, and he could remember the 1890s clearly. I tried to trip him up, but there was no way. That guy told you the same thing, every single time, from whichever direction you asked him. Because of my scientific training, I take things from different angles to see if the stories all fit together. And there was no way of tripping up Yates."

Kim does not have to ask questions, or even get a chance to; Don Dickson likes to talk. "I asked Rob Yates why Cherokee City declined. I told him, 'I've heard that Cherokee City was a popular resort town in the 1880s,' and I asked him, 'Why did it cease to attract people, do you think?' And he said that nearby towns such as Siloam Springs advertised medicinal waters for bathing, drinking, and so forth. Cherokee City had a good spring, and a hydraulic ram to pump the water from the spring up to the town, but the water was not medicinal. Then later, when the railroad bypassed Cherokee City in favor of Gentry, the town began to die. Still, it managed to support several stores before the automobile made it possible to visit Gentry easily. Before the railroad, before the motorcar, Cherokee City was much larger than Gentry."

Rob could remember the Indians' fondness for moonshine liquor. (Don Dickson had not asked, and Kim does not inquire, about young Rob's fondness for Indian maidens.) Hamp Woolridge continued to operate a corn-whiskey distillery on the south side of Hog Eye Branch, where the old town was. Woolridge had one of the better houses in town, still standing today although much altered and "modernized," and also ran a hardware store and a trading post, selling to the Cherokees ammunition, salt, coffee, tobacco, and other staples, including whiskey, for which the Indians paid in the barter of furs: fox, raccoon, opossum, mink, beaver, and muskrat. Well into the twentieth century, Hamp Woolridge dealt with the Indian fur trade, and with the specialty of the Cherokees: deer hide. The Nation, later Oklahoma, was a refuge for deer as well as for redskins; the latter shot the former and made an art of curing and tanning their hides. The hides were tanned with the animals' brains, which left them exceptionally soft and pliable and ideal for gloves, the best item of Indian leather goods. There are antique deerskin gloves still being worn today.

Doc Norris gave young Rob enough calves from the Norris farm to start him in business as a stockman, and Rob pastured his herds in the open range of The Nation, where his Indian friends kept an eye on them. Rob was friendly with the Indians all his life, although he never married one. When he reached his mid-twenties, convinced that Indian girls were just fine for the physical appetites but not suited for legal matrimony, he led to the altar a young white girl named Laura Shaw and had several kids by her, among them Elton. Rob let the Indians look after his cattle while he worked as a clerk in the stores of Cherokee

City, giving the Indians discounts on the merchandise; he was, according to his son Elton, "always good to the Indians." Kim had asked Elton, "In what way? What did he do for the Indians?" But Elton could only answer, "I don't know, other than more or less try to help 'em in different ways." Dovey had added, "Never had an enemy, I don't guess."

There was an Indian named Wofford, first name uncertain, about whom little is known. Elton Yates had mentioned Wofford to Kim as an example of how the Indians trusted Rob Yates and nobody else: when cattle were misplaced in The Nation, Wofford would find them and tell Rob where they were, but wouldn't tell Rob's brother or any other man. Don Dickson remembers his father telling of a Cherokee medicine man named Wofford who lived to be more than a hundred, and who collected herbs from the environs of Cherokee City. Rob Yates had told Don Dickson, "Some people liked ole Wofford as a doctor better than the ones we had, like Doc Norris. Doc Norris might bleed you or give you a bag of asafetida to wear, but Wofford would give you herbs and cure you." Kim has asked others about this Wofford. She recalls one of her Sulphur City informants, or correspondents, Marie Ball Wofford, a direct descendant of Peter Mankins, Sr., living in Jay, Oklahoma, whose husband, Dan Wofford, also a descendant of Peter Mankins, Sr. (both through Rachel, younger sister to Peter Junior), was a distant kinsman of the Cherokee James D. Wofford, a leader of the Georgia Cherokee on the Trail of Tears, and possibly the father or grandfather of this mysterious medicine man Wofford. When Kim asked Jewett Norris, "Do you remember an Indian named Wofford?", he replied that he knew a lot of Woffords but the one Kim had in mind must be "Ole Grandpa Wofford—I don't know which one he was—he translated the Bible into the Cherokee language—he was a well-educated Indian." (Possibly Jewett Norris confused Wofford with Sequoyah, whose "white" name was George Guess, and who was inventor of the Cherokee alphabet as well as eponym for the giant California evergreen.)

Kim mentions Wofford the medicine man to Carol Medlam; Carol has heard nothing of Wofford but suggests a "Cotton"

Blagg who runs a package store across the line in Oklahoma. Kim makes her first trip into Oklahoma.

The Mile Away gets its name from the fact that it is exactly one mile away from Cherokee City, westward, its eastern wall practically right on the Arkansas state line. Benton County, Arkansas, voted dry in 1945 and has revoted dry ever since, meaning that not even beer can legally be sold in the county. All Oklahoma counties are wet, but the hard stuff can be sold only in incorporated towns of three hundred or more, and The Mile Away carries only beer. It is operated by Cotton Blagg's son. Cotton lives down the highway a little ways. A man of fifty-five with sparse light-blond hair—hence his nickname—he has lived in this area all of his life. In fact, he was raised on Hog Eye Creek, not far from where the Indians used to buy their moonshine from the whites. In a curious kind of reversal ("Wofford's Revenge"?), the Indian of old traveled from the dry Nation into wet Arkansas to buy booze; now the white man in dry Benton County, Arkansas, has to cross the state line to get a six-pack of Coors. But Cotton estimates that less than 10 pecent of the business of The Mile Away is from Indians, whose drinking habits aren't really different, nowadays, from the white man's. "Most of your Indians over back this way," says Cotton Blagg, "you didn't have no trouble with. You take one occasionally—you know, they're just like everbody else, they'd get greased up a little bit, or try to, but, I mean, we didn't have no problems, 'cause they had to get off the premises; we sold 'em beer and just told 'em to get off and go somewheres else. They couldn't talk real good, a lot of 'em, but we never had no trouble with 'em."

"You must have gone to school with Indian kids," Kim says.

"Yes," Cotton says, "I did. Went to school with Indian children every day. They're easy to get along with. But you just kind of have to watch it: if you run into them and do 'em a favor or two, then they'll want you to do 'em some more favors."

"Did you ever know an Indian named Wofford?" Kim asks.

"Yeah, they used to be a lot of Woffords around here, and there's still some."

But Cotton Blagg has never heard of a medicine man called

Wofford. He tells Kim that she ought to talk to an old Indian woman named Kate Scraper, and he gives directions on how to find Kate Scraper off in the scrub oaks of eastern Delaware County. The roads are not paved, and Kim's car, Zephyra, fears the ruts and potholes, but Kim maneuvers her way to an old crossroads, still not far west of Cherokee City, still in Oklahoma, where there is a three-room "shotgun" house, painted gray, inhabited by a very old but spry half-Cherokee squaw and a large white house-cat. The interior is too plain and simple, too poor, to be compote, but it is meticulously neat and clean. Kim is fascinated by Kate Scraper, the first Indian she has ever talked with, and the first nonagenarian. Among half-breeds, Kate Scraper, age ninety-two, is that rarity whose father was a full-blood Cherokee and whose mother was a white woman, rather than the customary other-way-around. Arthritis has left Kate's hands extremely gnarled, but her face, although deeply lined, is still very bright and attractive, and her snow-white hair is well kept and neat. She was a child during the heyday of Cherokee City and the only living person who can remember not only the buildings—three general stores, two churches, livery barns, two hardware stores, the Odd Fellows Hall, Doc Norris's drugstore, the school, three hotels, and a café—but also a skating rink. Kate was fourteen (in 1907) before her parents would permit her (any day but Saturday) to go into downtown Cherokee City to roller-skate at the rink.

In her joyful, musical voice, free from the crackling that Kim has heard in the voices of other old women she has interviewed, Kate Scraper tells of the small but honest pleasures of growing up in Cherry-kee City. She wasn't born until the year after Harve Norris killed himself, but she can remember the story of it, if not the name of the girl involved. Her Cherokee grandfather fought in the Civil War with General Albert Pike's Indian Rebels at the Battle of Pea Ridge, which is in Benton County, not far from Cherokee City. Pea Ridge (or the Battle of Elkhorn Tavern, as it is sometimes called) has long been considered the most crucial Civil War engagement west of the Mississippi, responsible for the Confederates' loss of the trans-Mississippi and possibly the entire war, primarily because Pike's regiments of Indians proved to be totally ineffectual in the white man's style of warfare.

Kim asks, "Was your family thought of more as white or Indian?"

And Kate answers, "It didn't make any difference."

Kim asks, "Did you think of yourself more as Indian or white?"

And Kate replies, "Well, I don't know if I did! No, there was lots of Indians here, and lots of white people." In Cherokee City's population of five hundred, she points out, there were many Indians and mixed-breeds, and there was a lot of mingling, particularly at the church, the most important social institution in the wild, mean, woolly community.

"Did you ever hear of an Indian named Wofford?" Kim asks.

"Which one?" Kate replies. "The county is made up of Woffords. There's Charlie, and Bob, and Jim. . . ."

Kim thinks of Marie Wofford's mention of a James D. Wofford, and says, "There's a Jim Wofford?"

"There were *two* Jim Woffords, father and son," Kate explains. "The father lived to be over a hundred years old."

Kim would like to tell her about the two Peter Mankinses, or discuss the two John Milton Norrises, but there is no time. "Which was the medicine man?" she asks.

"Both of them were 'medicine men,'" Kate says. "They used wild stuff, wild roots and such. People came from far and near to be cured by them. White and red, but mostly red. Young Jim died, oh, ten or twelve years ago, although his widow is still living not far from here. Both Jims were fortunetellers, and both of them could tell you where to find something you'd lost."

Both of them could tell me where to find something I've lost, Kim is thinking, *but both of them are dead.* "Is that how they made their living?" she asks. "Curing people with roots and telling people how to find what they'd lost?"

"Nobody ever earned a living doing that," Kate Scraper says. "The Woffords had to farm, like all the rest of us."

Although Kate lived in The Nation (which became Okla-

homa when she was eleven), she and her family attended the
Baptist church in Cherokee City. The building still stands, whitewashed and neat, on the paved highway just north of the Cherokee Kid quick-stop. It was built over a hundred years ago by
Hamp Woolridge, who was a Baptist deacon despite being the
town's leading distiller (link to Peter Mankins, Sr.). Architecturally it is an archetype: small, white, the porticoed entrance in the
gable end, like a little temple. This is in contrast to the Sulphur
City Baptist Church of the last chapter, but almost identical to
Marble City's "Basin" church/schoolhouse of the following chapter. The belfries of the Cherokee City and Marble City churches
are identical, with louvered sides; both contain bells, real cast-
iron bells that ring, the latter echoing against the walls of the
valley, the former pealing and rolling out across the plains. The
only essential difference between the Cherokee City and Marble
City churches is that the former is a little bit longer, four bays
or four side windows as against the latter's three, reflecting a
larger population.

Kate Scraper shows Kim a clipping, kept in her Bible, from
a church newsletter, circa 1968, of the Cherokee City Baptist
Church: "We have some Cherokee Indians who come to our
services. They are nice and friendly, so we know all Indians aren't
as bad as we see on television." Kate does not comment. Nor
does she smile; that is, she does not smile any more than usual,
for she is usually smiling.

Kim asks, "Do you remember, back in the old days, any
stories of Indians' being mistreated?"

"No," Kate answers, "no, I don't."

A standard question put to the very old: to what do you
attribute your longevity? Centenarian Peter Mankins, Sr., had
cited, to the *Gazette* editor who asked it of him, the regularity of
his habits of chewing tobacco every day for sixty years, and drinking a whiskey tonic every morning (and perhaps getting his feet
washed as a Primitive Baptist). Kate Scraper's secret for a long
life is simply that she has never worried about anything, never
had a moment of anxiety or feared anything. There have been
no tenterhooks in her house. Grief and sorrow, yes, trouble and

hurt and poverty, certainly, but never any dread. To Kim, who is destined during this journey among lost cities to hear many "senior citizens" reveal their ways of having attained seniority, to learn what prescriptions have ensured the survival of the survivors, this comes as a revelation—especially because Kim has often accused herself of excessive worry, and because tension is her constant companion.

Kim wants to ask Kate Scraper *how* one can forestall care or banish worry, but she is afraid that the old woman might give some answers too easily had, such as: read your Bible, or chew peyote, or chant to the dawn. Instead Kim asks, "Do you ever wish Cherokee City had really become a city?"

"Oh, yes!" Kate exclaims, her eyes sparkling with double images: the remembered village of her youth, the possibility of a great place that would never be.

"What do you miss most?" Kim asks.

"Oh, my church. That's what I miss the most, going to church. I loved my church. I was sorry when they had to give it up."

The few Missionary Baptists remaining in Cherokee City in the late 1960s decided to abandon their small white temple, or, rather, to lease it out. There are three church houses still standing in Cherokee City, the other two almost unrecognizable as such, except for their shape: the gable end is the front. One, a whitewashed but rusting tin-coated edifice at the end of Main Street, is almost too tiny to hold a congregation, but was once the Pentecostal Holiness Church; the other, scarcely larger, out on the gravel road leading to the lost cemetery where "Jeremiah Woolly" is buried, is a grayish-green prefabricated metal building that once held the Assembly of God Church. Once there were many churches in Cherokee City; there is no irony in the fact that such a wild and mean town needed to sober up on Sunday mornings and atone for its badness through worship. According to the recent *History of Benton County* by J. Dickson Black, there were once Baptist, Methodist, Episcopal, Christian, and Congregational churches in Cherokee City. In modern times there was also a Church of Christ. The few remaining Missionary Baptists now go to Gentry for their religion as well as for their groceries.

The sign in front of the old Baptist church says "Church of God in Christ," which is a branch of Mennonites, of which the Amish are a sect. Kim remembers Amish in their buggies and black clothes in the vicinity of Beebe, Arkansas, but she has seen none of them around Cherokee City. She has heard of factions among the other denominations; the Cherokee City citizens did not confine their fighting to Saturdays but carried it over to their religious differences on Sunday. Don Dickson remembers that when the congregation in the Baptist church would sing "Will There Be Any Stars in My Crown?" the Methodists would chime in with a loud rendition of "No, Not One!" The Pentecostal Holiness Church—or "Holy Rollers," as they were called by others because they literally rolled on the floor or the ground when the Spirit overpowered them—were subjected to harassment that culminated in the dynamiting of their church. A milder form of harassment was simply to throw a live skunk through the door of the church and into the midst of the worshippers on Sunday morning.

Using Carol Medlam as her information center, Kim learns the name of the Mennonite minister, John Wiens. He lives in Gentry, but is too busy for an interview; he agrees to answer any of Kim's questions by mail. She makes up a questionnaire for him, which he takes weeks to fill out and send back to her. His full name is John Wiens, and he was born on September 1, 1920; before coming to Cherokee City he was with the Winton Mennonite Congregation in Winton, California. The Central District Mission of the Church of God in Christ, Mennonite, headquarters in Moundridge, Kansas, sent him to Cherokee City to take over the vacant Baptist church building, leasing it with an option to buy, paying rent by making the insurance payments. He does not know what happened to the former Baptist occupants.

He has not heard of the harassment and dynamiting of the Pentecostal Holiness congregation. He is not aware of the two other abandoned church buildings of Cherokee City, and does not know anything about their histories. His small congregation, which consists of six members and eight nonmembers, none of them natives of Cherokee City, has met with no hostility from the residents of Cherokee City.

Kim's last question: Are you and the members of your congregation familiar with, or interested in, the history of Cherokee City? Reverend Wiens's answer: "We are not familiar with the history of Cherokee City and have no particular interest."

Kim asks Dovey and Elton Yates, "Do you know anything about the Mennonites?" Dovey says, "I don't know a thing about 'em," but Elton says, "They's a family of Mennonites lives out east of Cherokee City, name of Zitzman or Zissman. You should talk to Joe; he used to work for 'em."

Joe who? Kim asks. Dovey says, "Our son the senator!" She gives Kim a fan, of the simple cardboard-on-a-stick type that ladies used to fan themselves with in rural churches and on porches on hot summer days. On one side of this fan are printed three photographs: a toddler climbing a washtub with an early wringer attached, above the caption "Candidate First Testing the Waters"; a formal portrait, circa 1900, of Rob and Laura Yates, the former looking like a very young version of Elton; and an old photograph of the Cherokee City Livery Barn, white false front, with all the Yates men standing before it, J. Yates, prop. On the other side of the fan is a red-white-and-blue message in support of "Joe Yates for Senator."

"I never give a speech or have anyone introduce me but what I point out the fact that I am from Cherokee City," Senator Joe Yates tells Kim when she visits his home in Bentonville, the county seat. Newly elected to represent the First District of Northwest Arkansas in the State Senate, Elton and Dovey's oldest son is proud of his hometown and his Yates heritage. A consummate politician, he knows practically everyone in his district. His master's thesis in geography at the University of Arkansas, entitled "Land Utilization of Cherokee Township," required him to interview all of the farmers around Cherokee City. For several years before running for the Senate he was a tax assessor and tax collector, a good way to get to know people. For a few years he also indulged in an ambition to own and operate a plant nursery in his hometown, called Cherokee Gardens, with his mother and father working in it.

Senator Yates tells Kim what little he knows about the Mennonites: they moved into and around Cherokee City twenty-five or thirty years ago and have kept a low profile ever since. As a young man, Joe Yates once cut hay for Mr. Zissman and noticed that the several young daughters wore long black dresses with black socks and hats, but otherwise the Mennonites were hardly conspicuous. "They're very nice people, make excellent neighbors, and they've never really expanded in size."

People are more tolerant nowadays. When Kim informs Senator Yates that the Reverend Wiens had never heard of the harassment and dynamiting of the Holy Rollers, the senator says, "That dynamitin occurred when my daddy was just a kid. . . . But when I was a kid they used to have a lot of brush arbors around. . . . They'd have revivals. They were very loud; you could hear 'em, oh, a half-mile away. Makin a racket. Probably the church got blown up from resentment. Makin noise. People were not real tolerant years ago."

Senator Yates was born in the house of his grandfather Rob, which had been the Cherokee House hotel. Elton and Dovey never forbade him to go into downtown Cherokee City, and he can remember from earliest childhood how mean the town was. "People were just ornery. I've seen a few knife fights, that kind of thing, and there was just a lot of fightin goin on. There were a number of people in Cherokee City who did not hesitate to shoot you, or cut you up, or beat you to death."

In preparation for interviewing the senator, Kim has found and read his thesis in the university library. The main conclusion of "Land Utilization of Cherokee Township" is that the use of the land at that time (1970) was the best possible type for that particular land. Variations of this theme are recurrent in the text: "The land use of the township is what one would expect to find in any area of similar topography in Northwest Arkansas" and "The author believes that the current uses of land in Cherokee

Township represent the most practical and economic uses at this time" and "In the opinion of the author, the present land uses represent the best possible types according to the capability of the land."

Kim asks, "Do you still feel that the land is being put to the best possible use?"

"There's been a tendency since I wrote that thesis," the senator answers, "that more people have gone to the city to work, and the farm has become more the hobby, a place to supplement their income by a few cattle, something like that. The poultry industry has tended to maximize itself. . . ." During the sixties and seventies, Tyson's, a giant of the poultry industry, headquartered in Benton County, subsidized the growing of chickens all over northwestern Arkansas, until the entire landscape was covered with long metal sheds for the hatching and raising and breeding of chickens. In Cherokee City as elsewhere, this chicken boom "has tended to maximize itself," a polite way of saying that many farmers found themselves stuck with acres of chicken sheds but had no profitable market for their flocks. All around Cherokee City there has been an almost total turnover in ownership of the land.

The apple orchards are gone. Early in this century, all of the land to the north of the village was in apples, four thousand acres of orchards, and these apples took all of the prizes at the St. Louis World's Fair of 1904. But the cycle of insects and pesticides and the development of pesticide-resistant insects, and the natural aging and dying of the trees, gradually killed the apple industry. "No one was willin to plant 'em back," says Joe Yates, "but while they lasted, heck, all those guys who had orchards made good money."

What about his nursery? Did he make good money at it? He had built two greenhouses, which Elton and Dovey had tended for him, but his parents had not been in the best of health for such labor, and "I got too busy playin politics. The peak seasons at Cherokee Gardens did not coincide with my political business, and I enjoy politics." Was there something about growing up in Cherokee City that had drawn him into politics? Most of Arkansas is staunchly Democrat; northwestern Arkansas for many years has been just as staunchly Republican, and conservative. Joe Yates is a conservative Republican, a distinct minority in the Little Rock legislature.

"My grandpa Rob Yates, more than anyone or anything, influenced me," he says. "He did not believe in the government doing *anything*. He would not accept an old-age pension. His philosophy was that the government should leave you alone. Strictly. And you had no right to ask the government for anything. That philosophy influenced me a great deal and made me very independent."

With the passing of his Cherokee Gardens, the village was left with only two businesses: Carol's Store and a place called Lapland, Inc. Carol had told Kim about Lapland, and Joe's parents had mentioned it. Dovey Yates had explained, "They get out and buy these dead animals and they, uh, they . . ." Elton had supplied, "Make dog food out of 'em. They cut it up, I think, and get it ready, and then they send it off, I don't know where to." Dovey: "I couldn't tell you their names. I've never saw 'em. They've been over there for a long time. Carol could tell you who they are. It doesn't bother us. Now, some of 'em on the other side have complained at times that they've had an odor." Elton: " 'Course, I think the county or state or law have made 'em refrigerate all that stuff, see, and that takes the odor away then, you know." Dovey: "Health Department's been out there a few times to check on it, but I don't know if they were—" Elton: "They're licensed and everything." Dovey: "They go all over the country and pick up dead animals, which makes it pretty nice, really. If it wasn't for that, why, a lot of people would just let 'em lay in the fields and do nothin with 'em and be really a lot worse than what this would be." And Kim had asked, "So, you consider their service a benefit to the community?" Dovey: "Oh, yeah, I think it is." Elton: "I do, too."

Kim asks Senator Joe Yates, "What do you think about Lapland?" Joe replies, "If I lived over there I wouldn't feel too good about it, but I don't think they've been much of a problem for anyone unless they live over there pretty close. It's a very low-key type of thing."

On one plat map of Cherokee City there is an area of a few square blocks designated as "City Park," which, according to Kate Scraper, had once actually been used for that purpose, with swings and merry-go-rounds and refreshment stands that sold taffy and lemonade. Now it is the site of the Lapland operation: a single large shed surrounded by dozens of rusting fifty-five-gallon drums. When Kim drives there and stops briefly, there is a large dead bloated black-and-white cow lying in the open entrance to the shed, but there is no person around, and no activity. She does not park her car and walk past the dead cow to see what is inside the building. Across the road is the house of Ken and Ivy Cossel, who own and operate Lapland: he does the actual dirty work, she answers the telephone. The house is nondescript, not one of the historical houses of the town. Mr. and Mrs. Cossel are not handsome people. Their kitchen, where Kim is required to stand for the interview, is not tidy.

In nature's scheme of things, the scavenger is all-important but somehow repulsive, a necessary evil. The early form of the word, *scavager*, meant "streetcleaner." Lapland cleans the highways of dead livestock. The scavenger in the animal world, the vulture or buzzard, whose job is cleaning up, is an ugly creature, almost as if the unpleasantness of his task were reflected in his appearance. Janitors and garbage men are never matinee idols. But Faulkner said, "You know that if I were reincarnated, I'd want to come back a buzzard. Nothing hates him or envies him or wants him or needs him. He is never bothered or in danger, and he can eat anything." The scavenger is efficient and utilitarian, and, as with all things utilitarian, design and appearance are secondary; looks count for nothing. Ken Cossel is tall and muscular but abominably abdominous; Kim cannot suppress the thought that his distended belly contains parts of a dead cow. Although blond and possibly of Scandinavian origin, he has none of the Finno-Ugric of the Laplander in him, and thus Kim's first question is not, as she would like, "What do you think of buzzards?" but, rather, "Why is your business called Lapland?"

Because, he explains, with the impatient patience that busy and manly men reserve for inquisitive females, it overlaps three states: Arkansas, Oklahoma just a quarter-mile to the west, and Missouri just thirteen miles to the north. "I could of called it Tri-State or something like that," he says, "but I wanted something different that would stick in people's minds."

Lapland is a small operation covering a large territory, around fifty miles in each direction. There is no competition. Neither Ken nor Ivy is from Arkansas; Ken has some relatives in Gentry, but he is from Kansas, and Ivy (he calls her Baby) is from Illinois. He was a trucker, driving a big semi, before getting into the disposal business. Now he works anywhere from four to sixteen hours a day, six and seven days a week, with Ivy on the phone twenty-four hours a day—"Calls late at night, and it may start ringin again at four-thirty, five in the mornin, when the dairymen get out and start milkin and they might find a dead one and call us right then. They don't give a damn whether we're up or not, they just go ahead and call!"

They do not pick up dead dogs or cats, only livestock—cattle, sheep, goats, pigs, horses. (Deadstock, rather.) Ken simply picks them up, carts them to his shed, cuts them up, and packs them into barrels, which are hauled to the renderer's plant in Russellville, Arkansas, some 180 miles distant. A truck from Standard Rendering Company, a division of Darling-Delaware, Inc., comes each day to carry off what Ken has packed into the fifty-five-gallon drums.

"Do you want to go watch me?" Ken offers Kim.

"Not really," she says. "I really don't." They both laugh. She asks, "Is the process of your cutting up the animal something you're very used to? Did it bother you at first?"

"Uh . . . a little bit at first. Some days it still bothers me. I wouldn't want to go in there with an upset stomach, I guarantee ya." Ken doesn't know what happens to the butchered carcasses when they leave his plant. He believes that the renderer converts them into bone meal and dry scraps that find their way into cattle feed, chicken feed, and, of course, dog food.

"Do you have Health Department standards you follow?" Kim asks.

"Yes, ma'am!" Ken says, almost defiantly, as if she had accused him of something. "You never know when the federal inspector's goin to walk in the door. And the reason he comes is to make sure that some of this meat is fresh enough to go on the kitchen table, by looks and smell—*but* that's the reason he comes in here, to see to it that we don't sell it for human consumption. I wouldn't do a thing like that, but it has been done at other places."

Kim glances around her at the cluttered kitchen, and cannot resist a final glance at Ken Cossel's stomach before she says, "That takes care of my questions," and makes good her leave. She begins to brood that she is just a scavenger, too, picking up carrion villages. In one of her dreams, she is swooping down, buzzardlike, on a dead and decaying town, and devouring it.

Her final interview is in Fayetteville, with Chris Yates, a twenty-two-year-old university student who is the first person younger than Kim herself whom she has interviewed. He is the son of Senator Joe Yates, grandson of Elton, great-grandson of Rob, a fourth-generation independent Republican Yates. He is not native-born, because his father and mother happened to be living in Anaheim, California, when he was born. Anaheim is a sort of enclave for displaced, adventuresome Arkansawyers—particularly Ozark Arkansawyers—who want to get rich in California. Most of them stay in Anaheim and die in Anaheim. Joe Yates came home and brought baby Christopher back to the place of his own boyhood, to grow up in the Cherokee House hotel of his grandfather. Chris Yates remembers Great-Grandpa Rob. "When my sister and I were little, we'd be out in the yard and he'd give us rides on his back, and chase us, and he was already in his nineties. I think the biggest thing I remember is, everybody talked about how honest he was. When he told you he'd do something, you could count on it."

Chris's hand sweeps across the map of Cherokee City that Kim has on the table. "He used to own all this land, and there were outlaws, and he used to talk about them." Rob's mother, Nancy Norris Yates, was a good friend of Jesse James's mother, and they exchanged letters that touch upon the adventures of their sons, Rob's at home, Jesse's in the field, holding up trains and banks and such, deeds of which his mother and everybody else was proud; he was never an outlaw to his own people. Chris Yates has only a vague memory of having heard of Harve Norris, the sixteen-year-old suicide; he knows none of the details.

Chris is already into politics, a senator of sorts himself: a member of the university's Student Senate, which has to deal with such hot contemporary issues as homosexuality on campus. Chris considers himself even more conservative than his father, although "We agree on practically everything. We're strong conservatives and Republicans." Senator Joe Yates is very proud of his son, who is a straight-A student majoring in finance and banking and a member of several honor societies and the Baptist Student Union, as well as the College Republicans.

"Aren't you pretty busy?" Kim asks with an understated smile.

"Yeah," Chris admits. But he has a busy career mapped out ahead of him, and he is impatient. As soon as he has finished graduate school at some distant but worthy place—Harvard or Stanford—he will come back to Arkansas, take a top job in the investment structure of a holding company, get into politics, and work his way up. Like his generation of college students at large, he has been frightened by the economy into seeking a strictly practical education: "I think it's possible to get a degree without really *knowing* anything. If you're going to get a job, if you're going to compete, you better be prepared, more so than in the past, when maybe just a college degree would take you a long ways. I think now you better *know* something along with the degree."

Chris goes back to Cherokee City whenever he gets a chance, especially during the summers. He doesn't go to see people (except his grandparents); he goes to see the *place*. He has explored

Hog Eye Creek all along its length, and he has ventured into the abandoned buildings.

"Did you ever try to imagine," Kim asks, "what the town would have looked like if all of the plots on the plat had been filled?"

"I've seen pictures of the turn of the century, all the people on Main Street, and I've thought about what it would be like if the railroad hadn't gone to Gentry. I've thought it would be nice sometimes if Cherokee City were still there and growing, but in other ways I'm glad that it's not, because it's such a peaceful place now."

One day Chris might well be governor of Arkansas, or United States senator. "One day I'd like to be senator," he admits, without specifying whether he will seek his father's seat or aim for higher office. Kim can imagine him at the turn of the century, in Washington, saying, "I never give a speech or have anyone introduce me but what I point out the fact that I'm from Cherokee City."

Marble City,
Arkansas

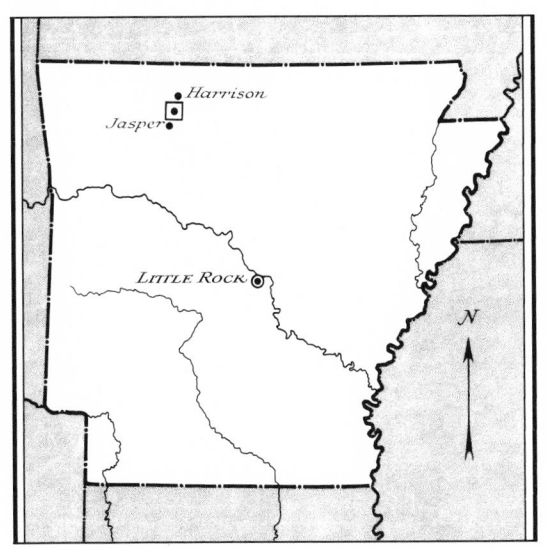

Harrison

Jasper

LITTLE ROCK

N

DOGPATCH USA
FAMILY
MOTEL CHALETS

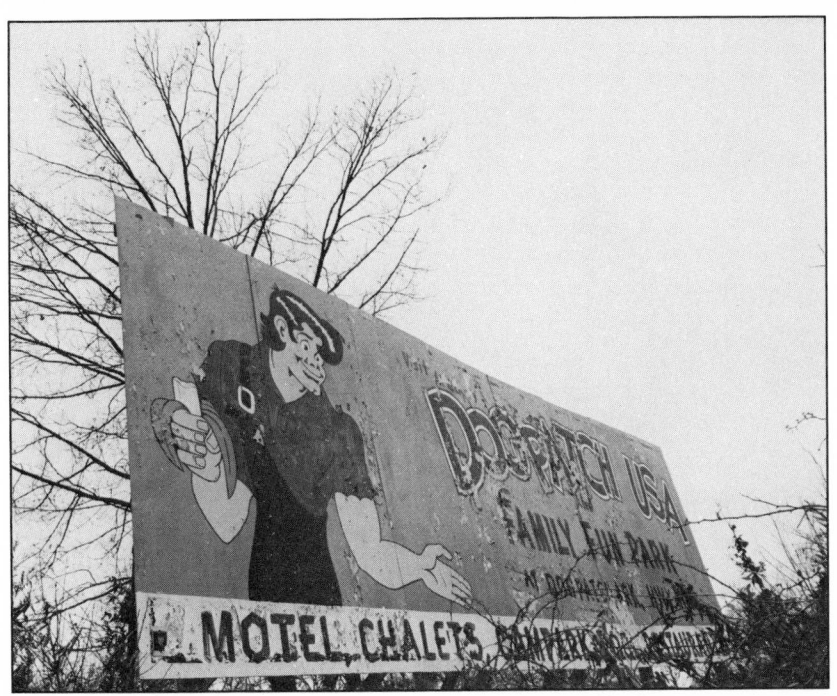

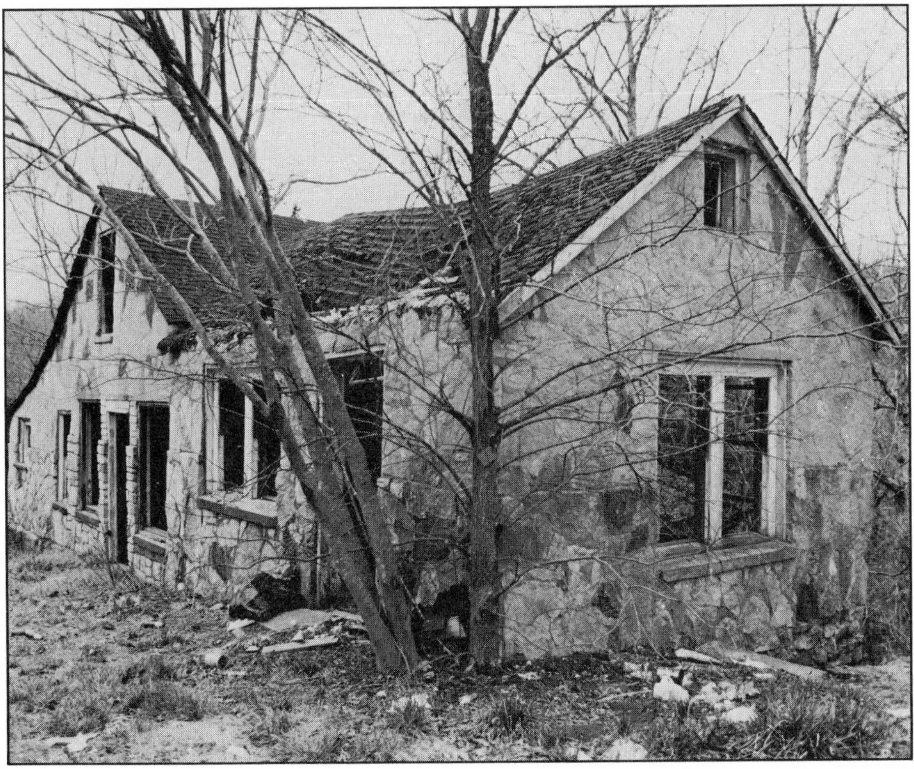

Did that there Dawg *Patch in the funny papers e'er even have ary* church*house nohow?*

—*local old-timer, 1985*

No TRACE OF THIS most ambitious of cities remains beneath the asphalt of a tawdry amusement park lifting its name, Dogpatch, from a defunct comic strip in which rustic yokels cavorted in a manner supposed to have originated in backwoods Kentucky, not Arkansas. Kim has never read the terminated "Li'l Abner" or heard of its long-dead creator, Al Capp, not because she is too young to remember them or because she feels some resentment at the false, shabby, ridiculing image that they presented of mountain people, but because she never was one to read the funnies much, having better things to do at breakfast time. Although this is her second visit to Newton County, the most "scenic," most isolated, most rural, most backward and primitive of Arkansas's seventy-five counties (on the first visit, she was hunting for a village less "comic," more "real," than Dogpatch, called Stay More, in another part of the county), Kim has never been to Dogpatch before and would not be going to it now, when it is off season and closed, except that she is curious and a bit miffed that the Dogpatch management has never answered any of her repeated but increasingly polite letters asking for some information about the Marble City that lies concealed like Troy beneath the hokey buildings and gimmicky rides of the "theme" park. Are they afraid of her?

All along the highways coming into this part of the Ozarks she has seen the billboards: "Have a heckuva day at Dogpatch

USA." She will indeed have a heckuva day (two of them), but not in the "family-fun" fashion that the billboards advertise. State Highway 7—running south out of Harrison, the only true "city" in this part of Arkansas—has been called one of The Ten Most Beautiful Highways in America (the parts that are visible beyond Dogpatch's billboards). It snakes through the heart of the Ozarks, which are the heart of the nation, dips through forested ravines and hollows, and trips along crests and ridges with spectacular panoramas. It is not a safe road—somebody is always getting killed or hurt around its curves on motorcycles or in cars, trucks, whole passenger buses that careen over the ledges—but it is reasonably well paved these days, after a long career as a mere dirt-and-gravel surface. Dirt roads aplenty fall away from it to wander among rugged hollows and gorgeous valleys where the way of life is still simple and earthbound enough, while not exactly unadulterated Anglo-Saxon yeoman backwoodsy, to attract new immigrants from the counterculture, young back-to-the-landers who may or may not be outmoded hippies, although some of them give one a *déjà-vu* sense of the sixties. Once upon a time this land seemed quaint because it held pockets of people still talking and dressing and acting like their eighteenth-century forebears, resistant to all change and progress from the outside world. Now it is beginning to seem quaint because so many of its home-steaders are people still talking and dressing and acting like their older brothers and sisters, who have long since given up the sixties' youth culture in favor of the yuppie life style.

Elsewhere in Arkansas the latest-blooming hippies have all cleaned up and moved back to the suburbs. Those who persist and endure in Newton County are the strong ones, fit survivors, like the real pioneers in the nineteenth century, who came as a kind of last spillover of the mountain settlement to the east. While genuine "residenters," as the old-timers are known, remain somewhat aloof if not uncordial toward the young "furriners" who move in, they seem to share one great trait: a desire for removal from the mainstream, an unwillingness to accept the common man's kowtowing to institutions and gadgets, bread and circuses, mammon and mores. The residenters wink at the newcomers' cash crop of choice, marijuana, remembering their own profits from distilled corn juice.

The newcomers, when they can get hold of a newspaper, read Trudeau's "Doonesbury" or Breathed's "Bloom County" with the same devotion that an earlier generation paid to "Pogo" and "Li'l Abner." Comic strips, like aspiring cities, become ghost towns. Something there is in the climate of Newton County that nourishes anachronisms and keeps the dead alive. Perhaps Dogpatch is no more outgrown and outmoded than the hippies and the hill people that it shares the county with. In time Dogpatch itself will fail and become a broken dream for those who are keeping it going.

When it goes, when the last ride closes and the last sham yokel gulls the last remnant of a crowd, it will have been the sixth or seventh broken dream upon the same spot, if we include whatever dreams the Choctaw Indian had, or go back even before him to the Bluff Dweller Indian who lived in and under Spring Bluff hundreds of years before and had no dreams whatever in the sense of aspirations or ambitions, other than the desire to exist and keep his belly full and be buried with dignity and ceremony. (Don Dickson of Cherokee City has been responsible for excavating some of the important Bluff shelters of Newton County and for transporting a "burial"—the mummified remains of one of these thousand-year-old Indians—to the University Museum in Fayetteville.) These Bluff Dwellers had died out, perhaps from disease or from conflict with other tribes, long before Newton County became Osage country in the early nineteenth century.

But the Osage were not "civilized." The first historical non-savage homesteading in the place that would become Marble City was not an Osage, or a Pawnee (who had a village a few miles to the west), but a Choctaw, named Archibald Toomer, or, as his name was entered into the Newton County land records, Ah-Che-To-Mah. The Choctaw people, originally from central and southern Mississippi and Alabama, were one of the "Five Civilized Tribes," but were of a Natchez-Muskogean linguistic group more closely related to the Creeks than to the Cherokees, and were politically more closely allied with the French than with the British. They were forced out of their lands in 1842 and dispersed across Arkansas and into southeastern Oklahoma (Indian Territory). There was no Trail of Tears for Choctaws, but the move was not painless; Ah-Che-To-Mah "escaped" and hoped to take up farming and hunting in the remote sunny glades of Newton County forests, and managed to hang on to his spread despite the influx of white pioneers from Tennessee, Kentucky, and Georgia.

Ah-Che-To-Mah was completely outnumbered by the Bellahs, the Willcocksons, the Alexanders, and the Harps when he sold his farm in 1852 to Richard Alexander and disappeared, perhaps to rejoin his brethren on the reservation in Indian Territory. Ten years earlier, the county had been established, and named, not for a president, general, governor, congressman, or river, or even for the celebrated discoverer of gravity, but for a mere mail carrier and marshal named Thomas Willoughby Newton. Thus, even in its naming Newton County broke with tradition and cast itself outside the mainstream.

About 1840, Peter Bellah, from Alabama, erected a gristmill on what would be called Mill Creek in what would become Marble City Township. Some living descendants insist that it is "Beller." Just as Archibald Toomer became Ah-Che-To-Mah, or vice versa, the Ozarker has a habit of pronouncing "er" sounds as "ah," and especially vice versa: hence, "tomato" becomes " 'mater," "Emma" becomes "Emmer," "Marcella" is always "Marceller," and so on. The logic is that if the actual spelling were "Bellah," then it would be pronounced "Beller"; since the pronunciation is "Beller," the spelling is therefore "Bellah."

Before coming on into Newton County, Kim took a motel room in Harrison; on the outskirts of that city she stopped to see Dr. Allen Robinson, a great-grandson of Peter Bellah. Dr. Robinson, who was eighty-eight (not as old as Kate Scraper), had only recently retired from a distinguished career as a physician, a pioneer in therapeutic radiology with a practice on Park Avenue in New York from 1921 until 1952, interrupted by service as a commander at the naval hospital in Long Beach, California, during World War II; during World War I he had been a young army doctor fresh out of Vanderbilt Medical School. But he had been born in Newton County, east of Marble City, the youngest in one of those typical ten-child families. All his years in Manhattan he was homesick for the Ozarks and came home on vacation every two or three years. Finally, after thirty years, a New York neighbor of his who was an architect had listened long enough to his talk about Arkansas and urged him to go home, recommending a fellow New York architect, a native of Arkansas named Edward Durell Stone, to build a house for him.

Stone (1902–78) designed "Robin's Hill" near Harrison for Dr. Robinson and his New York wife, Loretta, in 1952, and pronounced it his favorite of the many houses he designed. His best-known buildings range from the Museum of Modern Art in New York to the Kennedy Center in Washington, and a couple of entire college campuses, including the now defunct Windham College of Putney, Vermont, which went out of business the same year Stone died, 1978, leaving a great white ghost city of a campus in the small village.

For Robin's Hill, Stone cannibalized materials from the old Colonel Gaither homestead a considerable distance off toward Marble City: the large dogtrot "double house" of hewn logs was converted into a very modern bathroom, while the huge hewn timbers of the barn were realigned and scarfed and splined into a vast cathedral-ceilinged living room for the main house. Kim cannot help remembering the Alexanders' "Raheen" on its hilltop outside Sulphur City (whose architect, Fay Jones, was a disciple of Edward Durell Stone's); the similarities of site and scale are noteworthy, but the differences are more important. "More comfortable here," Kim wrote into her notebook, "more *used*, more habituated. This has been made into a home. Raheen is too new."

"We had to find a carpenter who wanted to use the old materials," Dr. Robinson told Kim. The very old physician was quite trim and spare, spry, scarcely stooped, wore no glasses to hide the twinkle in his eye, had a full head of white hair to cool his brain, and large, very long ears to hear perfectly with. "Not a carpenter who *could* use the materials, but one who *would*."

"Have you been to Dogpatch?" Kim asked, explaining that

she herself had not yet been there. "Have you taken the tour?"

"Oh, sure," the good doctor said. "With all these grandchildren . . ." His five grandchildren and five great-grandchildren had all had fun at the amusement park, but, like many others, he resented the name Dogpatch. He wished that its last "official" name, Marble Falls, had been retained, or even Willcockson, which was the name on the post office for many years. "Anything but Dogpatch," he said. He would rather have seen Marble City made into a state park than into a commercialized theme park.

From what little she knew about Marble City at that point, Kim had determined to concentrate on its physicians or its residents claiming to engage in the old-time practice of medicine, and she appreciated the coincidence of having her first interview be with a genuine physician. Dr. Robinson had heard of Marble City's "Dr." Silas Shruggs Stacey (1829–1915) but knew little about him. There is a great-grandchild of Stacey's living north of Harrison in a house trailer; it is on Robinson's great-grandfather Peter Bellah, who died before Stacey came to town, that this early part of the search must center. The name, Dr. Robinson assured her, was written down the way it sounded, "Beller," but was Bellah in the original. Allen Robinson may have been named for Allen Bellah, who was the first sheriff of Newton County. Did Robinson remember his great-grandfather? "He died in '62," the doctor told Kim; "I wasn't born until the nineties."

Kim and Dr. Robinson were joined by one of the doctor's grandsons, Jim Robinson, and his wife, Betty. They live on and manage the Robinson Farm Museum and Heritage Center at Rally Hill, east of Valley Springs, Arkansas, the fulfillment of Dr. Robinson's dream to have a living museum preserving the dwellings, tools, and artifacts of the early Ozark pioneers. Jim invited Kim to visit. Another day, she will.

That day, Jim Robinson told Kim of the Bellahs who were involved in the Mountain Meadow Massacre: in 1857, a party of 140 Arkansawyers on their way to California were stopped in Utah and slaughtered in cold blood by Paiute Indians at the instigation of Mormons who resented their trespass; there is a monument in their memory on the lawn of the courthouse in

Harrison. Jim Robinson also told Kim that Peter Bellah cut the block of marble that represents Marble Falls and the state of Arkansas in the Washington Monument at Washington, D.C., and suggested to her that she might want to talk to Doyle Harp, at his farm on Harp Creek, west of Marble City, who is a great-grandson (there are great-grandchildren of all the original settlers and central figures of Marble City still living somewhere in the neighborhood) of the Harp who helped Peter Bellah quarry the block of marble. There is a small monument to the accomplishment, and Kim decided that this would be the next thing she wanted to find, and to see.

Before leaving Robin's Hill, she put to Dr. Robinson the standard question about how to live so long. Would he also tell her that he had never worried? Surely a physician who tended the dying of both world wars must have worried a lot. No, he did not tell her he had never worried. His prescription was:

"Choose your ancestors. Live in the Ozarks. And marry a good cook!"

Now Kim heads her black sports car yclept Zephyra south on Highway 7, past the Dogpatch billboards, into Newton County. Just before the county line she sees on her right a stone ruin: once a gift shop or roadhouse or even a home (although much too close to the highway), it now lacks all of its many windows and its roof is caving in, but its flagstone masonry is still sturdy and intact. Kim is destined to ask several people about this derelict relic before she will learn, from the son of its builder, Albert Raney, that he had a dream of tourism long before Dogpatch but was finally forced to sell the gift shop (for such it was) to the Dogpatch establishment, which promptly forgot about it and let it deteriorate. Just beyond this handsome survival, Kim comes to Dogpatch itself, cold and deserted at this time of year, not yet ready for tourists, its hodgepodge of bastardized architecture sprawling through the little valley to the left. To the right is a tiny glade, scarcely noticeable, scarcely wide enough for Kim to pull off the highway; on it is a cairn of stones looking like a converted back-yard barbecue, encasing two marble blocks incised with letters, the upper one saying simply "ARKANSAS" and the lower one declaring, "This marker commemorates the Arkansas Marble in Washington's Monument taken by Beller and Harp Bros. from this hill in 1836 this marker erected 1954 by Newton Co. History Society, W. F. Lackey Pres. Manda Hickman Sec." The W. F. is Walter Lackey, a county historian who never lived in Marble City but knew everyone who did. Amanda Hickman did live here. Her name, of course, was pronounced "Mander," not "Mandy." (Another parenthesis: Mander Hickman was the last postmaster/mistress of the place before it became Dogpatch; Mander Willcockson was the place's first postmaster/mistress, appointed October 30, 1883, by order of the postmaster general of the United States of America, although Marble City had been a mail drop or postal stop for forty years previous to that. As so often happens, the name of a town is bestowed by the first postmaster, at least in the official eyes of the United States Post Office Department, and thus Mander Willcockson called Marble City by the name Willcockson, which it kept, officially, for the rest of its life, despite being Marble City in reality until, according to the backers or promoters of Dogpatch USA—though the figure, as we shall see, is of highly suspicious authenticity—60 percent of the local populace voted or signed X's on a petition to change the name from Willcockson to Dogpatch. Willcockson has the distinction of being the only post office in the United States to which an addressed piece of mail never had the post-office name spelled correctly [except by the Post Office Department, and then not always]. Some of the variants are: Willcoxson, Wilcoxon, Wilcoxson, Wilcoxsen, Wilcocksen, Wilcoggins, Millcocksing, and Wisconsin.)

There was never any town or even a settlement here before Peter Bellah built his gristmill; in fact, Peter Bellah himself did not come to live here, except when the business of the mill, which ran day and night, kept him overnight. He had settled eight miles northeast of his mill in the flourishing community of Bellefonte ("pretty spring," but quite possibly a play upon his name), where he quickly made a reputation as a millwright, designing and building and operating water-powered gristmills, which were as indispensable and almost as prevalent in those days as quick-stop convenience stores are today. His mill at Marble City (the exact year of construction, sometime between 1834 and 1837, is not known) was simply one more in his chain, but perhaps the largest, grandest, and busiest, thanks to the power of the spring as it bubbled up out of Spring Bluff. (Contrary to logic and popular belief, Peter Bellah's mill was built not at the waterfalls called Marble Falls but, rather, some six hundred feet upstream.)

Presumably, people didn't call him Peter but simply Pete: he called himself Captain, although there is no record of any service in any branch of the military. He was Cap'n Pete. Beller the Miller. Also, Beller Miller the Driller, drilling into the marble (actually a less compact, more grainy form of limestone) deposits for choice blocks. There were no houses at or near his mill. There would be no houses anywhere in Mill Creek Valley for years to come; Marble City would not become a dream until Cap'n Pete was dead, and even then no marble would ever be used in the construction of any house or other building there. Just what happened to the so-called marble quarried at Marble City is a mystery: some of it undoubtedly was worked into tombstones; some of it may have found its way to distant cities for banks, courthouses, churches; some of it may even have become sculpture.

One piece of it went to Washington, courtesy of Cap'n Pete, and perhaps the very name of Marble City derives from this one block, four feet long and two feet high. Bellah and the Harp brothers must have selected the whitest, most marblelike chunk they could find, for most of the Marble City stone, according to a description by Lee Randolph, who worked there in the 1890s as a marble cutter, "varies in color from light to dark gray, beautifully clouded gray and red, of dark and light shades splendidly mottled, showing all colors of the rainbow and excelling anything so far discovered for inside finish of buildings, and furniture work. The heaviest colors run from dark mottled red to the deepest wine color, turning into almost a blue black."

Cap'n Pete, his cousins, and the Harp brothers, seized with the dream of developing the marble quarry into an industry, went to the considerable trouble of building a special wagon that was pulled by three yoke of oxen, and hauling the ton-block of marble over the tortuous Boston Mountains a distance of ninety miles to the Arkansas River. The seven men and ten oxen required a month for the journey, and then the block was rafted out to the steamboat *Pennywit*, waiting in midstream; months more were required to float the block to New Orleans and thence to its destination at Washington, where it would remain locked up in a warehouse along with identical tribute blocks from other states, counties, organizations, and individuals, as well as ton-stones from China, Japan, Turkey, Greece, Italy, Brazil, and Switzerland, for years and years. The actual laying-in-place of the stones was commenced on the nation's Centennial—long after Cap'n Pete, most of his cousins, and most of the Harps were dead.

Kim decides to follow Jim Robinson's tip and interview Doyle Harp, who lives not far from the memorial to his ancestors and Peter Bellah. Nobody, Kim has discovered, appears to live *in* Dogpatch, or beside it, or close to it, or around it, except possibly the caretaker or someone like that. This time of year, like a stage between shows, it is empty of people: the props are there, all the sets are up, the scenery is in place, but if there are any people around, they are in the wings. Zephyra protests the dirt-and-gravel road that she must suffer a mile or so to get Kim over the hill and beyond the sham theatricality of Dogpatch. Doyle Harp, age sixty-one, is a farmer, and lives on a farm. The farm is in the Newton County mountains, without an acre of flat bottom land; his pastures and meadows roll all over the place, around the spring branch of Harp Creek; the land has been in the Harp family since the first white settlement. Doyle's son now owns the land where the ersatz marble for Washington's monument was quarried.

Harp Creek flows out of a place called The Basin, whose name is almost self-explanatory: a vessel of a valley, a washbowl of hills. There is a lovely little white school/churchhouse there, and not much else. One expects to hear the sound of harp music in the distance.

Doyle Harp went to school in The Basin; he was born and grew up near it; he has lived in this valley all his life. Like most of the farmers, he has had to work off the farm to supplement his income; once he worked for a feed company in Harrison, and before that he had his own feed business. Along with many other local people, he helped build Dogpatch, but despises it.

"I was on the carpentry crew," he tells Kim. "I didn't do anything but just drive nails in old boards." He says this almost as a protest of innocence. His crew put up all the buildings, using old lumber, old logs taken from old neighborhood buildings torn down, old homesteads robbed of their structures. The native carpenters at Dogpatch did a good job with the old boards: in fact, their work was *too* good, their carpentry too neat for the "rickety" look of hillbilly sloth that the Dogpatch management was after. Harp's crew was called back to smash the ridgepoles and make the roofs look slovenly.

"All those sway-back roofs . . ." Kim says.

"They decided they needed to be sway-backed, so they sent us back at 'em."

"Why?"

"To make 'em look more like *Dogpatch*." Harp pronounces the word the way Kim will hear it pronounced with emphasis by all of the native people she meets: with derision, with deep personal distaste. Not far west of Newton County is an actual locale called Dogbranch, and a timeworn Dogbranch Cemetery, and then of course there are dogwood trees everywhere, and also dogbane, dogtooth violet, dogberries, dog days, dog-paddling, dog sled, dogtrot, dog's life, and dogma, and though "dog" is pronounced "dawg" everywhere in Arkansas, the only pronunciation that comes close to the slurring utterance of "Dogpatch" is "doggone," a euphemism for "damn."

"You don't like *Dogpatch*?" Kim asks. She is learning how to say the word acceptably herself. "Why not?"

"I just don't like the way we got done," Harp says, "when they changed the name of it to *Dogpatch*. See, sixty percent of the postal patrons was supposed to be willin to petition, to sign it, that they wanted it changed. Nobody signed nothin! The dude that bought all that land there thought he had more money than the *state of Arkansas*. He just built the new post office all by himself up on the hill and decided to call it *Dogpatch*." Doyle Harp twiddles some imaginary dollar bills between his thumb and forefinger. "*Money*," he says. "I been in that new P.O. *one* time." He does not plan to go there again if he can help it.

Kim says, "What's this about sixty percent of the postal . . . ?"

"That means that percentage of the postal patrons was supposed to be willin for it to be changed to *Dogpatch* and move the P.O. up to the hill in Dogpatch park. And nobody signed the petition. Nobody. They just done it, and the postmaster told me one day if the local people don't start buyin stamps up here, it's goin to lower the rating of this P.O., and I couldn't cry for laughin: *let it happen*. That's the way I feel about it. I've never bought any stamps up there."

The Dogpatch Post Office serves not only the residents who once got their mail addressed to Marble Falls or Willcockson but also many newcomers in the housing developments and condominiums and chalets not directly connected with the Dogpatch establishment, as well as motels and a convention center independent from Dogpatch. Doyle Harp also worked in maintenance for these.

"I know you *worked* there at Dogpatch," Kim says, "but did you ever go to *enjoy* it, like anyone else?"

"Look, *Dogpatch* gives a lot of young people and several people my age employment. It employs a hundred, hundred fifty high-school graduates and college students for summer jobs. I drove a stagecoach over there for two years before it was blacktopped. Outside of that, I've been back inside the park only one time, just to look at it. It's the *hottest* place I've ever been in my life. It's all blacktop now, and, boy, when it's up in the nineties, and the sun beatin down on that blacktop . . . But there's sure plenty people moves through there. When it's open, you can sit in your car over here at the highway sometimes for thirty minutes just waitin to get on the highway. *Dogpatch*'s a nuisance, I'll tell you for sure."

There are no people moving through Dogpatch or along

the highway when Kim first enters the grounds, and the asphalt pavement is not hot but very cool, almost cold in the late afternoon with the sun already behind the mountains. Despite its absolute emptiness, Kim can imagine the hordes of families swarming among the rusticated buildings on a hot summer's day. The gate is open, Zephyra goes right through without let or hindrance, and for a while Kim just drives around on the broad blankets of blacktop, weaving in and out among the buildings and along the lagoon. The whole park begins at the sheer wall of Spring Bluff on the north and ends at the Marble Falls and the waterwheel on the south. Spilling out from under the bluff is a sequence of sizes of trout in a trout hatchery, ranging from fingerlings to lunkers; the cold spring waters are teeming with them. Kim, who loves to fish but has no tackle with her, could reach down and grapple one, if she had a place to cook it. She wanders on, strolling past the "sway-back" roofs with large, curiously bleached statues of goats perched atop them (nowhere in the Ozarks has a goat, no matter how sure-footed, ever been known to clamber upon a house roof). The other sculptural art of the village is equally cutesy and toylike—the Shmoo, a giant razorback hog, the "Kissin' Rocks," which Al Capp primitively plagiarized from Brancusi's famous *The Kiss* although he hated modern art, and the equestrian statue of General Jubilation T. Cornpone, Capp's satire on the military.

A few of the cannibalized, transplanted settlers' cabins in the park have been faithfully reassembled in a natural setting, although obviously selected with an eye for their "quaint" and impoverished rusticity: hewn-log cabins that have front doors but no windows, or a lone window on the side, with massive stone chimneys of the aggressive rubble masonry that gives backwoods architecture its character. A gratuitous picket fence has been strung along the porch of one of the best of these, but apart from this attempt at comedy, the cabin might have been found in its original setting away off in some locked-in holler of these hills.

Kim eventually parks Zephyra near one building without a sway-backed roof, with a sign on its porch, "Dogpatch Chapel," a belfry that looks like a tiny privy, and telltale sides that conceal what had obviously been the dogtrot or breezeway of a rural home. Compared with The Basin's church, which she has just seen—an authentic example of white temple-form rectangular and properly belfried vernacular ecclesiastic architecture—this Dogpatch Chapel is an obvious fake, although it easily fools the park's customers. More than a fake, it is an embezzlement of a real mountain cabin, the old Brisco place, uprooted from its hillside eight miles west of Marble City and burlesqued into this caricature of a church house as the Dogpatch establishment's concession to its customers' origins in the Bible Belt. Ironically, as a local fan of "Li'l Abner" has observed, there never was a religious building in the actual cartoon village called Dogpatch.

Doyle Harp's grandfather, Martin Brisco, built the exemplary dogtrot-style cabin and raised his family in it (there is a passage on Kim's tape in which Harp relates his boyhood memories of the place—"You had to wade the snow across the breezeway to get from the living room to the kitchen and up the stairway"—and explains how the cabin was actually taken apart, its logs numbered for the removal to Dogpatch), and even with its end chimneys torn away to make room for the chapel's entry, it still has a homey and cozy aspect. But beside it is a "joke cemetery": wooden crosses with cutesy Dogpatch-style names on them, making a laughing matter out of death, which was one of Al Capp's preoccupations.

From the sham chapel, Kim hears the sound of roaring water and walks down the slope to the Marble Falls, where stands a huge new waterwheel. The red mill itself has not yet been restored or reconstructed, but Kim has seen old pictures of it and can imagine how it would look: three tall red-painted wooden stories rising above a rock-and-cement cellar clinging to the cliffside.

High over the falls themselves runs a narrow-gauge railroad trestle of recent construction, designed to carry tourists on a miniature steam train over the gorge of the falls and creek. Kim imagines the train, too, but cannot even imagine herself, with her fear of heights, boarding the tiny "West Po'k Chop Speshul

Train" with kids screaming in delicious dread and one of them vomiting his hot dogs and cotton candy into the falls while Mommy holds him and Daddy admires the awesome workmanship of the waterwheel, slowly but powerfully turning, the world's largest wooden waterwheel.

The wheel is still now. The flume is closed, the sluice gates shut. Kim imagines the gates opening and pouring four thousand gallons a minute onto the wheel. She imagines the creak of the wheel above the roar of the falls. The place holds her. She is captivated, not by the awkward juxtaposition of the Dogpatch railroad and the accurate, faithful reconstruction of the water-wheel promising further restorations to come, but by the experience of being alone, or almost alone, in an entire deserted village with all of its buildings intact (if deliberately battered): Kim, who has been now to Sulphur City, of which only a vacant store and a couple of houses remain, and Cherokee City with its two dead stores and one live one still standing, is now surrounded by a completely unpopulated town where nobody really lives but where people long ago lived and dreamed and died. . . .

But it is late afternoon, increasingly cold, and Kim must get back to her motel room in Harrison and read what little she has found to chronicle the rise and decline of Marble City: a copy (given to her by Dr. Robinson) of the old mimeographed Newton County *Homestead*, a sporadic publication of the Newton County Historical Society, but written and edited almost solely by Walter Lackey. Born in 1892 in a one-room log cabin in western Newton County, Lackey was raised with a primitive education (three months a year for six years in a one-room log schoolhouse) to just a few notches above illiteracy, enough to write one book, a poorly written but highly readable history of his hills and their people. His semiannual *Homestead* managed to survive for three years (1959–61) despite an almost total lack of interest. "Those that have paid their 1962 membership dues will receive a refund," he announced in the final October issue, which, devoted almost entirely to Marble City, was thus, unwittingly, a Möbius strip: the last breath of a broken dream singing the elegy of a broken dream.

There is much in that last issue on Dr. Silas Shruggs Stacey,

born in the eastern part of Kentucky, the fertile crescent that
spawned so much of the civilization of the Ozarks. His mother,
Rebecca, was a full-blood Cherokee, the tribe that provided so
much counter-spawn for the white civilization of the Ozarks.
When the Cherokee were routed from their homes in 1837 and
forced westward on the cold and pestilential Trail of Tears, white
William Stacey took his wife and eight-year-old son and joined
the caravan, the forced march through southern Illinois and into
Missouri on which thirty-five hundred died. When the caravan
reached Springfield, Missouri, in the very flat Springfield plateau
of the Ozarks, William Stacey began to anticipate and dread the
flatness of Oklahoma, and he escaped the Trail of Tears and
took his family into a cavern in the Missouri hills near the present
town of Ozark. The cavern is now a tourist attraction with electric
lights, nicknamed "the Holland Tunnel of the Ozarks." Walter
Lackey visited it for the purpose of seeing where young Silas had
lived, and reported that "it is a wonder to see. The cavern front
is about 60 feet wide and about 40 feet high and the ceiling rock
tapers several hundred feet back. The floor is solid rock and
nearly level with a nice stream of water running down the center.
An ideal place for a home." The mouth of the cavern could
shelter several wagons at a time, and the Stacey stake-out became
a stopover for other displaced Indians. But restless William moved
on, into more remote Douglas County, where Silas grew up and
married a girl named Matilda, who would improve on the customary ten by bearing him eleven children. "Do it one better"
became Silas's motto throughout his life.

During the Civil War, Silas did it one better by joining the
Union forces, not just once but twice at the same time: he was
in both the Missouri Volunteers Infantry and the Missouri Militia
Home Guards. When the action was slow for one group, he
switched to the other, changing uniforms, then switched back.
Still not satisfied with this double duty, he assumed a third identity as "military surgeon," after months of watching real doctors
extract bullets and set bones and amputate limbs. His military
record as Corporal Stacey for one unit and Sergeant Stacey for
the other was undistinguished, but he was in wide demand as

Dr. Stacey. After the war, when all the limbs were amputated that were going to be, all the bullets extracted, and all the bones set, he did it one better by turning from surgery to internal medicine. No longer cutting people except in dire emergency, he began administering compounds of herbs and roots learned from his Cherokee mother, who had learned them from a tribesman named Wofford. He also became convinced that ingestions of, and baths in, sulphur water would cure almost anything—except whatever was ailing Matilda, who died after bearing the eleventh baby. He took his younger children and his parents and moved southward in 1874 to a sulphur spring in Arkansas called Sulphur Spring but not to be confused with two or three other places of the same name. Silas Stacey's sulphur spring was his very own, located in the wilderness beneath Sulphur Mountain, east of P D Flat in what would become Marble City Township at his insistence (Kim does not know yet how P D Flat got its name), and he did it one better by opening not only a medical practice there but also a resort.

"Dr. Silas S. Stacey's Mountain & Water Cure" was too inaccessible to become popular as a resort. It could be reached only on foot, but, ironically, the patients who needed it were not ambulatory. Over the years a few patients were carried in, but not enough to support his large family and parents, so in 1881 Dr. Stacey left an older son in charge of the resort and farm and moved westward a few miles into the community called Willcockson. Here he promptly did it one better by rechristening the town as Marble City, although the Post Office Department never would recognize it as such. He did his town clinic one better by also opening a general-merchandise store, which became the town's leading business. He married a dark-haired beauty with strange ways named Bettie Morgan, and the doctor used his growing influence in the town to get Bettie to replace Mander Willcockson as postmistress. Taking triple control of the clinic, the general store, and the post office, he did it one better by building and opening a hotel, then began buying up all the property in and around Marble City, building rental houses and becoming a landlord, and in his spare time doodling all over his prescription pad the placing of the streets and avenues and boulevards of his imagined Marble City. He named one of the grandest boulevards after recently assassinated President Garfield and the others after other presidents; he arranged his street plan not as a checkerboard in the customary rigid-plat perpendicular-and-parallel plan, but almost as a free-form, organic plat, taking cognizance of the roll and rise of the land, the hollers and hills. It is one of the most beautiful unfulfilled street plans of all our lost cities.

As the most prominent citizen of Marble City, Dr. Stacey was a kind and benevolent man, with a lively sense of humor, unable to stand solitude, and an excellent doctor who rarely lost a patient or failed to cure one, despite his lack of any formal medical education. He contributed regularly to the Methodist Episcopal Church and paid for the erection of the handsome white, steepled church house, although he himself never attended services. His nonreligiosity, if that is what it was, did not do him one worse in the eyes of his townsmen, although it provided an example for the Reverend Absalom Phillips, who could always build a good three-hour sermon around the doctor's supposed Satanism and would blame any of the town's misfortunes on the doctor; never mind that in private Phillips and Stacey were the very best of friends.

Besides the marble quarries in which Dr. Stacey had a large stake, he did his mineral interests one better by buying up all of the deposits of high-grade zinc ore north of Marble City. But the natural resources he was proudest of owning were his acres of medicinal plants. All of the two hundred known species indigenous to the Ozarks grew on his land or in his woods, and he hired people to pick them: mandrake, bloodroot, goldenseal, black snakeroot, lobelia gentian, sarsaparilla, ephedra, ginseng, springnet, senega, stramonium, colocynth, wahoo, wakefield crud, wafer ash, pleurisy root, catnip, horehound, pennyroyal. From a select mixture of these, compounds and distillations, he not only treated and cured his own patients but secured a patent for "Dr. S. S. Stacey's Sulphur Mountain Bitters" and did it one better with a patent for "Dr. S. S. Stacey's Perfection Universal Golden Elixir," found in every home's medical supplies but never perfect according to him, for he kept doing the stuff one better by adding one more ingredient each year of his life.

His life was long, and he never quit. In his eighty-sixth year he did the roofers of his house one better by carrying the shingles up a ladder to them, on a hot summer's day. A world war had already broken out in Europe, Marble City was declining rapidly, Stacey's friends and many of his family were dead, and those remaining had been convinced by the doctor, who loved white lies all his life, that he was actually 103 years old and had no business carrying shingles up a tall ladder on a hot day. His resultant illness was treated with all of the Stacey patent cures, and, to do them one better, he concocted a "Dr. S. S. Stacey's Black Nonesuch Draught," sold for years afterward as a death cure; it did not, however, cure Silas's ailment, and he was buried with sorrow.

His life would make a book, and no doubt will. He was a tall, red-haired, handsome man, a bit of a dandy. He loved good clothes and was an impeccable dresser at all times, doing it one better by wearing one of his twenty-seven hats to bed. He loved good horses and had an imposing stable full of fine steeds for riding and breeding, doing it one better by training race horses and building a racetrack. He loved good whiskey and preferred making his own, doing it one better by using the same distillery he used for his medicines and adding a few bitters for flavor, and doing that one better by the unheard-of practice of aging the whiskey in charred-oak casks and letting it sit for several years before drinking it. He loved good women and always did them one better. He loved good books and had the finest library in Newton County, doing it one better by actually reading it rather than merely displaying it, including leatherbound, buckram, gilt-edged, and gilt-stamped octavio full-sets of Robert Louis Stevenson, Sir Walter Scott, Nathaniel Hawthorne, Anthony Trollope, William Dean Howells, Henry James, and, to do them one better, George Meredith. Dr. Stacey was (and perhaps remains) the only person in Arkansas to start and finish Meredith's *Evan Harrington*.

"He lived in a big two-story white house and died in it and had his practice in it," Ethel Coker remembers, and tells Kim.

Her father's mother was Stacey's daughter, and she was born a Kilgore in 1906 on Boston Mountain south of Marble City. She was orphaned as a small child and went to live with her grandmother and her great-grandfather Dr. Stacey in the big two-story white house. "I used to help him there in his office when I was just a little girl," Mrs. Coker records on Kim's machine. "I'd come in, evenings after school, and I'd help him clean up his office. He used to say he would make a doctor out of me. Bless his heart, he didn't live long enough. I was only nine when he passed away."

Ethel Kilgore Coker, like Medea Dickson and many other widows Kim encounters among these cities, lives alone in a modern, efficient mobile home. Hers is parked off a secondary gravel road north of Harrison (address: Omaha, Arkansas). Kim gets lost twice trying to find the place, traveling on back roads that Zephyra disdains. The interior of the mobile home is pleasant, not cluttered but still compote, even boasting a compote radio— a big old late-forties wooden Art Deco radio cabinet, its innards still working, in lieu of a television set—and whatnot shelves in the corner and along the wall with whatnots on them. Does she perhaps have any of those books of Dr. Stacey's? Did he leave her anything of his?

"No, I don't have. And I wish I did. I wish I had even something he wore. He wore those old-timey hats, high top, high crown, real wide brim, all the time. And *suits*—I never seen him without a suit on. He had this suit with these tails, split duck tails, always dressed up, always had a white shirt on and a suit. As old as he was . . . It seemed to me like he got around awful good to be that old, as old as he was, or as old as I was told he was—over a hundred when he died. He used to use a walkin cane all the time, but he didn't use it to walk with, he just walked around and kind of flicked it around." Ethel Coker laughs and pantomimes the motion of his cane.

Kim asks, "Do you remember anything in particular about your great-grandfather that you loved?"

"Oh, everybody loved him, he was just a wonderful person, but he was just like a father to me, because I didn't have one. Everybody in that country came to him. People would come to him from miles away, and there was people came to him from St. Louis, Kansas City, Springfield, everywhere around, far and near, and when they came to him he would put up their horses and feed them and put up the people in the bedrooms upstairs."

Even after he officially closed his office in his last years and took down his shingle, he never turned away a patient. "They'd still come over there to him to get their medicine," Ethel remembers, "and he'd say to them, 'Well, I'll give it to you if you're not afraid to take it,' and he would not take a penny for it."

Ethel Coker lived through the decline of Marble City. The school, even though a typical one-room schoolhouse, was a large white building dominated by a male teacher (all the public-school teachers were male in those days) named Frank Carlton of whom we will hear again. The school closed about the time the United States entered World War I, and Ethel had only completed the fifth grade, the extent of her formal education. She watched the other buildings, one by one, empty and close. Her uncle Jim Stacey, Silas's youngest, was the village blacksmith for many years, and she watched the spread of the motorcar drive him out of business. Other Stacey offspring moved elsewhere. Silas's son Silas Monroe Stacey settled in the county seat, Jasper, where he raised a family and opened the town's leading general store and livery stable; he eventually gravitated back to his birthplace—Sparta, Missouri—where he operated a general store for the rest of his life. "His son taken it over," says Ethel, "and I suppose now that if it's still there, then some of his grandchildren are runnin it." The only known Stacey still around Newton County today is DeVoe Stacey, another grandson, who lives on Mount Sherman, west of Jasper.

Kim asks Ethel Coker the inevitable: "Have you ever visited Dogpatch?"

"Well, I've been there one time," Ethel says, "and, you know, I'd just give anything to go back to Marble City." It seems to Kim that she speaks of Marble City as different from Dogpatch, as if she feels that Marble City didn't simply become Dogpatch. "I'd love for it to be back just the way it used to be."

As Kim is leaving (and nowhere in Arkansas do you just

leave, without many minutes of idle chat in leavetaking), Ethel says to her, "I'm really glad you're doing this. It's really nice someone is interested."

Kim's next contact is with the oldest person she has ever seen or talked to, the oldest person Kim is to meet on her travels among these cities, and yet one of the youngest in spirit: hundred-year-old Dora Ervin Harp Curtis, who lives in a modest city house on a city street in Harrison, lucky to avoid a nursing home because she has been taken in by her eighty-three-year-old daughter, Elsie, who is also lucky to avoid a nursing home because she still has her husband, Willie McArtor, to look after her. The three of them sit with Kim in their living room on a warm sunny afternoon with all the windows closed and the shades drawn to darken the room and keep it cool. On the wall in the semidarkness is an ideal compote picture, the archetype of compote art: a 1920s octagon-framed glass-etched moonlight-on-a-lake-with-tent-and-campfire. Moonlight is the most compote of all images, Kim thinks, and realizes how appropriate it is for this darkened room.

Dora has good hearing, a pleasant smile and ready chuckle, a seemly hairdo not fully white, and an exemplary memory. She was born in The Basin in 1885 (the year *before* our key year), was raised in P D Flat, but went to Marble City for "church and for the mail and all stuff like that." Grown and married, she went with her daughter Elsie to live in Illinois for a while, in Missouri for a while, but always came back to Arkansas.

"Were you ever homesick for Arkansas?" Kim asks.

"Well, I don't know," Mrs. Curtis replies. "Wherever I was at, I was satisfied."

"That's a good way to be!" Kim observes.

Daughter Elsie offers, "She don't ever worry. . . ."

"You never worry about anything?" Kim asks the ancient mother.

"I never worry about nothing," Dora declares, "only sickness and death."

"Maybe I should pick up *your* habits!" Kim says. "*I* worry!"

"Do you?" Dora says, laughing. "You just cut that out. It won't get you nowhere!"

They progress to Dora's life in Marble City, the schools ("I never did go to a woman teacher, always men teachers"; but not many of them: "Tell you the truth, I didn't get much schoolin"). Kim quickly comes out with her stock question, "Have you ever been to Dogpatch?"

"No, I've never been down there," Dora says.

"Have you ever wanted to?" Kim asks.

"No, I don't want to go there! I tell ye, that used to be a nice little town, and I don't care a thing about *Dogpatch*."

So much for that. Kim brings up Dr. Stacey. Daughter Elsie remembers him well, but, surprisingly, Dora does not. Elsie explains: "To tell you the truth, the true fact, we didn't *have* doctors. Well, I guess my mother *did* have Dr. Stacey a few times, or, that is, my daddy would go over there and get medicine." Elsie recalls being afraid of Stacey's wife, Bettie—"She looked like she was part Indian, real black, and we was all afraid of her."

Elsie and her mother talk to Kim about the general stores and dry-goods stores and the coming of the daily mail hack, and the sawmill and cotton gin and gristmill. Willie McArtor chimes in to say that his dad bought the waterwheel and ran it for fifty years, but Kim has no McArtors in her notes and has been led to believe that Reverend Absalom Phillips owned the mill. When she asks them about Phillips, they don't recall that he ran a mill or a gin.

Dora says, "Was he the one that used to preach?"

Elsie says, "He didn't that I know about, now."

And that is about all we will learn, in these present days, of the hellfire-and-brimstone preacher Absalom Phillips, whose life would make a book—and no doubt will, despite his second wife's having disposed of all of his documents, notes, journals, letters, etc. Months later Kim will get a letter from a great-grandnephew of the reverend's, Bud Phillips, an author and a folklorist in Virginia: "When I lived at Harrison, Arkansas, a few years ago there then lived an old lady who had vivid memories of his preaching there in a tabernacle which stood near the big spring

in present Dogpatch." This old lady must not have been Dora
Curtis. This "tabernacle" must have been Marble City's Methodist
Episcopal Church Assembly building, a huge shed that was part
of the "permanent Methodist Assembly," accommodating several
hundred persons for both religious and social functions. Although this was erected "for the convenience of the Annual
Assembly of the Methodist Episcopal Church of the State of
Arkansas, which has selected Marble City as a permanent place
of assembly," it is not mentioned in the several histories of the
Methodist Church in Arkansas; the author of a *Centennial History
of Arkansas Methodism* laments, "I was unable to get much information on Newton County for lack of interest and co-operation
of the people." Walter Lackey encountered the same condition
in 1961—"no interest and less co-operation." Bud Phillips goes
on to describe interviews with those who heard one of the Reverend Phillips's sermons: "Uncle Ab would have fit well in the
U.S. Senate as an orator." In addition to his three- or four-hour
sermons, he also sang solo all the gospel songs and was thus "an
evangelist, not a pastor." Union hero, postmaster of Jasper, county
clerk, county sheriff, Republican bigwig, Methodist minister (as
of 1886), miller, cotton ginner and hotelier, Ab Phillips was Dr.
Stacey's best friend, but Elsie McArtor and her mother know little
of either. Their lack of knowledge can be explained by the fact
that they were not really townfolk, and knew well only the country
environs of P D Flat. They do *not* know how or why P D Flat is
so called. "It was *flat* when it rained, I'll tell you right now," Dora
says. "It was muddy and it stayed that way!"

One of their boarders at P D Flat was a young schoolteacher
named Delphie Henderson, one of the first female teachers in
the county, who lives just a few blocks away in Harrison, although
Dora and Delphie haven't seen each other in years. That is what
the city does to you. "I was thinking about her the other day,"
Dora says. "I used to talk to Delphie very often."

If Dora has never had a worry, Delphie Henderson has had too
many of them, and she shakes constantly. Kim goes to see her,

and they sit on the porch of the little house on Stevenson Street where she lives alone at the age of eighty-six, all of her eight children grown and moved far away. Her voice shakes, too, and on Kim's tape it is scarcely more than a high, hoarse tremolo. She apologizes to Kim for her shakiness, which could be Parkinson's disease, though Delphie explains that her nerves are the result of a bad winter icestorm that destroyed her roof and much of the contents of her little house.

Her name is Delphia. She says, "I was named for Philadelphia, or it was named for me, I've forgotten which! It's been so long!" Like Dora, she was born in The Basin, in 1899, on a Friday the 13th eighty days short of the twentieth century. Her grandfather, Elisha Massengale, settled and named The Basin, where her father, William Thomas Massengale, lived, and where the only residents today are Massengales. (A "furriner," or out-of-state retiree, living in the neighborhood of Dogpatch had written to Kim and suggested Hugh Massengale as a contact, but warned, "These mountain people are not too anxious to talk with strangers, and I don't think they trust outsiders too much.")

"I hate that name, *Dogpatch*," Delphie says. "I don't think a place as nice as that should have that name. It's a beautiful place." After teaching school in The Basin and P D Flat (yes, she boarded with Dora) and for a couple of years in Jasper, she "settled down and got married." She and her husband opened a little store in Marble City, and she was appointed postmistress just before the stock market crashed in 1929; she was storekeeper/postmistress throughout the Depression years, when "we never asked anyone to pay for their groceries, because they couldn't. We just did all we could for them, and we didn't have room in our little store for a feed store or we would've given 'em feed, too." The postmastership paid hardly anything, but they kept the store until they retired ("I told my husband that with the kind of customers we had, if you couldn't run a store, you just couldn't run a store") and some little miracle always happened. She tells Kim of the time her son was in college at Hendrix (a private college generally recognized as the best in Arkansas) and called home for tuition money, which she didn't have; she told him she would pray, and the next morning customers who had owed a large outstanding bill came in and paid it.

She recalls Dr. Stacey, remembers seeing him when she was a young girl, and remembers even better his son Jim the blacksmith. She tells of being given a gallon jug that had once held Dr. Stacey's aged whiskey and was later used to preserve medicine. "When they were empty, they gave 'em to their friends." Delphie meditates upon this fact, remembering the doctor's gifts of gallon stoneware jugs, each with its lower half glazed brown ceramic and a little ear for crooking one's finger through. "I thought it was the grandest thing, you know."

Kim lists, names, requests information about the others. Ab Phillips? He married Delphie's father and mother, and he was sheriff, and he ran the big red mill ("but it was gone when I was there"). Jonah Pruitt? He was sheriff, too, and "I went to school to him." Frank Carlton? "Yeah, I know Frank Carlton and all his family. I lived on one side of the hill and they lived on the other. He taught school, too."

Delphie takes pride in having been one of the first woman teachers, and she never had a problem with discipline. The pleasant white church/schoolhouse shown in our illustration was "her" Basin School. "I loved my children," she says of her pupils. "When I see one of 'em now downtown, they yell at me. They act like they love me. And I love them." Suddenly Delphie stops shaking and notices Kim's tape recorder. "Have you been recordin this?" she asks. *Yes!* Kim admits. "Oh, oh!" Delphie says. "Why didn't you tell me?!"

Before Kim can leave, she is shown photographs of Delphie's grandchildren. All grandmothers do this. Kim will be asked to look at photographs of grandchildren all over Arkansas. She admires Delphie's, but wonders, to herself, how often they come to visit their grandmother.

Next stop: the lost-in-the-backwoods, hard-to-find farmstead of Walter and Louise Mondy, east of Marble City, between P D Flat and Sulphur Mountain. Mondy, age sixty-four, who supplements his farming by building furnaces and heaters in his own little shop out back, was born in "downtown" Marble City, where his grandfather Luke Mondy had been one of the first settlers and had operated one of the general stores. "I could probably give you more information," Mondy says to Kim, "by bein down there and goin around and showin you where this and that used to set, you know. Where the ole blacksmith shop used to be and the store and the P.O. and all that stuff, you know." The busiest place in town, next to Jim Stacey's blacksmith shop, was Delphie Henderson's store. Luke Mondy used to own all of Marble City east of the spring branch, Mill Creek, and lived in a house that was later the home of "a fellow name of Frank Carlton."

"Who was Frank Carlton?" Kim asks.

"Well, he mostly got around, and dealt in land and stuff that way."

"And traded," says Louise Mondy. She asks her husband, "What was his nickname?"

"Well, I don't want that on her tape," Walter says, indicating the tape recorder. Instead, in the background on the tape is the sound of hail. It is very late in the afternoon of Kim's second day here, almost suppertime (or maybe the Mondys have already eaten); they are sitting on the long front porch of the farmhouse, and the driving rainstorm has changed temporarily to hail, the stones as big as marbles. Walter Mondy has not always stayed here on his farm; the search for opportunity has taken him, like many Arkansawyers, far afield—to California, to Canada, to Detroit, "following" welding and machine-shop work over the years. "I've been from east to west as far as you could go," Walter says. "We lived in Hartford, Connecticut, for four years." They are thus among the few Arkansawyers to live for a while in New England.

"You were homesick?" Kim asks.

"Lord, yes," Walter says. "This is the only place in the world that your neighbors cares about you. Only place. I'm an Arkansawyer. Born and raised here."

Kim smiles at that, loving his use of "Arkansawyer": so many modern, educated, but ignorant and insecure Arkansawyers make such a thing out of calling themselves "Arkansan," as if it were genteel.

She consults her notebook and asks one of her stock questions: "What scandals or crimes do you remember? Any suicides or murders?"

"Not over there at Marble City," he says. "That was a peaceful town. I never knowed of anybody gettin into trouble or anything." Kim considers how radically different this is from Cherokee City.

"How did P D Flat get its name?" she asks.

"Never did know," Walter says. "Only 'poor damn' . . ." He laughs.

Louise laughs, too. "Just Poor Damn Flat."

"You mentioned Frank Carlton," Kim says. "You're not going to tell me his nickname?"

"No," Mondy says. "I wouldn't want to tell that name."

"All right," Kim says, and asks her big one: "Have you been to Dogpatch?"

Mondy's face actually becomes red, and his neck muscles tighten. His words come rapidly and angrily: "Yeah, I've been down in there one time, made me so mad a feller had to pay to go in it and look around and see what used to be, and they got it all messed up now, it makes me so mad. I used to run all over that thing barefooted when I was a kid, and then to have to pay 'em seven or eight dollars to go down in there . . ."

Louise offers, "See, he'd like to see it back the way it used to be."

"Hell, yes!" Mondy says. "It used to be, anybody wanted to go down there and have a picnic or whatever, they could. If the kids wanted to get out there and play, they could. Why, Lord-a-mercy, you could ride your horse down in there, and tie it up. You knowed everbody, and you could talk, and you might have a little trade or somethin or other. You could *enjoy* it. And there's nothin you can enjoy over there now."

"You don't like the name *Dogpatch*?" Kim asks.

"Hell, no! It oughta be called Marble City!" Mondy is standing now, and gesturing. "Go down there and tear all them ole crazy buildings down, and put some decent roofs on 'em and put 'em all on there straight instead of all *humped-up*–like—you know—why—good gosh!"

It is too late in the afternoon for any more interviews, so Kim decides to take a different route back westerly toward Dogpatch and perhaps stop in the park again for one last look around. She drives the back roads across P D Flat (the name was "Piss Diddle," but the Mondys couldn't speak this onto her tape), taking the woodsy, bucolic eastern approach to Marble City, past Fodder-stack Mountain, on the same trail that Dr. Stacey rode in his buggy at least weekly from his farm into the village. On Zephyra's tape player she runs Beethoven's *Emperor* Concerto, one of the few classical cassettes she has. She drives very slowly, watching for ruts and potholes. There is no gate at this end of Dogpatch. The eastern side of the "theme" park dissolves into the woods and into this old township trail that she is on, and that Stacey traveled so often. As the trail nears the end of the woods and is about to emerge into the park beside the falls, she sees, on a ledge beside the road, the remains of a wagon: the oak spokes and felloes and staved hubs, the shafts and singletree and tongue and sideboards of a decaying wooden wagon. Seemingly in the process of dissolving into the ground, it reminds Kim of the skeleton of an animal. It is pointed eastward, away from Marble City, as if someone had long ago escaped from the town in that direction and the wagon had broken down and been abandoned. Thus the wagon, ignored by the Dogpatch management, serves as a true symbol of Marble City itself, the only thing authentic and original in the park.

Just across from it is the terminus of the West Po'k Chop Speshul Train, its narrow-gauge rails making a U-turn around a ramshackle outhouse-size hovel to head back toward the falls and the "civilization" of the village of Dogpatch. This little train runs on the only track that was ever laid in Newton County. Of all Arkansas's seventy-five counties, only poor Newton never had a mile of railroad track, although the developers of Marble City courted all of the major and minor railroad companies in hopes of a connection.

But the "real" railroad in the "real" Dogpatch of the "Li'l Abner" cartoon did not make safe round trips like this one. It ran straight up a mountainside to a point where it always fell back with a crash, killing all the passengers. Al Capp had an obsession with death and once declared, "Man is exhilarated by the thought of death. That's the basis of all the adventure in 'Li'l Abner.' It is always a flirtation with death; it is always a triumph over something that we all know will eventually triumph over us." When he died in 1979, his comic strip had been buried two years before, it and he suffering from terminal unpopularity. Ten years earlier, perceiving already the decline of his strip, he reluctantly consented to the establishment of the Dogpatch theme park in Arkansas and even went there, briefly, for the dedication ceremonies, where Orval Faubus appeared, no longer governor of Arkansas but now actually president and general manager of the Dogpatch corporation. Al Capp made a speech here. He stood on a platform with Faubus and looked around him at all these gimcrack buildings that have only the most superficial resemblance to the "real" Dogpatch of his mind and his drawing board, and he thanked all the local people like Doyle Harp who had made his "dream come true," and he said, "No one from either coast could have done as good a job. . . . I'm extremely pleased. . . . This *is* Dogpatch!"

Orval Faubus grinned his famous grin, although he did not like Al Capp. Orval Faubus was a genuine, dyed-in-the-wool Ozark hillbilly who faithfully read "Li'l Abner" but had no use for its creator, although Capp and Faubus were surprisingly alike. They were born just three months apart, Capp in September 1909, Faubus in January 1910, and they even looked alike: high foreheads with receding dark hair, and big mouths. But Faubus was born into the poverty of Greasy Creek, Arkansas, whereas Capp was born into the poverty of New Haven, Connecticut, a completely different world. In their teens, both of them ran away from home, Faubus to become an itinerant fruit-picker and hobo, Capp to have his first and only contact with real mountain people

in eastern Tennessee, where he remained only a few days, long
enough to be impressed by the fun-loving backwoods characters
but not long enough to learn to depict accurately their manners,
mores, and least of all their dialectic speech, which was always
terribly misrendered in his comic strip.

In 1934, the same year Faubus got his belated diploma from
the vocational high school in his hometown, Huntsville, Capp
was inventing and marketing his first "Li'l Abner" strips. While
Orval managed to become postmaster of Huntsville and edi-
tor/publisher of the weekly Madison County *Record* newspaper
(circulation 1,227), Al Capp was reaching a daily and Sunday
circulation of twenty-seven *million* with his Dogpatch saga. By
1954, when Faubus, through some strange flukes of Arkansas
politics, got himself elected governor, Al Capp's comics were
being compared to Gershwin's achievement in jazz, D. W. Grif-
fith's in the movies, and John Steinbeck was promoting Capp for
the Nobel Prize in literature.

Then, in 1957, Faubus focused the attention of the world
upon himself and upon a place called Little Rock, whose name
is still universally evocative of race hatred and the problems of
integration.

In the sixties, Faubus kept on getting re-elected to his six
terms as governor, while Al Capp gave Li'l Abner hippie-length
hair in concession to the youth culture, although his own politics
or ideologies were becoming increasingly conservative and he
finally lost his college audience completely by proclaiming, "The
martyrs at Kent State were the kids in National Guard uniforms."
Faubus was finally defeated by Winthrop Rockefeller, retired,
but kept attempting unsuccessful comebacks into politics, and
accepted the figurehead directorship of Dogpatch to earn his
keep.

The deserted grounds of Dogpatch are growing dark again. Kim
pauses only briefly at the village "square," beneath the equestrian
statue of Dogpatch's Confederate General Jubilation T. Cornpone, who fought in twenty-seven Civil War battles and lost every

one, and was decorated by the Yankees for his contribution to their cause. Quite possibly García Marquez was one of the many international fans of Al Capp, and modeled upon General Cornpone his Colonel Aureliano Buendia of Macondo, who fought thirty-two battles for the Liberal cause and lost every one of them.

Into the square comes another automobile, and Kim's first thought is that it is the park's watchman coming to run her out. She will explain that she came into the park from the east, where there is no gate. But the car, an old Chevy, does not look official, as if belonging to a Dogpatch security guard. Her second thought is that its lone occupant, a male, is the professor and novelist recently in South Dakota who has come to join her on her quest to Arkansas's lost cities. The car stops alongside Zephyra. The man gets out. Although she has never laid eyes on the professor/novelist, she would hope that he is younger than this man, who is quite gray, craggy, stooped, and has a nose like . . . She recognizes the nose, the famous face itself. She has met this man before, although she was only nine or ten the last time she saw him face to face, at the foot of the great staircase in his mansion at Little Rock. He had paused to shake her hand and that of her sister Michelle, and little Michelle, six or seven, had declared, "I will never wash my hand again!" Their grandfather, Julian Hogan, was standing proudly to one side, his hand across Kim's shoulders, where he rarely placed it. Julian Hogan, the father of Kim's and Michelle's mother, Jacque, was a big man himself, the director of the budget, a career employee, not a politician, but still one of the most powerful men in the capital, a man whom, Kim will discover in just a few more months, the *Arkansas Times* magazine considers one of the 50 Most Influential Arkansawyers of All Time.

The old man is wearing a necktie with a kind of country-western zippered jacket, black, and one can almost see the bulge of the pacemaker beneath it. "Howdy," he says. "Looks like me and you are the only visitors, this time of year."

To forestall his introducing himself, she says, "I'm the grand-daughter of Julian Hogan."

"Is that a fact, now?" he says, smiling. "Your grandpa was one of the finest men I ever knew, a great and dedicated public servant. He helped me shape my whole administration. How's he doin these days?"

"He's OK," she says. "He's in a nursing home." She has not seen her eighty-three-year-old grandfather for five or six years; her mother visits him regularly and reports that he is "beyond senility."

Kim has covertly switched on her tape recorder. She asks, "You don't work here any more?"

He laughs. "No, I'm just on my way up to Harrison to have supper with some friends, and thought I'd drop by and see what they've done to the place. Hasn't changed much."

They are standing directly beneath the statue of General Cornpone, who fought and lost his twenty-seven battles. This old man fought twenty-seven political battles and won them all . . . except the last two.

"Do you come to Dogpatch often?" she asks. She does not slur the word.

He looks around him, at the great emptiness surrounding them, as if searching for himself among the invisible crowds of people, the tourists who recognized him and crowded in on him, calling his name and yelling, "Howdy, Governor!" Is this the first time he has ever been in Dogpatch all alone . . . except for Kim? Oh, this is the story of—you know it, don't you?—not of lost cities but of lost people, who rose and stood their allotted time upon this earth, and then sat down again. "I was here early last year," he says, sitting on the fender of his car. "The new manager invited back some of us who had worked here before—sort of a reunion, in a way. So we came here and they had dinner for us and we just visited."

"If someone wrote a book about you," she says, "and no doubt someone will, how much would you like to see devoted to your time at Dogpatch?"

"About a paragraph!" he says, laughing. "Just to say that I was president of the corporation and general manager of the operation during the time I was here."

"When Dogpatch was constructed, was there anything left of Marble City at all? Any remains?"

"No," he says, and points north. "Perhaps a small building or so there at the fish hatchery, and that was all." He points south. "There wasn't anything down at the falls. It was just the falls and the remnants of an old mill that had been there years and years before. I think they're restoring it now."

"Did you ever read 'Li'l Abner'?" she asks.

"Oh, yes, I read that comic strip all the time," he says. "It was one of my favorites!" She asks him why. "Well, the philosophy expressed in it: here they were, these independent, benighted mountaineers, up against the federal government and the rest of the world and that sort of thing. It wasn't too authentic for portraying mountaineers, but it was humorous as a *fantasy*."

"Was there a dialect, a language that the employees of Dogpatch were expected to learn?" Kim wants to know. "Did they have to learn a language to portray the characters?"

"Oh, they mimicked the language and the phraseology used in the Al Capp cartoon. They were given *some* training. It wasn't difficult to learn a few words and phrases. And most of the people who were hired here—or many of them—were mountain people. They didn't have to *affect* any language." At this point the governor reaches into his jacket pocket and brings out a package of peanuts in the shell, opens it, cracks open a peanut, and pops the nuts into his mouth. He doesn't offer her a peanut.

"Did you ever meet Al Capp?" she asks.

"He came up to Dogpatch when they had the dedication, and I was with him off and on for two or three days. 'Course, Mr. Odom was there, and he was the owner, so Capp spent most of his time with Odom, not me."

"Did you like Capp?"

"Oh, I liked some of his philosophies. You know, he once remarked to the press, 'The trouble with Faubus was, he was prematurely right!' " The governor chuckles, then frowns. "But he was a very crude, rude individual."

Kim sweeps her arm in an arc and asks, "Do you think these buildings are crude and rude, too?"

The governor studies the architecture as if really looking at it for the first time. "Yeah, they are a bit extreme, just as the cartoon was extreme. Those sway-backed roofs there, all that stuff. A mountaineer erecting a building—even if it was just a log cabin, it would be better constructed than that. These buildings exaggerated the defects that you might find in houses, just as the cartoon exaggerated defects that you might find in people."

"Are there any displays in these buildings that tell of the history of Marble City, so that tourists could be aware of the history of the town?"

"No, but that's one of the things I thought we should've had. I would've liked to have seen a sort of museum here, with authentic tools and household items that were used by the mountaineers in pioneer days, not just in the Ozarks but all through the country." The governor gets a visionary gleam in his eye. "Because that's disappearing. A museum like that could provide a great deal of interest and entertainment for the old people who could remember it. Grandparents bring the kids in here and the kids can keep busy all day, but the older folks run out of anything to hold their interest."

"How much do you know of the history of Marble City?" she asks.

"Pretty little, I guess. First time I saw it, many years ago, there was nothin here but the big spring comin out of the mountain, and a fish hatchery."

"Governor, do you have fond memories of your time here at Dogpatch?"

"They're mixed memories. I had some very unpleasant things to deal with here, but I also had some pleasant ones. It's a happy occasion when you get out and work with young people, because young people are still honest. They haven't learned deceit. They haven't been disillusioned by experiences. I used to teach school, you know, and the happiest and most satisfying period in my life was when I was teaching. So dealing with these youngsters at Dogpatch was a pleasure for me." He pauses to crack and eat some more peanuts. "And those tourists, coming through here by the thousands, and many of them would recognize me and come up and talk to me, and some would come by my office on purpose to see if I was there and get acquainted with me. . . . That was quite pleasant. I've been working with the public and working with people all my life. You excuse me for eating peanuts!"

He says this not as a request but almost as a command or simply an observation, and pops a few more into his mouth. Kim asks another question: "Did you find that handling your subordinates at Dogpatch was any different from doing so while you were governor?"

"Well, I had a little better control as governor!" he says, laughing, but meaning it. He seems to believe that perhaps Kim will be one of his biographers, and he begins to talk about his career as governor, his real accomplishments neglected in the shadow of the Little Rock integration problem. Confident that her tape recorder will get it all, she is only half listening to him. ". . . the state park system, rebuilding the state hospital, building the Children's Colony, those things you just don't get done all at once. . . ."

In just another month, less than a month, the newspapers will carry the story that Faubus's estranged wife, Beth, will have been found dead, strangled in the bathtub of her Houston home and beaten to a bloody pulp for some senseless reason by a paroled convict attempting to rob and rape her, and that Faubus will be taken there by the police to view the scene and will say to the press, "How in the name of God can people do things like that to other people?" And Kim will cry, wondering how much the old man will have to bear, having borne the suicide of his only son.

Now she listens to him tell the story of his dreams that worked out and his dreams that failed. When he is finished, she asks him, "Governor, how would Arkansas be any different today if the whole Little Rock integration crisis had not happened?"

He thinks about that. Then he declares firmly, "It wouldn't. Everything went ahead just as I had planned it. I did what I had to do, and life goes on."

"What about your own life?" she asks. "What are you going to do now?"

He returns to his car and sits behind the wheel. "Well, first of all I'm going to go eat with those folks who are waitin for me. Then"—he grins that famous politician's grin one last time—"someday I'd like to write a book about the Ozarks. You know all these books like *Foxfire*? Well, I've read them, and everything in there was just a part of my natural life when I was growing up—we didn't think anything about it, that was just the way we lived, and now everybody thinks it was remarkable. I'm going to write a book. A writer who's a friend of mine told me, 'All you have to do is just describe the way you grew up!' "

Buffalo City,
Arkansas

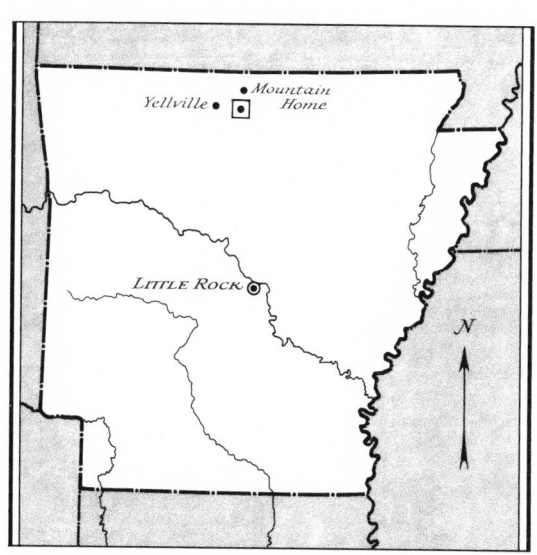

Yellville • • Mountain
Home

LITTLE ROCK ◉

N

YES, BUTCHER THOSE BUFFALO in that canebrake! At the very end
of Nabokov's most appreciatively read novel, the plaintive double
Humbert turns away from contemplation of his own and his
nymphet's death and waxes terminally poetic: "I am thinking of
aurochs and angels, the secret of durable pigments, prophetic
sonnets, the refuge of art." The auroch is, of course, the European bison, Old World Humbert's smaller version of the American buffalo. The auroch is the creature who most inhabits the
durable pigments of prehistoric cave painting. The buffalo sustained European man in his rise to art, just as it sustained the
Indian in his stewardship of the American earth while awaiting
the arrival of the European who would cultivate it and wipe out
the remaining buffalo as well as the stewards.

"Buffalo" is a misnomer. So is the eponymous "city" (or two
of them, twins) that took its (their) name(s) not from the animal
but from the river, which the National Park Service has designated America's first "National River," a spectacular, remote,
bluff-locked cascade down the middle of the Arkansas Ozarks,
immortalized in Kenneth Smith's *The Buffalo River Country*. The
American buffalo, so-called, is not a buffalo but a bison—in fact,
so much a bison that the taxonomists have labeled it officially as
Bison bison, a reduplication that we ought to honor by calling our
next destination Buffalo Buffalo City and letting it go at that,

instead of trying to sort out the schizophrenic distinctions between the two lost sister towns that are separated, not by the Buffalo River but by the White, which joins the Buffalo a few miles on down. Even the handful of residents remaining on the opposite shores are sometimes confused by the historical attempts to distinguish these places into Old Buffalo City and New Buffalo City, or West Buffalo City and East Buffalo City, or to rename the latter entirely by calling it Winnerva or Toney or Oredale or Sticker City, as it has been known at one time or another.

Buffalo City is the loneliest and most inaccessible of all our destinations, possibly because it is also the most beautiful physically. Beauty is not accessible; aestheticians speak of a requisite "distance," which in a nutshell means we cannot know and savor beauty up close, too close; we have to keep a space between our ordinary selves and the truly beautiful, lest our judgment be bedazzled by it. Beautiful people often give the erroneous impression of distance in the sense of aloofness or chilliness of manner, when in fact this is our own distancing from them; we cannot get too close to them, or we become aware of our own lack of their qualities. The same with cities, or with places; nobody wants to populate Buffalo City, because it is just *too* gorgeous, and remote, and dreamlike. Dreams are a nice place to visit, but we wouldn't want to live there.

Trying to anticipate getting lost in her attempt to find this lost city, Kim had made a special trip to see Ken Smith in his home at Fayetteville after she had interviewed Chris Yates of Cherokee City. Kim had read *The Buffalo River Country* and knows its lovely photographs by heart, but, apart from locating Buffalo City in its section maps, it has nothing to say about the place. So Kim had gone to see Smith, a shy, late-forties bachelor, and asked him, "Have you ever been to Buffalo City?" When he hesitated in his answer, as if trying to recall, or perhaps reluctant to discuss this Shangri-la, she declared, "I've asked several people about it, but nobody's ever heard of it."

"Yes," he said, at length. "I've visited or at least passed both Old Buffalo City and New Buffalo City, but there's not much to see in either place."

"How could you leave them out of your book?" she asked.

"They're not exactly in the Buffalo River watershed, and I limited myself to that." Ken Smith talked to Kim about the times he had landed his canoe near the sites of the Buffalo Cities and examined the few remains, scarcely ruins, of each. He had been more impressed by the natural, rather than man-made features: Stair Bluff, named simply because it rises like steep steps a thousand feet above the water; Laffoon Creek, which tears through Hathaway Hollow, past the lost and private cemetery of the long-gone Laffoon family. "Laf*foon*?" Kim asked. "Yes," Ken said. "Unusual name, isn't it? Laffoon."

The man to see, Smith told her, if you could find him, was a Baxter Hurst. "He's about the only one left in Old Buffalo City."

Expecting to find a hermit living in a shack (when in fact Buffalo City is the only one of these lost cities that never, as far as anyone remembers or the record can show, ever had a resident hermit), Kim goes off in search of Baxter Hurst.

Eastward from upper Newton County and Marble City, Marion County (named after the old Swamp Fox of the Revolutionary War, Francis Marion) is not so ruggedly mountainous as Newton but is thoroughly hilled and rolling, even the 628 square miles of it that lie beneath the waters of Bull Shoals Lake, the greatest impoundment of the White River. Kim keeps to the byroads of the southern part of the county, detouring, for the fun of it, through the hamlet of Eros, one of Arkansas's numerous four-letter towns. Who named Eros, and why, beggars both history and imagination. But Ozarkers are grandly euphemistic, and "love" was an indelicate word to the old-time Ozarker. Eros is only a winding wide place in the road , with no hint of eroticism or even cupidity, but as Kim lifts her foot from Zephyra's gas pedal and lets her coast over the summit beyond the village, there, stretching off immeasurably into the distance, are range beyond range of hills, and in her ear, range beyond range of tones, and themes, and instruments: evocations of a kind of heroic loneliness, with human voices choiring distantly in languages unknown.

As she pulls over beside the road to listen, she cannot remember whether she has passed through pale Eros or has yet to discover it, whether it is already history, a place passed and not again to be seen, or imagination, a place dreamed and yet to be. She is lost in music as these towns are lost in time, and decides at last that the sound comes from within her, the Theme of the Faraway Hills that invents itself inside anyone alone and tugged by distances.

How right and fitting, therefore, Kim thinks as she reaches beyond one of those hills into Yellville, the county seat, and discovers that the county newspaper is called *The Mountain Echo*, and that, further, this little newspaper was founded in the special year of 1886. Yellville? This "yell" is not from the same root as "yellow," and "golden," but from a cousin root akin to "call" and "calling," exulting and yelping. One cannot help thinking of Spillville, which is in Iowa, the lost town where homesick Antonín Dvořák, drunk as usual one Sunday afternoon, first caught an ear's glimpse of the Theme of the Faraway Hills (of which there are none in prairie Spillville), captured the notes before they could spill away from him, and changed and used parts of the Theme in a symphony (*From the New World*). This Yellville took its name from one Archibald Yell of Fayetteville, governor and congressman during the 1840s, who resigned his seat in Congress during the Mexican War to enlist with much publicity as a private, was quickly promoted to colonel, and just as quickly annihilated with his cavalry at the Battle of Buena Vista in 1847. His troops, guilty of atrocities against civilians, were poorly trained and overconfident, as was Yell himself. Yellville had been—like most villages, including Buffalo City itself—an Indian village, named Shawneetown; during his heated campaign for Congress, Archibald Yell visited the place and paid the residents $50 to rechristen it Yellville. Yell also had a county named for him without having to pay for it, but Yellville is the seat of Marion County, whereas Marion is the seat of Crittenden County. In Arkansas towns are rarely located in their eponymous counties: Conway isn't in Conway County; Hot Springs is not in Hot Spring County but in Garland County, while Garland City is in Miller County, while Miller is in Greene County. . . . It is very easy to get lost in Arkansas.

Kim's first stop in Yellville is the courthouse in the center of the town's square, a building of rough native ashlar stone in a World War II styleless style built to replace a lovelier one that burned after replacing a still lovelier one. . . . All over Arkansas the courthouses burn, and with them their records, making the historian's job difficult. Kim finds that the plat books in the county clerk's office have not burned, but the county clerk's clerk has only a vague notion of what Kim is looking for, and at first tries to get rid of her with an assertion that there aren't any old plat maps of Buffalo—*City*, did you say? But, sure enough, on page one of Plat Book Two is the dramatic map, Grand Avenue and all, Commerce Street with its railroad tracks that were never built, Maywood Park with Laffoon Creek meandering through it, the riverfront with steamboat landings (steamboats in the Ozark Mountains!), ore docks, a cotton gin, and a no-longer-existent or never-existent "U.S. Monument." A Lion Hill Road rises to the heights west of the city, and such fanciful addresses as Markham Terrace and Windermere Place await homebuilders who never built. So confident, even cocksure, were the planners of this city, on paper, that Kim almost begins to believe that there might be some trace of all this grand envisagement still remaining.

At the small office of *The Mountain Echo*, Kim makes the lucky acquaintance of Barbara "Corky" Craig, the *Echo*'s occasional folklore columnist, born in Marion County forty-some years ago, descendant on two sides of old journeymen sawmillers who once worked in Buffalo City. Like Faubus, Corky Craig did not realize until she was grown up that her whole life had been "folklore" and was thus worthy of interest; she now satisfies that interest with her column in the *Echo*. She knows Baxter Hurst and will be glad to introduce Kim to him.

Zephyra, that saucy Nissan Datsun 280-ZX, has a disinclination to traverse gravelly, pocked, chuckholed, or wrinkled roads. She is meant for city streets, and not would-be cities, either. Talk

about "Blue Highways": some of the byroads that Zephyra must
peregrinate in the course of this quest for the lost cities of Arkansas are olive-drab, or dun, or sepia, or positively taupe. Much
of the road that Corky Craig directs Kim and Zephyra to is sort
of henna, a strong reddish brown. The last few miles of this red
dirt road, Kim slows Zephyra to a creep. More than once she
asks Corky, "How much farther?", until the road drops down out
of the hills into the broad plain of a great river meadow surrounded by bluffs, and Corky says "Just right up yonder." The
road comes to an end approximately where the intersection of
Markham Terrace and Windermere Place was meant to be, at a
classic contemporary compote ranch-style house, seen so universally in suburbs across America that it seems almost out of
place on an actual ranch, which this appears to be. "What's this?"
Kim asks, seeing no sign of ruin or vestige of town. The Hurst
place, Corky tells her, and, gesturing toward the sweeping, cliff-
ringed, bare meadow, "Buffalo City."

Baxter Hurst, age sixty-four, is the baron and sole proprietor
of Old, or West, Buffalo City. He lives in this spacious ranch-
style with his wife, Geneva; his sister Ruby (Mrs. Fred Bearden)
lives in an older house nearby, and they, along with one other
family in a house built from the remains of the old Buffalo City
Hotel, make up the entire population of Old Buffalo City. There
are Hursts all over Marion and Baxter counties (Baxter got his
name not from the adjacent county but from an uncle who may
or may not have been named, like the county, after Governor
Elisha Baxter). There is a famous Hurst Fishing Service on the
White River and a Hurst Liquor Store, distant relations whom
Baxter does not patronize. He is an elder in the Church of Christ,
and he looks exactly like Kim's conception of what a Church of
Christ elder would be: mild-mannered, unassuming, almost
scholarly, equally at home behind the communion table and in
the fields of his cattle ranch. Although the house itself is thoroughly recent compote, the interior furnishings and paraphernalia are unassertive and make a modest distinction between the
more casual family room and the more formal living room, in
which hangs an ancestral portrait: Baxter has traced his forebears

to Thomas Hurst of the 1066 Domesday Book. The name Hurst
means "one who lives near a small wood." Baxter lives near a
very large wood. This is a hinterland peopled with Clinking-
beards, Bodenhammers, and Deatherages, with Derryberrys and
Blankenships, families whose histories are traceable not just to
the Domesday Book but to the first weddings of Angles and
Saxons, in the fifth century. There are no great heroes; these
yeomen and yeowomen overflowed from Tennessee, Kentucky,
and Alabama, where they had overflowed from Virginia and
North Carolina, and most of them settled in and did their jobs
in clearing the land and starting towns; some flowed on to Texas
and other points west. Of those who stayed to sink roots and start
families, no large tales are told. Marion and Baxter counties are
without mythopoeic heritage, without novelists, without trou-
badours except those who warble by rote the old ballads from
across the sea.

Baxter Hurst is an amateur historian himself, with a deep
and abiding interest in the fragments and traces of man's tenancy
of this land. He offers to take Kim out in his pickup truck for a
tour of the vast pasture that is all that remains of Old Buffalo
City. She is reminded of Buster Price and the ride to the Mankins
pasture, but that was only sixty acres; this one is four hundred
acres. Instantly Kim visualizes the large city that could have been
built in that pasture and on the heights and palisades around it
. . . and, of course, across the river, where New Buffalo City also
has a pasture, though not quite so vast, and heights, and a similar
dearth of man-built remains.

Baxter shows Kim the foundation of the old hotel, which
looks simply like a long stone wall, with the upper boulders spilled
in the sun; something there is that doesn't love it. True stone
walls are rare in Arkansas. Baxter tells her that this was the last
building standing in Old Buffalo. He does not remember the
name of it. (It was called simply Buffalo City Hotel in its last
years; in its early years it was Shoal House.) "I think it was '34,
might've been '35," Baxter says, "when my dad and my uncle
took it down. It was built of pine lumber, and they built two good
rent houses out of it."

A "rent house"—though the name suggests a ruin, a house ripped or torn—is a kind of country tenement. The vacant one in our illustration is just to the west of Baxter's house. It is a classic example of the two-door bigeminal board-and-batten shack, universal in its homeliness. All the junk on the porch of Baxter's rent house—part of an old school desk, a child's crib, etc.—is just a spillover from the interior of the shack, used strictly for storage and perhaps as a reminder to Baxter, who used to live there, of his less prosperous days. Was there an interior connecting door between the two rooms of the bigeminal shack? Yes, Baxter tells Kim, there is.

A mere trail running between the hotel foundation and the river, with a cowpath branch of it dropping down to the river, was once a county road, the beginning of a major freight-hauler's road that went all the way to Old Carrollton in Carroll County and was a primary lifeline to the first settlers of the whole region. Here at Buffalo Landing was the head of navigation on the White River, beyond which the boats could not go because of the shallow shoals (a redundancy) upstream. The freight unloaded here ("freight" in those days always meant the lightweight basic essentials that could not be homegrown or homemade: salt, pepper, coffee, etc.) would be transported by ox wagon over the most primitive one-lane trail to Carrollton, which was the chief trading point until it failed to get an expected railroad and faded into forsakenness.

The trees now along the river are weed trees, puny saplings, some losing their footings and falling into the rushing stream of the White River—which, however, sticks to the same basic course, unlike larger rivers, which meander all over the landscape. The White River sometimes floods these fields, but not nearly so often or so damagingly as in the days before the Bull Shoals dam was built. In modern times, the field has been less disturbed by the river than by the plow, which put all of these acres into cotton in the twenties, when Baxter's father bought the whole four hundred acres for $24,000. The plow also uncovered not only Indian artifacts but also Indian burials.

Kim asks Baxter how he feels about plowing up old Indian

cemeteries. "You'd rather not be plowin up a human being," Baxter says. "You'd rather not be runnin your plows through their graves. It doesn't seem quite right. But it happens, all up and down this river—once, after a big flood, there must've been fifty or a hundred burials revealed, just washed up out of the ground. The Indians probably didn't bury their dead too deep. They had a poor way of diggin graves."

There was once a large Osage village here, which, for want of knowing what they called it, we might call Tse-do Ton-won, which means "Buffalo City" in Osage. Tse-do Ton-won was here for a longer time than the Buffalo City of the white man has been here so far. At one time, along the mile of shoals in the river, there was a crossing for vast herds of buffalo (although a popular misconception about the buffalo, in addition to the misconception that he is slow and stupid, is that he joins herds numbering in the hundreds of thousands, whereas in fact each individual herd may have only from five to fifty, averaging fifteen; lump all these "villages" of buffalo together and you appear to have a "city" of buffalo). The shoals not only attracted an endless supply of mobile meat to the Indians, but also furnished an abundance of shoaling fish and the very popular freshwater mussels. These tasty bivalves, whose shells literally pave sections of Old Buffalo City, furnished the Indians with mother-of-pearl for inlays and decorative objects, and furnished the white man, particularly during the Depression years, with a whole industry for mother-of-pearl buttons. Among other artifacts excavated or washed up in the vicinity are stone hoes and digging tools, grinding bowls, and other objects indicating a thoroughly agriculturized society. The Osage, according to one theory, were once an extremely intellectual breed of people, living simply in their little cities, working hard to satisfy their few wants, cultivating their own gardens. Along came the buffalo and turned the Osage brave into a passionate, bloodthirsty hunter. He left his garden to his woman and went out on expeditions. His character became brutal, his feet became restless, and he forgot his intellect. He also substituted the ferocity of the hunt for the ardor of sex, and did not procreate enough to keep his population stable. No wonder he was a pushover for the white man.

Suppose that there were two Tse-do Ton-wons, even then, on opposite sides of the river. Those in West Tse-do Ton-won, with more access to the buffalo fording the shoals, became more aggressive and feral, while those in East Tse-do Ton-won, with fewer acres to cultivate, practiced "intensive gardening" and allowed no weed to sprout, and, in all the hours available to them between routing weeds, meditated or procreated, or both. Only the swift river separating East Tse-do Ton-won from West Tse-do Ton-won kept the two cities from warring with each other, but each was consciously aware of the other, and perhaps constantly afraid of the other. Thus do twin cities coexist, or two halves of the same city . . . or person.

In this same meadow, farther along, is a white man's burial ground, not very well cared for, and subject to the next great flood, should the Bull Shoals dam give way. This little city of the dead (the cemetery, not the lost village) isn't shown on the U.S. topographic survey map, probably because it is so easily overlooked, or so obscured by the masses of thick cane that grow in it. This cane, *Arundinaria gigantea,* cousin of Oriental bamboo but thrice as tall, is an evergreen grass that provided emergency fodder in early times but also tended to form impenetrable brakes and make clearing the land difficult. The only canebrake remaining in Old Buffalo City is right in the confines of the Old Buffalo cemetery. Baxter Hurst's kid brother Marlon is buried here, and Baxter shows Kim the grave, a headstone surmounted by a sculptured lamb. Several less artistic tombstones are lost among the cane and masses of wakefield crud, a pernicious viny weed that loves to choke anything made by man.

Kim moves gingerly through the cane, trying to step over the wakefield crud. "Do people come here?" she asks.

"Yes," Baxter says, "usually during the summer a few people will come, like maybe they live in Oklahoma or Texas and don't know much about their descendants that are buried here." Kim assumes it is just a slip: by "descendants" he means "ancestors."

"They like to come and put flowers on the graves and trim 'em up, but there's not a lot of people who come back."

Almost by accident, although surely not, Kim parts some vines of wakefield crud and stands face to face with the oldest headstone in the cemetery, "Sacred to the Memory of WILLIAM KENDALL HOGAN, 1820–1855." She asks, since the grave is so cluttered with the crud vines, "Has anyone ever visited this grave?"

"Not to my knowledge," Baxter says. "He was the man, we think, who was in business here with the old man Moreland in the 1850s."

"My grandfather was a Hogan," Kim remarks, "and his father came from this part of the country." Her great-grandfather's name was not William Kendall Hogan, she doesn't think, but *his* grandfather's name might have been that.

"Is that a fact?" Baxter Hurst says. "It's sure a small world." Apparently deciding that Kim would like to be alone with the spirit of her ancestor, he starts walking back toward his house, not far.

Graveyards do not frighten Kim. She is growing more and more accustomed to them.

William Kendall Hogan may or may not have been her ancestor, but he was the best friend of Everard Dickinson, who must serve as the theme hero for Old Buffalo City. The unusual first name, which undoubtedly was shortened to "Every" by those who knew him, means literally "strong as a razorback boar" in German, but Everard Dickinson was a spindly dude, a city slicker: in today's argot he might be called a wimp. Before coming to Buffalo City, he lived in Hartford, Connecticut, a poor relation of the "Up-stream Dickinsons" of Amherst, Massachusetts. His second cousin was a shy poetess named Emily, whom he met only a couple of times, conversed at length with, and possibly corresponded with, although none of his letters to her survive. Several of his letters to his parents, written after he left home and plunged into the Arkansas wilderness, are preserved in the files of the *Arkansas Gazette*.

> And so, as Kinsmen, met a Night —
> We talked between the Rooms —
> Until the Moss had reached our lips —
> And covered up — our names —

wrote Emily in 1862, when the moss had long since covered any trace of Everard's name. A bachelor as she was a spinster, he was still a comparatively young man of thirty-three, the age at which Christ was crucified, when he realized that he would spend his life as a poor shop clerk in Hartford unless he did something drastic. In 1848, gold had not yet been discovered in California. Horace Greeley had not yet enjoined such shop clerks to "go west." (Greeley in fact cribbed this quote from one John Soule in the Terre Haute, Indiana, *Express* of 1851, three years after Everard went west to Arkansas.) Everard left New England in the spring of 1848, determined to escape forever the clerical class that his station and training had predestined for him. It takes a lot of footloose shop clerks to blaze a frontier.

Everard was industrious but not particularly adventurous, and he wanted to find a relatively "safe" wilderness where he could become a small-business man without being eaten up by bears or scalped by Indians. He chose Arkansas primarily on hearsay: it was a frontier without being an especially dangerous one. Just how he wound up in Buffalo City, which had recently received its hopeful name either from William Hogan or the one other man living there at the time, William Moreland, is not certain. Soon after arrival, he wrote to his parents:

> The roads are bad and there is no stage route to this place and the only way travellers can get along is on horseback. This is a wild, romantic region of country and has been but little known about until within a few years. *Although this place is called a city*, there are only 4 male inhabitants in it; myself and Mr. Hogan of the firm of Hogan and Tunstall and the old man Wm. Moreland and his son, and their families.

Italics added: even though the place was "best known by the name of Buffalo Shoals" (one more of its many appellations), the name had already been changed to Buffalo City by one of the two Bills, Hogan or old Moreland, likely the latter, "the proprietor of this city," with whom Everard and Bill Hogan were boarding. Moreland had settled at the Shoals in 1829, just ten years after the first white settler, Major Jacob Wolf of Kentucky, had come into the area as President Thomas Jefferson's appointee to serve as Indian agent and maintain peace between the Arkansas Cherokees and Osages.

Jacob Wolf, about whom a major book remains to be written, built the still-standing, oldest house in Arkansas a few miles downstream, at Norfork (which he called Liberty): a majestic two-story dogtrot (or "saddlebag") log cabin with four great rooms, each eighteen feet square, one of the upper ones serving for many years as the courthouse. From the porch of this house, Jacob Wolf dealt both with the red residents of Tse-do Ton-won who brought furs and peltry in exchange for weapons and whiskey, and with the white immigrants like Everard Dickinson who came up the river in search of places for settlement. Quite possibly the landscape around Major Wolf's settlement at Norfork reminded Everard of the hills around his boyhood home at Belchertown, south of Amherst in Massachusetts. The westering pioneer often stops and settles when he finds a visual reminder of home.

Jake Wolf took a shine to Everard and tried to persuade him to stay, and this friendship remained in the back of Everard's mind throughout his early experiences at Buffalo City. He wrote to his parents that if he should decide to leave Buffalo City and go back to Norfork,

> I shall board with old Major Jacob Wolf, one of the oldest settlers in this country and bearing the name of a strictly honest and honourable man—he lived here for years when the country was inhabited by Indians and always retained their respect and good will. I have been down to see the old Major and he says if I will come down he will have the house

put in good repair and send his ferry boat up after my
things—when the water will admit. If I move, I will let you
know—and I think now, I shall go there as it is more of a
publick place and there are some very good settlements up
the North fork and below on White River the trade of which
I shall get and here at Buffalo City we are so hemmed in by
mountains that the nearest settler to us (out back) is 5 miles
off. But I think one day there will be a considerable *town here
at this very spot.* [His italics]

But his new host, old Mr. Moreland, had taken an even greater
liking to him, and offered him free board in exchange for help
on his farm and the possibility of getting Everard interested in
his eighteen-year-old daughter, Agness, who was illiterate and
backward in other ways, including her appearance.

Whether Everard had ever had a crush on his cousin Emily
(not likely) or (more likely) remained stuck on another cousin,
the flirtatious Clarissa Stebbins of Northampton, Massachusetts,
his "sweet-pretty" for whom he had long had a hankering but
was too poor to propose, his dream of a new life in the frontier
wilderness, where there was no poverty because everyone was
equally poor, must have included fantasies of an exquisite, primitive pioneer daughter who would homespin his clothes and cook
his venison and warm his shuck mattress. Agness Moreland did
in fact cut and sew a pair of homespun pants for Everard, for
which she charged him only 50¢, and she did his laundry for
$1.50 a month, but the food she served him consisted of two
items, which he was not able to distinguish, and their conversation
was severely limited, not because she was shy but because she
knew of nothing to talk about. "That's cornbread," she explained,
"and that's hawg meat," she added, and had nothing whatever
else to say.

"I see you've met Agness," Bill Hogan said to him, when
first they met, and merely pointed to the pants Everard was
wearing. Perhaps Hogan recognized the fabric, or the style, or
the cut. The two men—Everard was six years older—hit it off
splendidly from the beginning, although Hogan was clearly going

to be competition for whatever mercantile operations Dickinson had in mind. Hogan boarded with the Morelands and, like them and so many other new Arkansawyers, had come from Tennessee. He bought supplies from Major Wolf and resold them to settlers in remote parts of the White River country. Occasionally he made purchasing trips to Memphis, and offered to take Everard along on his next one.

Business at Buffalo City was slow—one customer a week was considered heavy trade—and Hogan spent most of his time hunting and fishing, two activities he began to share with Everard. They hiked for miles together over "the foot of the spurs of the Ozark mountains," as Everard called them in his letters home.

> I believe I had rather live out in these mountains and enjoy the free mountain air and be an independent man—with a buckskin hunting shirt on and leather breeches—than wear a ruffle shirt and silk stockings and be a hireling and a slave, as all poor people are in those old thick settled countries.

He explained that gold and silver were the only "circulation" and that money was scarce; a man couldn't do a large business for cash and it wouldn't do to give credit. "I never intend to sell goods on a credit any more." He traded directly for peltry, bear skins, otter skins, "and etc., and took in about 40 fur skins yesterday." The reader of his letters to his parents surmises that he had gotten himself into real trouble in his job back home in Hartford by giving credit, and more recently gotten himself into trouble in Memphis by overextending his own credit with a "Mr. Candee," who had supplied him for the wilderness. William Moreland offered to help him out of debt to Mr. Candee in return for a vague pledge that Everard might settle permanently in Buffalo City and perhaps take Agness off the old man's hands.

Credit is both the bane and the boon of aspiring cities, and citizens. Forty years before, Goethe had observed, "Let us live in as small a circle as we will, we are either debtors or creditors before we have had time to look around." Buffalo City was a very small circle, and Everard had scarcely had time to look around before he was in debt to both Moreland and Hogan. Without mentioning Agness, he told his parents of the little problems he faced: winter was coming on, and his log store had no chimney; to have one built would cost him $25, which he did not have; he needed a well dug, which would cost him another $25; he could draw water from the river, but the banks were too steep and slippery, especially after a rain. For all his frontiersman spirit, Everard was apparently too much a weak man-about-town to build his own chimney, dig his own well, or clamber up and down the bank for water. Is not a "city," after all, a place where one can pay to have others do these things?

He was full of the future. In one letter he suggested his parents might want to come and join him (as Peter Mankins had done). His brother William had recently died at home; the other brother, Henry, had gone to far-off Wisconsin (perhaps to found the town called Buffalo City there); Everard was guilt-stricken at the thought of his now childless parents at home. "If you choose to come here and live with me, I will try and make a living for us all," he wrote to them, although "this is entirely too new and wild a country to suit you." Mr. Moreland invited him to try his hand at farming during the September harvest: "I have been out binding oats and gathering corn once or twice. I begin to think I should like farming very well. . . . You can buy a good cow for six or seven dollars and hogs are a dollar a head."

But he had to make the ultimate choice between being a countryman and a townsman. Land was his for the asking; he explained to his parents the phenomenon of "pre-emption," whereby he could pick out a parcel of land, build a cabin on it, raise corn, and pay no taxes for the rest of his life—but he couldn't build his own chimney, let alone a cabin. Daily he felt that he had stepped too far into the back country without any training for it. A century and a quarter later he would be followed by hordes of "back-to-the-land," counterculture young people, who would meet similar obstacles and face similar difficult choices . . . and give up.

Everard Dickinson gave up, or retreated a bit, back down the river to Major Wolf's settlement at Norfork, the "more of a publick place" where he would not have to worry about chimneys and wells and Agness. There were more girls in Norfork; he wrote his parents that he kept on the lookout for a chance "to hug and kiss the gals a little" and expected to marry soon. But his dream of a mate seems to have been as airy as the dream of gold that in the year of 1849 began to infect all the settlers and draw half of them to California.

His very last letter to his parents, in June 1850, ends with a postscript: "I may go to California (but do not say I even think of it)." On this page of the letter, ten years later, his mother wrote in her own hand, "read over by his Mother alone in her house." What happened to him? Quite possibly he went on to California, or tried to, and joined the hundreds who perished there or on the way.

"But do not say I even think of it." That ambivalence, that conflict between his will to change his luck and his fear of the unknown, lost him to this story even as it made him this story's classic example of faded ambition, of the futility of aspiration or mere anticipation, of the vanity of dreams. Everard personifies Buffalo City itself: divided, irresolute, and temporary.

The town went on without him, though. Maybe William Hogan married Agness, for want of anyone better, but there is no further record of him except the lone tombstone marking his death a few years later, at the age of thirty-five. If he sired a child who lived to become Kim's ancestor, there is no proof at all.

The Ozark mountaineer, fiercely independent and almost reclusive by nature, traditionally avoided the city, even the would-be city, as a sink of corruption and iniquity, and he looked upon citydwellers as contemptible wastrels of a different race. Everard Dickinson could not have defined it for his parents, but his expedition into Arkansas was doomed in advance by the rural population's distaste for the epithet "city." Never mind that Buffalo City would not amount even to a hamlet for some years to come;

its name repelled countless backwoodsmen who wanted nothing to do with any urban manifestation.

Everard had gone on to try his fortune elsewhere when the first steamboat arrived at Buffalo City, in the 1850s. The steamboat is a kind of floating city, and some of them were even christened as such: *Queen City, Delta City, Mound City, Empire City.* These very names frightened off the hill folk who had not already been frightened by the roar of the engines, the whistles, the sight of black people on deck. Even today, the popular imagination refuses to associate the steamboat with the backwoods mountains and sees it instead chugging down the broad, level expanses of the Mississippi. Flat delta country is the abode of the big boat, just as the flat plain is the abode of the buffalo, and flat land is the "natural" habitat of the black man.

Indeed, Buffalo City was as far as the steamboat could ever penetrate upstream into the hills. The shoals at Buffalo City were too shallow. Some accounts of the fragile history of the place indicate that Buffalo City came into existence because it was there that the steamboats had to dock before or after turning around. In fact, the keelboat and the barge had antedated the steamboat by years, and there was a landing waiting for the first steamboat when it came.

The steamboat was responsible for splitting Buffalo City, amoeba-like, into two cells. The only advantage that the *other* Buffalo City, the second one, had over the older, western location is that it was just a bit closer downstream to the steamboat, which did not have to approach the shoals to turn around there, on the east side of the river. In the bustling days of the late 1850s, just before the Civil War broke out, this division of the city into two halves created in equal parts a spirit of competition and a sense of confusion. On the western bank, at the older location, Captain John Quisenbury began to develop the Port of Buffalo City, surveying the town into lots, marketing choice riverfront lots ($150 each), and building a hotel and tavern called Shoal House, which would be a stagecoach stop to take the steamboat passengers and freight into the interior of the remote Ozarks.

At almost the same time, across the river, another immigrant from Tennessee, young Jonathan Cunningham, bought and cleared five hundred acres of land and established a rival steamboat landing, as well as the indispensable gristmill, which the west bank did not have. It would be too pat to say that if Everard Dickinson personifies one Buffalo City, in its older days, then Jonathan Cunningham personifies the other, newer one; but the separate identities of the two Buffalo Cities do reflect the differences between the two men. Cunningham, who was only twenty-two when he left Tennessee, refusing his mother's offer of sixteen slaves to accompany him because he had come to Arkansas to escape the institution of slavery, was a strong person, in both body and spirit, and he endured. Sickly as a child, he was nursed into strength by slaves, who would carry him out into the shade of a tree to cool his fevers until after dark, when he would lie studying the stars, learning their names and movements in order to prepare for his dream of becoming a steamboat pilot and navigating by the direction of the stars. It is a romantic image. Though Jonathan never became a steamboat pilot, he did become a harbormaster at his landing in the new Buffalo City, and remained so opposed to slavery that he would not permit the steamboats carrying slaves to land at his side of the river.

Thus the split between the cities reflected in microcosm the split between the sides in the Civil War, and Jonathan Cunningham's own part in that war symbolizes the North's opposition to the South. East Buffalo City is not only east but also north of West Buffalo City. Back home in Tennessee, two of Cunningham's brothers joined the Confederate Army. He, like the majority of Ozarkers, walked to Springfield, Missouri, and joined the Union Army.

Though one major skirmish of the Civil War occurred in Buffalo City (West), there is no evidence that the participants were from opposite sides of the river in the same town; that would carry the microcosm idea too far. Just as many of the able-bodied men in Baxter County on the eastern side of the river fought for the South, and just as many of those on the western side fought for the North, and they were fighting not because any of them supported or opposed slavery but because of clan loyalties and misplaced chauvinism and simply an urge to fight.

When the fighting was all over, Jonathan Cunningham returned to Buffalo City to discover that his home and businesses had been destroyed and that the worst part of the war was just beginning: the looting and pillaging by bushwhackers, jayhawkers, and other free-lance guerrillas. For the Ozarks at large, this was the ugliest aspect of the entire conflict. As if the war itself had not satisfied the urge of men to kill and torture, the former soldiers—called "bushwhackers" if they had worn gray and "jayhawkers" if they had worn blue, but otherwise not distinguishable one from another—turned their aggressions away from the ordered battlefield and focused them on the innocent, neutral, and helpless citizens. The old, the sick, the female, and the young were the victims of this strange episode of sadism. The horror stories Jonathan Cunningham heard from his wife when he returned home were worse than anything he had seen in the war.

After restoring his farm to life, rebuilding his landing and its warehouse, and putting the gristmill back into operation, he established a whiskey distillery, as if to satisfy a most urgent need for elixir against the memories of the war. To make his product available to his cross-river neighbors in Old Buffalo City, he established a ferryboat, which continued to operate until modern times. But even with this link between the two sides of the community (there was never a literal bridge, not even a pontoon), the rivalry and enmity between them only continued.

All over America, "sister" cities grew up despising one another. The residents of Kansas City, Missouri, have no use for their neighbors in Kansas City, Kansas; in St. Louis they make terrible jokes about the people in East St. Louis, Illinois. Minneapolis and St. Paul, together at the head of Mississippi navigation, are not only hostile but of different religions, the one Protestant, the other Catholic. San Francisco and Oakland hate each other. When the cities are separated by a national boundary, the problem is worse: El Paso, Texas, and Juarez, Mexico, have a real problem in their interpersonal relationships, while Nogales, Mexico, and Nogales, Arizona, are scarcely on speaking terms, in Spanish or English. Children in Sault Ste. Marie, Michigan,

are told that if they are bad they will go not to hell but to Sault
Ste. Marie, Ontario.

Even today, as Kim discovers in trying to give equal time to both
sides of the river, the two Buffalo Cities are worlds apart. The
last ferry ran in 1949. Baxter Hurst, who remembers it well, tells
Kim that his father owned the ferry all the years that Baxter was
growing up. In those days, the grocery store and post office were
on "the other side" of the river. "We'd go over there almost every
day," Baxter says. "This is kindly funny, but this old man, Sam
Beavers was his name, we called him 'Uncle Sam,' he had a
blacksmith shop over there where he lived, and he run the ferry
for my dad. Now, my dad, who owned the ferry, had it in the
deal that his family would get free ferriage. Us kids would traipse
over there ever day, or some of us would go over there almost
ever day, because we'd need some groceries and we got our mail
over there, and, you know, that was a good reason to go, just to
get the mail. And I guess we caused Sam Beavers a whole lot of
trouble: he'd have to put us all across the river, free ferriage. He
was a good farmer as well as a good blacksmith, and he might
be out there hoeing in his corn patch or workin in his shop when
somebody wanted to go across, but he'd have to stop and set us
across the river." Baxter Hurst laughs. "People needed the ferry
would have to holler pretty hard to get his attention."

"When the ferry ceased running, in 1949," Kim asks, "did
you feel cut off? Did you feel the world got a little smaller?"

"Why, no," Baxter says. "By then, we were gettin our mail
on the route on this side, and we had transportation to get to
Flippin, so we just went to Flippin for our groceries."

"When was the last time you went over to *that* Buffalo City?"

Baxter thinks, but shakes his head and says, "I caint recall."

Kim turns to Corky Craig and asks her the same question.
But Corky says, "I don't remember when I was *ever* in that part
of the country."

* * *

So Kim, first giving Corky a ride back to Yellville, goes alone to "New" Buffalo City. It is not easy. Only a few hundred yards as the crow flies (or the trout swims) from Old Buffalo City, it is miles and miles by car, back up the road to Flippin to U.S. Highway 62 and eastward to Cotter, over the high bridge there on the White River. Cotter calls itself the "Trout Capital of the World" and is still a station on the Missouri Pacific Railroad, which runs through but doesn't stop at Buffalo City. Night is coming on as Kim approaches Mountain Home, the seat of Baxter County, and she does not want to hunt for the "other" Buffalo City in the dark. There is a Holiday Inn on the highway in Mountain Home, a town that is booming with an influx of retirees from Chicago, St. Louis, and other big cities of the Midwest, people looking for the good, simple, cheap, clean, healthy life of the Ozarks. Kim decides to check in at the Holiday Inn. All of the other license plates are from out of state.

Bright and early in the morning, she resumes her quest for Buffalo City, off the highway and onto the secondary roads and then the tertiary roads of Baxter County. The last few miles are on a dirt-and-gravel road, henna-colored. As she nears the end of it and her destination, Kim can see the river and, in the distance, on the other side, Baxter Hurst's wide pasture.

At the road's end, at the water's edge, with Stair Bluff rising steeply behind them and vapors rising from the river, sport fishermen are putting out their small motorcraft to begin a morning's try for rainbow trout. There is a sign, "White Buffalo Resort," with a logo of an albino bison. A cluster of small buildings, cabins or camps, stands where Jonathan Cunningham's homestead had been. Kim observes, wryly, that whereas Sulphur City, Cherokee City, and Marble City had all aspired to become resorts but failed, Buffalo City never intended to be a resort but was reduced to one in the end.

At the office of the White Buffalo Resort, Kim talks to the young man and woman who manage it, Darrell Rose and Elaine Watkins; they have been on the job only a few months, since the resort opened to the public after several years as a private camp. The absentee owners, two sets of them, live in Texas. The resort is so called not because of any albino buffalo who might have anything to do with it but because of the conjunction here of the two rivers, the White and the Buffalo.

Kim asks, "Do you know anything about the history of Buffalo City?"

"As far as I know anything about it," Darrell says, "all I know is what I've been told. Because all this was before my time."

"What *have* you been told?" Kim asks.

"Well, that it used to be a booming town. It used to be on both sides of the river, used to be a ferry. Used to be a *rough* town. Killings and fights and gambling. Things like that."

Kim has not heard of any violence here. She asks, "Do the people who come here to fish ask any questions about why it's called City?"

Elaine says, "They want to know *where* Buffalo City is. I tell 'em they just missed it!"

"I must have missed it, too," Kim observes. "Where is it?"

They point out to her that back up the road she came in on, just beyond the railroad track, are a couple of commercial buildings, vacant, abandoned. "That's *it*, far as I know," Elaine says. She tells of a lady from Batesville who comes regularly to stay at the White Buffalo Resort, and who claims to be a native of Buffalo City and sometimes visits those vacant buildings. "She just sits out there and daydreams all the time."

Kim drives Zephyra back to the railroad track and stops to look at the vacant buildings on a rise of ground east of the track. In the early-morning sunlight, it is a scene that Edward Hopper would have loved to paint. He cherished another White River, far away in Vermont. He adored abandoned houses beside railroad tracks. Above all, he celebrated such sunlight, a lonely kind of light, if light itself can be lonely.

This railroad, which contributed so much to the growth of the newer Buffalo City, was built as part of the St. Louis, Iron Mountain, and Southern, a name revered by train buffs. Hopper would have loved that name, Iron Mountain. The track is still maintained by the White River Division of the Missouri Pacific, and freight trains still carry coal each day. Baxter Hurst told Kim of still hearing the train's distant whistle, long and lonesome, several times a day. It was built as a passenger line, completed in 1906, one of the most spectacular mountain railroads in the nation. Six years of blasting away the sides of bluffs and carving tunnels through five mountains were required to lay the roadbed. The original plan was to run the road to and through Old Buffalo City, which helped that side of the river continue its end-of-the-century boom, but after the crews had labored to hack the path along the west side and below the treacherous Stair Bluff and into Old Buffalo City, orders came down from St. Louis that the whole roadbed, twelve miles of it from Norfork, would have to be repositioned on the east and north side of the river, just in order to raise the grade some four or five feet. Relocating the railroad spelled the death of Old Buffalo City and gave brief rise to the growth of New Buffalo City.

But a new natural resource gave a temporary revival to Old Buffalo City and changed the name of New Buffalo City to Oredale, because it became a principal shipping point for zinc ore, mined in all the surrounding hills. Zinc, which can galvanize iron and keep it from rusting, as well as turn copper into brass, came into great demand during the years of World War I, and towns all over the Ozarks of Missouri, Arkansas, and Oklahoma boomed because of the zinc mines. The name Oredale lasted only as long as the boom and was favored only by the mine owners; the zinc miners and the railroad men, enlivening the place with their carousing, continued to call it Buffalo City.

Kim gazes at the two vacant buildings set back on their knoll above the railroad track, then parks her car beside them for a closer look. The white wooden building on her left was the Beavers Hotel. Over its long-opened doorway are the letters painted in red, "OPEN." Kim is reminded of the upside-down sign in the store at Cherokee City, "WE ARE OPENED." The back-roads motorist is warned to avoid any motel with "Vacancy" painted on the side of the building: be suspicious of permanent paint. The Beavers Hotel (two guest rooms downstairs, four up) might have accommodated an occasional tourist, but mostly it was where the railroad crews stayed, or the transient schoolteacher, or a lost peddler. It contained a barbershop, too. It appears to have been remodeled in comparatively recent times—a "Chicago window" upstairs, wide clapboards all over—but it has not been occupied in recent memory except by mice, owls, and cockroaches. It sits pale cheek by ruddy jowl next to the stonemasonry edifice that was Buffalo City's last post office, last general store, and last hope for rebirth of the dead village (it carries a "FOR SALE" notice; a Batesville realtor waits for any buyer. And waits).

This stone store was, through most of the thirties and forties—the last days of the real Ozarks in modern times, before the coming of electricity and the dominance of the motorcar—the bustling enterprise of a man from New York City named Clarence Vance. If not a book, at least a lengthy article could be made out of his life. The stone building had been erected early in the century by B. R. "Bud" Hudson, a merchant in Old Buffalo City who left that town at about the same time the railroad decided not to go there. When Bud Hudson grew old and decided to put his General Mercantile up for sale, not simply with a "FOR SALE" sign but with ads in newspapers that might reach a distant readership, he was approached by Clarence Vance and his wife (whose name, as best anyone can remember, was Lola), who paid cash for the building and moved in. Vance was a college-educated cosmopolitan, and his New York City manners and accent made people suspicious of him. There were other stores in town then, and they took most of the business away from him. But he devoted himself to learning the ways of the mountain people and winning their acceptance. Baxter Hurst told Kim, "He would do things just to get the feel of it and know what it was like. He'd come over here and pick cotton all day on this farm, just to know what it was like. He was that kind of fellow."

The best way to ingratiate oneself with the hill folk is to acquire their religion; Clarence Vance offered to teach Sunday school in Buffalo City. His pupils began to patronize his store, and in time he had a thriving business. In his spare moments he was writing a book, according to Baxter Hurst, who cannot, however, remember if the book was ever published or what its subject was. Also in his spare time, Vance was patiently marking out the form of a large white cross on the ground atop Stair Bluff, using white stones and painting other boulders white in order to lay out a great Christian symbol that could be seen for miles (and is still visible from certain spots, although Kim does not find one). If Sulphur City's heraldic pennant was the imagined yellow banner, then Buffalo City's must be this white cross, like a gravestone a thousand feet above the town.

Vance became postmaster of Buffalo City and founded the Buffalo City Historical and Improvement Society, persuading some of his neighbors to join. Like Walter Lackey's Newton County Historical Society, it had a short life, for lack of interest. During this time it contributed a few pages to Frances Shiras's *History of Baxter County*, but very little, unfortunately, on the history of Clarence Vance himself, who remains largely a figure of mystery. "They left here and went to California," Baxter Hurst told Kim. "We lost touch with them after that."

The little white hotel and the little stone store beside the railroad track are not the only remains of Buffalo City. There is a little brown schoolhouse someone has converted into a fishing camp, a few older houses used only as summer homes, and one used as a year-round home by a couple of old-timers who, along with Baxter and Geneva Hurst across the river, make up the only permanent population of the Buffalo Cities. Harvey and Laura Stevens, ages eighty-two and eighty-one, have lived in Buffalo City since 1924, when Harvey was hired as a crewman on the railroad.

Harvey and Laura remind Kim a good deal of Buster and Margaret Price of Sulphur City. They have been married for sixty-three years. Harvey, a stoutish man, wears fresh bib overalls and is cleanshaven (as if he were expecting company, Kim thinks; so many of these people seem to have been waiting for her). The interior of their house is compote: there is a reproduction of the popular painting *This Daily Bread*, an old man alone saying grace over his humble lunch. A large china hutch contains Depression glass and a representation of the Last Supper that gives the illusion of three dimensions. From the ceiling hangs a quilting frame for Laura, a quiltmaker, who proudly shows Kim some of her work, including one with all of the states' flowers and another with all of the states' birds (Arkansas's are the apple blossom and the mockingbird). Laura makes these quilts not to sell but as gifts for her children and grandchildren.

When Kim asks who they consider the most colorful character during the years they've lived in Buffalo City, they both cite Clarence Vance. "Old man Vance," says Harvey, "he drawed more people here than anybody I know about, and he put that big cross up there, and he give the Fourth of July."

Laura explains, "They was people come here from everwhere on the Fourth of July to his picnic. They had dinner on the grounds, and stands that sold stuff, and they come from all states here. He advertised it, you know." Laura's voice is sweet, almost girlish, calm and clear.

Vance's annual celebration of the Fourth attracted regular notice in *The Mountain Echo*, which announced that the Missouri Pacific Railway had ordered all of its fast express trains to stop in Buffalo City on July 4 so that passengers could alight to participate in the dances, watch fireworks "shot off from atop the majestic and awe-inspiring White River Palisades that overlook the village," and enter the great variety of contests and games, such as hog calling, a turtle race, climbing a greasy pole, and catching a greasy pig. Prizes included a can of gasoline for the motorists who brought the most people, an inner tube for the motorist who had come the greatest distance, a sack of flour for the largest family, a pair of Big-Fit overalls for the best old fiddler, and a permanent wave for the most beautiful young lady.

Clarence Vance was the planner behind all such details. "Why did he leave?" Kim asks the Stevenses.

Harvey and Laura exchange glances and Laura says, "Well." After a while, Harvey clears his throat and says, "Well, they were just givin him a bad time." Who? "People. They never done nothin mean to him, but they just give him trouble, and he left, went back to New York, where he came from."

"Baxter Hurst says he went to California," Kim tells him.

"Does he? Well, maybe he did. I thought it was New York."

"He done a lot of good for the people here," Laura says. "He visited the sick and everything. He was somebody we could be proud of, not like that Arnold Comer."

"Who was Arnold Comer?" Kim asks.

Again the Stevenses exchange glances, as if trying to determine how far they can go in telling the secrets of the town's past. Again it is Harvey who tells it. "He was just a boy. Fourteen years old. This was back in the twenties, I reckon. He killed some folks. Several folks."

The story of Arnold Comer is sketchy, not well documented, and subject to imperfect memories. His father, Will Comer, was a dirt-poor man with a large family. They were not one of the old, established Buffalo City families. Will Comer, not respected in the community, was sometimes disparaged for his lack of cheerfulness and inability to take a joke, tell one, or listen appreciatively. About once a year his wife left him and their children and went back to her mother's home, across the river (in the 1920s the ferry ran several times a day, or on demand). Once, as a child, Arnold begged to go with her and was taken, but stayed one night and came back on the ferry by himself. His father beat him. Will Comer "took a stick" regularly to all eight of his children, and sometimes to his wife, but Arnold seemed to be his favorite target. The father claimed the boy had no sense, no manners, no respect for his elders, no ambition, no abilities, no goodness, and not even the redeeming boyish cuteness that some kids possess.

There was speculation in the community as to whether Will Comer's harsh treatment of Arnold caused the boy to become mentally unbalanced or whether Will mistreated the boy *because* his mentality caused him to do stupid and contemptible things. Arnold took to sitting on a corner of the porch for hours on end, doing nothing, lest anything he did be censurable. But if he was spotted thus by his father, he would be given a task to do, usually some feat of strength or dexterity that was beyond his resources, and, on failing it, would be thrashed severely for his mistakes.

"Finally," says Harvey, "he started out runnin away from home and go back over yonder in those hills, you know, to git as far away as he could." Arnold would sometimes disappear for days on end but would eventually come home, because Buffalo City gave him at least the security of the familiar, which the woods, or wherever he went, did not. His father told him that starving himself out in the woods was the dumbest thing that anybody had ever heard tell of, and whipped him especially hard for that.

One day in 1926, when Arnold had just turned fourteen, his tolerance (if that is the word) took leave of him, and he went berserk. Feeling himself innocent of all that he had been accused of all his life, he decided to kill the most innocent person he could find. He stole his father's pistol and ran down the road until he came to a house where an old woman was sitting in her rocker on the porch, holding a baby, her granddaughter. He shot the woman. The baby fell on the floor and began crying. Arnold did not want to shoot the baby, too, because a baby to him was beyond innocence: to be innocent, you have to be old enough to be guilty. But the baby kept crying. Arnold snatched it up and took it with him, attempting to hush it, but it would not hush. He took a rock and beat its cries still.

When Arnold saw himself covered with blood, he decided he needed some other clothes, and some transportation to get him out of Buffalo City, and determined to kill the first horseman he came across. Soon thereafter he shot a fur trapper, Charles Moore, off his mule, but the mule escaped, though wounded. Dressed as a fur trapper, Arnold fled to the woods. His father told the sheriff that they had better find him before he himself could get ahold of him, because if he got ahold of him first, there would be nothing left of him to bring to justice.

The sheriff and a considerable posse found Arnold first, but not before spending days and nights in the search. Will Comer was kept away from the captive, who was tried, found guilty, but, because of his youth, sentenced to twenty-one years in the Boys' Industrial School, a reformatory. There he remained only a year before being transferred to the State Hospital for the Insane. The last anyone heard of him—some years later, in 1933—was a small item in *The Mountain Echo* to the effect that he had killed his asylum roommate with a window-sash weight.

Few other people remember Arnold Comer. Kim's last interview for Buffalo City is not in the town itself but in neighboring Gassville, back on the highway. It's an ugly name for a town to have, and the inspiration for jokes having to do with gasoline and stomach gas and empty talk, flatulent talk. In a very modest house too poor even for compote, right beside the busy highway and the roar of trucks, Kim finds Stella Beavers, age eighty-nine, being examined by a nurse from the Health Department.

Stella Barton Caststeel Beavers grew up in Buffalo City and is related by blood or her marriages to nearly everyone on both sides of the river. The Caststeels were descended from Doctor William Caststeel, the head of one of Buffalo City's first families, and the father of both Jonathan Cunningham's first wife, Minerva, and his second wife, Tabitha. The Beaverses, of her last husband's family, came from Virginia by way of Illinois and Missouri, and totally dominated the last years of New Buffalo City, owning the hotel, a general store, and the blacksmith shop, and running the ferry for Baxter Hurst's father. Stella married John Caststeel when she was thirteen, too young for her to remember how many years she remained married to him; he drank and lost his mind and ran away. She worked hard most of her life, beginning as a cook for the railroad work gangs, and later as the stationmaster downstream at Cartney, where she tended the switch lights, sold tickets, met the passenger trains, carried mail from the post office to the train, and logged the freight shipments for a salary of $18 a month. Stella is tired, and her memory, she warns, is not reliable.

But she remembers Arnold Comer and Clarence Vance; the Vances, she says, were the nicest people she ever knew, and the

Comers were the worst. Arnold she recalls as "just a big ole stripe of a boy," whose "mind wasn't good enough." As for the Vances, they left not because of any trouble but because "things just got dead, I guess."

"What's your best memory of the days you lived in Buffalo City?" Kim asks her.

"Well, when my husband was section foreman on the railroad and we lived in a section house right at the end of the bluff there, with no back yard except the river and just enough room to walk between the house and the bluff, I used to keep boarders, used to cook for all the men who worked on the railroad, cooked dinner for 'em every day on an old woodstove, maybe twenty-five of 'em I cooked for."

"You must have been a good cook."

"I don't mean to boast, but I did used to be a good cook. I've cooked for the public in cafés and hotels."

"How much did you charge your boarders?"

"Five dollars a week, it was." Stella chuckles. "You'd pay that much for one meal nowadays."

"And that was your happiest memory, cooking for all those men?"

Stella frowns. "I've lived an awful life." She seems to be searching her buried store of imperfect memories for something better than her hours at the cookstove. Or something worse. Kim does not have to ask her if, like Kate Scraper, she has never had a worry in her life, because her wrinkled face, unlike Kate Scraper's, has worry written all over it. "I had some babies, three of them, but they . . ." Her voice trails off. Moments pass. Stella studies her gnarled hands. Kim studies Stella and wonders what she looked like in the days when she was, as Kim has read and been told, "the prettiest stationmaster on the White River line," and undoubtedly the object of kidding and courting from all the railroad men. Kim, who has always regretted marrying at sixteen, cannot conceive of what marrying at thirteen would have been like, so she asks.

"Well, I don't know. It was rough. I've had a rough life. I

didn't have any home, just my father. My mother died when I was six, and my two sisters got married and left home."

"When you were thirteen, were you in love?"

" 'Love'? Girls that age don't understand love; they don't have any idee what it's all about. I just wanted a home, was all. That was the main thing."

Stella's voice becomes increasingly weary, and Kim decides to ask one or two more questions and go. "Did you like living in Buffalo City?"

"Oh . . ." Stella says in preface, and ponders the question for a while. Her inward gaze seems to watch again the passing railroad trains and even the last steamboats (she was eleven when the last steamboat came up the river). She stands again in the shade of Stair Bluff and Turkey Mountain and looks around her. And tells Kim, "I didn't ever know nothin better."

"Do you ever go back?" Kim asks.

"What's there?" Stella asks. "No, all it lacks is throwin the dirt over it."

Kim does not go back to Buffalo City for a final look around, either. It is the sort of place that looks better in memory.

Cave City, Arkansas

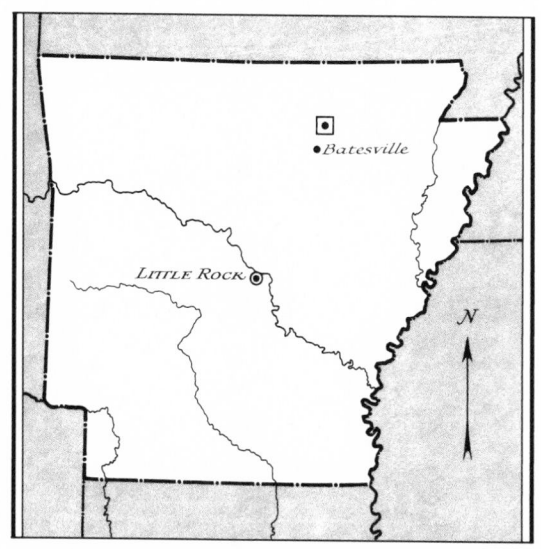

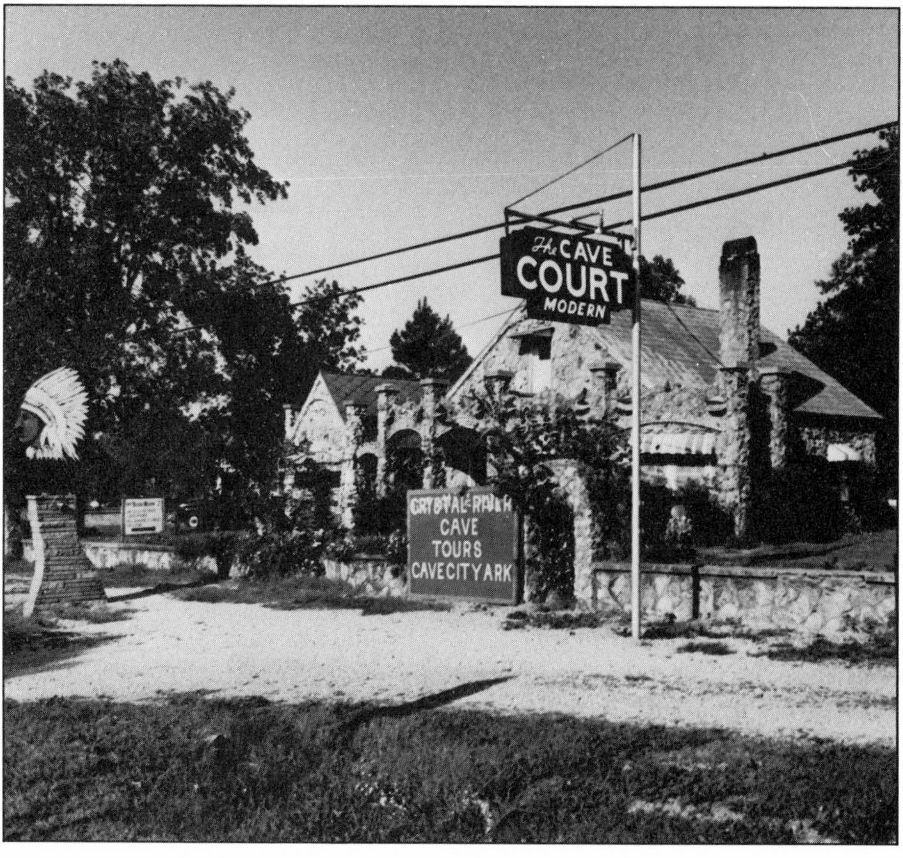

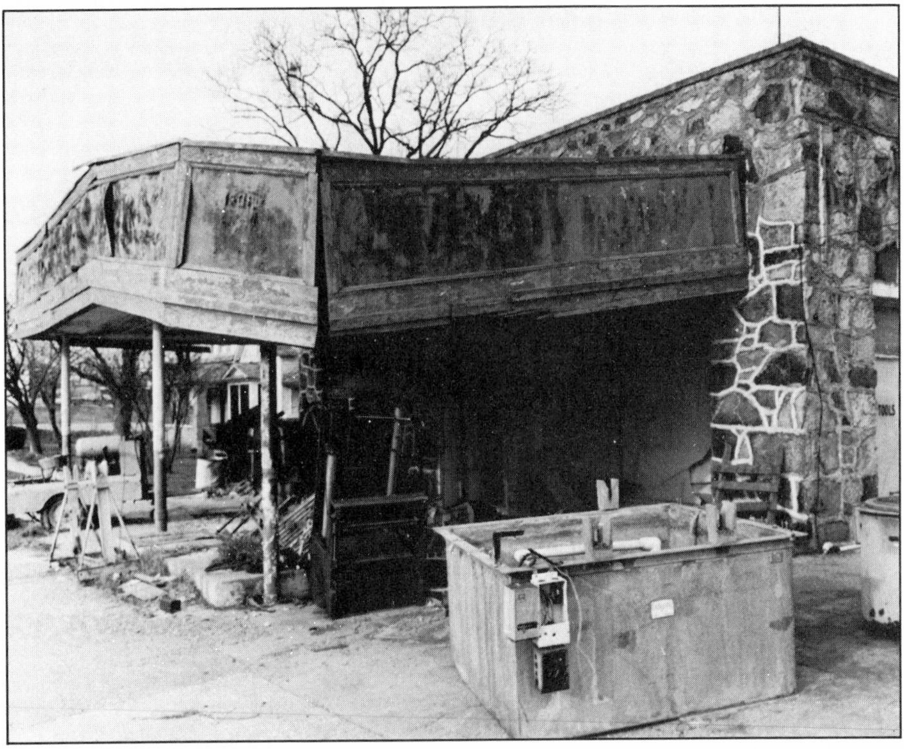
TOOLS

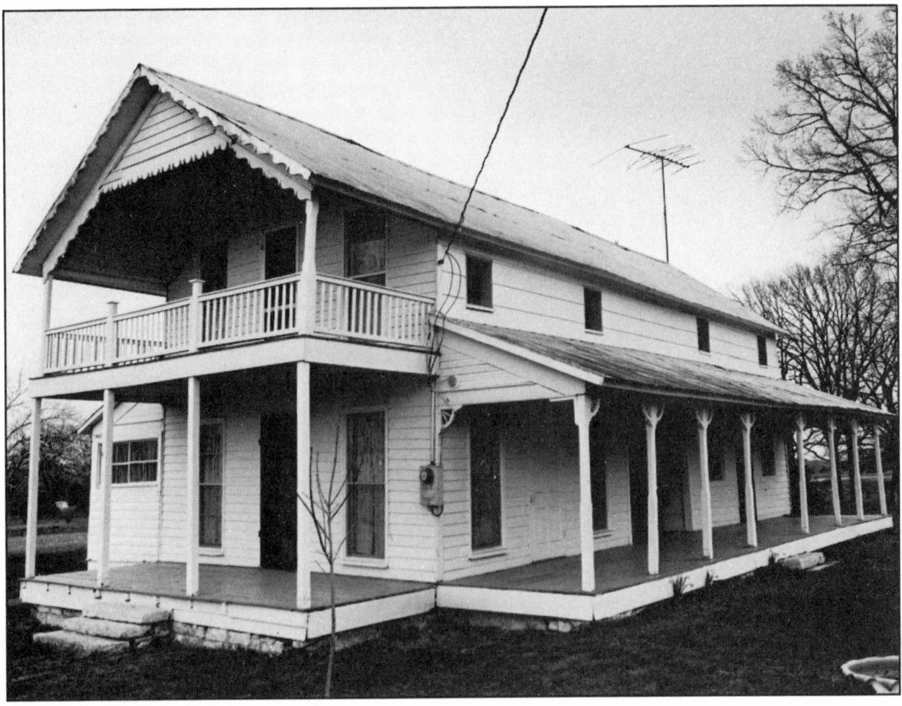

Nothing evil had been in the cave, but she had
not enjoyed herself; no, she had not enjoyed herself, and
she decided not to visit a second one.
—*E. M. Forster,* A Passage to India, *1924*

THIS IS THE FIRST TOWN Kim visits that is still a town. Among these places that have hoped for cityhood, it alone has not given up, although it has a long way to go, and many scars of the effort: the abandoned stores and houses, the awkward attempts at face-lifting, the plastic surgery that is too plastic. But there are a comparative lot of people here, who stubbornly refuse to leave, or who have left and come back, because it is home.

Cave City is large enough to have a Chamber of Commerce, which prints a little brochure with the motto "Small Town Atmosphere with Big City Pride," without knowing that such pride is not found in big cities, that pride is a mark of hopeless smallness, fierce and doomed nothingness, blind loyalty. The original name of this place was in fact Loyal, because, it is said, the settlement was founded by a man who remained loyal to the Union when all the neighborhood hamlets seceded. The other towns in Sharp County have pretty names or quaint names like Strawberry and Evening Shade. Ash Flat and Hardy. Poughkeepsie and Ozark Acres. Ben-Gay, Grange, Calamine, and, right in the center of the county, Center.

Unlike our other lost cities, where a river or a creek spills nourishingly alongside, Cave City has an invisible stream; it is entirely subterranean and runs through the strange cave that gives the town its name, a cavern as much a mystery to contemporary scientists and explorers as it was to the Osage who once inhabited or at least enshrined it. No one has ever been able to discover where the Crystal River originates, or where it goes. It has no known association with the far-distant Mississippi, and yet its water rises and falls with that big river's rise and fall. Just as the original settlers remained loyal while their neighbors' allegiances were muddied, the Crystal River remains crystal-clear and blue and calm when all the local streams are flooded and brownly roiling.

The fish who inhabit the cave are not merely blind: they have no eyes. Centuries of evolutionary darkness have removed any vestige of eyeballs from them, but given their other senses such sharpness that they are nearly impossible to catch. There is no subtle symbol here for the human inhabitants of Cave City, who are for the most part just as sighted as anybody, if somewhat myopic to the blight around them, and are very slowly tearing down the faded ruins along Main Street only to replace them with "contemporary" atrocities such as the shingle-hooded Bank of Cave City, built not as a bank but a car dealership.

Cave City is not on the way to anywhere. Highway 167, which is Main Street, is a United States highway, with a shield-enclosed number on maps, but is not a link, much less an artery; it begins at Bald Knob, Arkansas, and lazes northward to the pleasant town of Hardy, Arkansas, where it dies. Hardy, always a resort town with quaint native-stone buildings, has filled up with retirees from Chicago these days, as has the nearby boomtown of Cherokee Village (no relation whatever to Cherokee City), the first retirement community in the United States, a city that has made almost an industry out of providing homes and services for well-to-do old folks. Hardy, not named for the great English novelist but evocative of his villages, is best known for its Arkansaw Traveler Folk Theatre, stocked by musicians (including Orilla Pinkston, whom we will meet later) who commute from Cave City, a kind of enclave for old-timey Ozark folk music.

But Cave City is not in the Ozarks; that is one of its minor misfortunes. It modestly claims to be in the "foothills" of the Ozarks, but those feet are flat: the biggest hill, where the Cave City Cemetery rolls over the top, is scarcely two hundred feet high. The WPA Federal Writers' Project's *Arkansas: A Guide to the State*, published in 1941, quietly mentions: "State 11 continues south to CAVE CITY, 23.6 *m.* (659 alt., 427 pop.) a resort village whose field-stone buildings straggle along the road. The CAVE *(adm. 10¢)* consists of three chambers, the largest of which is about 80 feet wide and 10 feet high." One of those fieldstone buildings straggling along the road is shown in our photograph, still straggling: the last picture show, the sagging marquee of the Cave Theatre (Shorty Thompson, proprietor), its last film (starring Randolph Scott and Ida Lupino) but a matinee memory in the minds of children grown middle-aged (or was it something on the TV late the other night?), who also remember the rest room's being behind the screen instead of off the lobby, and recall the theatre's transformation into a Ford dealer's auto-repair shop before its gradual decline into a roadside eyesore.

Whatever people in Cave City do, most of them who work commute to the factories of Batesville, fifteen miles south, and thus Cave City is usually referred to as a bedroom satellite of Batesville. Batesville is one of the oldest towns in Arkansas, founded in 1818 and still preserving much of its nineteenth-century appearance. It is most noteworthy as the home of Colonel Charles Fenton Mercer Noland (1810–58), an early soldier, duelist, newspaper editor, and raconteur who wrote humorous sketches for the Eastern journals under the name Pete Whetstone and thus fostered the Easterner's conception of Arkansas as a hilarious backwater.

The backwater of Cave City is all underground, crystal-clear and populated by those eyeless fish; the same proportion of the citizenry has actually explored the cave, or simply visited it, as the proportion of New Yorkers who have visited the Statue of Liberty: less than a few. The cave has its obligatory legends, of Indian chiefs and suicidal maidens, of lost explorers and accidents, nothing terrible or especially forbidding, just enough to entice the tourist's curiosity if the simple fact of the hole's yawning openness, a gynecological wonder, does not: Kim will not go into that cave, not yet, and perhaps not ever. She will approach it in time, imagining in advance its damp, cold, dark confines, and she will hesitate to deliver herself into its maw for the sake of journalism or of art. Kim will discover that the dark, unbeckoning opening into the cave becomes a metaphor for a life's passage she is not ready to face: growing old.

In a letter to Professor Harrigan, Kim has written:

> It's a new experience for me, talking to so many elderly people. Some have been quite friendly and helpful, talkative and interested. Some have been less eager to converse. At any rate, it has been an experience that has led me to wonder what I'll be like as an elderly person, assuming I live long enough to earn that euphemistic epithet, "elderly." It's a scary thing, imagining the health problems of aging, although the ones I've spoken with who are especially well preserved don't really exhibit pronounced aging difficulties; they seem healthy and happy. Two *very* old women have told me that they never worry, and that they feel this is the reason for their longevity. I'm still young and healthy (although I worry entirely too much), but I wonder what I'm going to be like when I'm seventy-five or eighty or older. Will I be cheerful? Dependent on others? Depressed? Lonely? Active? Sociable? Reclusive? Poor? Likable? Bedridden? Diseased? And most important, mentally alert or mentally feeble?
>
> Never before have I questioned this, or been aware of the vast differences in the elderly and the effects of aging. I see wrinkles, arthritic hands, very slow movements, hear crackly voices, and wonder what is ahead for me. Who that I have met will I be like?

Kim will want to try to get a room for the night in one of the individual rock-rustic cabins of The Cave Court, a thirties motor court, father of the motel, built during a period of American history, early in the Depression, when Americans were seeking an escape from reality by way of the picturesque, romantic, rustic, roadside tourist camp with its grove of trees (why were the trees always painted white partway up their trunks?) as an oasis along the bland, relentless highway.

The architecture of The Cave Court is the product of the imagination and hands of one Charles Prince Matlock (1893–1974), a local farmer who taught himself stonemasonry and set himself up in business to contract the occasional dwelling or commercial structure, and who left his mark scattered hither and yon over the local landscape. It is presumptuous to compare Prince Matlock with Antonio Gaudi, the great visionary Barcelona architect, and yet the points of similarity are indubitable: Gaudi (1852–1926) was also of very humble origin and began designing with an eccentric but colorful medievalism that hinted at such prophetic shapes as the parabolic arch; there are also hints of the parabola in Prince Matlock's motel. Both men were "originals" with a highly developed sense of the intricacies of space, structure, color, and particularly texture, especially textures that verge on the absurd, such as Gaudi's "chocolate-fudge sundae" sheaths and Matlock's "spitball" coverings, which are actually assemblages of strange geologic material called "petrified foam." Matlock also embedded into his cement surfaces quartz crystals, geodes, Indian stones, fossils, broken glass and pottery, etc.

There are Prince Matlock buildings in Strawberry, Evening Shade, Ash Flat, Calamine—all of the local communities, including Batesville—but his main work is in Cave City, the motel as well as the older buildings of the "campus"—Home Economics and Gymnasium—of the Cave City Schools. The schools' mascot, naturally, is "The Cavemen," inspiring the artistic imagination of students doing posters and homeroom decorations, mostly in a "Flintstones" motif. Perhaps the prevalence of rock in Prince Matlock's work is a kind of aboveground advertisement for all of the underground caves. He himself was an avid spelunker and holds the record for having ventured as deeply as it is possible to go into *the* cave, entering the fifth or lowest of five chambers by boat launched into the Crystal River and floating southward in the dark until he was stopped by a ninety-foot vertical wall beyond which there is no visible passage.

Both Prince Matlock and Antonio Gaudi were essentially "biological" in their approach to architecture, but Gaudi, perhaps the supreme individualist in architecture, never repeated himself; Prince Matlock, on the other hand, except for his fanciful child's sand castle at The Cave Court, is just one more rock mason, and no student of architectural history will justify devoting a thesis to him.

The Cave Court, Kim discovers with surprisingly little disappointment, is filled with customers, an unusual circumstance; she is told that a family of far-flung Cave citizens having a reunion is responsible. "PLEASE DO NOT TAKE ROCKS OFF," a sign warns Kim as she leaves the grounds.

Across the highway from The Cave Court, in a house of Prince Matlock's more conventional stonemasonry, Kim finds Hubert Carpenter, age eighty-seven, a former postal worker and route carrier who had used up his savings to commission Prince Matlock to build The Cave Court; Carpenter operated the place himself until he was too old to sign in wayfarers in the middle of the night.

All his years as a postman, Hubert took his vacations in the same Western states where Nabokov collected butterflies, but instead of bringing home butterflies, Hubert brought home rocks, to be used in the construction of the motel. Friends as well as tourists brought configurations of seashells and coral from Florida and the Gulf Coast. Prince Matlock himself, a rockhound, contributed prized specimens from his collection. Prince and Hubert went to Eureka Springs to hunt rocks there and look at its distinctive stone architecture.

Hubert Carpenter tells Kim that he, not Matlock, designed The Cave Court. "I had it marked out on paper just exactly like I wanted, the driveways and cabins and everything. I marked it out. I could go off and be gone for a month, and Prince knew just exactly what to do and how I wanted it done."

Through the Depression years, Hubert and Prince supervised the construction of The Cave Court as a kind of public-works project. Out-of-work men would come to Hubert for loans and he would put them to work at $1.50 a day, hauling and lifting rock for the buildings. But none of the rock was broken. Hubert points out to Kim the difference between stonemasonry and rock masonry: the former always implies the working of the rock in some way, cutting it or shaping it; but at The Cave Court, "We didn't break 'em, we didn't carve 'em, we put 'em there just like God made 'em."

"All those little rough round rocks," Kim says, "look sort of like . . . like spitballs."

Hubert laughs. "Them are *geodes*. Found 'em about twelve, fifteen miles east of here, and brought in seventeen truckloads of 'em." These geodes are small hollow rocks with crystals lining their inside walls. A pity: the beauty is all in the interior, unseen.

Hubert and his wife, known to everyone as Miss Eunice (a long-time teacher of home economics, especially sewing, at Cave City High), ran the motel for thirty-eight years, kept chairs and a swing placed around the lawns where they could sit and visit with their guests, and never had any trouble other than the usual problem of petty thefts (Hubert ordered the imprinted ashtrays by the hundreds and hoped they would be stolen, as a form of free advertising). For years after Hubert sold out and retired across the street, people from all over the country would call the motel and ask, "Is this Hubert?" The motel has had three or four different owners since Hubert left. He doesn't keep track. He doesn't even have any idea what the rates are these days; he guesses about $6.00 or $7.00 (much too low), but in his day the rates were $1.50, $2.50, all the way up to $4.00. Kim asks him if anything unusual ever happened during all those years he owned the place. Didn't anyone ever die in the cabins? Only once, Hubert relates: a Mr. Logan with a heart condition, a frequent guest when he was auditing the county books, checked in one night, failed to appear the next morning, and was found dead in bed. Cave City, it must be remembered, is not on the road *to* anywhere: people do not pause at the motel so much as make it their destination.

When Hubert bought the cave and the land above it for his motel, the cave was not developed and opened to tourists. The town was already called Cave City, but was hardly more than a crossroads hamlet; Hubert had no idea it would become a town of the size it has. He had bought the land from Dr. Laman (more about the name Laman to come), who had done nothing to make the cave accessible to the public: "It wasn't worth a thing in the world to him." Hubert, with Prince's help, set about turning the cave into a tourist attraction, installed electric lights at a time when even houses didn't have them, and made the town into a destination.

Kim asks the gentle question that she puts to all of her old-timers: "Did you have any hopes or dreams that never came true?"

"No, no, never did," Hubert says without pause. "No, I'll tell ya. My wife and me, we both filled our duty, I think."

She likes the way he puts that: "*filled* our duty," as if each of us has a duty yawning like a big cave in the ground, to be filled up. Let every man fill his allotted cave.

Hubert Carpenter was one of eight sons in a family who kept trying for a girl on the way to the proverbial ten children and finally succeeded with a lone female whom they named Orilla, an Anglo-Saxon form of a bird name, Oriel, "the golden." Golden Orilla lives across the street from her big brother Hubert, just north of the cave, in the old Carpenter home, where she was born and grew up with Hubert and her other seven brothers. In the blossoming year of 1886, this house was built by Henry Horn, the second house in town; the first no longer stands. Horn altered the house to accommodate his growing family, and Joseph Carpenter, father of Hubert and Orilla, altered it more, until today it defies description (which is one reason there is a photograph of it). Does it "address" the street? Or does it address the cave and motel? If the former, then it speaks with a portico of balustraded balcony and gingerbread trim. If the latter, it barks with a dogtrot and a house-long porch. There is no chimney. The roofline is topped with the obligatory centipedal TV mast, but there is no smokestack of any sort, not even a flue. Kim asks Orilla why there is no chimney.

"There was a big chimney," Orilla says, "but we took it down and used it to underpin."

"Underpin?" Kim says, and Orilla tries to explain. Olaf Pinkston, age eighty-three, Orilla's husband, tries to help in the explanation. Despite his name, Olaf is not Scandinavian; his name
is just a form of the good old English "Oliver," meaning "peace."
He doesn't look his age; hale and hearty, he has just come in
from preparing the seedbed for his garden, a busy spot. Olaf
plays well on the guitar, the bass fiddle, the mandolin, and several
other instruments, especially the harmonica. Orilla is excellent
on the mandolin, the accordion, the guitar, and especially the
piano and organ. Together they know by ear hundreds of old
folk songs and ballads. Together they have taught thousands of
young people how to play and sing.

They helped to organize and serve as musical directors for
the Arkansaw Traveler Folk Theatre in the village of Hardy. The
theatre and its popular (with tourists) one-act pageant running
all summer long commemorate a famous folk song, "The Arkansaw Traveler," which itself is based upon an apocryphal but
characteristic Arkansas folk tale. (Misspelling the state as "Arkansaw" is a venerable sop to the outsider inclined to rhyme it
with Kansas.) The song and the tale manage to evoke the pioneer
spirit of Arkansawyers, the simultaneous gullibility and "exper-
tise" of outsiders, and to take into consideration a whole slew of
subsidiary themes: hospitality, or the lack thereof, squatterhood,
the ten-children family with which we are becoming so familiar,
and, in the interplay between the squatter and the traveler, the
whole matter of Arkansas's relations with the rest of the world.

The clever repartee delivered from the Squatter to the Traveler centers on the latter's famous jibe, "Why don't you patch
the leaks in your roof?," to which the Squatter replies, "It's been
raining all day." This elicits the Traveler's setup question, "Why
don't you do it in dry weather?," bringing the Squatter's punch
line: "It don't leak then." This interchange is much older than
Arkansas's squatters; scholarship has traced its origins at least to
1832 in this country, down east in York, Maine; and to 1842 in
Russia, the date of publication of Gogol's *Dead Souls*, in which
Gogol describes the decrepit huts in a Russian village: "It seemed
as though the owners themselves had removed the laths and

shingles, arguing, and no doubt quite correctly, that as huts cannot be roofed in the rain, while in fine weather the rain keeps
off of itself, there is no need to mess about indoors, while there
is plenty of room in the tavern and on the high-road."

Currier and Ives made and distributed a popular lithograph
of the Arkansas Traveler astride his horse, arriving at the Squatter's cabin. The print was based upon Arkansas artist Edward
Payson Washbourne's painting of the subject, done in 1858. The
Squatter's crude hut or cabin is typical of those of the time in all
particulars except one: it has no chimney. If this was an oversight
on the artist's part, Currier and Ives did not bother to correct it.

Kim has become a kind of latter-day Arkansas Traveler herself, sometimes seeking shelter for the night and being turned
away, as she was at The Cave Court, and asking questions about,
if not leaking roofs, missing chimneys. The "point" of the Arkansas Traveler legend is that the sophisticated newcomer is put
to a test by the raw, shrewd rustic, and, passing it by dint of his
musical skills, is accepted. On one level, it could be taken as the
conquering of the frontier by civilization; on another level, the
taming of savagery by art; on still another level, cultivated man's
triumph over his own base instincts. It is easy to imagine Everard
Dickinson arriving at Buffalo City to find himself in a predica-
ment similar to the Arkansas Traveler's but having no violin
mastery or other art to get him out of his fix. The Arkansas
Traveler tale is the story of our continual confrontation with the
residues of the pioneering, frontiering, westering instinct that is
part of our programming. It helps to explain why our urge to
"get back in touch with our roots" or "return to nature" hardly
ever succeeds.

Here are Orilla Pinkston's activities, keeping her too busy,
at seventy-seven, ever to grow old: in addition to being musical
co-director of the Arkansaw Traveler Theatre, she is active in
the Church of Christ, whose new building is right across the
highway, north of Hubert Carpenter's place; in the Church of
Christ she has given vocal-music lessons (that denomination is
opposed to instrumental music, on the grounds that the Bible
tacitly forbids it). She gives both vocal and instrumental lessons

to the Girl Scouts, Cub Scouts, and 4-H Clubs. She is on the county-fair committee and the community-development council.

An excellent cook (she began by cooking for her eight brothers; her earliest childhood memory is of rising before the sun each morning to bake sixty biscuits for them), she organized the lunch program for the Cave City schools, worked in the school kitchens with other mothers until her four children were grown, provided food for the kitchens by organizing the Cave City Parent-Teachers Association to start a school garden, then organized a food canning area on the school grounds at harvest time.

She teaches both music and art to grown-ups through the Federal Rural Adult Education Program. Her own artwork is limited (limited?) to the production of ceramics in her own kiln and to her specialty, apple-head dolls, George and Martha Washington dolls, which she began to create in commemoration of the American Bicentennial and which were chosen to represent the state of Arkansas at the national contest in Virginia. Shrunken apples make faces full of character.

A bonus of this high profile she has kept over the years has been her selection by a national organization as a home tester for a variety of consumer products from the research-and-development laboratories of American corporations. She is constantly given things to try out: foods, cosmetics, household products, pet foods, paints, automobile accessories, what-have-you. She tried out the first instant coffees and the first chocolate-chip cookies.

She belongs to the Audubon Society and is a conservationist; she belongs to the White River Art Association and is active in the Mountain View Folk Culture Center, as well as in the Rackensack Folk Society. "Rackensack" is an old anagrammatic word for "Arkansas," an ultimate play upon the many possible mispronunciations of the state's name; some years ago, an apartment hotel in Little Rock was going to be called The Rackensack, but the image-conscious newspapers inveighed against and killed it; today the word has passed into folklore, and the society bearing its name is an occasional and thinly populated organization.

Orilla and Olaf Pinkston have a book of their own, coauthored with Leo Rainey, *Songs of the Ozark Folk* (Branson, Missouri: The Ozarks Mountaineer Press, 1981), which contains capsule biographies of themselves as well as other Cave City folk singers, most no longer living, who learned the words and music of their ancient "ballits" from their mothers and grandparents. Some of the story-songs in their book are of modern invention, but others have been identified as venerable Child ballads.

One would expect a woman as active and energetic as Orilla to look larger than life, huge, even muscular, whereas in fact she is small, thin, and extremely pretty. Kim decides not to ask her whether or not she ever worries: all of those activities, organizations, clubs, crafts, and music keep her too busy to worry.

"Do you still have musical gatherings here in Cave City?" Kim asks.

"Every second Saturday of the month," Orilla says.

"Where?" Kim asks.

"Right out there on our porch, when the weather's good," Orilla says. "People can bring their lawn chairs, and we serve them cookies and some Kool-Aid."

"Is it mostly ancient folk ballads that you do?"

"Well, we don't do any country, but we do bluegrass, and of course bluegrass is *all* folk music."

Bluegrass is the modern musician's compromise between rural tradition and urban speed. It is a clever disguise for the old music, to make it unobjectionable to an era aroused by rock. The fiddle is fast anyway, and the conversion of a sprightly old tune like "The Arkansaw Traveler" into bluegrass is merely a matter of adjusting the rhythms in banjo, guitar, Dobro, mandolin, and bass. Bluegrass is clean, wholesome, "family" music. It even lends itself to gospel songs. Such sentimental moods as lonesomeness, homelessness, and unrequited love can find expression in the cool of the grass that is blue. A broken dream that must remain untold in jazz, rock, even blues, can quickly be developed and descanted in bluegrass, the Kool-Aid of music.

"What was your earliest memory of Cave City?" Kim asks Orilla.

"There was just one store, and a post office," Orilla says. "An old school building, and one church. A doctor had his office in his yard. He rode a horse, and I would climb up on the upper porch to see the doctor pass. Clop-clop-clop! I remember sometimes there'd be some colored people up here, they'd get something to drink, and they'd be cursing and things like that. One day the men picked one of them up and brought him here and tied him to the porch out there and began to whip him. They all took turns whipping that colored man. My mother went out there and said, 'If you're going to kill him, take him away from *my* house.' Maybe it saved him: they put him back in the wagon and took him away."

"Apart from that, was it generally pretty peaceful?"

"No," Orilla says. With Olaf's help, she explains: there was a lot of family feuding. The origins of these feuds were obscure, distant memories. Kim cannot understand what there was to feud about. "I don't understand it, either," Orilla says. "There was one family right next door to us, and another family across the street, and a third family up the road a ways, and the three families were at it all the time, feudin with one another. I've seen people carry a gun just to take their cows to the pasture."

"Does Cave City need anything today?" Kim asks as a last question.

"We could use one of those Wal-Marts or K-Marts," Orilla says. "Yes, it would be very convenient if we had a Wal-Mart."

Wal-Mart, founded and largely owned by billionaire Arkansawyer Sam Walton, bills itself as "Discount City." This kind of "city," which Sam Walton has decreed will be placed on the outskirts of towns, not larger cities, is the small town's city of the future, a market for everything under one roof, making "downtown" obsolete.

Because the family reunion has taken over The Cave Court, Kim spends the night in Batesville, in a family motel, The Powell. Powell is a common name hereabouts; as far as she can determine, there is only a coincidental connection between the name of her motel and the name of her next contact, Wilson Powell, who is general manager of *The Batesville Guard,* a local newspaper that has its best circulation in Cave City, where 75 percent of the families, according to Powell, get the *Guard* either by home delivery or in the mail. Cave City, says Powell with affection, is "one of those towns which is still trying," still attempting to keep up with progress and the problems of simultaneous growth and decay. Powell at seventy-one has become a fixture of the *Guard* office and has no plans to retire. He doesn't anticipate joining the army of local citizens who get tagged with the label "senior" and need manufactured activities to while away their sunset years, but he takes a very strong interest in their problems.

In her motel room, doing her homework, Kim has studied the stories about old people in communities like Cave City all over the state. Next to Florida, Arkansas has the highest percentage of "senior citizens" in the population of any of the states: 14 percent are sixty-five or older. This reflects not merely the desire of outsiders to retire to the beauty, climate, and economy of Arkansas, but the longevity of the native populace in one of the healthiest states in the world. The old people of Cave City are a mixture of immigrant retirees from other states, natives who never left home, and natives who went away to spend their working years in Indiana, Illinois, or Kansas and then came back to retire.

Entering Cave City, Kim had noticed some of the ladies walking Main Street in what seems to be almost a costume for their time of life: pink slacks, glasses with the corners turned up and rhinestone-studded, an elaborately curled hairdo frosted or sometimes colored lavender.

Old people seem to have a need to be uniform, and to function under uniform programs for their benefit or welfare, each with initials for a name. There is the RSVP for Retired Senior Volunteer Program, with its SCP for Senior Companion Program and its FGP for Foster Grandparents Program. The OAV is the Older American Volunteers; there is also the RVSC, Retired Volunteer Service Corps. There is RVPP, Retired Volunteer Partners Program; HOME, Housing to Match the Elderly; MAPS, Mature Adults Personnel Service; and CHORE, Community

Helpers Organization for the Retired Elderly. The proliferation of initials seems to hark back to the New Deal's alphabet soup, which all of these folks lived through. Kim thinks perhaps all the programs should be lumped together into COO, Community Oldsters Organizations.

"The WRPA is a fine outfit," Wilson Powell tells her.

"What does that one stand for?" she asks.

"The White River Project on Aging," he says. "It works out of the Community Center in Cave City. That gives them a place to get together and carry on their activities, and that's important to them. If you don't have a meeting place, usually your activities don't mean much."

"How does the WRPA specifically affect the lives of the old folks in Cave City?" Kim asks.

"It gives them something to look forward to," Powell says. "The center's always open, and at least once a week they have get-togethers, and it gives people with absolutely nothing to do something to look forward to."

Orilla and Olaf had told her about a recent get-together of the WRPA, which they had helped to organize. The men of seventy or older had staged a "beauty contest," dressing up as women. One of Orilla's brothers (not Hubert) had dressed as if pregnant.

"Some were afraid he wouldn't make it!" Olaf had said, laughing.

"It was so much fun," Orilla had said.

Like the majority of people, who are not old, Kim has great trouble identifying with the viewpoints and problems of the elderly. Old is cold. Old is soiled and sad. A great wrinkled face is a fearsome warning of what will become of oneself. The withered heart demands our respect but gets only our pity. And there are fewer wrinkles in the face than in the mind, which is beyond repair. Like a ghost town, the old person is hollow and forgotten. Abandoned dreams embitter the strongest mind and weaken the firmest will. The only blessing is that one ceases to care.

"I keep hearing the name Joe Weston," Kim says to Wilson Powell. "Can you tell me anything about him?"

Powell, whose expression is always friendly and courteous, gives her a sharp look. "I'm not sure he's relevant to Cave City. Sure, he lives there, just outside of town, and he published a newspaper there, but it never qualified as a real newspaper, he had no permits, no mailing permits for it, and he is a very controversial figure still, even a sensational figure." Powell searches his files and finds an example of the *Sharp Citizen*, Weston's typewritten and hand-lettered "newspaper," its title a pun upon the citizens of Sharp County, of whom Joe Weston considered only one to be truly sharp: himself.

During the six years of its life, the *Sharp Citizen* contained no news other than the news of Joe Weston's continuing battles against the establishment. He couldn't have cared less about church socials, local births and deaths, marriages, or community events. He regularly slandered, if not libeled, persons in power, bankers, the county sheriff, machine politicians, the governor. He was caught in a kind of vicious circle: he would attack those who he imagined wanted to attack him; his attackees would then attack him; he would attack his attackers, who would attack him for attacking them; then he would attack them for attacking his attacks on them.

It was his whole life, all he did or seemed to know how to do. A man of seventy-two dying of diabetes and its complications, Joe Weston was not a native of Cave City but of Little Rock, an air force veteran, and a "real" newspaperman in San Diego and Salt Lake City, where he was converted to Mormonism, took a Mormon wife, but was later excommunicated; he came home to Arkansas to nurse his illnesses and his grudges against mankind. After getting a sense of power from starting the *Citizen*, he ran for governor as a Republican against Senator-to-be Dale Bumpers but won almost no votes; then he waged a vicious campaign against Senator-to-be David Pryor, using in his campaign the same style he used in his newspaper: "I'm going to hold my own press conference and come out with a sensational, personal charge against the governor. He'll spend his Wednesdays answering my Tuesdays." But Governor Pryor ignored him, mercifully, and his campaign was another of his lost causes.

His latest lost cause was a multimillion-dollar suit against all of his real and imagined enemies, including the Supreme Court of Arkansas, the Mormon Church of the United States, various local judges and district judges, politicians and officials. Somehow the suit had managed to reach the Supreme Court of the United States, where it was awaiting a hearing and giving a whole new meaning to the word "plaintiff": it was both the most complaining of suits, in the sense of petulant griping, and the most plaintive, in the sense of melancholic and mournful.

"Should I talk with him?" Kim asks Wilson Powell.

"If you can," Wilson says.

She phones Weston in advance, tells him her purpose, and asks for directions to his house. "Are you armed?" he asks her. She laughs and says of course not. "Should I call out the squad?" he asks. She doesn't know whether to laugh again, even nervously. She is more than a little frightened of him. He gives her the somewhat complicated directions to his place.

He lives north of the village, on a little farm, one of those subsistent but self-sufficient organic farms, with lots of goats and vegetables. A beautiful blonde girl, teen-aged, is riding a pony in the meadow. Weston's present wife, Ann, looks not much older than the girl, and the place seems to be full of her kids, including a little boy who is named Free Press Weston. It is not fair to name a child that; as he grows up his peers will nickname him "Freep." The boy and his brothers and sisters and Ann's mother, Lou Jean, who, Kim is to learn—later, elsewhere—is actually Joe Weston's previous wife, come in and out of the room, and sometimes stay, as Kim talks to—or, rather, simply listens to—Joe Weston. Heavyset, overweight like many diabetics, he has a full head of crewcut graying hair, and beady eyes; his face is expressionless, and his mild manners belie his fiery character.

Kim's fear of him rapidly gives way to utter boredom, for he is a terrible windbag. She is permitted to ask him only one question—"Why did you decide to move to the Cave City area?"—and from there on he does all the talking, recounting his long past, his career in the air force, his injuries in World War II, his association with the Mormon Church and his experiences in Salt

Lake City. Kim is acutely aware of his speech—quiet, slow, with exact phrasing and precise pronunciation—of which he, too, is aware: "I have an excellent command of the English language," he comments during his never-ending story.

She wishes he would pause long enough for her to ask her next question. He never does. He launches into the story of his lawsuit now before the Supreme Court, as well as the various suits against him and his countersuits, which have led up to it. "I expect a victory; I will be quite surprised by anything less." He talks of his newspaper endlessly. "No one has ever brought to Arkansas such an extensive journalistic background as I possess." She only half listens. Occasionally she hears a name she knows: "Fulbright . . . McClellan." Like most braggarts, he is a shameless name-dropper. Many of the big names he mentions she does not know but feels that she ought to know. She has so little interest in politics. She never reads political news in the papers, and though she has lived all her life in Arkansas, and voted, she never knew that Joe Weston was running for governor. She really wishes he would shut up. She begins to feel like crying. Or screaming. Her notes dutifully record: "jurisdiction districts, pay-offs to a judge (or is it pays-off?), indictments by grand juries, prosecuting attorneys, liquor in dry counties, call-girl operations, stays in jail, counts of perjury, double jeopardy . . . What is 'double jeopardy'?"

There is the briefest pause. Now hurry: she has time for a very quick question: "WhydidyouaskmeifIwasarmed?"

"We've been shot at at least a hundred times," he declares, and uses the question as an excuse for telling the long story of all the harassment and persecution he has been subjected to. His wife, Ann, sits listening, never nodding her head or shaking it, never registering any emotion, never seeming either to indicate that she has heard all of this before or to suggest that it is all news to her. On the walls of the living room, in a house that is not a shack or a ranch-style but something in between, are her paintings, still lifes mostly. She has an M.F.A. degree, Master of Fine Arts. So young and pretty, she must have her special reasons for bearing so many children to old Joe Weston. In James Agee's

Let Us Now Praise Famous Men, there is a tenant family named Woods in which the multiparous young mother, Ivy, married to fifty-nine-year-old Bud Woods, has her mother, Miss-Molly, who is the same age as her husband, living with them in their crowded cabin. But Miss-Molly is not Bud's former wife, as Ann Weston's mother is Joe Weston's former wife.

When, finally, Kim manages to get up and begin backing off toward the door, Joe Weston thrusts into her hands a copy of the sixty-page booklet printed for his case before the Supreme Court, and then another booklet, *The Sharp Citizen Story,* on the history of his newspaper, and then various other pamphlets he has published. She takes these back to her motel to study.

Wilson Powell had told Kim, "Weston and I have been personal acquaintances. Note I didn't say 'friends.' We haven't had any problems between us, but I don't think the man has any close friends. Everybody is afraid of him. He can take a simple rumor and make it really rough." The primary target of his magnification of simple rumors, Kim discovers by reading the material Weston gave her, is a man named Eagle Street, Cave City's banker. Born with the century, Eagle Street founded the bank in 1920 at the age of twenty, and retired in 1980 at the age of eighty. Street might serve as an archetype of the small-town banker everywhere: shrewd, lean, upright, poker-faced, political, and very tight-fisted. If in his old age he is not loved, he has the consolation that throughout his adult working life he was too feared to be even liked. One of the cardinal rules of banking is "Never give a loan to anybody who needs one," and Eagle Street adhered firmly to this rule all his life, making enemies everywhere. One of Joe Weston's biggest mistakes, when he first tried to start his newspaper, was to ask Eagle Street for a loan.

The head of the Bank of Cave City today, housed in a crewcut flat-top building that was once the Street Motor and Tractor Company, one of Eagle's numerous sidelines, is Eagle's grandson James Mack Street. Kim discovers that he is not lean and unsmiling like his grandsire Eagle but is a young-looking thirty-four, friendly and inclined to pudginess: he looks and dresses like a banker of the current yuppie crop. Kim is eager but uneasy about asking him questions concerning Eagle, who, according to Joe Weston's "newspaper," was a rake, playboy, and debaucher, and who retained such sexual power into his seventies that he continued his wanton seduction of all the women in the county, married or not. Joe Weston's journalistic accounts of Eagle Street often read like a bad pornographic novel.

Although young James Mack Street is executive vice president of the bank and Eagle is officially retired, the old man "still comes in for a couple of hours on Mondays and a couple of hours on Fridays, enough that he thinks he still has control, you know, and that he's still calling the shots. I guess he is!"

Kim has never talked to a banker before without needing money, and after all these days of talking to people past seventy it is easy, relaxed, and refreshing to talk to someone her own age. "Have you ever had any robberies or holdups?" she asks.

He smiles. "We've never had an armed robbery, but we've had a lot of people rob us with a pencil." He explains, "They would say, 'I promise to pay,' but they really didn't mean that when they said it."

"How do you feel being called a 'bedroom community' for Batesville?" She hopes that isn't construed as an off-color question.

"I find it very comfortable to be just fifteen miles from Batesville. I grew up there and went to school there."

She wonders if the mention of Joe Weston would anger him, or if he would make a polite effort to conceal his anger. But because there is no problem of the poor hearing or weak voice or wandering mind that she so often encounters in the aged, she comes right out and asks, "What do you know about Joe Weston?"

There is no anger or even irritation in his expression, but a kind of amused tolerance. "He's our resident outlaw . . . or a real kook, I'm not sure which. He was really down on Granddad. Weston got his start picking on local politicians and then graduated to the state level."

"Why was he down on your grandfather?"

"Mainly because Granddad wouldn't loan him any money, that's all. It's always a motive like that. Weston would very skillfully pick up an ounce of gossip and make it look as if it was very close to the truth. It was so absurd it was funny, really. Some of his accusations . . . 'Eagle Street, the bastard tyrant of Sharp County . . .' " James Mack Street laughs.

"What was your grandfather's reaction?" Kim asks. "Was he amused?"

"Granddad took it that if people were going to believe that kind of garbage there was nothing you could do to change their minds about it. He did explore a potential legal action, but he finally decided it would do more harm than good to try to counteract it, so he just shrugged it off." James Mack Street tells a little story. "There was one lady that Joe Weston wrote about, who was going around with some other man, not Granddad. That kind of gossip. One day Joe Weston parked his car on Main Street and walked over to the post office. We heard all this ruckus and going-on out there, and looked out to see the lady working him over with her shoulder bag." Street chuckles. "She was really letting him have it with that shoulder bag. He ran across the street and into the restaurant, and she just walked up and down the sidewalk, waiting for him to come out. Then she went into the hardware store and bought a can of black spray paint and sprayed it all over the windows of Weston's car! I guess he suffered about as much as he dished it out," James Mack Street concludes. "His is the kind of reputation the town doesn't take pride in, and we would've gladly shipped him anywhere else."

So many of Kim's contacts will die before the year is out, she will become afraid to read the *Gazette*'s obituary columns. But it is hard to avoid seeing the *Gazette*'s headline: "Editor Joseph Harry Weston, 72, Dies; His Prose Led to Controversy, Lawsuits." The obituary will say, "Still pending is Mr. Weston's appeal to the United States Supreme Court in his lawsuit for $39 million in damages from Independence County, the Supreme Court of Arkansas, the Mormon Church and various public officials."

Not long after that, the Supreme Court will turn down his appeal.

Considering the importance of the Streets to Cave City, it is remarkable that the town does not have a Street Street, but the humor of this redundancy has escaped them. There is a Matlock Road leading out toward the treeless subdivisions with street names like Melody and Tammy Drive, and on the development's edge a short lane called Laman Street.

Most of the Streets and that street are descended from Laman. James Mack Street, among his other civic volunteer positions, has served as the chairman and master of ceremonies of the First Annual Gathering (reunion) of the Laman family, three hundred descendants coming from coast to coast to honor their ancestor George Washington Laman, who came from Tennessee to Arkansas, not to found Cave City, but to sire the two brothers who did.

The name Laman, family tradition says, comes from France, where it was originally LeMan. "The Man" in French, as Faulkner has pointed out in explaining the genealogy of the Chickasaw patriarch Ikkemotubbe, is "l'Homme," which Ikkemotubbe himself anglicized to "Doom." But for our purposes we might think that Laman means "The Man" as much as Mankins does, and if Peter Mankins can serve as a metaphor for mankind as it came to Sulphur City, then George Washington Laman can represent the patriarch of the family of man moving into Cave City. But little or nothing is known about him; he first settled in Arkansas near another "city," Lake City (next chapter), but found the swamps and the flatland there too conducive to malaria and moved on into the highlands of Sharp County. In the Old Testament another patriarch, Isaac, was buried by his two sons Jacob and Esau in the cave at Machpelah, one of the Bible's famous caves; for their part, the two sons of George Washington Laman, Jim (James Andrew) and Jack (John William), became the founders, planners, plotters, and platters of Cave City.

For our purposes it would be nice to relate that Jim and Jack fought on opposite sides in the Civil War, but they were young boys at the time of the war, and it was not until the last decade of the century that they set about changing the name of the post office of Loyal to Cave City. Jim founded the Cave City bank that his great-grandson and partial namesake, James Mack Street, now runs, and Jack founded the Laman Mercantile Store for general merchandise, although Jim built another, competing La- man Mercantile Store for general merchandise. The two brothers built side-by-side houses on Main Street, moved into them the same day with their side-by-side wives, Martha Elizabeth and Elizabeth Ann, and planted most of the rest of the town to fruit: Jim to strawberries, Jack to apples. This bigeminality of birth, house, spouse, job, and crops ought to provide for fabulous par- able or allegory.

Eagle Street married one of Jim's granddaughters. One of Jim's sons, George Thomas (Doc Tom), studied medicine and became the town's doctor when other physicians, having discov- ered the place was too healthy, moved out. Doc Tom's practice was not a busy one and he was often broke, but he stuck it out for forty years, until his death, because Cave City was home and he couldn't leave.

When all the descendants of the Lamans congregated for their first family reunion, it was at the behest, urging, and or- ganizing of Doc Tom's only child, Ruthel. The other 274 des- cendants presented her with a framed citation as "Patriotic Citizen Initiator of the First Gathering of the Laman Family."

Ruthel Laman Johnson Heasley, now seventy-eight, lives by circumstance in Batesville but dreams of buying a house on Main Street in Cave City for her last years. On one of Batesville's quiet back streets Kim finds her house, two stories that are neither modern nor quite old and have not a trace of compote but many tasteful antiques. There is nothing compote about Ruthel, either; although she is old enough to have been Orilla Pinkston's original music teacher, she is ageless. Like almost everyone of her gen- eration, she must take daily medicine (in her case cortisone, which sometimes leaves her dizzy to the point of seeming drunk), but she has an elegance of appearance and of manner that gives the lie to her years.

Kim and Ruthel (it is accented strongly on the first syllable) begin by talking about her best pupil during the twenties, Orilla, when Ruthel herself was only a teen-ager; Orilla, slightly younger, would in turn become a music teacher at seventeen. Because Orilla had to do all of the sewing and washing and ironing for her eight brothers, "she was bothered by arthritis and she had a great deal of trouble with her hands," Ruthel recalls. "She would come to my house for music lessons and she would've ironed shirts for eight boys. I don't know how many shirts they each had, but even eight would've been an awful amount. She was real tired and her hands were sore."

Ruthel remembers her grandfather Jim Laman very well, but not her great-uncle Jack. When she was just a very little girl, Jim, who lived just a few doors down Main Street, would come and ask her, "Would you like to go *knocking around*?" She would be thrilled, because it was her favorite means of travel: "I would put my right foot on his right foot and I would put my left on his, and he would hold me by the hands, and I would walk on his feet, you know. And we would go places."

Jim would take his granddaughter knocking around to his gristmill to watch the wheat being made into flour, and to his gin to watch cotton being hulled.

Ruthel's father, Doc Tom, owned the cave for many years before he sold it to Hubert Carpenter, who developed it. Kim remembers Hubert Carpenter replying to her question "The cave itself is mysterious and interesting to me, but I wonder if the people who live here find it mysterious and interesting?" "No, no," Hubert had said. "I bought it from a doctor and it wasn't worth a thing in the world to him. He wouldn't ever do a thing with it." Doc Tom had no desire to commercialize the cave, and for years left it as it was: a big hole in the ground, which he and his neighbors used as a refrigerator in hot weather in the days before even "iceboxes." Olaf and Orilla had explained to Kim how each family had its own lard bucket in which milk and butter were kept cool in the cave. Olaf had explained, "Each one had a different-colored ribbon so you'd know his bucket, you know! But now you wouldn't dare leave anything down there!"

Ruthel remembers playing in the cave as a child. In the hottest part of the summer, "I would take my paper dolls and take my lunch in a little sack and go down into the cave and play . . . because it was so cool, you know. I'd play all day in there, and it seemed like a long time to me. And then there was—up at the mouth of the cave, up at the top of the bluff, where the mouth opens down into, you know—there was a little path which ran right along there. Little calves would fall off that path and fall right into the cave and break their necks. I remember hearing people talking about it, saying, 'Oh, how terrible. So-and-so lost a calf.' It was quite a drop, you know. The path overhangs the open mouth of the cave, and those calves would just fall off. Well, I reckon that was enticing to me, and I must've wanted thrills or something. I can remember running just as close to the edge of that path to see whether I'd fall in or not."

"That was brave!" Kim says, and asks Ruthel another question: "Did you ever wish that Cave City would actually become a city?"

"I don't remember ever thinking that," Ruthel admits, "but I remember hearing my grandfather—'Uncle Jim,' everybody called him—I remember hearing him tell my dad that someday out on that highway—I call it Strawberry Road but they call it Center Street, I believe, and I'm sick of the way they named some of the streets—it should be called Strawberry Road, because it's the road that goes to the town of Strawberry—oh, out that way was where the old, old school used to sit. When I was a kid, it sat out there, and on about a mile, there was a little creek and there was some houses started building up, and I remember my grandfather saying to my father, 'There will come a time when this will be the center of town.' He could envision that back then. But it seems it has spread more to the north, building toward Evening Shade. He thought it would develop toward Strawberry. I never thought about it. I was perfectly happy with it the way it was. It was real quaint and nice. Still is."

There is that house on Main Street that Ruthel would like to buy so she can leave Batesville and go home. Friends ask her if she would be satisfied there. "Yes, I would love to live there again. My earliest recollections are of the old Christmas trees at church."

Kim mentions Joe Weston and asks, "Do you know anything about him at all?"

"I know he's been in the courts a great deal," says Ruthel, who spent her working years as a court recorder. "I don't know the man. He's a *real* individual, real independent in his thinking. I've seen some of the articles he has written about Eagle Street and they're pretty bad."

Ruthel's father met her mother when the latter was a student at The Cave City Institute Boarding School, a private academy founded at a time when public schools were inadequate or non-existent. Students at the Institute came from a radius of a hundred miles or more and were subjected to a rigid discipline of "all study and no play": dating was confined to certain hours on Saturday afternoons, and curfews were strictly enforced. A photograph here shows the large house, with wraparound porches on the upper and lower floors and a tall stone chimney, that served as a boardinghouse for the Institute, pupils and faculty together, and, with old porch rockers, swings, and other porch furniture on its galleries today, still has the look of a comfortable boardinghouse, the only one in any of these lost cities. Here lived as a child one of Cave City's most successful sons, Eugene McNeeley, who became president of "Ma Bell," the American Telephone and Telegraph Company in New York.

Like Orilla Pinkston, Ruthel has rare memories of blacks in Cave City, and these only of people passing through. "There were no black people in town at all. As a small child, I remember there were a few black people in Evening Shade and Sidney, and they would drive through Cave City to get to Batesville with their big wagons. They would have these black drivers hauling merchandise. . . ." Ruthel remembers that she would hide under the bed when they drove through town. She traces her fear of blacks to the common fear children had because their parents kept them in line by threatening punishment from imaginary Negroes, in her case, a certain Old Black Jobe. Whenever she was naughty, her mother told her that Ole Black Jobe would come "get" her and haul her off.

Does she, Kim asks finally, have any hopes or dreams of her own that never came true? Yes, says Ruthel Laman Heasley, "when I was a young person, when I was going off to college, I wanted to go to the University of Missouri, because Robert Frost was there at that time. I wanted to study under him, and be a writer. But my folks sent me to Galloway, a little college for girls here in Arkansas. I always wanted to be a writer, and I wanted to study with Frost. That was one big ambition that never came true."

This time—unlike Buffalo City, where Kim could not bring herself to go back for one last look around—she does return to Cave City briefly, for a specific reason: she has forgotten to find the cemetery. She makes a point of searching out the cemeteries of these lost cities early on, but it has slipped her mind here. In the southwestern corner of town, right on the county line, is the town's lone eminence, and upon the pleasant knoll the cemetery, with a view of sorts, of the town. The cemetery seems so new; Kim cannot find any ancient headstones in it, and no distinctive or original headstones. She hopes that Prince Matlock, at least, will have a bizarre or original tomb marker. She searches for it, and at length finds it lost among numerous others of the same factory-cut, corny compote style. Charles Prince Matlock, a native genius of indigenous architecture, lies beneath a stone not just ordinary but of suffocating banality. Surely he did not choose it for himself.

In August the Lamans of America will forgather for their Second Annual Gathering, and the people of Cave City will hold their annual Watermelon Festival, opening the Arkansas watermelon season ahead of the town of Hope, down in southeastern Arkansas, which has the biggest (over two hundred pounds) watermelons in the world but not the tastiest, which are grown around Cave City and get the flavor, according to legend or truth, from the rocky soil. Jim Laman's apples are mostly gone, and a few descendants of Jack Laman's strawberries straggle on, but everybody raises and eats the watermelon, and people come to the town from far and wide to buy them, people who couldn't care less about the cave itself and never go near it, except perhaps to sit in the shade of the trees around it on a hideously hot afternoon in the worst month of the year, cooled by the cave's breath and the mouth-drenching squish of bites into red-ripe melon.

Lake City,
Arkansas

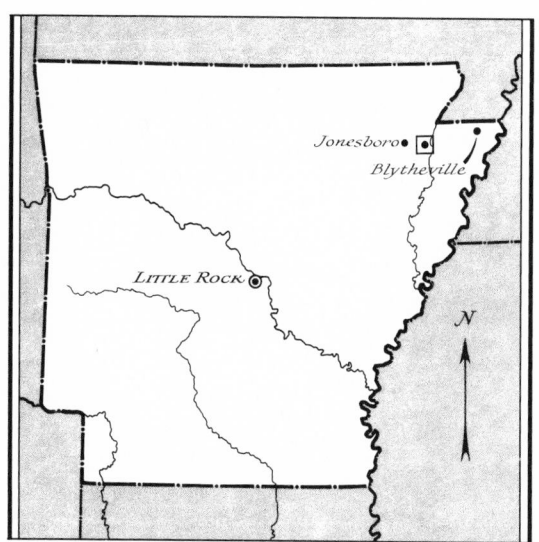

UNITED STATES
POST OFFICE
LAKE CITY
ARKANSAS 72437

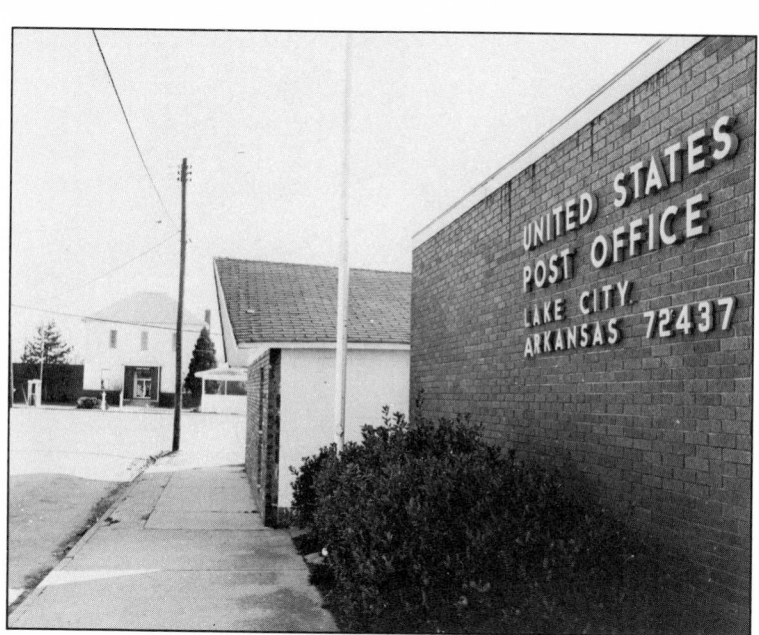

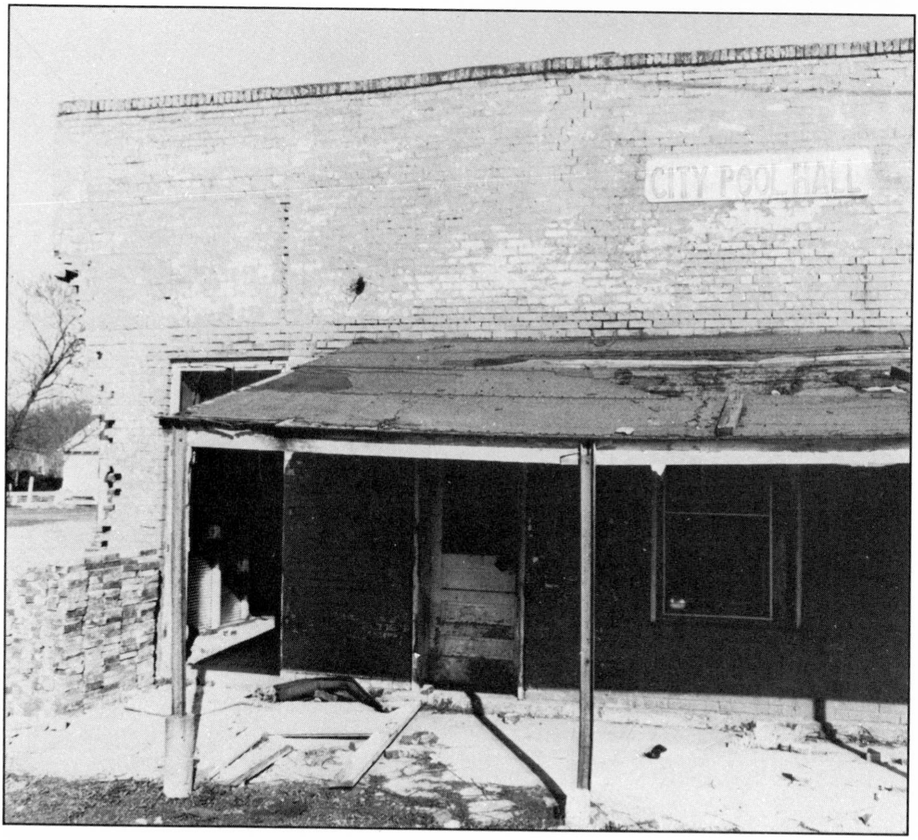
CITY POOL HALL

Cain was the first builder of cities.
—Rabelais, Works, *bk V., ch. 35, 1551*

BETWEEN THE STORMS upon the earth and the storms beneath the earth, Lake City has had a hard time of it. (The "lake" from which the town takes its name was never that, only a wide place in the St. Francis River, not a pond or a pool of water, but a flowing stream. Lakes do not flow; they are inland *bodies* of water. There is no body of water here, just the sluggish brown little St. Francis, whose stuporous tranquillity belies its occasional spree of flooding, and gainsays its rambunctious past in the earthquake-ridden formative years of these pocked and pimpled "Sunk Lands," which was Lake City's official name for a long time.) There was an Indian village here, as in Buffalo City and in Cave City (and in Mound City to come), when, in the winter of 1811–12, one of the worst cataclysms known to man (but barely known to history, because so few lives were taken, miraculously) shook and tore this region, with the epicenter of the seizure somewhere just to the northeast of here. Farther northeast is the village in the bootheel of Missouri called New Madrid, pronounced New *Mad-rid*, which, because it was the only populated place affected by the upheaval, gave its name to the disaster. Kim is in northeastern Arkansas now, just a few miles from the sharp toe of that "boot-heel," all vestiges of hilly countryside far behind her; she will not see hills or hear the Theme of the Faraway Hills again on this journey until she has completed a swinging loop down through the southeastern and southwestern parts of the state.

For now, there is this somnolent, stagnant village in a top-ographic freak of earth shaped within the memory of man, even if unrecorded by those men who lived here and, being Indians, had no need for records. The white man's records kept not far away in New Madrid that winter were awesome: the *sense* of the earth, the smell first, the strange organic smell, as of the very bowels of the earth putridly eviscerated. Then the sound: de-scribed by the literate earwitnesses as an ominous subterranean rumble, not like the growling of an empty stomach but like car-riage wheels on cobblestones, impatient and threatening, and growing in intensity until the sight came: the terrifying sight of trees falling everywhere, whole massive masts toppling, forests flopping, and then the ground, the earth itself, becoming like gelatin, rock and soil viscously quivering.

The New Madrid Earthquake—unlike the more famous San Francisco Earthquake ninety-four years later, which was all over in one day (although the fires went on for weeks afterward)—lasted for three months in recurrent jolts, like a long-drawn-out orgasm, with trickling aftershocks for a whole year (and tales are still told of innocent lovers' blaming the earth's jolts on their own blissful shudders, a misconception Hemingway echoed in his "moving earth"). Seismologists have declared that the sequence of New Madrid shocks surpassed any other recorded earthquake in the history of the North American continent in terms of the number of shocks, the length of the disturbance, the size of the area affected, and the estimated severity on the Richter Scale. Furthermore, the prospect of another great, more destructive earthquake in this same area is certain and appalling. But nobody cares; nobody has heard of New Madrid.

It would be wrong, however, to blame the dermatological disfigurements of the landscape hereabouts on the New Madrid Earthquake alone; the pocks and cracks and sinks, the pits and sloughs and donnicks, are the result of an ancient attempt by the Mississippi River to change its whole course westward, an aban-doned attempt, like so many of the fickle waywardnesses of that Grandfather of Waters. The Mississippi today dodders along forty miles to the east of Lake City, as the alligator gar swims, and yet its former detour through these Sunk Lands can be detected in the quality of the soil, a beautifully rich mud-born delta silt which makes some of the best farmland in the world, even after a sesquicentennial of hard use by farming man.

A blemished face can protect the privacy of an overflowing heart. No tourist comes to Lake City to see these Sunk Lands and disturb this isolation. Even though Lake City has the highest population of any of our lost cities, it is in its own way more lost than the others, which have some attraction for the lover of scenery, or of architecture, or of ruins, or of nature's steady determination to reclaim its land. It is also one of Arkansas's several lost "second" county seats. Roads were so bad in the nineteenth century, streams were so deep and unpredictable, and, in the case of the Sunk Lands of eastern Craighead County, the rich land itself was so inaccessible, that it was necessary to have more than one county seat simply to make government available to all the people. Jonesboro, the first or primary county seat, is only twenty miles from Lake City, but it was an all-day trip by wagon—during those seasons of the year when it was dry enough to make the trip at all.

So Lake City was given its own courthouse, of sorts, and its own chief deputy sheriff, and its own county clerk, although it has to share the county judge with the other county seat. Kim decides to start at the top, with this man. His name is Roy Bearden and he is called "Red" by himself and everyone who knows him, because of his rufous hair, with freckles and a rotundity to match. Judge Bearden's office is in the Art Deco–style courthouse at Jonesboro; he has no other, smaller office in the courthouse at Lake City. Jonesboro (with thirty-two thousand people, the seventh-largest city in the state) is also the home of Arkansas State University, homely stepsister to Fayetteville's main university, a school associated with templed hills and towers of learning, whereas the Jonesboro campus is for flatlanders, farmers, and swamp dwellers. There is just as much difference between eastern and western Craighead County, and Kim begins her all-too-brief session with the very busy judge by asking him about this distinction.

Despite his appearance of a well-fed good ole boy, Judge

Red Bearden is impatient and no-nonsense, nonjovial. He explains to Kim, "I would not really say it is differences beween the two as much as it is, uh, personality, uh, especially wunst you cross that St. Francis River into that country beyond Lake City, where they feel like a bastardly child as far as the rest of the county is concerned. And they probably have some concrete reasons for feeling that way, I don't know. Sure, they've got a courthouse over there, but this here is really the courthouse. They're just sort of like a branch bank."

"Why don't you just consolidate the two?" Kim asks.

The red judge winces. "That would be political suicide, lady," he says. "The courthouse over there is very personal to the people in the eastern part of the county. It's something they've held on to over the years. Besides, if we was to move that courthouse over here we wouldn't save very little monies."

"Isn't it personally inconvenient for you to have to sit on both benches, over there and over here?" she asks.

"I don't do that," he says. "I'm not a judicial judge. I'm just an administrative judge. I go over there purely on administrative business."

"You *run* Lake City, then?"

"No, the mayor does that. Talk to her."

"Her?" Lake City, Kim discovers, has a woman mayor.

The March morning sky darkens and clots with heavy, looming clouds as she drives eastward toward Lake City. All her life she has known this pattern to herald the need to look out for fierce cyclic winds: what the radio, now she turns it on, would call a Tornado Watch, as the first stage in a public anxiety leading up to the second stage, Tornado Warning, and sometimes even to the third: Tornado!

In terms of the number of deaths resulting therefrom, Arkansas is the worst tornado state in the country. Farther west, the flatlands of Oklahoma and Kansas have a reputation for a storm cellar in every back yard, as well as daily alerts in anticipation of the big funnels, but Arkansas, especially *its* flatlands (in which Kim now finds herself), has the most destructive of the big twisters. For some reason perhaps having to do with the whirling wind's preference for the line of least resistance, the tornadoes do not like the mountain country of the Ozarks and are comparatively rare there; none were ever seen in Marble City or Buffalo City. In Lake City, there is nobody who has never glimpsed or endured a tornado.

The word "tornado," of relatively recent usage, replacing the synonym "cyclone," is from the Spanish for "turn" but also from the Latin for "thunder," suggesting the heavy rain and sound effects that accompany the storm; whereas the quiet, more classic "cyclone," from the Greek for "coil" or "wheel," does not evoke such special effects. Most old-timers prefer the latter, but there are superstitious people who avoid calling the storm by either name, lest the utterance of the name itself bring on the beast. A circumlocution thus replaces it: "monster storm a-brewin," or "hell wind a-churnin," but most likely a euphemistic "somethin bad a-comin."

The usual true accounts of automobiles and heavy trucks swept off the highway and carried great distances by the tornado are matched by unauthenticated stories of people being lifted high into the air and returned unharmed to a walking (or running) position, of a sack of meal that was hanging on a porch being hit with a gust that blew away the sack but left the meal hanging, of water wells being turned inside out and pouring well water all over the country. More likely are such stories as (according to one old-timer) that the tornado momentarily sucked the St. Francis River dry and poured the water out of the top of the spout of the funnel, or lifted the roof off a house without disturbing a table set for dinner. Indian legends favor the identification of the cyclone with a wild horse; farmers report numerous "sightings" of horses being lifted bodily from their stalls, blown around the decapitated barn, and returned alive to earth.

Along with recurrent droughts, equally recurrent floods of the St. Francis River, and the not recurrent but always possible earthquake, the seasonal, cyclical cyclone appears to be less a destructive force than a theatre for displays of heroism, exhibi-

tions of charity, outpourings of kindness, bringing out the best
in people who never knew what resources of goodness they had
in them until the storm demanded their mettle. If Lake City is
a hazard area—a dangerous climate and a menacing geography—
it compensates by lacking the boredom and lethargy that attend
the safe backwaters of society. The excitement of the weather is
also reflected in the excitement of misadventure of another sort:
crime. Lake City has a history of misconduct to match its goodness
and render it the most wicked of our lost cities.

In a little shopping plaza in the "new town" on the western
fringe of "old" Lake City is a small "modern" brick shed that
serves as a city hall, and here Kim locates the mayor, who is just
hanging up on a phone call with Judge Bearden when Kim arrives to see her. Pat Qualls is a very young and pretty forty-three,
a farm girl, ex-teacher, and, like Orilla Pinkston, long-time music
teacher; she still teaches piano and voice. She grew up in Monette,
across the river from Lake City, but married a Lake City farmer.
"Judge Bearden and I have a good working relationship," she
tells Kim, in her little office.

"What's your main headache as mayor?" Kim asks her, getting down to business after the two women have exchanged pleas-
antries and comments on the weather: tornado watch for the rest
of the morning.

"Jobs," Pat Qualls tells her. "We need jobs in this town. We
need an industry. Who doesn't? Without jobs, nothing else will
flow. Businesses won't do business. The empty houses will stay
empty."

"I guess a lot of people here have to drive to Jonesboro to
work, don't they?" Kim asks.

"Jonesboro." Pat Qualls nods. "Also Trumann, Monette,
Blytheville, anywhere. There aren't any jobs in Lake City. A
woman came in this morning to see me, a sixty-two-year-old
woman, and she said, 'I've gotta have work. If I don't find a job,
I'm going to California.' "

"But your population is growing. . . ."

"Yes, it's doubled since 1970, when the census showed nine
hundred seventy. We've got twice that now. And I'd like to see

it get really *big*, say to about five thousand. If we could get jobs, everything else will take care of itself."

"Then you would *be* a city."

"And behave like a city. One thing I've found is, the people here don't *want* progress. They want it like it was fifty years ago. They want to dump garbage in their back yards! When we instituted mandatory garbage the first year I was mayor, I got all kinds of criticism over that!"

Kim asks, "Whom should I interview? In your opinion, who is the most colorful or interesting person in town?"

Mayor Pat says, "That's a tough question. Offhand, I would guess Cotton Taft. But maybe he wouldn't talk to you. What you'd probably need is someone who knows him to take you down there and introduce you to him. Let me make a couple of calls."

Mayor Pat tries to reach her husband, who is a good friend of Cotton Taft's, but he isn't home: out watching for a tornado, probably. She makes another call, without luck. And then a third. This time she reports to Kim that another man, by coincidence another "Cotton," Cotton Williams, might be able to arrange for her to meet Cotton Taft. She gives Kim directions on how to find the Senior Citizens' Center, where Cotton Williams works. Kim is impressed that the mayor has been so helpful, and she thanks her profusely.

(A few weeks later Pat Qualls will be appointed by the governor of Arkansas to the three-member Public Service Commission, will be given a salary higher than the governor's and an enormous power over public utilities and their regulation, and will be continually in the news for her tough but fair-minded decisions on the commission, doing battle with the electric and gas companies. She will be quoted as blaming the utilities for the lack of jobs in Lake City. "Why would an industry come to Lake City when it could go west to Jonesboro and have lower utility rates?")

Kim decides to have lunch at the Riverfront Café, the town's lone eatery, located in the same malled "new part" that contains the city hall. She hasn't even seen the real Lake City yet. "Riverfront" is a misnomer for the café, since it isn't on the river, but the menu does include catfish. Kim orders a cheeseburger. All the other customers are men wearing farmer's bill caps who are observing her appreciatively.

A police car stops outside, and an Arkansas state trooper gets out and comes in. He points a finger at one of the customers and says, "Hiya, Hambone." He shifts the fingerpoint to another man and says, "Whattayasay, Watermelon?" All of them call him "Plug."

The state trooper notices Kim. He looks at her, and then at Zephyra parked outside. He walks to Kim's table, looks down at her. He jerks his head in the direction of Zephyra. "That your car?"

Yes, she says, but realizes the words haven't come out. "Yes," she says aloud. "Is something wrong?"

He shakes his head. "Pretty," he says. She doesn't know whether he means her or Zephyra. Is he flirting? He is not a tall trooper or a spare one, but looks something like Dick Tracy gone to seed, or Dick Tracy with a double chin instead of the chiseled jaw.

She makes a show of pushing the "RECORD" button on her tape recorder. "Why are you called Plug?" she asks. "Do you shoot a lot of people?"

He laughs, then sits down at her table, studies the tape recorder for a moment, laughs some more, and addresses the tape recorder: "Naw, I've been called Plug since I was a little kid, too young to remember who called me that or why." Then, from behind his hand, avoiding the tape recorder, he whispers to her, "What's this gonna be printed in?"

"A book maybe," she says, and she tells him her name and explains her mission in as few words as possible. "Do you know anything about Lake City?" she asks him.

"A little," he says. He sips the coffee the waitress has brought to the table. "What do you want to know?"

"Has there ever been any crime in Lake City?"

Corporal Plug chokes on his coffee, inadvertently spitting a bit of it out in holding back a laugh. Then he swallows, clears his throat, and *laughs*. After getting control of himself, he says, earnestly, "Kim, honey, you came to the right man."

She has indeed. Arkansas State Police Corporal Hershel L.

"Plug" Eaton, age forty-six, grew up in Lake City, and has spent all of his spare time and holidays for years researching the history of his hometown. Every lawman has a hobby. Some off-duty police collect butterflies or injustices, breed dogs or flies, raise gardens or rackets, play golf or dead, or simply polish their arsenals. When State Trooper Eaton is not in the line of duty, he is on the track of the years, preserving the past for his personal pleasure, and is the author of a thin but unique pamphlet, *History of Lake City, Arkansas*.

As soon as Kim finishes her cheeseburger, he says, "Let's go," and he takes her out and puts her in his cruiser—not in the back seat, where the felons and drunks go, but in the passenger seat beside him. The car is white with a dashing blue stripe and a toplight and siren. She has never been inside one of these as prisoner, suspect, or violator of road laws. Nice to ride in one as a friend of the force.

Trooper Eaton (he is taking the afternoon off, she learns) drives her all over what's left of the town, a tour guided and narrated by the most knowledgeable historian she could hope to find.

"Might as well start here," he says a couple of blocks east of the Riverfront Café. The first abandoned building, looking like some forlorn warehouse, was the town's ice plant, erected after years of bringing in ice by train to pack out by train the river's enormous daily catch of fish. "They sold the ice machinery out of there, and some old boy took it to South America," Plug explains. "This South American went around buying up all the ice plants in the world and taking 'em home with him. Gets hot down around the equator, you know. Now, right there sat the old railroad depot. . . ."

There are no rails, no traces of them remaining—the tracks were taken up and sold for scrap—but the roadbed for the Jonesboro, Lake City & Eastern railway line is still visible. Kim can imagine an early morning at the time of World War I and the considerable activity around the old depot as the first of several daily trains arrived from Jonesboro, bringing in drummers to sell their wares to the town's shops, along with people returning home from a night on the town in Jonesboro and travelers to the east, to the bigger town, Blytheville. The train also brought the mail car, the baggage car, and a few empty flatcars to carry out the quickly dwindling timber from the sunk lands and saw-mills to the east. The post-office wagon and an express wagon for the freight waited, along with a hack driver hoping to pick up a fare going to the hotel or a drummer going to a Main Street mercantile. In the shade of the depot there would be assembled the usual club of men loafing and watching the comings and goings of trains, the waking up of the town, and whatever river traffic remained, a short distance away.

All across America, hamlets grew into towns, and towns into cities, with the coming of the railroad; and with the going of the railroad, cities faded into towns, towns into hamlets, and hamlets into ruins. As if it were a vessel supplying blood to the brain, the shutting off of the railroad brings on stroke, paralysis, and death; Lake City is a stroke victim. The highways and roads all around are now paved, all-weather, all-season, and the trucks pound upon them, but it is not the same as in the days when the long freight trains of the J.L.C.&E. came into town ten times a day.

The railroad was built out to Lake City in 1898, when the town was still remote, isolated, accessible only to the traffic of the river, an occasional steamboat or other watercraft. Like most shortline railroads, it was short-lived. If its mission in life was simply to open up Lake City and the eastern timberlands to the progress of lumbering and, after the woods were taken, agriculture, then it served its function well. But the men who chartered it for "ninety-nine years and a day" were as ambitious and as shortsighted as the men who anticipated that Lake City would become a city, and who incorporated it as such the same year the railroad steamed into town. Like the roots of a cypress tree spreading outward into the muck, the tracks of the J.L.C.&E. extended year by year eastward into Mississippi County and to branches reaching the Big River itself, then began to shrink back-ward until, fifty years after its beginning, it was dissolved and the last tracks were removed. In recent years the old Lake City depot served as an Assembly of God church, but today, says Plug Eaton, "it's just sittin there empty and vacant."

Also empty and vacant are the town's pool hall and its drugstore. The letters of the sign above the former are vaguely visible—"CITY POOL HALL"—the "CITY" giving some dignity to a place that in many other towns is called "recreation parlor," a hangout for men and boys exclusively. It once held a barbershop, too, like the ruin of a hotel in Buffalo City, and in its own vernacular way it appeals to our *Ruinenlust* as well as any abandoned building in Lake City. One corner of the brickwork is fallen and jagged, unintentionally like the intentional jagged corners of the Best & Co. store in Houston designed by postmodernist James Wine as one of his visual jokes, to crumble the dumb edges of box architecture and appeal to the public's fascination with disaster and ruins. Archaeologists of the future centuries who might uncover this sign and investigate the ruins would be equally divided over whether CITY POOL HALL was a kind of natatorium or possibly one more of those shrines in which the priests and their acolytes took sharp sticks and poked at hard colored balls on a table of green felt, all symbolic of the many ball-into-hole rituals of nineteenth and twentieth century man.

Around the corner, on Main Street, is a better-preserved ruin, the drugstore, with its plate-glass windows still intact, its overhanging marquee still unfallen and level, and its abutting alley not yet overgrown with brush and weeds. Although the interior of this drugstore was once a busy place with an ornate soda fountain, whose marble surfaces and counter echoed the marbled wainscots of the entrance (the soda fountain was given a new life recently as a museum piece in Fayetteville, on the other side of the state), it was not so much the store itself as that alley alongside which was the impromptu social center of Lake City.

The druggist for fifty-five years was Ab Davis, whose death on the floor of the store in 1977 was to bring about the building's abandonment, even by the fraternal organizations upstairs, Woodmen of the World and the Masons, for whom Plug Eaton was once secretary-treasurer (he is a 32nd Degree Mason). "Ab would get his ice cream in those huge cardboard cylinder-type things," Plug recalls from his own boyhood, "and when they'd get *about* used up, he'd sit 'em up there in the alley. And there's where we kids spent our afternoons, scraping the leftover ice cream out—" Plug interrupts himself with laughter at the pleasure of the memory.

"Did this place have a name?" Kim asks.

"Just 'The Alley,' " Plug says. "Volumes could be written about the goings-on of The Alley . . . the fightings, the stabbings . . . that's where everybody went to fight. That's where all the winos went to drink. That was the main thoroughfare, right there!" Doctors had offices conveniently leading off The Alley; there was also a stairway leading up to the "Office Upstairs" of another doctor, Old Doc Roberts (about whom more later).

This Alley and this corner were the town's social center, more than the pool hall, and when Ab Davis died, efforts were made to keep the place running as a secondhand store, as in secondhand stores in secondhand towns all over secondhand America in these times.

Now, here, where the new little official-modern United States Post Office sits behind its Zip Code, the corner of Main and Walnut, was a whole block of buildings, called "The White Elephant": a store, a café , a movie theatre, another store. All gone. There, look, is the courthouse: that's it.

Craighead County Courthouse (Eastern District). You wouldn't know it as such; looks more like just somebody's white two-story house, wooden. The only all-wood courthouse in the state of Arkansas, a tall frame building in a styleless design that might be called Georgian simply because of its simplicity and lack of ornamentation, it has nothing whatever fancy except a hipped roof instead of a gable, and a few tall, narrow windows. The whole thing is such a strong contrast to the Art Deco courthouse of the Western District, in Jonesboro, built in the middle of the Depression. Lake City's courthouse, despite being of wood, is one of the oldest unburned courthouses in Arkansas; construction was started in 1883 and finished in our key year of 1886, the same year the town's name was changed from Sunk Lands to

Lake City. Inside, the staircase is all-wood, too, and leads up to the big courtroom, where all those murderers and thieves were tried and found guilty.

Plug Eaton shows Kim the spot where one of those murders occurred, up an alley. "You want crime? Right out the back there was where Bill Pace was shot. Five times with a .38 Special."

"It must've set a record for shortness of distance to where the culprit was found guilty," Kim observes. "So close to the courthouse . . ."

"*Every*thing's close to the courthouse here!" Plug says. "Did you ever know a town where the courthouse faced the whore-house?" He looks sheepish and says, "Pardon me, but right over there was our resident bawdy house, back in the twenties and thirties. There was a saloon next door. Another one over there."

And here, where there is just a one-chair barbershop, which before that was a sort of speakeasy, was once the office of Judge Craddock, where he could look out his windows and watch every-thing that was going on in town. "Let me tell you about Judge Craddock," Plug invites.

He wasn't a real judge. Horse trader, realtor, lumberman, banker, farmer, cotton ginner, mayor, and kangaroo jurist, William M. Craddock was the son of Welsh immigrants who foaled him in Pennsylvania a year before Fort Sumter was fired upon and took him to far-off Kansas and Oregon to pioneer the settling of both of those states by breeding, raising, and selling horses, indispensable to man's mobility in the widening West. Raised on a horse ranch, young Craddock had his earliest job taking boxcar loads of horses back east to sell in the big cities. For some reason known only to himself, he brought a trainload of horses in 1898 not to New York or Boston but to the end of a new track just opened to Lake City, then an isolated quagmire that had more need of oxen than of horses but which eagerly accepted Crad-dock's load and persuaded him to stay and start a horse trading market and barn, just in time for the J.L.C.&E.'s expansion and opening up of the town to the outside world.

Bill Craddock quickly branched out into real estate, until he owned most of the Lake City business district; then into lumbering, until his sawmill processed the virginity of thousands of acres of prime timber around Lake City; into banking, until his Lake City Farmers' and Merchants' was the first and only financial institution in town; and into the planting of cotton upon the vast acres his sawmill had cleared of lumber, until his Independent Gin Company handled all the cotton harvest in the eastern part of the county. By this time Lake City was almost a city, and he was mayor of it as well as best friend of U.S. Senator Thaddeus Caraway, a local boy whose career in Washington had begun under Craddock's tutelage and patronage years before, when Caraway established his first law office in Lake City.

Caraway never persuaded his friend Craddock to open a law book or take other than a business interest in the affairs of the courtroom, but Craddock held his own court, of sorts, in his little office. A jovial lifelong bachelor (rendering him suspect of homosexuality among his few enemies), he liked a good joke as much as the next fellow (unless the joke was about his own proclivities) and would occasionally call into session a court where he would "try" his friends, or an unwary visitor, on some charge such as "flagrant misrepresentation of the observable truth" or "inclination to wear the wrong garment out of season" or "failure to observe the laws of nature." With no more worlds of finance or commerce to conquer, "Judge" Craddock used these kangaroo courts to amuse himself and others. The defendant was always found guilty, and sentenced by the judge to stand a round of coffee or a box of cigars for the other attendants of the court.

When a city has finished growing, it turns to entertainment. An actual judge who tried a moonshiner in the Lake City courthouse and sent him to the state penitentiary was afterward hailed into Judge Craddock's court and charged with "raising the price of whiskey," found guilty, and ordered to buy coffee for all the spectators. Throughout the Roaring Twenties and Depressed Thirties, *the* annual event of Lake City was not July 4 but April 12, the birthday of Judge Craddock and two of his cronies, who gave themselves an annual birthday party and all-day public picnic, wingding, and blowout.

When Judge Craddock died, at age eighty, he owned most

of the eastern part of the county, but, for a reason as strange as his reason for coming to Lake City in the first place, he requested that his remains be sent back to his boyhood home in Kansas for burial.

Or perhaps the reason isn't hard to find. Plug Eaton drives Kim to the Lake City Cemetery, which is not on a hill like the Cave City Cemetery (there are no hills or even knolls here) but squeezed between the town's eastern side and the river, right on the edge of the Sunk Lands, where it has been flooded by the "lake" on several occasions. Judge Craddock wouldn't have wanted to be buried here. The few trees in this amphibious cemetery are, of course, cypress, the water-loving evergreen whose branches (appropriately or coincidentally, but probably unbeknown to those who lie beneath them) are ancient symbols of mourning. Cypresses standing in swamps with their knees above water suggest the forbidding gloom of death. Here some of the graves are entombed, New Orleans style, above the ground. Later in the afternoon Plug will take Kim all the way up and out to the Pine Log Cemetery, twenty miles northwest of Lake City, where there are knolls and rises that contain the burials of many of the town's best people, including Allen Springer, who owned most of those knolls and rises as well as the best plots here in this cemetery.

Every foundling town should have a founding father with a name like Springer. Twelve years before Bill Craddock stormed into town with his load of horses, Allen Springer had sprung upon the town to open Lake City's mercantile store and buy up the land that was to constitute the new Lake City when Oldtown, as the first river port was called, faded away. This road past the Lake City Cemetery, now officially called Lake Street, fronting the Sunk Lands, had been the Main Street of Oldtown, where two Hungarian Jews, Moskovich Morris and Leopold Rich, had opened separate businesses in the pre-Springer era. This was almost a prehistoric era, in the sense that nothing is known about the two Jews, their business, and their later departure; when the remains of Oldtown burned in a fire in 1904, they were already gone. Allen Springer was coterminous with Mark Twain, whom he resembled, at least insofar as his mustache: his manner was quiet and reserved. He lived in his native Indiana until the Civil War, when, as a Union foot soldier, he fought at Shiloh and Vicksburg, marched to the sea with Sherman, and came to know and love and remember the South. However, he did not return to it until ten years after the war, when he bought 240 acres to farm near Lake City, still called Sunk Lands or Oldtown. This area was populated by Confederate veterans who were suspicious of him until he sprang upon them the fraternal spirit of Freemasonry and organized them into a Masonic brotherhood and lodge of which he served as Worshipful Master for twenty years, throughout the springing of the town into cityhood.

When Lake City acquired a post office in our key year of 1886, Springer sprang an appointment as its first postmaster. When the railroad came and a site was needed for a terminal and a new town, Springer sprang his 240-acre farm upon both the railroad company and the subdividers platting out the blocks of the new city (which shows on its various parts "Springer Addition," "Springer's Grove," "Springer Estate," and "Springer Block"). When the town was incorporated in 1898 as Lake City, he sprang upon it his candidacy for mayor and was elected its first mayor while getting himself reappointed perennially as postmaster. What wars of competition between Springer and Judge Craddock were settled in the wooden courthouse can only be imagined. One can assume that the town was big enough for both of them, or was in the process of becoming so as a result of their competitive efforts. When Craddock started his sawmill, Springer started one, too. But Springer was almost twenty years older than Craddock, and all that was left for Springer to spring upon the town, now that it had reached its optimum life, was an establishment to take care of its dying: he opened an undertaker's parlor.

Although Lake City Cemetery would be eschewed by Springer himself (as well as two of his wives, and his children), the customers of his funeral home are buried here. Plug points out the grave of B. J. Harrison, who, with Judge Craddock and Allen

Springer, makes up the triumvirate of the Lake City power establishment.

Befitting a tycoon, Benjamin J. Harrison (not named for his contemporary, the United States president from 1889 to 1893) was known simply as "B.J." to his associates, friends, and family. A year younger than Allen Springer, he fought on the opposite side in the Civil War, a sergeant with the Rebels; unlike Springer, whose three wives came from Indiana and Illinois, B.J. married a local girl in Craighead County and set up their postwar farmstead south of Lake City. In the Reconstruction years, beset by carpetbaggers, ex-Rebel B.J. organized a local chapter of the Ku Klux Klan, and when that organization was declared illegal and forced to disband, organized a kind of antijayhawker band of vigilantes who made life rough for the lawless bandits roaming the countryside. B.J. personally killed the ringleader of the gang and drove the rest of them into retirement, bringing a decade of peace to Lake City.

During the bustling 1880s, Harrison began a daily commute from his farm to his general store in Lake City, Harrison Mercantile Company, competition for Allen Springer's store at a time when Lake City's population was only seventy-five. One day a fur trapper visiting his store became drunk and disorderly; B.J. evicted him with force and humiliation; the trapper returned in the night and set fire to the store, ending the Harrison Mercantile Company. B.J. sold his southern spread and bought a new farm right on the eastern edge of the village, adjoining the cemetery ("That white house you see right up there," Plug points out, from the cruiser parked beside the cemetery, "that was B. J. Harrison's farm when he moved to town"). On this farm he started an orchard of twelve hundred trees, and, walking distance from downtown Lake City, began to operate a cotton gin in competition with Judge Craddock's, a gristmill without competition, and the Lake City Hotel.

Carefully he rebuilt his burned-out mercantile store and reopened for business, only to lose it again in the fire of 1904 that wiped out Oldtown and destroyed half of the new Lake City.

His son, George, married a beautiful but high-strung woman named Pearl. Plug points out her grave. "You want to hear about a murder?" Plug says to Kim. "Here's one."

"Who killed her?"

"It's the other way around, maybe," Plug says, and tells her the best of his many stories about crime in Lake City.

The summer of 1921, Pearl Harrison was the cook for the road gang of a construction company that had a contract to hard-surface the main road westward to Jonesboro (Plug makes quotation marks with his fingers around "hard-surface," explaining it meant simply covering the dust with crushed rock, creating what the locals called a "rock road" to distinguish it from a dirt road). As the work progressed farther out of town, a new camp was established at the crossroads for Webbs Mill, a sawmill station, and Pearl, who did not want to leave Lake City to move into the Webbs Mill camp (or whose husband, George Harrison, would not let her go), offered the job to a friend of hers, Alma Curry. One imagines both Pearl and Alma as camp cook counterparts of Stella Beavers of Buffalo City, the pretty cook for the railroad gang. Pearl's father-in-law, B.J., was quite wealthy, but his son, George, wasn't, not enough to keep his wife from working as a cook. Or perhaps she enjoyed the opportunities the job offered her to get out of the house and meet people, and to have a lot of men appreciate her cooking.

Alma Curry readily accepted Pearl's offer, but Alma was shackled with a twelve-year-old daughter, Verne, and decided the only way she could take the job at Webbs Mill would be to bring Verne with her; Verne could help peel potatoes and wash dishes. Meanwhile, the road gang at Webbs Mill was getting hungry, waiting for their new cook to show up and replace Pearl. They speculated whether the new cook would be as pretty as Pearl and as much fun to tease.

But the new cook never showed up. She was supposed to come by rail, and the road gang eagerly met each incoming passenger train, but Alma Curry wasn't on any of them. A week went by during which they cooked for themselves and complained.

One hot evening in July, two boys who had been squirrel hunting in the dense woods near Webbs Mill, south of the railroad tracks, came upon the rapidly decomposing bodies of a woman and a girl. The sheriff and the coroner found that both bodies had been severely beaten, the woman's head almost severed from her body, and the child's head completely cut off and thrown some fifteen feet away. A search collected only fragments of evidence: the bloody wooden club, broken in three, which had been the murder weapon, and a letter torn to shreds and scattered. The July heat had caused the bodies to rot so thoroughly that they were shoveled into makeshift coffins and buried on the spot.

The letter, pieced together, was from a man named Lovejoy, in Pine Bluff, who had written to ask Alma the whereabouts of her husband, Jim, and to offer him a job. Alma and Jim had been separated for a year. Jim Curry was arrested at Caraway, southwest of Lake City, by his landlord, Deputy Sheriff J. H. "Boogerman" Jenkins (who makes another story later), but Jenkins convinced detectives that Jim Curry had been in Caraway at the time of the murders.

The investigation turned to Pat Ryan, foreman of the road gang that Alma Curry was to cook for, and to Pearl Harrison, who had relinquished the job to her. Ryan had suddenly quit his job and was preparing to leave the country, which placed him under suspicion, and under arrest. Pearl Harrison . . . Well, it was a tangled web, leading to one Asberry Webb. Testimony at various meetings of a grand jury revealed that Webb had been "on intimate terms" with Alma Curry before the crime, and had been seen by a witness running out of the woods at Webbs Mill and boarding a train three days before the bodies were found. Subsequent evidence revealed that Asberry Webb had also been "on intimate terms" with Pearl Harrison, and that George Harrison had caught Asberry and Pearl together on the wagon bridge at Lake City and given Webb a terrible whipping.

The best explanation for a motive was that Webb and Pearl had believed that Alma was so jealous she had tipped off George Harrison as to their whereabouts.

But a grand jury meeting in August would not indict any of the suspects, and Pearl was released, along with Jim Curry, Asberry Webb, and Pat Ryan. When the governor of Arkansas offered a hundred-dollar reward for the solving of the case, a Memphis "psychic detective" went into a trance and diverted everyone's attention to a "yellow skinned negro" who was the lone black man within miles of the scene of the crime; the sheriff questioned, but could not find any evidence against, a black man who was found to fit the description. Later in August the county's habitual crook, a little man named Whitey Davis who had been arrested several times for pandering, operating a bawdy house, and petty larcenies, was taken into custody, inflated into the role of prime suspect, grilled at length, but managed to produce an airtight alibi.

Finally, and suddenly, Pearl Harrison was arrested again in September and formally charged as an "accessory before and after the fact of murder." New evidence had suggested that Pearl had met the train on which Alma and her daughter had arrived at Webbs Mill, had escorted them to the cookhouse at the camp, and was seen leading the two of them off into the woods.

Before she could be taken to Jonesboro to stand trial, Pearl Harrison swallowed an ounce of carbolic acid and died, leaving a note To Whom It May Concern: "God knows I am innocent of what they got me charged with and God is above all. I'll tell you again that I am innocent and had rather die than go out to Jonesboro."

The investigation appeared to end with her suicide and was never seriously reopened, although amateur sleuths, as well as Corporal Plug Eaton, are continuing it to this day. Popular sentiment refused to accept the possibility that Pearl Harrison herself could have bludgeoned and decapitated the two victims, and if she was in collusion with the man who did, she took the secret of his identity to her grave.

Plug has pointed out to Kim where she died, B. J. Harrison's large white two-story house at the end of Main Street near the river and the cemetery. A roomer in that house at the time was Will Nash, who had once been sheriff of all Craighead County and who was later to become sheriff again . . . and again. To newspaper reporters, he mentioned that as he was leaving his room shortly before the suicide, Pearl waved to him and said good-bye. "That was the first time in my life she had ever said good-bye to me and when I learned of her suicide I really understood the meaning of her parting farewell," said ex-Sheriff Nash.

Just why Sheriff Nash was rooming with the Harrisons instead of with his own mother, who took in boarders, is a mystery. One of Mrs. Nash's boarders at the time was Dr. Fred Roberts, age forty-six, a lifelong bachelor like his friend Judge Craddock, with whom he had bought and subdivided Springer's Grove. Doc Roberts, remember, had his office upstairs on Main Street, and he was an old friend of Pearl's; indeed, he had posted her thousand-dollar bond himself both times she was arrested. He was the first on the scene after she took the poison, and worked frantically to counteract the poison and revive her. Doc Roberts lived another decade before a stroke took him. His tombstone at Pine Log Cemetery bears the inscription "Office Upstairs."

Will Nash had a passionate distaste for spirituous beverages, which made him the man of the hour whenever Lake City's problems with liquor got out of hand. He was the son and brother of lawmen. His father, Samuel Nash, had been a pioneer native-born sheriff of Craighead County who later served as postmaster of Lake City when it was still called Sunk Lands by the Post Office Department; he died before the name was changed, in 1886, to Lake City, and his grave is one of the earliest of those that are sometimes flooded in the Lake City Cemetery. Samuel's wife, Virginia, was forced to take in boarders after his death, including Doc Roberts. The older son, Alanson (Lance) Nash, was to become town marshal of Lake City in the Gay Nineties, but not before the younger son, Will, became town marshal at the age of seventeen, when Lake City was only a small "sawmill town" with a saloon on every corner and a reputation for miles through the virgin timber as a "wild and woolly" town (shades of Cherokee City, but for a different reason: these hard-drinking Lake City men spent their weekdays in the woods felling timber and were thus lumberjack drinkers, not cowboy drinkers, who were a gentler breed of tippler).

Young Marshal Nash was so successful in handling the drinkers that he ran for, and was elected, chief deputy sheriff of the Eastern District in 1902, and then, in 1908, on a promise to "clean up the county" of its illegal liquor traffic (commonplace "moonshining" and bootlegging), was elected high sheriff of the whole county. The prosecuting attorney with whom he worked was Judge Craddock's crusading protégé, Thaddeus Caraway, later to become U.S. senator (and to be followed after death by his wife, Hattie Caraway, who became during the Depression the first woman elected in her own right to the United States Senate), and with his help Sheriff Nash kept good his promise for four years. Nash then went into retirement and watched during the Prohibition years as the liquor problem grew to enormous dimensions, stills were brewing in every backyard, and gambling interests were joining organized crime to manipulate the liquor industry. "Lake City was the capital of the moonshine trade," says Plug Eaton. Citizens called on Will Nash to come out of retirement; re-elected sheriff, he once again set about his countywide clean-up.

During the early years of the Depression, after his four-year term as sheriff ended, Will Nash was allowed to return to his farm for a while, but he was again called out of retirement to become a United States marshal throughout the years of World War II, when most younger men were in the service. His next "retirement" was equally short-lived: the wild postwar years saw a return of illegal liquor manufacturing and gambling, and once again, at the age of seventy-three, forty years after his first election to the office, Will Nash was elected sheriff of Craighead County, to serve notice upon all the county's malefactors and illegal operators that "Nash has returned." The mere mention of his name seemed sufficient to clean up the county this time, and he was permitted to serve out a quiet four-year term. The principal street on the south edge of town was named Nash Road.

Sheriff Nash died peacefully in bed. Two other sheriffs died with their boots on. Boogerman Jenkins, who had operated the hotel in Caraway where Jim Curry was arrested and provided the alibi that sprang Curry, later sought promotion and election from deputy to chief deputy. When Will Nash came out of retirement in 1928 to handle the Prohibition-inspired liquor problem, the Boogerman ran for the office of chief deputy of the Eastern District, where throughout Prohibition he had fought the moonshiners who had nicknamed him. He had accepted, even welcomed his nickname, and used it in his campaign literature: "If you want the law enforced in this fair land, cast your vote for the Boogerman." This was bad rhyme but clever politics: he defeated nine other candidates for the job.

But shortly before he was to be sworn in as chief, the Boogerman went out one morning on a routine errand to collect some taxes; a mail carrier found his body beside his car on a county road. He had been shot twice, once in the back and once in the chest. Other deputies arrested two youths and a boy who had been operating a moonshine still. The younger, Rayford Ransome, age fifteen, was charged with actually firing the shots that killed the Boogerman, but while free on bail was hit by a train. He spent six months in a hospital, and his trial was delayed for two years. The boy did not deny the shooting, but claimed that he did not know the Boogerman was a deputy sheriff, and that he had fired in self-defense. Because the jury was deadlocked six to six, the judge declared a mistrial. Ransome had to be brought to trial a second time before a jury would convict him of murder in the second degree. He was given twenty-one years.

Plug explains to Kim that murder in the second degree is without premeditation, not planned, a spur-of-the moment thing. The boy Rayford Ransome was carrying a weapon because most moonshiners were armed.

Liquor was also involved in the shooting of Chief Deputy George Spencer, though this was after the Prohibition years had ended. There are other points of comparison between the killings of Chiefs Jenkins and Spencer: both were shot twice, Spencer in the arm and in the chest; both were shot in the country outside of Lake City, Spencer in the "suburb" of Lunsford, south of town; both assailants claimed in court that they had shot in self-defense; both were convicted not of murder in the first but in the second degree; and both were sentenced to twenty-one years in the Arkansas State Penitentiary. But the young Rayford Ransome, unless he had been sampling his own moonshine, was sober when he shot the Boogerman; Alf Wood was drunk when he shot George Spencer.

Chief Spencer had gone to Croppy Bryant's beer joint, south of Lake City, on a report of a disturbance by the intoxicated Alf Wood, but just as he entered the door of the establishment Wood shot him. At his trial Wood claimed that he had mistaken the chief for a man who had threatened to kill him that same day, had been expecting the arrival of the other man, had become drunk in expectation of it, and had responded wildly when someone in Croppy's yelled, "There he is!"

In recent years, continuing his own investigation of all these crimes, Plug Eaton has interviewed a brother of Alf Wood. Alf died in the early sixties, after serving only seven years of his sentence. The brother presented a more complicated story, involving another man's passion for Alf Wood's pretty wife, a rape committed by Croppy Bryant's son, an investigation of the rape by Bill Clements, constable of Lake City Township, and a frame-up in which the drunken Alf Wood had been expected to shoot and kill Bill Clements but had shot Chief Spencer instead, by mistake.

Constable Clements, to whom all these links lead—not just Spencer and Wood but several lawmen in Lake City—was a classic example of a man on both sides of the law: keeping and preserving it for years, then violating it. And his is the saddest of these stories. He was born across the river, in the wilderness of Cane Island, of an old family who had settled the area right after the Civil War as refugees from the more strife-torn killing grounds; all his life Bill Clements would have a special affection for the river people, the dispossessed squatters and vagrants who wrested a living from the fish and game of the swamps. Growing up on Clements Donnick, a peninsula of cleared canebrake jutting out into the "lake" of the St. Francis just north of Lake City, he watched the town grow. From childhood he had aspirations, like Plug Eaton, of becoming a law officer, not for the state police, which did not exist then, but for the township of Lake City. He became constable of the village during the worst years of the Depression, when Lake City and his home ground across the river were filling up with migrants, failed farmers, the shiftless, the same scared wanderers his ancestors had been when they came to Cane Island.

Many people died, starved, or were killed during those Depression years, and Constable Clements was required to investigate along with, or in place of, the county coroner, the sheriff's deputies, and the health officer (or at least whatever temporary undisillusioned physician had replaced Doc Roberts, who ascended to his Office Upstairs at the outset of the Depression). One of the people Constable Clements went out of his way to help was a homeless pregnant woman named Nellie Hart who had come from God only knows where in search of shelter and a place to birth her child. Bill Clements gave her a bed in his own modest cottage on Clements Donnick (his wife, whose name was also Nellie, had left him, taking their three children to California), fed her from his table—or, rather, supplied the food with which she prepared a table for the two of them—and assisted in the birth of the baby, a girl, who was named Doris Jean, a good common country name.

"Let's drive out to Cane Island," Plug suggests to Kim, and heads the cruiser toward the bridge. En route he points out ("I guess you could call it crime, too, in a way") the house where lived the poor mother of the Reverend Jim Jones, whose 911 disciples killed themselves with lethal Kool-Aid at Jonestown in Guyana; Jonesboro was named for an ancestor.

They approach the long bridge, which has a shorter span of steel that is meant to lift ("That was built to let the steamboats pass under, but it never has been raised"); the bridge does not arch gracefully but shoots straight as an arrow for a mile out into the marshland of Cane Island. It is a two-lane state-highway bridge, built in 1934, just after Doris Jean Hart was born, not quite soon enough to replace the rickety wooden one-lane bridge that had extended that mile out across the "lake." The same year the new bridge was opened, Lake City had put together its first Chamber of Commerce, and the Chamber celebrated both its birth and the completion of the bridge with a big ceremony, a three-day affair, including live music and dancing and a beauty pageant, a contest to choose a Bridge Queen who would christen the new span.

"This was before I was born, of course," Plug relates, "but I've got newspaper accounts of the festivities. They elected this girl, a Jonesboro High graduate named Ida Frances Metz, as 'Miss Bridge,' and all these girls paraded in their formals and all, and they gave the Bridge Queen a bottle of beer to do the christening with. Oh, we never had heard of champagne in Lake City then, and during the Depression we couldn't have bought any if we had it. So Miss Ida Frances Metz takes this bottle of beer and says, 'I christen thee, the St. Francis River Bridge,' and smashes the bottle over the cement banister there." Plug chuckles. "In my researches, I thought how entertaining it would be to locate Miss Ida Frances Metz and talk to her. I didn't even know if she was alive or what, but just the other day I opened the paper and there was a picture of the fiftieth reunion of her high-school class, and who should be in it but Miss Ida Frances Metz, from California. I couldn't find her, though, but I tried."

The present mile-long span of cement is just a few yards upstream from the location of the old railroad bridge, of which no trace remains, and from the old wooden bridge, long ago carried away by floods. The present bridge not only serves to join Cane Island (which is not actually an island, any more than the river is a lake) to the "mainland" but is also the only link between northeastern Arkansas's two largest cities, Jonesboro and Blytheville. As they come to the end of the long straight stretch of cement, and Plug turns off onto a dirt road, he explains,

"Now, this is Cane Island. There's a little church, Bethabara, and that's the real name of the place, but nobody calls it that: it's just Cane Island. Here's the cemetery."

In Cane Island Cemetery, a grassless expanse of poor dirt without even a trace of wakefield crud, Kim is shown the headstones of a few of the early settlers, and then she is not taken to, but allowed to find on her own, the grave of baby Doris Jean Hart. It stands out: upon it someone (her mother? Bill Clements?) placed the iron bedstead of the crib in which she lived her short life. The sun is out again; whatever tornado had been watched for is off scaring people miles away; in the bright sunlight stands the iron crib, painted white and then repainted by recent, unknown hands. Someone long ago, carefully but clumsily, handlettered a wooden sign and hung it over the head of the frame: DORIS JEAN HART 1934 1935. In more recent times, someone (there are no Harts on the Island, or anyone remotely related) has placed a small, carved, compote chiseled headstone with the same letters and numbers at the head of the bedstead. There are no other bed frames serving as grave markers anywhere else in the cemetery; in all her travels through the cemeteries of the lost cities of Arkansas, Kim has never seen, nor will ever see, a child's bed used to fence a grave. She turns aside so that Plug will not see the single tear running down her cheek, and she wipes it away. Plug says, "You know, I've talked to people who've lived their whole lives here on Cane Island, one of them eighty, and no one remembers anybody named Hart. I've spent a lot of time trying to find out about her or her mother, and no one even knows where they came from, who they were, and where they've gone to." He pauses and looks around at the other modest headstones. "But it's a free cemetery," Plug observes. "Anyone who wants to can bury here or be buried here. Bill Clements wanted to. That's his grave right over there."

After the death of Doris Jean Hart, her mother, Nellie, wandered on, as aimlessly as she had drifted into Bill Clements's life, and the constable turned his attention to another woman, who perhaps reminded him of his lost Hart, for she was also twenty years younger than he, and went by the name of—get this—

Nellie McClish, his third Nellie. "How do you spell that last name?" Kim asks and wants this carefully preserved on her tape recorder. It could be McLish or some other variant of the ancient venerable Scottish name MacLeish, as in the grand poet Archibald; but Plug spells it M-c-C-l-i-s-h. Once again, as with William Hogan of Buffalo City, Kim wonders about her own links to these people: the man who took Kim as a child bride of sixteen was a McClish, from eastern Arkansas; she will always wonder, but will never know, if Nellie McClish might have been an aunt or at least a cousin of his. Constable Bill Clements had two children by Nellie McClish and at her urging gave up the hazardous business of law enforcement, retiring to his beloved river to build a houseboat.

The houseboat may not be the same one shown in our picture beside the bridge. If not, it was identical to it, in architecture identical to dozens of houseboats on the St. Francis: the simplest of vernaculars, with a gable on a rectangle, painted white and floated upon oil drums or great logs or whatever will float. This was the home Clements provided for Nellie McClish and their two kids for six or seven years, throughout the duration of World War II, until the day Nellie had had all she could stand of the river, or of the fish that Bill caught and she had to clean for the market, endless schools of catfish and buffalo fish. As one more winter approached, they fought, and she took the kids and left him.

He brooded until Christmas, thinking of a Christmas morning without the usual delight he took in being Santa Claus for the kids. He drank some whiskey to help him endure the morning, but instead of soothing his sorrow it raised his anger against Nellie for her desertion of him. The last he had seen of her was when she got on the little bus that took Cane Islanders across the bridge into Lake City, and she seemed to have been flirting with the bus driver, who was a man she knew, and a man whom the former constable knew too well. On that Christmas morning Bill Clements got out his old service revolver, a little .32 owlhead, and polished it; he could find only five of its six bullets.

He went into Lake City to the home of Nellie's brother, Clyde

McClish, with whom she was staying. Nellie was out in the back yard plucking a chicken for Christmas dinner. He told Nellie he wanted the children. She said no. He asked Nellie about the bus driver. She would not talk about the bus driver. He hit her with the butt of the owlhead, in the face. She dropped the chicken she was cleaning and began to cry. He shot at her three times, two bullets going wild, one hitting her in the temple, killing her. He had two bullets left, one for each of the two children. But it was Christmas; you can't shoot a kid on Christmas. So he poked the snub barrel into his own ribs and squeezed the trigger. The bullet disappeared somewhere into his innards but didn't hurt too much. He took more careful aim at his heart and fired again; this time the bullet, the final one, almost got him, but still left him standing. He took out his pocketknife and attempted to finish the job by cutting his own throat.

Blood was everywhere when the sheriff's deputy arrived and exclaimed, "My God, Bill, who has done this to you?" "I did," Bill said. He survived somehow, and, recovering after months in the hospital, came to trial almost a year later, after the obligatory month-long examination at the Arkansas State Mental Hospital, where he was declared sane. He was found guilty of first-degree murder, because the crime had been premeditated at least for a day ("Good example of premeditation," Plug explains to Kim: "The day before the murder he went to the funeral home and inquired if their burial insurance had been paid up, and was told that it would expire in fifteen days. The man at the funeral home asked him if he wanted to renew it after the fifteen days was up, but Clements said, 'No, that'll be plenty of time.' That sealed his fate.")

He was sentenced to life in prison, and served twenty-one years of that sentence (the same number of years as the killers of the Boogerman and Chief Spencer) until, at the age of seventy-four, he was released. Then he returned to the river, found his houseboat gone or stolen or confused with several others, and spent the last few years of his life as a hermit in a shack on Clements Donnick. "Up that way," Plug points out, is the donnick, where the shack stood. Nobody lives around there now. What's a "donnick"? It is one of those words in common usage among local citizens; Plug has heard it all his life to mean a kind of little peninsula created by the meandering of the river.

Leaving Cane Island, Plug asks, "Well, is that enough crime for you?"

Kim nods. It is, indeed, more crime than she will hear of in all the other lost cities put together. But where else has she made, or will she make, friends with a lawman who is a historian?

Back across the bridge, Kim points out the houseboat anchored on the river, the one with the signs painted "NOW OPEN" (although it appears to be closed) and, on the door, "OPEN COMIN," and, on its roof, "LIVE CATFISH." She asks if that might be Clements's boat. It could have been. "See that old man there?" Plug points out a white-haired man in rubber waders strolling along the riverbank. "That's Cotton Taft."

"Oh, I've heard of him!" Kim exclaims. "Mayor Qualls told me a little about him."

"I doubt if he'd talk to you," Plug says. "If you just walked up there and started quizzin Cotton, he'd tell you the biggest yarns you'd ever heard in your life and there wouldn't be one ounce of truth in any of 'em. But he's the last of a dyin breed, one of the old trappers and fishermen, and he lives right there on that *other* houseboat—calls it his 'mansion'—been here all his life and is just an ole recluse."

Everybody in Lake City knows Plug Eaton, and everyone is his friend . . . except Cotton Taft. Plug will make no effort to introduce Kim to Cotton.

"He won't talk to me?" Kim asks.

"Especially not to a stranger. He might say a few words to you, but if he thinks you're trying to pump him he'll tell you a yarn that won't ever quit!"

In her notebook Kim has the name of a man Mayor Qualls has mentioned, Cotton Williams, who might introduce her to Cotton Taft.

"No wife?" she asks Plug.

"Aw, yeah, I've got a wife and two kids," he says. "Two beautiful, healthy, wonderful children."

"I meant Cotton Taft—is that his real name, 'Cotton'?"

"Just his nickname. Elvis is his real name. Yeah, he was married once. Wife left him."

"Like Bill Clements?"

"Sort of like that. He and Bill were good buddies."

Because she has decided to spend the night in Jonesboro (there are no lodgings to be had in Lake City), Kim decides to retrieve Zephyra from the Riverfront's lot and follow Plug's cruiser the twenty miles out to Pine Log Cemetery. It is fun tailing a police car, but there is hardly anyone en route to see them—a flat, broad cotton country that once contained individual family "forties" of cotton land but now is mostly abandoned houses.

At Pine Log they park their cars, and Plug shows her the graves of Allen Springer, "the grandfather of Lake City," and other notables who had chosen this high ground west of town to be their final resting place, including the tombstone of Doc Roberts with its letters, "Office Upstairs."

Kim decides that this cemetery would be a good place to ask Plug the questions about his own aspirations, dreams, and reflections upon mortality. She begins, "What would you like to see written on *your* tombstone, Plug?"

He answers immediately, as if he has given it some thought before: " 'An honest man who did his best to bring a little happiness to his fellow man.' "

"And woman," she says. "You've certainly brought me happiness, to give me so much of your time today," she tells him, and thanks him for the long tour. Then she asks, "Did you ever have any hopes or dreams that never came true?"

He reflects only a moment before answering, "No, because I've got the job right now I've always wanted. I'm very happy doing police work, and I think I do a halfway creditable job. I don't get too many complaints. I've got a good home, much better than I ever dreamed about having." He pauses and glances around him at the tombstones in this third and last of the cemeteries he has shown to her, and adds with sincerity, "I'm on a first-name basis with Jesus Christ, and I know where I'm going when I get through down here." He gets into his cruiser and starts the motor. "So, really, what more can any reasonable man ask?"

A week later, Kim will read in the newspaper an account of a school-bus accident south of Jonesboro. Loaded with teachers and students on their way to Little Rock early in the morning for a convention, the bus will miss a curve, crash, and kill nine and injure thirty. It will be the unpleasant job of State Police Corporal Hershel Eaton to meet parents and friends at the hospital and tell them who has died, who has survived.

The next morning, in contrast to the stormy day before, is bright and sunny, with fluffy white clouds hanging in the blue. Kim will remember this for a long time as her "Cotton Day": her last day in this cotton city, beneath a canopy of cotton clouds, on a riverbank levee with cottonwood trees (the river doubtless inhabited by cottonmouth moccasin snakes), the grass sprinkled with the cottony seed-fluffs of dandelions, and she, wearing all-cotton things, talking to two men dressed all in cotton, *both* of them nicknamed "Cotton."

First Kim goes to the Senior Citizens' Center to meet Floyd "Cotton" Williams, age eighty-four, who is not so much an inmate or a patron of the center as he is its caretaker and general factotum. Most of the patrons under his supervision are not so old as he is. Despite his age, he is vigorous and healthy ("I didn't realize you *work* here!" Kim says to him). He has lived in Lake City all of his life, except for three or four months when he went out to California but couldn't wait to get back to this place: his "folks has always been here . . . lived here, died here, buried here."

It's just a coincidence, he says, that he and his old pal Cotton Taft have the same nickname. "When I was a kid I was just as white-headed as I could be," Williams tells Kim. Cotton Taft got his nickname because he could whop a baseball out into the cotton patch. Unlike Taft, Williams is not a bachelor, but has been married for fifty-six years: he and Edna live right up there beside the Lake City Cemetery. Cotton's daddy brought a three-room cabin boat to Lake City and was a commercial fisherman all his life but also operated a kind of resort on the St. Francis—swimming, boating, bathing, and fishing—which he managed until 1925, when Lake City's "resort" days faded away. Cotton Williams lived through all of the floods of this century and could tell Kim about each of them.

Yes, he knew Bill Clements, very well, used to work on the river with him day in and day out, hunting and trapping with him.

And, yes, he knew Pearl Harrison and can recall the details of her supposed crime and her suicide.

Yes, he remembers Sheriff Nash and can see him walking tall as if it were just yesterday. Best of all, he remembers Sheriff George Spencer, who was "a very close friend of mine. We grew up together. I know exactly what happened when he was shot down by that Alf Wood."

Cotton Williams will be glad to take Kim (in his own car, which he still drives without any problem) to the river to meet Cotton Taft, but first he has to feed lunch to the senior citizens and then close up the office for the afternoon. While Kim waits, she prepares the questions she'll ask.

The two Cottons, who haven't seen each other recently, greet each other like the old friends they are, old rivermen, and Cotton Taft scarcely notices the young lady who's with Cotton Williams and holding a tape recorder in her lap as they sit on the bank of the levee, steps away from Taft's houseboat, beneath cottonwoods and cotton clouds. The two men begin talking about some subject as if they had just left it, a subject not too familiar to Kim, who keeps her mouth shut and her recorder silently running.

"... never took a drink from that still on the donnick," Cotton Williams says.

"... know you didn't, Cotton, nor me, neither," Cotton Taft says. He seems only vaguely aware of Kim; when he gives her one glance, his eyes stun her with their blueness, as if a whole life spent out under the open sky had absorbed the bright color of the air and sky. "Who's this?" he says finally to Cotton Williams.

"Just a little ole girl," Cotton Williams says. "Might want to ask you a simple question or two."

"You aint a reporter?" Cotton Taft says to her.

"No," she says, timidly but truthfully, "I'm not."

"There was a lady reporter here just this mornin," he says. "Or maybe it was yesterday mornin; I get so many of 'em, I caint tell 'em apart."

"Why are you so popular with reporters?" she asks.

Cotton Taft laughs. "I guess I'm an old goat! I'm a real character, caint you tell?"

"In other words," puts in Cotton Williams, "it's because you and me saw Lake City develop from when it wasn't nothin."

"And back to nothin," Cotton Taft says. He stares around him defiantly, as if challenging the dead town to rise up again.

The two men talk of the old days, their memories of the coming of the first Model T Ford, the days when cows and goats roamed the dirt streets, which were edged with wooden sidewalks. They talk of their first boyhood jobs for *real* money": killing frogs at night for a dollar a dozen. They talk of the war—not Number I but Number II, when meat was rationed and people had to have stamps to buy it, so they ate fish instead, and Cotton Taft had a fish market that was running night and day. That river right now, Cotton Taft observes, wouldn't hold all the fish he had taken out of it during his life. He used to catch three or four hundred pounds a day.

"How's your fish business these days?" Kim asks. Immediately she wonders if it's a bad question; there seems to be no business of any sort along the riverbank. But Cotton Taft answers quickly:

"It's good! If I could only catch 'em. Right now I'm havin the biggest trouble catchin fish as I've ever had!" Both Cottons grumble about the condition of the river: several drought years have hurt and lowered it, and those folks up in Missouri who control the Mappapello Dam won't open the gates and let old St. Francis come the many miles down into Arkansas. There is also suspicion that the state never restocks the St. Francis, since the river is used for commercial fishing more than sport fishing.

Worst of all, the fish have been poisoned by insecticides running off from the cropland.

Both Cottons look at the sky. "We need a rain right now," Taft says. "Just an eench. Not one of them floods, but about an eench, for the gardens and flowers. . . ."

The two men talk of drought years past, of flood years past, of storms, tornadoes, of the best ways to predict the weather. Kim enjoys just listening to them. She realizes something: of the lost cities she has been to (or will go to), this is the only one in which she has not sat indoors, in somebody's compote living room. She likes being out here on the riverbank.

After a lull in the conversation, Kim asks Cotton Taft, "Did you know Constable Bill Clements?" The two Cottons exchange glances, and Taft does not reply. "Was he a friend?" Kim asks.

"Yeah, yeah," Cotton Taft says impatiently, "but he'd kick you right in the butt. Pardon me, lady." He ruminates and grinds his teeth. "I didn't trust ole Bill. See, we used tackle to catch fish and traps to catch coons, but Bill, he'd take *any* of it! He was a booger-cat." Taft points upstream. "Lived on the donnick over there, last years of his life. Because of the things he done, you know, and other people, I'd think he was pretty lonely them last years." As if to divert his friend from thoughts of *that* tragedy, Cotton Williams begins reminiscing about worse things that happened: a friend of theirs who got literally scalped, and other killings they knew in the rough days of the town, including a liquor-syndicate war in which nine moonshiners were killed.

"Why was there so much violence in Lake City?" Kim asks.

"Well," says Cotton Williams, "this used to be a timber town. Come payday, they'd all get drunk, and cut up, and—"

"—and whore around!" Taft adds. "Pardon me, lady, but there was *two* whorehouses up there, one of 'em over the hamburger joint. You'd get you a hot dog or a hamburger and pay the man fifty cents and then you could go upstairs, where all the girls were. I don't know where all the girls come from. I never went to none of them places."

"Were you married?" Kim asks.

"Yeah," Cotton Taft says, and begins to tell the story as if he's rehearsed it through frequent repetition. Like Bill Clements, he had a wife and two kids, whom he raised right there in a houseboat on the river. Not that he ever felt like shooting them, but, like Bill's Nellie (the third one), Cotton's May up and left him, "flew the coop." "We was makin so much money here in the fish business we didn't know what to do with it, so one day she just grabbed her an armload of money and left. By herself. Me with the two kids. I raised 'em. She was on her way out to Californy, stopped in Las Vegas, lost all her money, got beat up, but stayed twenty-five or thirty years, then she come back home. . . . She didn't come home for *me*, she just wanted a place to stay, and I was dumb enough to give it to her. I hardly knew her. She'd weighed about a hundred forty when she left, a real pretty gal, and come back weighin about ninety and looked *awful*, looked like she was ninety years old and had been in the dope." Taft shakes his head sadly. "Oh, I paid her hospital bill for a while, but I wanted out, so I got me this lawyer and he told me what to do. I went down and talked to my wife and she said she'd give me a divorce for a thousand dollars. 'You got it, kid,' I said to her." Taft pauses, squints at the river, spits, and adds, "But I tell ye right now, you don't know how sick you can get lookin at someone you thought so much of, and was so pretty, and then see her when she's been thrown down the hole. All I could do, lady, was put her on the plane and send her back."

Suddenly Kim realizes that the desertion of a town is like the desertion of a spouse: you never know what will happen while you're gone. "Do you ever go down to where the old abandoned buildings are, where there used to be a drugstore beside an alley and—"

He shakes his head. "It's lonesome down there, lady."

"Why does it bother you?" she asks, wondering if it isn't much lonesomer here on the riverbank, except when the reporters come.

"Well, I used to go down there and everybody in the world was there. Why, I remember when you could hardly walk, there were so many people, and there were *five* cafés and you'd have to git you a plate of grub and eat standin up because there were so many people. *Now* . . ." He shakes his head. "You go down there now, you can holler and there aint nobody to hear ye."

"Do you ever see your children?"

"My boy was just here yesterday. Drives a truck. Fifty years old, bald-headed and fat. I understand my girl's in California; aint seen her in ten or fifteen years, but I understand she's big and fat, too. She married off and just got to eatin! I like to remember her the way she was: just a little blond-headed girl, like you."

And these two old men like to remember the town the way it was, and go on talking about it, recalling the glories of its past and the good times they used to have.

Cotton Williams cracks, "But the next fifty years will be easier for both of us!" Both men chuckle over that.

"I hope so!" Cotton Taft says. "But, Cotton, we've had it. We've had fun. Doggone it, I tell you right now . . ."

"We've had a rich life."

"Yes, we have. Cotton, right there when we run that river together, we had fun. . . ."

"Oh, yeah, we had fun."

Lake City was incorporated as a city in 1898. Elvis "Cotton" Taft may (or may not) have been born the same year, or the next, or, as he has told Kim, with this century. Perhaps he himself doesn't really know. "No, he doesn't really know," Cotton Williams tells Kim, driving her back to her car. "He thinks he's three or four years older than me, but the truth is, I'm three or four years older than him."

"I wonder how a person loses track of how old he is," Kim remarks, just making conversation.

"Oh, there's a million and a million that don't know their age."

"He's got the bluest eyes I've ever seen," she says.

"Yeah, he has. Cotton was a real nice-lookin young man, too."

"Do you remember when his wife left?"

"Oh, sure. I knew him before they was married, even."

"Seems he had some good memories of her."

"That's right," says Cotton Williams, who still has his wife of fifty-six years. "We still have some good memories of her."

Mound City,
Arkansas

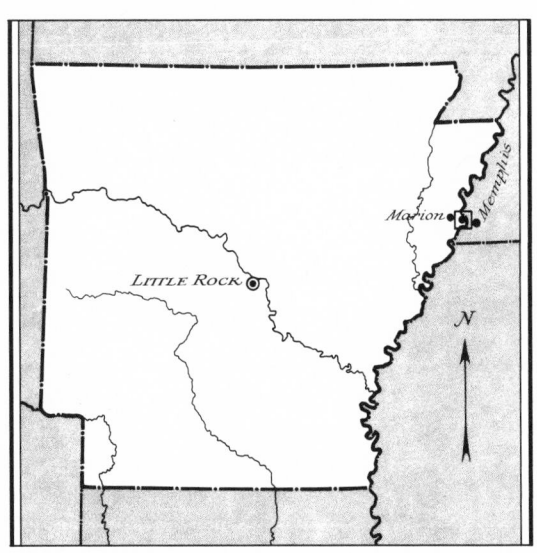

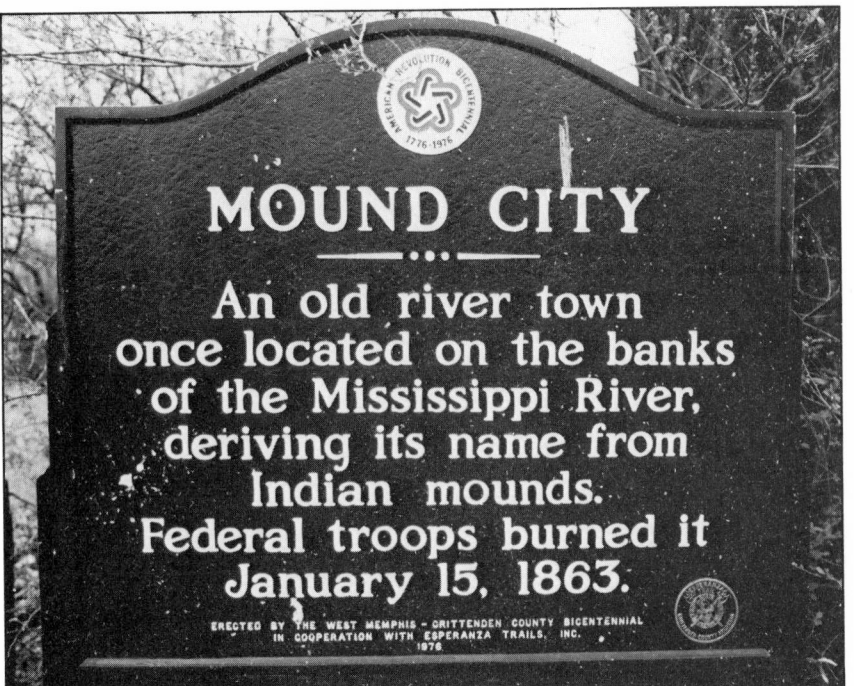

AMERICAN REVOLUTION BICENTENNIAL
1776-1976
MOUND CITY
An old river town
once located on the banks
of the Mississippi River,
deriving its name from
Indian mounds.
Federal troops burned it
January 15, 1863.
ERECTED BY THE WEST MEMPHIS - CRITTENDEN COUNTY BICENTENNIAL
IN COOPERATION WITH ESPERANZA TRAILS, INC.
1976

2nd St. JOHN MB Church
Sunday School 10 AM
Morning Worship 11 AM
Evening Worship 230

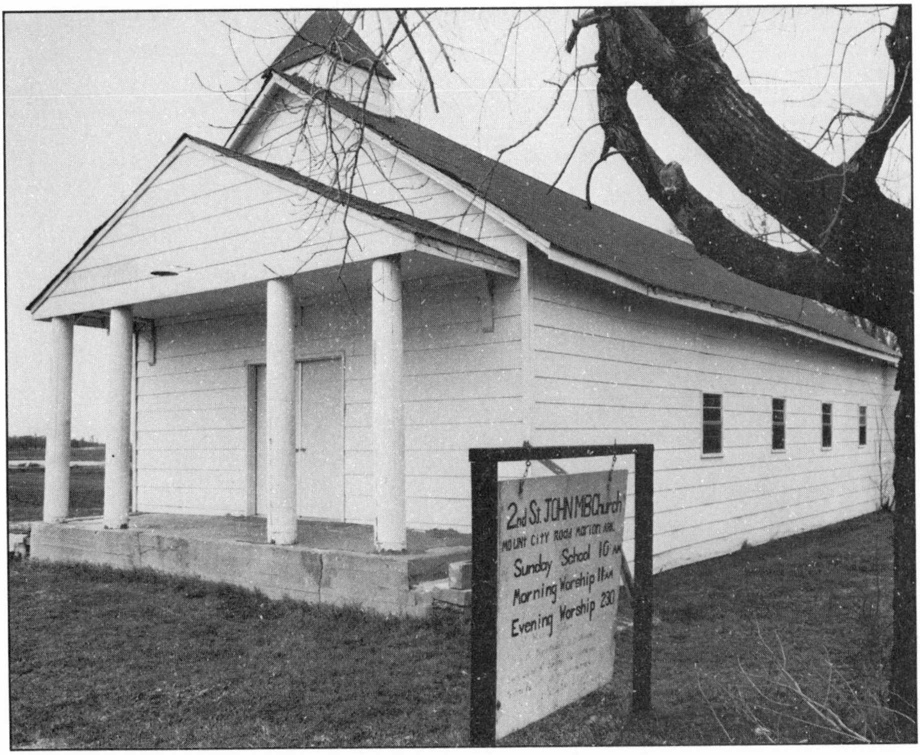

Mound City is nothing more than the barest resemblance of what it used to be.
—*Goodspeed,* Biographical and Historical
Memoirs of Eastern Arkansas, *1890*

No ONE KNOWS WHERE de Soto crossed the Mississippi River into Arkansas. Five different landings have been conjectured as his *entrada*, the northernmost being the future site of Mound City, which was already a village with mounds even then, even then deserted, or temporarily abandoned in fear of the armored Spaniards and their sophisticated weaponry. Perhaps the name in the language of those inhabitants ("Aquixo," as spelled by the Spanish) meant "mound-wanting-to-be-city."

It would have been the only eminence and clearing in all that marshy woodland, and if de Soto espied it rising across the great awesome roil of muddy water, he would have deliberately chosen the mound as security against a possible flood, in that late springtime of 1541.

Those same sunbrowned natives who called their city Aquixo called their stream a name derived from Algonquin that sounded like "Mizzissibizzibbippi," the very utterance of which was meant to convey its feeling: Old Big Deep Strong Turbulent Muddy Winding Grandfather of Waters. Not simply Father of Waters, as it is so often mistranslated, but *grand*father, ancient and venerable. These "Indians," like so many others, worshipped the sun when it was rising in the east, and all they could see to the east of themselves, besides the morning sun, was the Big Muddy Grandfather. Their own grandfathers had first heaped up a pile of dirt on the bank of the river to protect the interred bodies of their grandfathers from being washed away in the floods, just as their dark-skinned counterparts were doing alongside another flooding river, the Nile, with a more durable sort of mound-building, brick mastabas and blocks of stone pyramided into great mounds. The original Mound City is the necropolis at Saqqara—the cemetery for, coincidentally, the archaic Egyptian capital of Memphis. Just across the river from Mound City, Arkansas, is another Memphis, named after the first.

A digression on language ties it all together; Memphis, in Egypt, was named after its founder, Men, the Greek "Menes," related in the dark mother-mewlings of etymology to the Latin *manus*, for "hand," which gives us not only the multitude of "handiwork" words—"manipulate," "manage," "manufacture," "maneuver," "manure," "manuscript," "legerdemain," etc.—but also any concept involving extension of the hand—"command," "demand," "mandate"—or a failure of the hand—*manqué*, as in cities frustrated or unfulfilled (not to speak of Peter Mankins again)—and finally the Old English (as well as Dutch and Old Norse) word for both "hand" and the protecting hand, or protection, as from floods: *mund*, which is the origin of our word "mound," as in Mound City.

"Mound" and "mountain" are not to be confused: the latter comes from a related root meaning "projection." A mountain projects; a mound protects. It is nearly as simple as that. The mounds at Mound City were piled up to protect man primarily from the river and secondarily from fellow men, from the coming of bellicose de Soto and his starving, once-proud knights, who had sold all their possessions in Spain to finance this expedition, and whose numbers had been decimated from the six hundred who had landed in Florida two years before. The mound protects both the living man and the dead man: somewhere deep beneath the dirt lies entirely decomposed the grandfather who established the city and decreed the heaping up of the dirt above him. Somewhere on top of the pile once stood a temple of sorts, and more recently stood animal and human refugees from the flooding of the Grandfather of Waters. We can only conjecture the flexed position of the corpse and the log-and-mud architecture of the temple; we have photographs of the men and chickens and cows and squirrels held suspended barely above the deluge.

That torrent and tide, commencing two thousand miles away in the lake country of Minnesota, in a river named after the same Schoolcraft who explored early Arkansas, has been captured in the art of the people who were creating it long before de Soto came. Etched or stamped or painted onto the sides of their ceramic ware are abstract representations of the behavior of the Grandfather, his endless, fickle meandering, his sudden dance into whirlpools, his spinning around within the vortex, his bending and doubling and occasional rising into the hallucination of a familiar creature—bear, opossum, frog, squirrel, duck, rabbit, raccoon—around and about the contours of a vessel shaped by protecting hands from a mound of river clay into a bubble magically endowed with permanency, unless it be shattered into shards. The hands that mound the clay caress it with ritual motions symbolic of the Grandfather's slow, inexorable cruising, which turns and counterturns down and down the center of the continent. The result of this artisanry, dismissed as a bunch of pots by schoolchildren taken to the museums, is a more durable tribute to the Mississippi than anything from the hand of Sam Clemens. In a universal language of spirals and swastikate symbols used in Austria four thousand years before Christ, in neolithic China three thousand years before Christ, and in Ireland two thousand years before Christ, to mention only three examples of the widespread diffusion, artists have tried to convey these same feelings about water, its elusive illusion—the theme and function of art: to seize the fickle.

The fickle Grandfather two thousand years after Christ has writhed eastward yet again, to leave Mound City no longer on its very banks but stranded miles to the west of its course. The Mississippi's continuing hilarious mockery, a running joke, is to change the whole eastern boundary of Arkansas constantly: thousands of acres of Arkansas soil lie on the eastern shores of the river in what ought to be Tennessee and Mississippi, while thousands of acres of Tennessee and Mississippi lie on the western shore in what ought to be Arkansas. (All those fluid, sibilant *s*'s are in the names of all three states. Walt Whitman said of the Mississippi that "the word winds with chutes," but he might not have noticed that "Arkansas" and "Tennessee" each have at least two of those chutes, too; in fact, of the ten states along the river's route, all but Iowa and Kentucky have an *s* in their name.)

Would Mound City have become a city if the Grandfather had not abandoned it? From its earliest aspirations to cityhood, it was in competition with the place across the river called Memphis, which had the rock masses of the Chickasaw Bluffs to protect it against the fickle shiftings of the course of the current of the stream. Mound and Memphis were sister belles primping up for the steamboat's attention in the 1830s. If Hernando de Soto first saw the river from the heights that are now a park named after him in Memphis, he stood then in wilderness and beheld a "civilized" destination on the other side. If the fort built by the French on the eastern bank (and taken subsequently by Spain and then by Great Britain) passed into the possession of the United States in 1797, that same year the Spanish built a new fort on the Arkansas side of the river and called it Esperanza, for aspiration or hope or ambition or whatever you call the swelling in the heart created by any new enterprise. If "the Gentleman of Elvas" who accompanied de Soto became his bard and persuaded him to cross over the river, and then recorded his destiny and doom in Arkansas, another Gentleman named Elvis would make Memphis famous in our own time.

With wry hyperbole William Faulkner wrote of his native state, "Mississippi begins in the lobby of a Memphis, Tennessee hotel and extends south to the Gulf of Mexico." With less exaggeration we might say: Arkansas begins at a mound in the mud in the shadow of Memphis and extends west to the Great Plains. The Arkansawyer would never have tracked that mud into the lobby of the Peabody; he would have tracked it west into the lobbies of Little Rock. The building of a major road through the swamp and wilderness, from Memphis to Little Rock but starting at Mound City, was the state's first highway project, in 1832, and the cutting and laying of that road, called "the Old Military Road" because soldiers helped build it and soldiers used it to conduct Indians on their "removal" to concentration lands in the territories of Arkansas and what would become Oklahoma, was largely responsible for opening up Arkansas to statehood four years later, besides making possible the whole nation's movement to and settlement of Texas and the Wide West.

What's left of that road, over which thousands of Indians were marched to their unwanted new homes, and tens of thousands of settlers poured into Arkansas to stay or to stop on the way to Texas, appears on the right side of our photograph of Mound City's "Main Street," where there is nothing except a long, false-fronted store building deserted, and a historical marker. It is still a dirt road.

Of all our lost cities, Mound City, which was never platted into streets and avenues, is the only one designated by the United States Department of the Interior's Geographical Names Information System (GNIS) as not a populated place but a mere "*locale*—place at which there is or was human activity; it does not include populated places, and includes such sites as a landing, crossroad, ruins, ghost town." According to the GNIS, two other states, Texas and Utah, have a "locale" named Mound City. There is a populous county seat in Kansas named Mound City. Another county seat in North Dakota is called Mound City, and still another Mound City is located in Missouri. The state of Mississippi itself is confused by having not one but *two* populated places named Mound City.

Then there is Mound City, Illinois. This is *the* Mound City, which gave its name to the ironclad steamboat sent by the Federals to put down the Rebels in Arkansas, a gunboat that became the victim of "the most destructive single shot of the War between the States" when a Confederate Captain Fry, sent to stop it near the mouth of the White River, noticed a porthole left open in its armored flanks. He fired a single lucky cannon shot that scored a bull's-eye: it hit a steampipe within, scalding all the occupants and forcing them out on deck, where they were picked off by sharpshooters, resulting in a loss of 150 men. This *Mound City* sank in the White River and remained visible for many years after the war as a symbol of one of the few Rebel victories. The

boat had been built at the naval yard in the Illinois town of Mound
City, on the banks of the Ohio, down which had floated the man
or men who may have been inspired by that "city" to give the
same name to the place they founded in Arkansas.

If Missouri has its "bootheel," then Illinois has a "slipper
toe," and this is where its Mound City is located, just above Cairo
(another Egyptian name). This Mound City is also a county
seat, for Pulaski County, and in addition to being the chief naval
depot for the Union's "freshwater fleet," it furnished hallowed
ground for a national cemetery for 5,555 Civil War dead. The
whole surrounding area of southern Illinois is a seedbed for
"locales," a ghost-town hunter's paradise. One of these hunters,
Glenn Sneed, without the help of the GNIS, located 840 (eight
hundred forty!) ghost towns in the hills of the seventeen counties
that make up southern Illinois, and, without the help of any
experience at writing, put together a book, *Ghost Towns of Southern
Illinois*, a marvelous compendium of primitive literature and oral
history, which no publisher would touch and which he published
himself in 1977 (out of print; a paperback edition is available for
$11.95 postpaid from Austin Periodical Services, Route 37 North,
Johnston City, Illinois 62951).

If this part of Illinois is a hundred miles upstream from the
part of Arkansas that concerns us here, and if it is a flagrant
digression to shift attention, even momentarily, in that direction,
then Sneed's labor and his naïve art beckon us with messages
that shed light on the whole journey in search of lost cities (seventeen of the places Sneed found have—or had—"City" as part
of their name). Traveling what must have been thousands of
miles without leaving his corner of Illinois, Sneed researched as
best as he could the known facts about each of the 840 places,
interviewed any survivors, and wrote a précis for each lost town,
concluding the pieces with variations on a theme that, strung
together, make up a kind of poem to lost America:

> Two houses stand. There is a single man in each house. The
> village that was once the home of 125 people now has a
> population of two.

No one who had not known there was once a village there would ever guess that this was once the site of commerce.

One may drive through it without ever dreaming that it was a thriving village for ten years.

No one driving by the crossroad would ever guess that once a town was there.

Today nothing remains of the village where once lived two hundred and fifty souls.

One driving through the village knows that he is in a hamlet but he would see only the ghost of the thriving city of a century ago.

The place where the village stood has grown up in underbrush and trees and is now a wilderness.

The ghost of the once populous village roams the memories of the few folk who still live there.

Who can but tell that the ghost of this community may rise again?

In the auspicious year of 1886 *le douanier* Henri Rousseau painted in Paris the first of his dreamlike landscapes-with-figures-in-them, which would be laughed to scorn by sophisticated art lovers everywhere but would have an indelible influence on all attempts by modern art to seize the fickle moments of the unconscious. Certain primitive writers—Walter Lackey for his chronicles of Newton County, and certainly Glenn Sneed for his monumental exploration of ghost towns in southern Illinois— deserve recognition for handling the word with the same awkward, direct, intuitive innocence that Rousseau brought to pigment.

A traveler passing through will never know a town was there. The ghost town's sense of melancholy reminds us of our deepest fears of never having an identity of our own, of failing to find anyone who can answer the awful question, "Do you know why I am me?" If no one knows that a town was ever there, no one knows that you were ever here.

Kim misses Mound City, Arkansas, the first time she goes looking for it. A wrong turn in a Y in the poor county road puts her on an empty, straight road, exasperatingly flat and barren except for two huge silos standing tall in a vacant field. In silhouette the silos could almost be the twin towers of the World Trade Center in Manhattan, were it not for the complete lack of anything else around them. These silos represent all that is left of "industry" in Mound City, but the dull road stretching straight to the horizon takes Kim farther away from the "city" in the direction of the Big Road, Interstate 40, that leads to the Big City across the river, Memphis. For all the emptiness of these wastes, it is an area of high traffic congestion: besides the busy six-lane interstate, three major railroads coming from the north, south, and west, the Burlington and Northern, the Missouri Pacific, and the Rock Island. No sign along their route marks the spot where the first rails were laid westward into Arkansas soil in 1853. When Kim reaches the end of this straightaway, she finds a closed-up roadside shed with a big sign, "FIREWORKS CITY," not a city that interests her, and then, just before an access interchange to Interstate 40, a smaller sign pointing in the direction she has just come from: "Mound City." She turns around.

Again the desolate straightaway, again the Y in the road, a few dwellings—white farmworkers', a few shanties, blacks', sharecroppers' or hired farm hands'—shotgun architecture of the sort that is found all over eastern Arkansas, particularly in the Mississippi delta: without lawns, or with mud for lawns, a few scraggly trees that may in summer provide shade but now are like witches summoning foreboding weather from the sky. Later, when Kim has met blacks in another town and grown accustomed to talking to them, she will regret that she could not summon the nerve to stop at one of these wretched shanties and knock at the door, if only to ask, "Is this Mound City?"

Kim passes a small church, a very tiny white church, "2nd St. John MB Church." Is there a *first* St. John Church elsewhere? Or formerly on this spot? Or is the name taken from the Second Epistle of John, shortest (thirteen-verse) book in the Bible? "And now I beseech thee, lady, not as though I wrote a new commandment unto thee, but that which we had from the beginning, that we love one another." It is certainly the shortest church house Kim has ever seen, with a belfry or tower hardly more than a rakish cap, and four white columns too plain to be even Doric. The announcement that Evening Worship is at 2:30 reminds her that in rural Arkansas "evening" is still thought to be any time after noon. The address is given as "MOUNt CitY ROad Marion ARK." If the people of this small congregation do not know the difference between the protecting Mound and the projecting Mount, how is Kim to find it? She drives the short way back into Marion.

Marion was named for the same Swamp Fox as the eponymous upland Marion County, where Buffalo City is located. But this Marion is the seat of Crittenden County, named after the dashing Robert Crittenden, born in Kentucky in 1797, the same year Fort Esperanza was built; at sixteen he was a soldier in the War of 1812, and at twenty-two the first secretary of the new "Territory of Arkansaw" (as it was spelled in the act of admittance). Indeed, he was the dominant figure in the early history of Arkansas politics, and was called "Cardinal Wolsey" by his friends and enemies, one of whom, Congressman Henry Conway, challenged him to a duel. Crittenden was a notoriously poor shot; urged by friends, including his second, Ben Desha (for whom the next county Kim will visit is named), to practice his marksmanship, he fired three times at a tree and missed three times. But somehow he managed to hit Conway with one lucky and mortal shot, and went on after the death of the popular congressman to dominate politics in the young Territory of Arkansas, to build the most aristocratic brick mansion in Little Rock, and to publish an influential newspaper, before his own early death, hastened by disappointment over the failure of his glamour to get him elected to Congress.

When George Fogleman (who had come in middle age from Europe to America) landed in Arkansas in 1824, the Territory was only five years old and the steamboat only seventeen, an unruly teen-ager; Carnot had just published *Réflexions sur la puissance motrice du feu*, that pioneer work of thermodynamics in which he showed that heat does not work unless it is let down from a higher to a lower temperature. The same principle underlies the use of nuclear energy in our own time; for Carnot's time and for Fogleman's, it meant the rapid development of the steam engine into a power that built the entire nineteenth century, as the combustion engine built the twentieth. Fogleman did not read Carnot; he did read the announcement that Congress had approved the sale of certain public lands for 10¢ an acre. Even at such an outrageous bargain price, George Fogleman could afford to buy only about forty acres of Mississippi waterfront—he was that poor—but his land was thick with virgin trees, which he began chopping down by hand and, with the help of his wife's strong back, carried down to Fogleman's Landing to peddle to the few steamboats that stopped. As the years passed and more and more steamboats began stopping, so Fogleman bought up more and more of the woodland, and could afford to buy a team of mules and a wagon, and a Negro slave to help. Thus he slowly founded a dynasty based on steam. Two of his grandsons became steamboat captains, as we shall see. When he died at the close of the war in 1865, having lost to freedom the sixty-five Negro men and their numerous wives and children who were his chattels, but owning twenty-one miles of the Mississippi waterfront and twenty thousand acres of land that had been cleared of its timber (the steamboats had burned up all the wood and were running on coal by then) but planted with a far more lucrative crop, cotton.

Most of the actual cities along the Mississippi, from New Orleans to Minneapolis, owed their growth to the steamboat, and all of the aspiring cities, including three named Mound and several no longer existing at all because they were swallowed whole by the fickle Grandfather, were founded upon the expectation of aggrandizement by steamboat traffic. In a lonely microcosm of its own, Mound City is the story of the coming of steam, the rise of steam, the dangerous unruliness of steam, and the evaporation of steam into nothingness. Carnot's philosophy that heat must come down from a higher temperature to do its work applies to towns no less than to molecules.

But what sort of man was George Fogleman? Kim can find nothing on the Fogleman dynasty in the Crittenden County Library. For a moment she is tempted to ask Mrs. McCarter, the helpful librarian, "You wouldn't happen to know of any state troopers in this district who collect local history?" But Virginia McCarter volunteers, "Really, you ought to talk to Julie Longnecker. She lives not far from here."

Local citizens are proud of young-fortyish Julie Ward Longnecker, who has published articles on local history and recently won the prestigious Arkansas Historical Association award for the best scholarly article on Arkansas history, "A Road Divided: From Memphis to Little Rock Through the Great Mississippi Swamp," a study of the building of the Old Military Road, which began at Mound City. When Kim phones her, Julie invites Kim over to her house, where her husband runs a day-care center, not operating on weekends. Julie is a slender, vivacious woman whose appearance suggests what Kim may resemble in another decade. History writing is only a passionate hobby for her; she works full-time doing research and statistical studies in the marketing office of a Memphis hospital.

Julie and Kim have a lunch of fried chicken snatched at the convenience store on the corner, and Julie shows Kim her article published in the *Arkansas Times* monthly magazine, "The *Sultana*: At Mound City, An Old Horror Lurks Beneath the Silt."

"What was the *Sultana*?" Kim asks Julie, in all innocence.

"You don't know, do you?" Julie observes, without censure. "Not many people have ever heard of it. You didn't study it in your history books. But it was the greatest marine disaster in this country's history." She gestures eastward, in the direction of Mound City. "And it happened right out there on the Mississippi."

Kim remembers something about Sam Dunlap, the eulogist at the funeral of Peter Mankins in Sulphur City; Dunlap had been a passenger on the *Sultana*, but Kim doesn't remember having heard just how many were killed. "I thought the sinking of the *Titanic* was the biggest marine disaster," she says to Julie.

"Read the article," Julie advises. Although she has written about the *Sultana* and about the Old Military Road, both having connections to Mound City, she confesses to Kim that she doesn't really know very much about Mound City itself. There is hardly any written history of it. Julie suggests that a fellow member of the Crittenden County Historical Society, Margaret Woolfolk, might have some information on Mound City, and after lunch she takes Kim to Miss Woolfolk's house. Here, in one of Marion's finer but still-unassuming homes, with many windows opening onto her lawn and trees and quiet street from the confines of her study, Margaret Woolfolk, age sixty-six, writes regularly for Marion's newspaper, the *Evening Times*; she also uses her personal computer and its modem, printer, and associated hardware in the service of her ongoing attempts to put together a history of Crittenden County.

Miss Woolfolk is old enough to remember seeing Mound City when some of its buildings were still standing, including the ruins of the old two-story hotel. But for the last forty years or so, nothing has been there except the plantation store.

"You know, of course, that like most river towns Mound City developed primarily out of woodcutting," Miss Woolfolk begins, uncertain of just where to begin. "They would chop timber to provide fuel for the steamboats. Mound City was but one of scores of river towns that went out of existence when the steamboats declined and the levees were built." She goes on explaining how they were built to keep the Mississippi from flooding the rich cotton lands, and how the levee in relatively modern times dealt a final death blow to Mound City by being constructed between the city and the river, cutting it off from the river; of course, the river had already cut itself off from Mound City by shifting its course miles to the east.

"Was there ever any time when Mound City could have been called a boomtown?" Kim asks.

Margaret Woolfolk shakes her head. "I don't think it was ever a boomtown in the sense we think of them. It was just a place where people could get on the steamboat, and for a while it was designed to service those people and those boats. It had, at most, a dozen places of business, accommodations for river passengers, a barber, and a doctor or two . . . but in those days we used to have doctors running out our ears."

"In the year of, say, 1886, what would Mound City have been like?"

Margaret Woolfolk smiles. "Now, if you take *that* year," she says, "it's kind of late already. That was just before the post office of Mound City closed down for good." She consults her computer printouts. "There's no record of a post office there after 1888. And of course 1885 was the year the *Mark Twain* blew up."

The steamboat of that name, not the writer, Miss Woolfolk explains, although the writer was known to blow up on occasion, too. Just opposite Mound City, the *Mark Twain*, which was being captained by Gustavus Fogleman, grandson of George, suffered a boiler explosion that killed two white men and seven black men. Captain Fogleman had his leg broken in two places in the accident, but returned to the ship after it was rebuilt and renamed the *Alace*, and continued for several more years as a pilot, before retiring to devote all his attention to his five hundred acres of cotton plantation. Gus's wife was Mamie Barton, one of the lovely Barton girls of Mound City (his brother LeRoy married another one), but for that matter most of the Barton men married Fogleman girls. It is confusing: the Mrs. Barton who was a passenger on the *Mark Twain* when it blew up was Gus's mother-in-law, but her husband's first wife was a Fogleman, Gus's sister.

The Bartons and the Foglemans intermarried throughout the life of Mound City. (A town is often either a tournament between two families or a marriage between them.)

James Barton, the patriarch of this family, born in Kentucky the same year George Fogleman came to Mound City, 1824, did not settle in Crittenden County until 1852, after spending enough time in Texas to earn the money to buy large tracts of land and be prominent in local politics from the moment of his arrival on the scene. He was a Union sympathizer, but when Arkansas seceded early from the Union, his slaveowner friends in Mound City, and his two younger brothers, Frank and Bob, persuaded him to shift his allegiance to the Confederacy. He organized a company of Crittenden County men over which he was appointed captain, and, near the close of the war, became major of a battalion, which he surrendered at Mound City in 1865. He was not, like his brothers, a cotton grower, but opened in Memphis, across the river, a mill for extracting oil from cottonseed. The principal use of cottonseed was the planting of cotton, and although the oil squeezed from it had been used for fuel in ancient China, it was not until Barton's time that it became widely used as a foodstuff: James Barton helped establish an industry that grew into a major source of cooking oil, shortening, salad oil, and margarine. His brothers across the river in Mound City operated a cotton gin that supplied him with most of his raw material. However, his career as the tycoon of cottonseed oil was cut short when he was forty-nine and succumbed to an epidemic of yellow fever, from the bites of mosquitoes, which swept over Memphis in 1873, carrying away hundreds. His son, Jimmy, carried on the business, leasing thousands of acres of Crittenden County cotton, and Jimmy's son, also called Jimmy, kept it going into the twentieth century.

In 1859 Frank Barton, James's younger brother, built a handsome mansion near Mound City; here he ensconced his bride, John Fogleman's firstborn, Alice, mother of the bachelor Frank Barton who continued to run the Mound City Cotton Gin for years after his father's death. When Alice died in 1865, shortly after the death of her grandfather, old George Fogleman—both in the same year as the *Sultana* disaster—her husband married another woman and sired Mamie, who became the wife of Captain Gustavus Fogleman, he of the *Mark Twain*. Thus the captain had a father-in-law who had formerly been his brother-in-law, and a nephew, Frank G. (the bachelor) Barton, who was also his half-brother-in-law (it is very confusing), with whom he conspired late in life to build the levee that reclaimed two thousand acres of their cotton from the Grandfather of Waters but also drove the last nail into the coffin of Mound City.

The third brother (of James and Frank) was Bobby, known as R.B.; he raised cotton and supplied it to Frank, but after Frank's death sold his cotton plantations and plowed the money into a railroad westward to Bald Knob. This growing town took its name from a treeless rise that supposedly offered de Soto and his men the only high-and-dry spot after their trudge through the eastern-Arkansas marshes and sloughs (eventually, however, the Great Flood of 1927 covered everything on all four sides of Bald Knob). Bobby Barton married Fannie, another of the daughters of John Fogleman.

If the skimpy history of Mound City has a central character, it is John Fogleman, who was eleven years old when he rode down the Ohio and the Mississippi on the keelboat of his father, George, and lived for seventy years through the history of Mound City. George Fogleman might have been the founder and namer of Mound City, but John was its builder and squire, until his death in our critical year, 1886. Two of his three sons were steamboat captains and later cotton growers on a plantation scale, and both married into the Barton family, as did two of John's daughters, Alice and Fannie; a third daughter, named Mississippi, a lovely name for a girl and one that could easily be shortened to Missy, married aboard a steamboat at Fogleman's Landing a man named Morris, Memphis's first steamboat agent and later steamboat magnate until the Civil War.

When he was nineteen, John Fogleman witnessed the building of the Military Road commencing at Hopefield and turning westward at Mound City, and the "removal" of thousands of Indians over it. He watched the steamboat traffic on the river grow from an occasional brave boat or two to a constant flotilla of vessels. And he was a principal actor in the tragedy of the *Sultana*.

When Kim and Julie leave Miss Woolfolk's house, they agree to meet later in the afternoon at Mound City, where Julie will take Kim to meet a man who is trying to exhume the skeleton of the *Sultana* from the soil of his soybean field. Kim drives Zephyra back along the country road to the cemetery at the St. John Church, where she pauses just long enough to confirm that no Bartons or Foglemans are buried there, only their slaves and descendants of those slaves. Then Kim confronts the Y in the road again, and this time takes the one less traveled by, which leads her into the heart of all that remains of Mound City: the abandoned general store beside the "Hanging Tree" and a historical marker erected during the Bicentennial celebration of 1976, which states that Mound City is "An old river town once located on the banks of the Mississippi River, deriving its name from Indian mounds. Federal troops burned it January 15, 1863." There are several other historical markers in the vicinity and along the twelve-mile Esperanza Trail, which begins here and continues to the site of Hopefield, but this is the only one that offers any information about the town itself.

The store is bare of signs. No printed words on colored tin exhort the customer to drink Coca-Cola or Royal Crown, smoke Camels or Chesterfields, or spread Vicks VapoRub. These red-white-and-rusted rectangles of metal probably once crowded one another along the façade, but have been removed, like the store sign itself, whatever it once proclaimed: "Mays General Merchandise" or "Mays Plantation Store." It never said "U.S. Post Office," because that sign came down in 1886. Stripped of all signs, the building takes on even more of a classical purity of line. (Were the Greek temples at one time festooned with cloth banners of advertisements?) Its false front is not merely a raising of corners to give the illusion of a second story, but an honest echo of the roof pitch at the same time the roof pitch is denied. Like the false front everywhere in nineteenth-century architecture, its chief function is an aspiration to cityhood by imitating the city's verticality, at least up to the level of the second floor, which isn't there. In a way, the ancestor of the false front is the medieval cathedral, whose towered façade conceals the sloping roof, hiding unstable diagonals with assertive verticals. The retention of diagonals in the façade of Mays Store gives it almost a baroque flavor, like the Alamo. The porch is wide and deep, and without effort of imagination Kim can see the storekeeper and his customers relaxing there, shaded from the blistering sun or umbrellaed against the peltering rain.

The peltering rain has left this road unsuitable for traffic, especially such traffic as low-slung Zephyra, who absolutely detests Kim's apparent intention: to climb the levee with her, to see if the Grandfather can be seen. He cannot, but with much slithering and spinning of wheels Zephyra ascends the road up to the levee's level top, where she balks and refuses to descend into the quagmire beyond, though in good weather she could go all the way to Hopefield. Kim stops, gets out, and surveys the scene. Although there is no sign of the river itself, the filled-in oxbow lakes, which were once channels or chutes of the river, are now lined with willows and cottonwoods and turned into fishponds. The one directly below her, although she does not know this, is the Mound City Chute, which once held Fogleman's Landing. A couple of fishing shacks stand there now. It was there that, in April of 1865, the *Sultana* exploded. . . .

In time of war, luxury boats become troopships. One of several sometimes metaphysical definitions of "transport" is "a ship used to transport troops or military equipment." Transportation is, unfortunately, the only way to get home by water. Sam Dunlap, private in Company B of the 3rd Tennessee Cavalry, Army of the United States, was on his way home in 1865, toward the close of that cruelest month, April: on the 9th, the Confederacy had surrendered; on the 14th, the President, Abraham Lincoln, had been mortally wounded by a pistol shot to the back of the head; and on the 3rd, Private Dunlap had been "paroled" from a Con-

federate prison camp called Castle Morgan, at Cahaba, in Alabama. Cahaba is not as infamous as Andersonville, in Georgia;
at the latter, thirteen thousand men, a third of the prison population, were allowed to die of starvation and disease. Cahaba
had comparable conditions of overcrowding, exposure, water
pollution, abominable rations of food, and mistreatment by the
guards, but not quite so many died; those who did not, like Sam
Dunlap, had a fierce, irrational desire to go home, to see the
familiar contours of their land and their people before they died.

Sam had been eighteen when he enlisted, in 1863, in Blount
County, Tennessee; nineteen when he was captured, at Sulphur
Branch Trestle in northern Alabama; and twenty when he was
transported homeward, from Vicksburg, Mississippi. In between,
he had seen a lot of different places, on foot, on horseback, on
trains, and on boats. Of these means of transport, the forced
march of the prisoner was the most familiar to him, and the least
pleasant: as often as not, it had been a forced wade, or a forced
swim. Twice he had escaped during these treks—once on the
Tennessee River by swimming underwater for three minutes or
long enough to be presumed drowned by his captors, and once
on the Cahaba River by diving deep enough to elude the bullets
fired at him—but both times he was recaptured after a few days
and forced onward to Castle Morgan. This camp was so-called
by virtue of its fortification, a twelve-foot-high fence of thick
boards that Sam could not climb, although once, after months
of being fed nothing but a supposed cornmeal that was actually
ground corncobs softened with stagnant creek water contami-
nated by human refuse, he tunneled beneath the boards with his
bare hands over a period of two weeks of spare-time nightly
digging, only to have the escape foiled when he broke through
the other side to face a snarling dog held on a leash by a snarling
guard. As punishment, he was denied even the supposed cornmeal thereafter, and kept locked in a dark, airless wooden box
of solitary confinement; one side of this was the plank wall or
palisade of the enclosure, but, weakened by starvation, he could
only scratch feebly at it with a kind of small pick fashioned from
what remained of his belt buckle. Slowly, over a period of a week,

he pricked out a hole large enough to admit his body. This time he waited until the patroling dog outside the wall had been led around to the other side of the camp, then squeezed through and dashed into the woods to freedom.

Sam managed to get as far as Selma, twelve miles away, where on a March day one hundred years later—almost exactly—marchers would hike to protest the same continuing cause of human rights he had been a soldier for. There, like some of the later protesters, he was caught and jailed. The local civilian provost marshal who was Sam's jailer gave him the first food he had eaten in weeks, a plate of beans, and carelessly locked him up in an unwindowed room on the second floor of a brick building. The room did have a fireplace, unlighted, and a chimney, up which Sam climbed and from the top of which he flapped his arms and flew into the branches of a tree.

From that tree to the outskirts of the city of Selma was less than a mile, but the roughest mile Sam Dunlap ever traveled. The streets were full of Rebel soldiers. Under the cover of night and of the chimney soot, which had blackened him thoroughly, he sneaked down alleys, narrow lanes between lots that were like those alleys Peter Mankins had planned for Sulphur City and doubtless shown to Sam, who was reminded by them of his attempted escape from Selma. An alley is both an access and an impasse. The Rebel soldiers, who were fidgety and sleepless while waiting for the Federal attack on Selma that would come any day now, and hearing the rumor that a Yankee had escaped from the redoubtable Cahaba, made a sport of blocking off all the alleys of Selma. Sam was caught twice, both times convincing his captors, because of his soot-blackened flesh, that he was a local Negro; the third time, his captors decided to have some fun with him anyway and, in the course of submitting him to their games, discovered that he was not a Negro. He was returned under heavy guard to Cahaba.

This time he was not put in the box up against the wall but chained to a stake out in the middle of the compound, supposedly where the other prisoners could watch him starve to death as an object lesson to them. But the other prisoners, thousands of them, were beyond the point of caring or even observing what personal suffering Sam was enduring. There were no longer any corncobs to be ground into mush. "Them fellers would've et each other," Sam observed to Peter Mankins years later, "but nary one of 'em had the strength to butcher a chinch bug."

There is a point in starvation beyond which hunger pangs are no longer felt. The despair in camp was such that when news reached the prisoners that General James Wilson's "Lightning Brigade" had struck Selma and captured it, no one seemed to care that Wilson might move on south to liberate Cahaba. Before that could happen, though, the entire population of Cahaba was made to stand and file out through the gates on their last forced march, westward, out of Alabama. The men were so weak and listless that only a few mounted guards were required to keep them moving, but Private Dunlap was assigned a guard of his own to prevent any further escapes. He had no idea where he was being taken.

Hundreds of men died on this march; the ones who did not were allowed to capture anything edible that moved or stood along the route. Ironically, it was springtime, and things were coming up out of the earth. They ate reptiles and at every stream they crossed caught minnows with their bare hands. Somewhere in eastern Mississippi they were herded aboard the cattle cars of a train, but it was not exactly a rest from their march: they were packed so tightly they could not sit. The train moved slowly westward. Sam Dunlap no longer had his personal guard but was packed in with the others; though he considered escape, he was too curious to know the destination of the train, which proved to be Jackson, Mississippi, the capital of the state, and still a Rebel fortress. It was full of alleys; Sam did not attempt escape, but remained with the thousands of prisoners as their march resumed, again westward, again with men dying at every mile along the route, until they had only one more river to cross, the Big Black, and there was an encampment of thousands upon thousands of men, all prisoners, more human beings than Sam Dunlap had ever seen at one time in one place in his life before. On the heights above the far side of the river were rows of neat white tents beneath a flagpole on which Old Glory was flying, the first time Sam had seen his flag since the previous September, and his voice was not alone in cheering it.

But the immense throng of prisoners crammed into the fetid fields on the east side of the Big Black were not celebrating their impending delivery into Union hands, which was still uncertain. The Confederacy was not beaten. Lee had not yet surrendered at Appomattox. This encampment of prisoners, many of them taken from the dread Andersonville and the remainder from Cahaba, was not technically under Federal control. It was a "neutral" ground, a chessboard on which the pawns were still negotiable. For days, weeks, the men waited, watching from afar the daily raising and lowering of their flag across the river. Catholic nuns called "Sisters of Charity" moved among them, distributing hardtack and jerky: rockhard dried bread and leathertough dried beef, a banquet compared with their former fare. The number of daily deaths from starvation dropped, but still prisoners died of old wounds, scurvy, cholera, and dysentery.

Then one morning word spread through the camp that its inmates were being taken across the Big Black to be officially "paroled": released to the Federal side on condition that they never fight against the Confederacy again. Few of them were able or willing to violate that condition if they had been given the chance, or if the Confederacy itself had had any chance to live a little longer. The Rebel guards ordered the men to fall in with their respective regiments and prepare for muster. Since Sam Dunlap could find nobody from his old Tennessee regiment, he fell in with a company of Germans from Ohio, who were soon swallowed up by a battalion from Michigan and surrounded by a regiment from Indiana. In droves they were ferried across the Big Black, and put aboard a shuttle train that conveyed them to the bluffs of Vicksburg, where they marched down to the waterfront of the biggest water of all: the Grandfather, muddier than ever, swollen with spring rains. Only when Sam caught sight of all the steamboats docked on that river did he allow himself to believe that he was truly going home, heading north toward home. "Goin home," he said aloud to the man next to him, and the man replied, "You bet."

The riverbank was lined with steamboats being boarded one at a time by long files of soldiers, who stood in their ranks patiently waiting their turn. These steamboats were not troopships but luxury sidewheelers, spotlessly clean and decked out with pennants. The passengers already on the promenade decks, silently watching the soldiers beginning to board, were well-dressed civilians, women and children, rich old men. Sam became acutely conscious of his attire: his once-neat blue uniform was reduced to grimy rags, though all around him were thousands of men no more soldierly dressed than he. Many were standing with the aid of crutches or canes, or being supported by their fellows; Sam was one of the few who stood, if not at attention, at least on his own unassisted feet. There was not a clean-shaven jaw in the throng, or a head of combed hair, and the civilian passengers already on the big boats were obviously not happy; they became less happy as the ex-prisoners, by the dozen and then by the hundred, began boarding the vessels. While he waited his turn, which might take hours, Sam counted the troops being loaded upon a smaller steamboat named *Olive Branch*; he knew enough of the story of Noah and the Ark to know the significance of the name, and the symbolism of peace. When he had counted to seven hundred, and the boat could not possibly hold any more, he stopped counting, but still soldiers were ordered to cross the gangplank and find room.

"Where are we going?" the man next to him asked Sam.

"Cairo, Illinois," Sam said, pronouncing it "kay-row," as he had long known how to do. "If they don't run out of boats first."

The next boat, whose name, *Henry Ames*, had no symbolism that Sam would have appreciated, took much longer to fill. There were a thousand when he stopped counting, and he still wasn't very close to the head of the line waiting to board. The man next to him, who must have observed Sam's lips moving as he counted, asked him how many; when Sam replied, "One thousand, so far," the man swore an exclamation and said, "She wasn't meant to hold more than two hundred."

When the *Henry Ames* finally left the dock, its absence revealed the bulk of three more steamboats, and the largest had
her name in big letters across the sidewheel house: *Sultana*. In
the complicated system of Muslim polygamy, a sultana is not
necessarily the bride of a sultan; the name is reserved for a sultan's mother, his sister, or his daughter, but if his wife becomes
the mother of his first heir, *then* she can have bestowed upon her
the title of *sultana hasseky* and is entitled to fifty eunuchs of her
own. But that is so much Arabic mumbo-jumbo; throughout the
American South, "sultana" is the nickname of the purple galli-
nule, or water hen, or swamp hen, a freshwater bird, and to Sam
Dunlap this was the meaning: she was the bird that was going
to fly him home . . . if he ever got aboard her. Night was coming
on, making it hard to keep count, but twelve hundred or so men
had already boarded the big boat, and still there were many ahead
of him, between him and the wharf. A sergeant came into the
midst of the ex-prisoners and said, "At ease, men. That's all
they're going to take tonight. Maybe we'll get aboard in the morning." Through the night Sam waited. He really had his heart set
on the *Sultana*, but wouldn't be disappointed to take one of the
next two boats; they might be less crowded. He was a patient
man usually, except when he was trying to escape, and right now
he wasn't trying to escape from anything. The other men, too,
although excited to giddiness by the prospect of going home,
were patient; some of them had spent two years as prisoners at
Andersonville or Cahaba; they could wait a little longer. Instead
of sleeping, they listened to the sounds coming from the *Sultana*,
where the soldiers who had already boarded were singing, playing harmonicas and a banjo, and celebrating their leavetaking
from the South.

The next day the loading was resumed, and Sam's place in
the long line crept closer to the boat's staging. By noon the rails
of the ship were crowded shoulder to shoulder by the lucky
boarders gloating at the men still waiting on shore. "If I aint
number two thousand," Sam said to himself, still counting, "I
aint goin to make it." But that number was passed, and still he

had not boarded. When at last his turn came, he was Number 2,231. The legal capacity of the *Sultana*, one of the biggest boats then on the river, was, including the crew, 376 persons.

But Sam was aboard. The problem now was finding a place to stand, or occasionally sit. It was a four-day passage to Cairo, maybe five nights on the water, and the only prospect of sleep might be an hourly exchange of sitting or half-reclining positions among the packed hordes. There were only a hundred civilian passengers on board, and each of them had a tiny stateroom with a bunk, but none of them had any intention of sharing their space with the sick, lame, filthy soldiers on board. They kept their cabin doors tightly shut and latched. Once, on the next morning out and up from Vicksburg, the door against which Sam was leaning nudged him, and he let it open a crack to reveal a beautiful young woman, the first lady Sam had seen up that close in ages, wearing the fanciest, fluffiest, pinkest dress he had ever seen. She stared at him with obvious distaste but confessed, "I cannot summon the steward. He will not answer the bell."

"Probably caint git here through all the crowd, ma'am," Sam observed. Then, "Can I be of any service to ye?"

She studied him. Hesitantly she told him, "My chamberpot needs . . ." But she stopped. "It's all right," she said. "I can manage." She closed her door. Hours later the door nudged him again, and again he let it open. "Why are you leaning against my door?" the lady all in pink asked him.

"Sorry, ma'am," he said. "It's the only place I got to lean." He indicated the two soldiers who were leaning against the wall on either side of the door, then asked, "Could I empty that pot fer ye?" But again she hesitated. "Lady," he told her, without politeness, "I been up to my chin in worse dung than yours for the last six months. A little more won't hurt me." She let him into her cubicle. He took her chamberpot, carrying it gingerly so it would not spill, worked his way through the crowd, usually moving backward like a crawfish, to the taffrail, where he dumped the contents of the pot overboard, then returned it to her cabin.

"Thank you," she said, and asked, "Where are you going?"

"Back out to my leaning post, against your door."

"I mean," she said, smiling, "what is your destination? I am going to St. Louis."

"If they muster me out at Cairo," he said, "reckon I'll try to git on back to Blount County, Tennessee, up in the Smokies, where I'm from."

"Would you like to sit down, instead of leaning against my door?" she invited him. There was a chair in the cabin. He tried it. It was the first chair he'd sat upon since . . . he couldn't remember the last time he had sat on a chair. It was so nice, he was afraid he might fall asleep any minute. "My name is Adeline," the young woman said. Sam told her his name. She told him about New Orleans, where she had been visiting. He told her about Cahaba, where he had been visiting. She seemed to understand. They talked a long while. They exchanged birthdates, hers only a month after his. She seemed to need to talk, out of nervousness, and out of a great fear: would the boat ever reach Cairo, let alone St. Louis? "I've heard," she told him, breathlessly, "that if we make Cairo, it will have been the greatest number of people transported on one boat in the history of the Mississippi River." Then she told him, sadly, "We weren't even supposed to stop at Vicksburg. I have heard that the only reason we stopped there, and then had to take on so many of you, was because one of the boilers was leaking, and had to be hastily patched. Do you know anything about boilers? This trip was supposed to be such a pleasant outing, and everything has gone wrong." Sam, who knew nothing about boilers except that they had a bad reputation for exploding, told her that he hoped everything would be all right, that she would be in St. Louis before she knew it, even if she had to endure a few inconveniences. It was pity that a pretty gal like her couldn't get out on the promenade deck and show off her several dresses, he said. Could he see them? One by one she took her dresses out of their trunk, unfolded them, and held them up before her. "Them sure is pretty," he said. That night she told him that he was welcome to stay and stretch out on the floor if he liked. She slept in her bunk, fully clothed. He did not touch her.

When the *Sultana* docked at Memphis the next day, Miss Adeline told him that she was joining her fellow cabin passengers for a few hours on shore and would return before dark. Sam wouldn't have minded going ashore, too, to see what Memphis looked like, but the ex-prisoners had orders not to leave the boat. Several of them sneaked off anyhow, or jumped from the decks to the wharf. One of the ship's officers began rounding up able-bodied men to help unload the cargo, mostly heavy hogsheads of sugar. The pay was 75¢ an hour, and after working hard for three hours, Sam had money in his pocket for the first time in half a year. He joined some of the other men on a tour of an alley called "the Whiskey Chute" because it had fourteen saloons in it, a fine use for an alley. They tried to visit each one. It was the first liquor of any sort, and good liquor at that, that Sam had tasted since the previous summer. He had enough to feel good, but not enough to get drunk, as most of the other fellows were. Some of them were so drunk they couldn't make it back to the boat; they couldn't even be carried back to the boat, and had to be left behind. A few hours later Sam would stop feeling sorry for the ones who were left behind.

The young lady, who had changed to her purple dress, opened the cabin door for him but began to close it before he could enter. "You've been drinking," she told him, wrinkling her nose. "You can't come in here if you've been drinking." She would not let him in. He resumed his former position, leaning up against her door, and watched as the lights of Memphis dwindled into the darkness. He listened to the steady threshing of the paddle wheels in the black water and reflected that he was feeling so good, it was just as well Miss Adeline wouldn't let him in; he might even have tried to kiss her, or worse. One night of good sleep on her floor was enough for him. He could get through this night without any sleep.

In the distance across the darkened river he could just make out the trees on shore, and on small islands along the shore, or donnicks projecting from it, and what looked like a mound. The water of the river was so high that only the tops of trees were visible. There were no lights left burning that late in Mound City;

all the Foglemans were asleep, and all the Bartons, too. He watched the far shore drift past, knowing it was Arkansas, where he had never been, although friends and relatives of his from back home in Blount County had migrated to the Ozarks and had written back such glowing accounts of what an unspoiled and uncrowded paradise it was that Sam had often dreamed about going there. Now that the war had been won, maybe he could.

The *Sultana* moved on imperceptibly upstream. Dark clouds further blackened the night, and there was a smell of rain, with small distant lightning flashes and peals of thunder moving closer. When the *Sultana*'s boiler suddenly exploded, Sam thought at first that the boat had been hit by a lightning bolt, but he had seen what lightning bolts can do to trees, and no lightning bolt was powerful enough to do what this one had done: smash the texas to flinders, rip apart the hurricane deck, topple the twin smokestacks, twist the whole boat slaunchways, and cause the raining down of boat parts and body parts, a great downpour of pieces of wood and iron, sections of human arms and legs, heads, torsos. The roar of the explosion had not faded when it was replaced by a scarcely lesser noise: human voices screaming, a great inarticulate howl of protests and pleas, lamentations and declarations of impossible pain, followed by the complete pandemonium of those still living trying to move, all at once, in every direction.

Clouds of hot steam obscured his vision, but Sam moved to inspect the source of the explosion, and found amidships a great gaping volcanolike crater, at the bottom of which were the remains of the engine room: exposed live coals with bodies burning on them, the bare fireboxes shooting their flames into all the surrounding woodwork. Soon the whole center of the boat was up in flames, which illuminated the whole scene all around him more garishly than his worst dream of hell: throngs of men were still standing though their skin was falling from their bodies in strips; others, blinded by the scalding steam, were bumping into one another in panic, while all the men not burned were pushing and shoving one another, trampling one another, in a senseless rush with no direction except a general direction toward the water, which was already littered with the bodies of hundreds who had willingly or unwillingly gone overboard.

In the next few minutes, more people were killed before Sam's eyes than had been killed in the explosion: people killed by falling decks and collapsing timbers, people killed by flames they could not escape, people killed by people endlessly milling and stomping and running down one another, and most of all people killed by the Grandfather, who waited for those leaping into him, for the swimmers and the nonswimmers alike, for the would-be floaters. Mercifully the Grandfather consumed the non-swimmers first, almost instantly, although their last, panicked moments of consciousness were without mercy. Sam saw in the light of the flames a human "raft" of four hundred or so people together in the water, each of them clambering to get on top, each of them pushing or dragging others down under, until the entire raft of people disappeared beneath the surface. He turned away to watch the scenes on board: of the burned, the crushed, and those who, after the failures of Andersonville or Cahaba to crush their spirits, were driven insane with fear. At every moment a dozen or so leaped from the decks into the river, while another dozen crowded and kicked one another away from the rail. The *Sultana*'s captain was loudly addressing the survivors, trying to calm them but further panicking them with the urgent loudness of his implorations, asking them to keep calm and orderly. As the captain wildly exhorted the crowd to patience, a group of women passengers came out of their staterooms, dropped to their knees before the captain, and began praying loudly. Sam thought they were beseeching the captain, but they were only using him as an intermediary, as one used a priest or a parson between oneself and God; they were clearly trying to get into direct touch with God. Sam noticed that one of them was wearing a lovely purple dress. He moved to her, and raised her to her feet.

"Git up, Adeline!" he said. "Prayin won't do you no good."

She turned her attentions immediately from God to Sam Dunlap, and threw her arms tightly around him. "Save me!" she beseeched.

He pried her gouging fingernails out of his arms. "We got

to wait!" he insisted. "Can you jist wait? And be easy? Jist a little while?" She searched his face, trying to understand, but could not. "Look at 'em!" he said, and pointed at the hundreds in the water, the dozens leaping from the rail. "The ones that go first are the first to die! We got to wait till the time comes."

"I can swim!" she yelled at him. "I know how! I've done it before!"

"In this purty dress?" He fingered her violet taffeta. She began to rip the garment from her body, until she stood stripped of purple, in her white crinoline undergarments. She looked at him defiantly, as if challenging his decorum and his authority. "No, Addy, where would you swim *to?*" he asked. "The nearest bank's a good mile of swift water over yonder. Can you swim a mile through a flood? No, stay close to me, and wait."

But the flames were rising higher and hotter. He was uncertain himself how long they could stay aboard without being burned, and between drowning and roasting he would choose the former. He took Adeline's wrist and led her toward her stateroom. Its ceiling had caved in, and someone had ripped off the door to use as a float, but he found beneath her bunk one life preserver, a cork-padded cummerbund, and he tied it around her waist, then led her out of the cabin and forward across the jumble of corpses to the *Sultana*'s bow, the only part of the boat not engulfed by flame and smoke, where a mob of several hundred passengers who were not injured and not inclined to try the water were huddled together watching the last act of the drama. The boat had been drifting stern-first ever since the engines stopped, and now the great paddle wheels and their housings were aflame and beginning to fall away from the sides of the boat. A fore-to-aft breeze was prodding the fire southward, downriver, across the entire length of the boat, whose upper decks had collapsed into the pyre; the last living passengers on that end of the boat were leaping from the taffrail.

Then the dying *Sultana*, as if diabolically determined to submit all her sides to the holocaust, began to swing around. As the paddle wheels fell away and their burning housings collapsed, the bow, on which the refugees huddled, began to drift toward starboard, slowly at first but then, as the wind and water rushed against the larboard side, swiftly, until the hull had spun completely around, with the bow pointing downstream and downwind . . . and downflame. The hundreds of procrastinators who had sought out the bow as a safe refuge were now being covered by billows of black smoke and red cinders. In the panic and confusion, Sam discovered that he had let go of Adeline's wrist, and could not find her. "ADELINE!" he yelled, but his voice was lost in the screams of the crowd as they surged in a body up against the bow's rail, knocking it down. Sam was pushed helplessly overboard and into the water.

The height from which he fell plunged him deeply into the dark water. In the depths, he struggled to right himself and climb to the surface. Other bodies fell against him, other struggling hands clawed at him. He felt his ankle locked in a clasp that would not be released by his most frantic kicking and seemed to draw him deeper beneath the surface. With hands and feet alike he kicked and thrashed and tore upward through the pile of bodies until his head surfaced and his lungs sucked in air for only the briefest space until other hands encircled his head and pulled him under again. Trying to find open water, where nobody struggled or begged for help, he back-paddled away from the drowning masses. But while he was seeking to avoid them, he was still searching for one of them: Adeline, whose survival had become nearly as important to him as his own. He realized that all this time, from the moment of the first explosion, his mind had kept itself calm with a serene fantasy: of Adeline attaching herself gratefully to him for life in some pleasant valley of the Ozarks, of the two of them becoming lovers and outwitting this disaster.

Suddenly he caught sight of the bow of a steamboat bearing down on him, and for a moment he feared that he was in the path of the drifting *Sultana*. But the bow light illuminated the name *Bostonia II*, and it was not a maimed and deserted steamboat but a whole one, peopled, moving fast, coming right at him. He thought it was only the product of his imagination, a dream of rescue, like his fantasy of the pastoral future with Adeline, but there were other men in the water around him and they saw it, too. The swimmers, and the drowners, began to wave their arms to attract the attention of the men aboard the *Bostonia*. However, the rescue boat, if it was bent on rescue, did not slow, let alone stop: it seemed to be heading for the wreck of the *Sultana*, drifting toward the western shore downstream. The *Bostonia* paddled onward until it was lost in the darkness. The drowners went on drowning, in despair. The swimmers, too, one by one, gave up this last hope.

Sam knew he could never make it to the distant shore, with nothing to hold him up except his own lungs and his tired arms. He hoped that in another minute, when he would have to give up and let the Grandfather have him, it would be quick, without pain, without any more last-second hopes to be dashed. But when he gave up, he would be one of the last to do it; the other men around him had all disappeared, gone under . . . except for one, who was not a man.

Oh, it was Adeline, and she was alive, and floating in the cork cummerbund he had tied around her! She was smiling at him and holding out her arms to him, and he swam to her and embraced her and spoke her name, lovingly. "Dear Sam," she said, and held him tightly in return, then helped him float. Somehow she had managed to put her pretty purple dress back on, and although the taffeta was wet and dark and clung to her, she was still radiant in it, the most gorgeous creature he had ever seen, and right on the spot he said to her, "Adeline, will you marry me? If you will but consent to be my wife, it will give me strength to deliver us out of this hell unto the salvation of a happy land where we may live happily forever after." Or words to that effect; he may have been babbling, so happy was he to have found her and to be making his proposal to her.

She kissed him and sealed the pledge of their troth.

They began to swim toward Arkansas, but both were tired, and after several long minutes their arms began to fail them. Sam rolled over onto his back and pulled her to him, and held her to him while he continued back-stroking the water with one arm and kicking with his feet. It was slow, but it kept them afloat and gave her time to rest so that she could swim some more.

When the sky began lighting up in the east, it was not the fire of the smoldering *Sultana* but the beginning of dawn. Something grabbed his ankle, and he feared that once again he had been caught by a desperate drowner; this time, however, it was the topmost branch of a tree that had snagged him. He turned and looked and saw other treetops nearby. The shore itself still could not be seen.

He was completely exhausted. "Adeline, sweetest," he said, "I jist caint swim another blessit lick. Let's grab aholt of one of these treetops and rest a while." Though he picked the stoutest tree he could find, the branches of the top of it were still not strong enough to bear their weight, and just barely strong enough to provide a handle to keep them above the surface of the water. The water was not so swift here as in the middle of the river. In the gentle eddies of this protected spot they would wait until rescue came or their strength returned enough to swim to land. While they waited, he spoke to her at length, soothingly, telling her of his bright dreams for their ultimate haven in the Ozarks. Could she endure living in a small town? Or would she rather live on a farm? Then the mosquitoes began biting them. Not a lone scout looking for flesh, but whole hordes of them, clouding the lightening sky, hovered over them, and bit, and bit. They slapped themselves and each other. Soon, as full daylight came, the mosquitoes were joined, or replaced, by buffalo gnats, so called because, although mere black flies, they can bite through a buffalo's hide, and bite with a venom that swells the surrounding flesh. Sam tried periodically dunking his head and shoulders beneath the water to keep the bugs off and urging Adeline to do the same, but this was only a momentary solution: they were chewed to pieces. He began to wonder if this were not a worse fate than either burning alive or drowning. He talked faster to Adeline, as if this might divert the both of them from their miseries. He told her his whole life's story in the vales and hollers of Blount County, but his constant voice was punctuated by the sounds of their palms slapping their flesh, until he thought he would go mad.

He was still babbling the story of his life when Frank Barton of Mound City, maneuvering a canoe among the treetops, found him and pulled him into the canoe.

Frank, late a lieutenant of the defeated Confederacy, had been awakened during the night by his father-in-law, John Fogleman, who had been awakened by the explosion of the *Sultana*'s boiler, although it was miles upstream and could be so easily mistaken for thunder. John Fogleman had become a light sleeper because of the high water, and when he heard the sound he knew it for what it was: the instant fragmentation of boilerplate by the uncontrolled expansion of steam. "Get up and start coffee," he told his wife as he dressed. First he went to the homes of his sons LeRoy and Gus, and roused them from sleep. John Fogleman knocked at the "mansion" of his son-in-law Frank Barton, and told him to get his brothers Jim and R.B. The only other families in Mound City were the Malones, the Lumberstons, and the Berrys; John summoned the head of each household. By the time the summoning was finished and these men had dressed, the *Sultana* had already drifted downstream into view, a ball of fire. None of the men owned a skiff or any other boat except Frank's canoe, and he wasn't going to paddle out into *that* water.

One of the men was sent upstream to the Mound City woodyard, fuel stop for the steamers that still burned wood, to alert Bill Boardman, who ran the woodyard and who owned a skiff. Then the other men, directed by John Fogleman, began the construction of a makeshift raft, twelve-foot logs lashed together with rope. With homemade paddles and long poles to propel and steer the raft, John Fogleman and his sons set out into the tide, and, during the long night and the day following, with innumerable trips back to shore, they saved at least seventy-five of the survivors and recovered the bodies of twice that many, until the veranda of John's house, and his parlor, too, became a morgue; the ladies of Mound City brewed endless pots of coffee and tried to feed and clothe the survivors and treat their injuries. The dozens who were badly scalded by steam could only be tem-

porarily soothed by the application of salves and talcums before
they died.

Almost from the beginning, it was apparent to John Fogleman and his townsmen that these men they were saving or recovering were Union soldiers, and there was still bitterness in
Mound City toward the Yankees, who had burned the village
two years earlier, during a senseless raid. Major James Barton
himself, along with his brother Lieutenant Frank Barton, had
just recently surrendered what was left of their units to Union
officers from Memphis. Now all of these ex-Rebels were risking
their lives to rescue the ex-Yankee parolees. Frank Barton in
particular, with his canoe, swifter and more maneuverable than
the Fogleman raft, was finding a large share of survivors. As
dawn broke to make visibility possible, he seemed to discover a
Yankee or two in every treetop; since he could take only one or
two at a time back to the safety of land, he sometimes had to use
his paddle to fight off swimmers desperate not to be left behind.

Frank Barton was a very tired man and a very bug-bitten
man, who had already rescued two sergeants, several corporals,
and a captain, when he found Sam Dunlap, whose sleeve revealed
the remnants of a private's single stripe. He recalled feeling like
a fisherman who is tempted to throw the small ones back in. But
he prodded Sam with his paddle to see if he was going to fight,
and then told him to get into the canoe carefully so as not to
capsize it. Sam said he would not go without "her." An argument
followed, during which Frank sought to convince Sam that there
was no "her." Finally Frank made as if to leave him and demanded, "Are you coming with me or not?" Sam came.

Sam was taken to John Fogleman's house, where the ladies
sought to feed him and apply some salves to the hideous swellings
of his insect bites. He refused food, accepted some coffee, and
sat on the edge of the veranda for the rest of the day, not even
watching the constant comings and goings. The hull of the *Sultana* had drifted to shore almost within shouting distance of Fogleman's house. There had been a few men still clinging to the
unburned bow, and Fogleman's raft had removed them. As
the last raftload of survivors was leaving it, the *Sultana* contin-

ued burning and slowly sank into the shallows off Fogleman's
Landing.

That day and the day after, steamboats and ferries from Memphis
came to Mound City, removed all the survivors to the hospitals
of Memphis, and took away the dead. Mound City returned to
normal. But one survivor remained behind, at his own insistence.
"I aint fixin to cross that river again," he said, and refused to go
with the others. John Fogleman gave him a room of his own,
where he stayed for several days, until the bloated disfigurements
of his face and head began to subside and his appetite returned;
then he joined the Foglemans at table and listened silently to the
continuing news of the disaster. Each day hundreds of bodies
were found along the river's banks, or floating miles downstream.
Crows and hogs were seen feeding on the corpses. Of a total of
six hundred survivors in Memphis, two hundred died of their
injuries and burns. It was estimated that fifteen hundred of the
Sultana's passengers had perished, making this the worst mari-
time disaster in the history of man's movement on water.

The ladies of Mound City put together a new outfit of civilian
clothing for Sam Dunlap, and the men of Mound City made him
a present of a horse. For the first time in six months, this former
cavalry soldier found himself upon his favorite means of transportation. One of the men gave him a demijohn of whiskey, and
another gave him twenty Confederate dollars, still spendable in
parts of Arkansas, although the war, everybody told him, was
entirely over, done with, finished. He thanked everybody and
turned his horse northwestward, toward the Ozarks.

In the weeks that followed, he never found a single person
who had heard of the *Sultana*. When he stopped at small towns—
Lake City, Loyal, Buffalo City—he would declare, in response to
inquiries, that he had survived the *Sultana*, and be required to
explain what the *Sultana* was. When he reached a place called
Sulphur City, whose name reminded him unfavorably of Sulphur
Branch Trestle, where his whole regiment had surrendered, he

met a man named Mankins who had heard of the *Sultana*, and, despite his dislike for the name of the place, he stayed.

Years later, in the beginning of our key year, 1886, some men in Ohio, veterans of the Ohio regiments who had mostly drowned at Mound City, organized a *Sultana* Survivors' Society and planned a big reunion at which the survivors could renew their thanks to the Lord for their deliverance and swap thrilling stories of their experiences during the disaster. They went to great effort to locate each and every one of the known survivors, including Sam Dunlap in Arkansas. But though they invited him to join them, he was indisposed. Later he was invited to contribute his personal narrative to a book written by a fellow survivor, now a minister, the Reverend Chester D. Berry, *Loss of the "Sultana" and Reminiscences of Survivors: History of a Disaster Where over One Thousand Five Hundred Human Beings Were Lost, Most of Them Being Exchanged Prisoners of War on Their Way Home After Privation and Suffering from One to Twenty-three Months in Cahaba and Andersonville Prisons* (Lansing, Michigan: Darius D. Thorp, 1892). But Sam Dunlap, who by that time could not even recall what Adeline's last name had been, declined to participate in the project.

Kim notices that the black mud is rising toward her ankles, and she steps carefully back into Zephyra and removes her shoes. She looks for something to wipe the mud off her shoes and the floor mat. There is the copy of Julie's article in the *Arkansas Times*, and her eye falls upon the information that the *Titanic*'s sinking took thirty or so fewer lives than the sinking of the *Sultana*. She does not wipe mud with the magazine but finds a box of Kleenex and uses up several. Then she gets herself and Zephyra down off the levee and goes to meet Julie Longnecker, whose car she follows along the base of the levee a short distance to a ranch-style house where a man named Sam Oliver lives.

Sam Oliver, age forty-two, is the second son of Dearmont Oliver, a Missourian who bought up six thousand acres that had once belonged to the Bartons and the Foglemans. For his father he cultivates several hundred of those acres in soybeans, the cash crop that has replaced cotton throughout most of the Arkansas delta, and the oil from which has replaced James Barton's cottonseed oil as the main ingredient of contemporary shortening, margarine, or salad oil, but is just as likely to be metamorphosed into paint, printing ink, cosmetics, or pharmaceuticals, while soybean meal makes up the larger part of the diet of all our beef and poultry.

Recently one of Sam's hired hands, driving a tractor out in the soybean field, plowed up some pieces of iron that looked like the boiler of a steamboat. Since a 118-year-old local legend had it that the *Sultana* sank in that vicinity, Sam, who came from Missouri only four years ago, began poking around in that soybean field, collecting more fragments of scrap metal: an iron grate, lengths of chain, strips of copper, pieces of plumbing that wouldn't have been found in a building on the banks. He took them to an expert, who examined them and said they came from a nineteenth-century steamboat.

As legends will, the legend of the *Sultana* had locally grown to the point where its hull was filled with gold and silver and the skeletons, if not the preserved bodies, of hundreds of the victims. But Sam Oliver had no greed for the treasure, and he went ahead and planted the field in soybeans, which grew tall and obscured the site, until one day he encountered a stranger sitting in a car beside the field, with a bunch of maps and charts spread out before him. The stranger asked Sam Oliver if he knew where the *Sultana* was buried. Oliver, suspicious of him, said, "Naw."

The stranger showed him the map in his lap and pointed to a spot on it, saying, "I've done a lot of research on this, and I believe the *Sultana* is right there."

Sam studied the map. "You're wrong," he said, and jabbed his finger at another spot. "It's about fifty feet north. My tractor driver plowed up pieces of boiler when I cleared that field."

The stranger was Jerry Potter, a young lawyer whose office in Memphis has a twenty-first-floor view of Mound City and environs. He has made a consuming hobby out of the story of the *Sultana*, and hopes to write a book about it. Now that he had located the owner of the soybean field, if not the exact location where the steamboat was buried, Potter had an ally in the search. He and Oliver devote all their spare time to it.

Wherever the *Sultana* finally went down, the fickle Grandfather has long since covered her beneath twenty feet of sand and silt. One popular theory was that the boat, coming to rest at the head of the Mound City Chute, had blocked off that chute and forced the Grandfather to take a different course eastward. All along the Grandfather are his little grandchildren: bowed lakes which were once his main course but in the endless process of his meandering and cutting off have become closed away from him. The mass of soybean acreage between the Mound City Chute and the present course of the Grandfather is still known as Chicken Island, one of the brood of "Paddy's Hen and Chicken Islands," and somewhere in that thick alluviation of rich silt is buried the *Sultana*.

Jerry Potter and Sam Oliver are using a magnetometer and a water probe to hunt for her. The magnetometer has helped them zero in on an area of 100 by 300 feet within which the 40-by-260 hull of the *Sultana* probably lies, and the water probe, a jet-spraying pipe inserted through a four-inch casing, has flushed up telltale debris, particularly charcoal, which could only have come from the burnt timbers of a steamboat.

The next step is to begin actual excavation, but that would be a very costly process, perhaps $500,000 or more. Sam's wealthy father, Dearmont Oliver, is willing to subsidize the project in the hope of recovering the whole hull, building a museum around it, and turning it into a tourist attraction. Bright dreams surround this endeavor, although few of the people involved in it have stopped to wonder why any tourists would go out of their way to see the remains of a steamboat that nobody has heard about. Still, anything that might bring life back into Mound City . . .

Kim finds Sam Oliver to be a patient but quietly excited adventurer with a respect for the past and an honest, unselfish approach to the quest for the *Sultana*. "Are you sure of its location *now?*" Kim asks him.

Sam nods eagerly. "Uh-huh. We sure are." He tells her that

the next step will be to dig a test trench down to about twenty feet and then, if they find the hull, excavate a gradual slope that will accommodate heavy earthmoving machinery. "We don't think we'll find anything inside the hull," he says. "But what's important is just the history, and proving that it *is* the *Sultana.*"

"What do you think is really there?" she asks.

"Oh, maybe just some brass buttons off the uniforms. There might be some bones. There were so many people died on that boat. Sometimes when you're out there digging around, you get a kind of weird feeling, almost gruesome, like digging in a cemetery, so I don't know how I feel about getting into that boat. At one point we thought we might as well leave it alone once we found it: just mark it and let it be. But I've said this before, and I'll say it again: it might be *my* boat, because it's on my land, but the history belongs to the people, and we owe it to the people to uncover the boat. The phone calls and letters I've been getting—and Jerry, too—some of them from descendants of the people who died in the *Sultana* . . ."

As if in response to the mention of his name, Jerry Potter arrives. He doesn't look like a Memphis attorney; he is dressed to go rabbit hunting, or to probe for buried steamboats. Kim reflects, not for the first time, upon the habit people have of becoming her contacts promptly when she needs them. After the introductions, Kim asks him the same question she asked Sam Oliver: "Are you absolutely certain that what you've found is the *Sultana?*"

"*I* would probably be the most surprised person if it's not the *Sultana,*" he declares, but he presents the lawyer's case against the evidence: the charcoal they've found could have come from, say, a burning log jam in that area, or the remains of a burnt building that washed away into the river. But they've also found fuel coal, which could only have come from a steamboat's engine room.

Sam Oliver says, "I think the next day we work over there we'll hit the hull. We've gone through the elimination process, and we're ready to hit it. We'll be excited. . . ."

Both men are clearly obsessed with the search, and Kim

wonders how they will really feel when they do find the *Sultana*. "I'll probably become depressed," Jerry admits. "I'll have to find a new hobby. My wife will be relieved—I've been so devoted to this thing for years. But we'll have such a sense of accomplishment, as if we've uncovered a page of American history that very few people know about. It's amazing how few people know about the *Sultana*."

Kim knows all too well that the romance of the search is greater than the joy of the actual finding. In her explorations through these lost cities she hasn't found very much, not even the ruin of a major building that would be comparable to the ruin of the *Sultana*, but the search itself—the questing, the asking, and the wanting to know these towns and their reasons for existence—has been enough: the means better than the ends, the questions better than the answers, the looking better than the seeing.

She never even *saw* any mound at Mound City.

Arkansas City, Arkansas

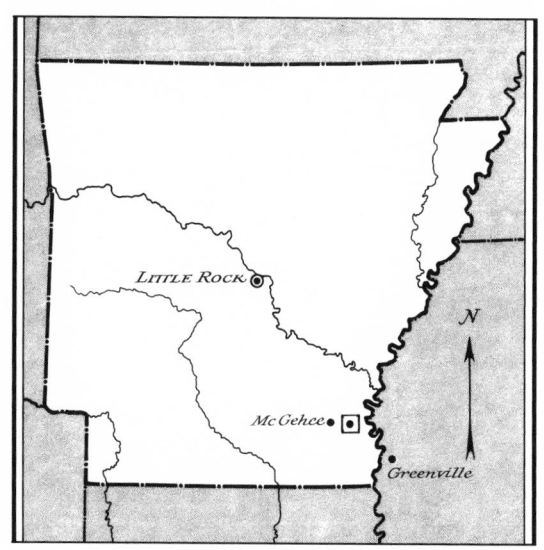

LITTLE ROCK

McGehee

Greenville

N

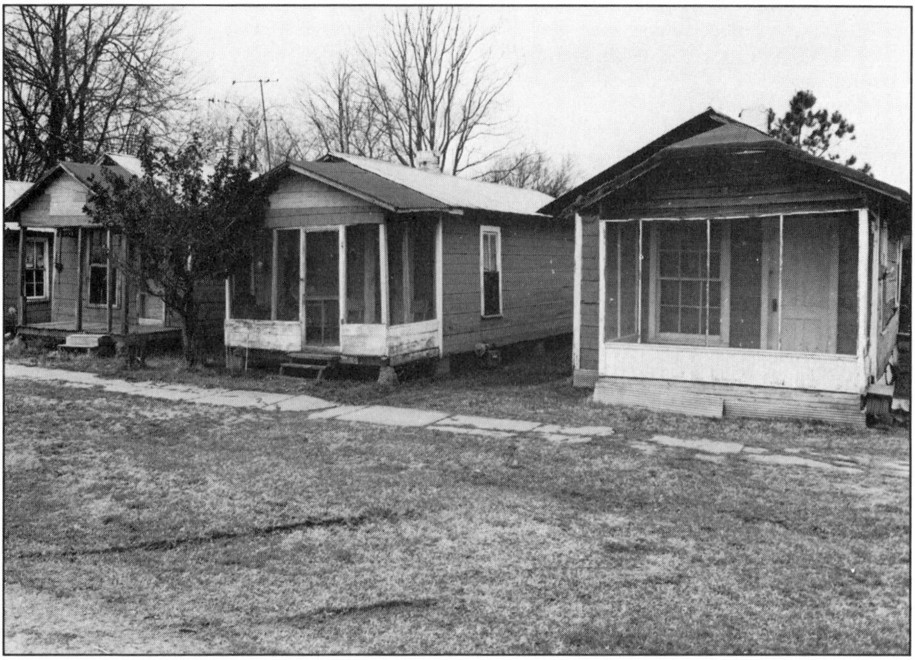

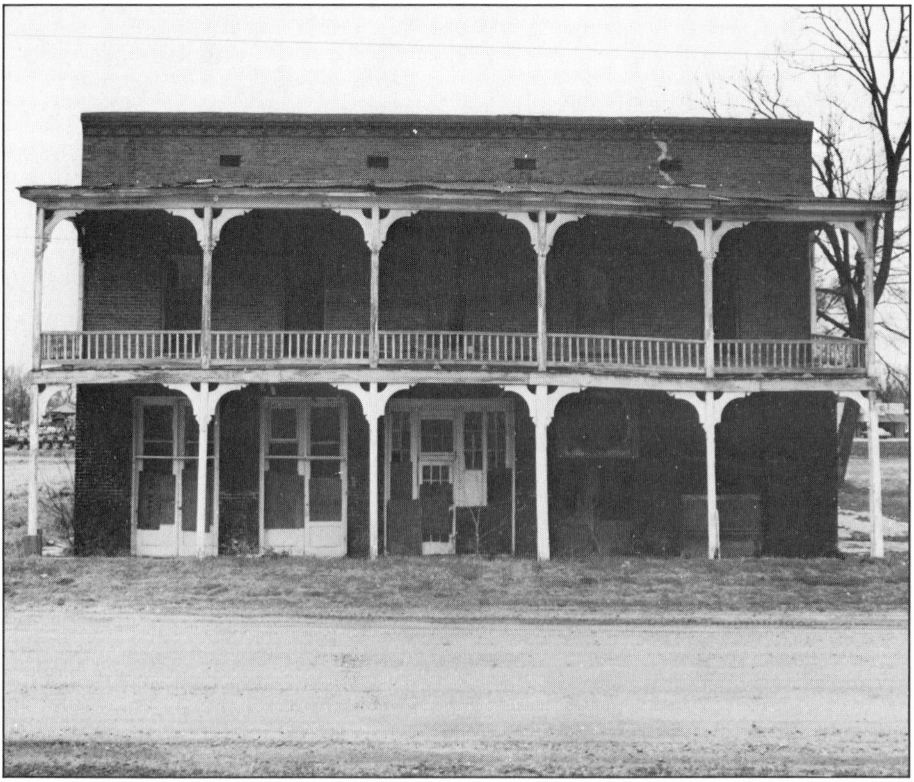

IF SAM CLEMENS STOPPED to visit it today, supposing he could find his way inland several miles from the Mississippi, which has left it more forsaken than Mound City, he would be struck by its silence, an eerie quiet without even a trace of the hell-of-a-place atmosphere it had in the time of the steamboat, when he knew it. He knew how fickle the Grandfather of Waters could be, and what it had done to towns along its banks, but even he would be stunned into melancholy by the changes that time and the river have wrought upon this once-noisy metropolis.

Because of its name, it is our flagship city, but Arkansas City is no more typical of Arkansas than, say, Virginia City is of Virginia; that one, which is not the famous Virginia City in Nevada or even the one in Montana, but a remote hamlet lost in the Blue Ridge Mountains of *Virginia*, has no suggestion of the piedmont or the tidewater, as this one has no suggestion of the Arkansas uplands. This is all delta. It is the only truly *Southern* place of these lost cities, and by very virtue of being Southern it takes on the flavor of Mississippi or Louisiana more than of Arkansas, which is not a Southern state, despite its misguided association with the Confederacy.

Half of the nation's states have their eponymous state cities: some of them, like Kansas City or Oklahoma City or especially New York City, became the largest metropolises in their states; others, like Iowa City, Texas City, and Jersey City, managed to become true cities; but most did not, and some, like Alabama City, Montana City, and *that* Virginia City, are little more than locales or ghost towns. Arkansas City *could have* become a major river port rivaling Vicksburg and Helena, if not Memphis or St. Louis. But the Grandfather first abused it, then abandoned it.

Ironically, the best-known Arkansas City, the much more populous one, is the one in Kansas, where they pridefully but mistakenly pronounce the name of the city and the river that runs by it to rhyme with the state: Ar*kan*ziss. For years, until the invention of the Zip Code, much of the mail, including perishable baby chicks, destined for the fourteen thousand people in Arkansas City, Kansas, was misdirected to the town of seven hundred in Arkansas, to the chagrin of both postmasters, and even today some crosscountry truck driver will negotiate his eighteen-wheel rig along the narrow blacktop that runs eleven miles from the nowhere highway to the nowhere town, and, finding that he is not in Arkansas City, Kansas, but five hundred miles off course, he will vent his trucker's displeasure on whatever quiet, modest citizen informs him of his error. Usually this happens to be Mr. Robert Montgomery, the postmaster of the small third-class post office, recently moved from its old brick storefront facing the levee to a more official-looking building beside the volunteer fire station and the outdoor basketball court.

Monty, who gets kidded for his lack of resemblance to the Hollywood star of the same name, just as Arkansas City gets kidded by those who know the big one in Kansas, is Kim's first contact when she arrives. Had she known where to look, she might have found the small village library, in an old house, but the post office is more conspicuous. In a city as small as this one, the postmaster will know everybody.

"Well, there's a few young couples here I don't know," Mr. Montgomery admits to Kim. "Just moved in the last year or so. But everybody gets their mail right here: we don't make any deliveries."

Postmaster for "only" fourteen years, he tells Kim he doesn't know anything and she ought to talk to Verna Reitzammer, who was postmaster for forty-two years. As he is giving her directions to Mrs. Reitzammer's house, a woman comes into the post office to check her box. "Wait a minute," the postmaster says to Kim. "Maybe that's who you want to see first: the mayor's wife. She can show you everything."

He introduces them. Judy Bixler, forty-three, who looks as young as the youthful mayoress of Lake City (although, as Kim will later learn, she has three children in their twenties; the eldest, Cherie, works as a fashion designer in New York, where so many young people go), seems to have come into the post office at this very moment almost by design, for she will prove to be Kim's primary contact. Kim will never meet Judy's husband, His Honor Richard, who is now in his third term as the town's mayor, although it is strictly a part-time activity, taking a share of his active career as a beekeeper. B & B Honey is, next to the giant Potlatch Corporation (paper), the town's biggest industry, although the business is "operated" by the bees themselves, and their busy apiarist, Bixler, has found time as mayor to improve the streets, install drainage ditches, build a new water tower, a small "city hall" with recreational facilities, and a senior citizens' center, and acquire a new fire truck.

Judy Bixler apologizes for not being able to take Kim to the mayor himself: Richard Bixler is out in the fields with his bees. "There aren't any farm crops in bloom yet," she explains, "but there's always something in bloom along the river for the bees."

She herself is a busy hairdresser, but at the moment the town's lone beauty shop has no customers waiting, and she will be glad to answer any questions or show Kim around. "What would you like to see first?" she asks.

"Is there a cemetery?" Kim asks.

"Sort of." Judy smiles. "Follow me." In her station wagon she leads Kim in Zephyra through the platted streets, each lined with sidewalks, ancient sidewalks cracked and tossed and weedy, sidewalks that run past mostly vacant lots, past the impressive courthouse, not on a square but in a neighborhood surrounded by houses, and on out to the northern edge of town, out a street called Avalon (although Avalon was the ocean island where King Arthur was buried, most of the streets in Arkansas City were renamed in the 1950s after the steamboats of old: "Delta Queen," "Kate Adams," "President," "Morning Star") and to the Arkansas City Cemetery.

Such as it is. Flooded more often than the Lake City Cemetery, it was not even intended for the graves of the "better class of citizens," as old maps once referred to the house lots of the white population, but became, rather, a potter's field for the "low class of citizens," or blacks, who have always been in the majority of the population here. But nowadays blacks and whites alike are buried in higher ground at Trippe, a community to the west, or elsewhere. John Campbell, whose slaves cleared a small plantation here in the 1830s, lies here with his wife in unmarked graves, not in the amphibious bogs of the cemetery proper but within a small mound rising up from it, possibly an ancient burial mound of the same Indians who established the larger mound several hundred miles upriver at Mound City.

Kim *sees* this little mound and starts to climb it to look at the few headstones there, but a snake lies coiled in her path and frightens her away. If the snake is seeking to sun itself, it will have to wait for several days: the sun will not shine during the time Kim is in Arkansas City. She returns to her car and remarks to Judy Bixler, "I won't find much of the historical past here."

"The past of Arkansas City wasn't historical," Judy says. "It was hysterical." She invites Kim to go home with her, to her house-and-beauty-shop just a few feet from the post office (everything in this miniature city seems to be just a few feet from everything else). The Bixler residence is a modern house that looks to be reconstructed from old bricks, although Judy explains that the bricks are "antiqued," new bricks made to look old; the interior walls, however, are paneled with old boards taken from a sharecropper's shanty, weathered with a silvery patina. The street that runs out front, parallel to the levee, is called variously Front Avenue or De Soto Avenue or sometimes just Main Street, and throughout the town's heyday it was a one-sided main thoroughfare on the riverfront, lined with shoulder-to-shoulder shops and stores. Judy Bixler's house occupies the former site of one of the hotels. Another hotel, of two stories, is still standing, a scant two blocks away, the only really old relic along the street.

One room adjoining the Bixlers' living room has been equipped as a modern beauty parlor, with a row of chairs and floor-model hair dryers, although there is no sign out front advertising it, no B & B Beauty to match the B & B Honey. Maybe, Kim reflects, the double B's don't stand for "Bixler and Bixler," but for "Beauty and Bee." During the next two days she will see quite a lot of the Beauty, but never meet the Bee.

"Do any of your customers ever get to talking about the size of the town—whether they hope it will get bigger or go on getting smaller?" Kim asks.

"Most people like it just the way it is," Judy says. "The older people, who remember it as a large place bustling with activity— I don't think they would wish for it to be like that again."

Now Judy is on the phone, trying to line up some people to be interviewed by Kim.

The landing on the river was there for years before it was called Arkansas City. For steamboats coming up the Mississippi from New Orleans, it was the first place to stop and take on fuel wood after Vicksburg. Most likely it got its ambitious name, Arkansas City, simply because it was the first stop in Arkansas for a boat coming from Louisiana and Mississippi. Upstream from Arkansas City is the place where the Arkansas River flows into the Mississippi, and an equal number of miles up the Arkansas is the first white settlement of the Territory, Arkansas Post, established in 1686, two hundred years before our commemorative year. This place has been marked by events that may have been hysterical but are surely historical: it became in 1717 the center for a scheme far more ambitious than the naming of an aspiring town "City." The Scottish-born financier and mountebank John Law, who hoaxed all Europe with an investment scheme that came to be known internationally as the "Mississippi Bubble," actually intended to colonize large tracts of wilderness near Arkansas Post, but the closest he came to it was to ship five hundred black slaves from Guinea to clear the way for eight hundred Alsatian

Rhinelanders. The Germans had no experience with frontier life but held out as best they could, with the help of friendly Indians, until the bubble burst and they emigrated to New Orleans, there to settle a more civilized area that is still known as the German Coast.

Arkansas Post changed hands from the French to the Spanish and back to the French until it became the first capital of Arkansas Territory. One of its residents, John Patterson, the first white child born in Arkansas, in 1790, lived on until that fateful year of 1886 and wrote his own epitaph: "I was born in a Kingdom; / Raised in an Empire; / Attained manhood in a Territory; / Am now a citizen of a State; / And have never been one hundred miles from where I live." He did not identify any particular place one hundred miles away where he had never been. He could not have been thinking of Little Rock, which is farther than that; more likely it was Arkansas City, which became called such as early as 1850. If the city was fated to spend its later years being confused with Arkansas City, Kansas, it probably suffered very early from confusion with Arkansas Post, which thrived as a major steamboat port even after it lost the capital to Little Rock.

During young Sam Clemens's days as an apprentice steamboat pilot in the late 1850s, he knew the fuel-stop woodyard not as Arkansas City, but only by the name of whoever owned the woodyard after John Campbell died and it was no longer called Campbell's Landing. Three miles upstream from it, and in competition with it, another landing tried to call itself "city" in the early 1870s, though it succeeded only in giving its name to the new county, Chicot (from a French word meaning "stump of a tooth" and referring to the snags or stumps of trees left littering the swamps after the timber was felled for steamboat fuel). Chicot City was very quickly thwarted in its ambition to become even a village, let alone a city, although Chicot County thrived, and Lake Chicot, formed in an old abandoned oxbow of the Grandfather, is the largest of Arkansas's natural lakes.

If young Sam Clemens did not know Arkansas City, he knew the only major Arkansas town on that stretch of the river, called Napoleon, which was founded in 1820 by a French general from

Arkansas Post, a subordinate of Bonaparte named Frederick Notrebe. For years during the booming of the steamboat era, Napoleon flourished as the principal Arkansas port on the Mississippi; because it was located at the confluence of both the Arkansas River and the White River with the Mississippi, it was the transfer station for cargoes and passengers on the smaller streams whose sternwheelers could not manage the Grandfather. When Sam Clemens first saw Napoleon in 1854, it was "a good big self-complacent town. Town that was county-seat of a great and important county [Desha, of which Arkansas City later became, and still is, county seat]; town with a big United States marine hospital; town of innumerable fights—an inquest every day; town where I had used to know the prettiest girl, and the most accomplished, in the whole Mississippi valley . . ." But when Mark Twain came back twenty years later to look at it, he found "a town no more—swallowed up, vanished, gone to feed the fishes; nothing left but a fragment of a shanty and a crumbling brick chimney."

Is it better to be consumed by one's spouse than abandoned? The Mississippi River swallowed Napoleon whole; many years later the river went away and left Arkansas City miles inland. But by 1874, when an especially devastating flood drove the few remaining citizens of Napoleon southward to Arkansas City, the newer town had already been incorporated; in 1879 it was declared the new seat for Desha County (it is pronounced Dee-*shay*, named after Ben Desha, that early settler and politician who was Bob Crittenden's second in his duel with Conway). The day would come when only its function as the seat of county government and jurisprudence would keep Arkansas City alive, and the citizens of thriving McGehee, centrally located eight miles to the west, would clamor to take away those functions.

The people Judy Bixler is trying to contact are not available today, she reports with regret to Kim after several phone calls. For once, it seems, Kim's interviewees are not lined up and ready for her.

Judy suggests that they go out to lunch. Where? Kim did not notice anything approximating a restaurant or café when she came into town. Except for Cave City and Lake City, none of these lost cities were large enough to support an eatery. But there are two restaurants in Arkansas City, and although Kim would not notice them she was fated to eat in both of them. For lunch today: Grundy's Blue Front. Located on Delta Queen Avenue, not far from an out-of-place ultramodern complex of the Arkansas City Schools, it is scarcely more than a shack, one large low-ceilinged room with a few tables and chairs haphazardly arranged on a dirty wooden floor. The exterior is painted a once-bright, now dull blue, but the name may as well refer to the menu. A permanent blue-plate special is meatloaf, white beans, lettuce salad, and cornbread. A large black woman (Mrs. Grundy? or just "the help"?) bakes her own pies fresh daily, but the dessert today is simple pound cake. Despite the cool weather, the beverage is iced tea, and it has been presweetened. The few other customers are either workingmen or farmers in town for the day. Judy tells Kim that her husband won't let her eat here alone, so she is glad to have Kim with her.

Kim remarks upon the quietness: even here in the Blue Front their voices seem to be the only sounds; there is no banging around in the kitchen, no talk from the other customers. Judy apologizes that Kim won't be able to hear a thing from any of the people that Judy is trying to line up for her, not today. Could she come back tomorrow?

The afternoon is free, but not empty: Kim goes for a walk. Leaving her car at Judy Bixler's, she climbs "Judy's Hill," the levee. She walks along the roadbed atop it, looking down at the remains of storefronts along De Soto Avenue, at the whole town spread out before her, platted evenly and orderly, but sparsely planted with buildings, as if a selective tornado had plucked out from each block a handful of stores or homes. On this levee where she walks, the tents of refugees during the Great Flood of 1927 were planted side by side for miles; the western slope of the levee became a boat dock for hundreds of skiffs bringing the homeless to this island, while the eastern slope of the levee, where

the risen waters of the Mississippi were actually lower than the
waters of the Arkansas on the western side, was crowded with
rescue steamboats, houseboats, and makeshift motor launches
coming and going over the overBig overMuddy. But Kim does
not know this; she has not yet seen the photographs of the human
congestion atop the levee during the flood. With no sound from
the far-distant river now, with no sound at all except the wind
blowing her hair back, she sees not the flood, but the town as it
must have appeared at its best, in the Gay Nineties: excursion
steamers and showboats lining the waterfront before the levee
obscured it, the floating opera and the floating palace, elegant
ladies on their way from the elegant hotels to the opera house,
gambling men in vests and string ties going and coming from
the thirteen saloons along the Front Avenue (there was not a
church in town in those days), and the carriages driving away
from the railroad depot, where a spanking new passenger
train has pulled up. In all this quiet, it isn't hard to imagine the
sounds, the noises, then: of bells, whistles, gongs, calliopes,
brass bands, the songs of roustabouts, cries of vendors,
and laughter everywhere, of people having the time of their
lives.

Kim is having the time of her life. She is the happiest she
will ever be in any of these lost cities, save one, toward the end.
She has not yet seen the detailed maps that the Sanborn Map
Company, purveyors to the fire-insurance industry, who in-
spected every building in every city of any size in the United
States and left detailed dimensions and data, made of Arkansas
City in our cartographic year of 1886, in which Front Avenue
already had its two-story Parker Hotel ("new, not finished inside")
on the same block with two saloons, a dry-goods-and-grocery, a
candy-and-fruit store, a drugs-and-stationery, and a millinery,
but even without the map Kim can already imagine that ladies'
hat shop, and the sort of trimmed and untrimmed flats and felts
and frilly bonnets with plumes and ostrich tips, aigrettes and
jetted ornaments, ribbons and wreaths. For a moment, Kim's
head feels naked. In those days, she would not have dared to
let her long blond locks blow free in the breeze as she walked

here along the levee, above the town drowsing in its afternoon tranquillity.

There on the corner, empty now except for the fenced basketball court, stood the proud Desha County Bank & Trust Company, red brick turret and tower and battlemented escutcheon with a block of stone deeply engraved "1 8 8 6," the year that Henry Thane built his romantic "skyscraper," tallest edifice in town (he would not put up the much bigger courthouse until 1900). Northeastward, toward the end of Front Avenue—not its actual termination so much as the place where it is deflected into a curve by a big house that blocks it—stands the home Henry Thane built for his second wife, Stella, in the newly popular Tudor style of fake half-timbered gables common after World War I. Since the bank was torn down, this house is all that is left of Henry Thane in Arkansas City; he was buried in its yard, but when Stella died in 1974, their son had his body removed to the Trippe Cemetery to join hers.

The rise and fall of Arkansas City can be measured in the rise and fall of Henry Thane, its self-styled "tycoon." Faulkner would have loved him; in fact, maybe Faulkner *did* love him, since Yoknapatawpha is but a buzzard's short flight across the river into those northwestern counties of Mississippi that provided the mother lode of Faulkner's fictions, wherein the tycoons are named Sartoris or De Spain or even Snopes, the selfsame ambitious honorable captains of finance or industry or at least striving, who rose, or never ceased trying doggedly despite all obstacles to rise, above the humble beginnings and lack of fortune that heritage or simple genetic ontogeny shackled them with, who fought their way savagely out of the brambles and thickets of the primeval unpitying wilderness and out of the even denser thicker brambles and thickets of their creator's labyrinthine baroque congested prose style and syntax, not for monetary gain so much as for sheer survival, to keep from being swallowed up, as a town will be swallowed up by the river, into the dark maw and oblivion of that ornate and convoluted reduplication of sentences.

Henry Thane could not talk like that. Try as he might, he could not think, *Yes, even with this golden stud in my collar bobbing up and down with the slow rise and fall of my Adam's apple I am not able, I am not disposed, to transmute the humble straightforward pedestrian sentiments of my avaricious heart into noble highsounding honorable oratory, not because I am bereft of extraordinary intelligence and lacking in all mellifluousness of utterance but because the people of Arkansas City, if they caught me speaking this way I am thinking, would ship me off to the state lunatic asylum at Little Rock.*

The closest he ever came was when he paid his $100 to Goodspeed for the privilege of having his capsule biography (self-written) and even a capsule autographed portrait printed in the 1890 *Biographical and Historical Memoirs of Southern Arkansas,* when he was already a tycoon at age forty. The portrait shows his dark handlebar mustache, like a riverboat gambler's, drooping down both sides of his jowls to points beneath his chin; his eyes large, fierce, and penetrating; and that golden stud in his tieless collar motionless over the unbobbing Adam's apple in a throat about to utter these words: *Let a man be industriously ambitious, and he will rise, whether having the prestige of fortune or the obscurity of poverty.*

But Henry Thane never talked like that. Or ever again wrote like that, either. His surviving writings, other than a piece of paper on which he jotted down his childhood memories for his son, consist of a series of newspaper articles, almost senile ramblings, that he wrote for the local weekly at the age of eighty, after his empire had fallen in the floodwaters of 1927. With titles like "Early Days in Southeast Arkansas," "The Passing of Chicot City," "Some Tales I Was Told," and especially "Arkansas City," they provide fragmentary information from one man's imperfect memory of the past, but do very little to explain or even reveal his character.

The loquacious people who think and speak too much throughout Faulkner were of Scottish descent, or French, or African. Henry Thane was German. Not just of descent: he was born in Prussia, although at the age of two he was brought by his father, Franz, to this country. The romantic name, which suggests the Anglo-Saxon king's soldier granted land for his military service, coming from the Old English *thegn* for "freeman" or "warrior" and related to the Germanic *thegnaz* for "boy" or "man," has no equivalent in modern German. One thinks, of course, of Macbeth's reiteration, "I am thane of Cawdor," and of Lady Macbeth's babble, "The thane of Fife had a wife: where is she now?"

A simple solution to avoid the triteness of naming an aspiring metropolis something "City" is to name it simply "Metropolis," and Franz Thane settled with his wife, Margareth, and son, Henry, on a farm near the ambitious hamlet of Metropolis, Illinois, which never became a metropolis. (The name also conformed to the growing American fad for Greek-sounding places, *polis* meaning "city," and *metro*, "mother," therefore Mother City, which no American city was ever actually named, though there are an abundance of *poleis*, including Indianapolis, Minneapolis, and such as Arkopolis, as we shall see.) Henry grew to young manhood tending chickens and living in a one-room log house with a mud chimney in a forest, neighbor to other German immigrants trying to farmstead the American wilderness, not unlike those duped by John Law in 1719 to brave the forests of Arkansas Post.

At the age of sixteen he left home for better schooling at Warrenton, Missouri. Almost certainly, at such a small place, he knew young John Milton Norris, later of our Cherokee City, who was only one year his senior and enrolled at the same small college: one imagines them talking together of their casual notion for the "cities" they later built, one occupying a position in northwestern Arkansas corresponding diagonally exactly to the position of the other in southeastern Arkansas. But neither man graduated, Norris learning just enough to prevent him from protesting the title "doctor" later attached to him, and Thane so little that he would later claim his only education was in "the school of hard knocks."

Dropping out of college during a winter's blizzard that left him yearning to see the sunny but still-recovering and reconstructing South, he went down the Mississippi to Memphis, where he found a job driving an ice wagon for the marvelous new ice plant that actually manufactured the wonderful stuff. He came to know Mound City across the river and to wonder if a railroad would ever be built to it, for he was newly fascinated with land steam. Water steam, in the form of steamboats, did not captivate him, partly because he had an aversion to water in any form, never having learned how to swim. To cure this phobia, he tried for a while to work as a boom rat or slough pig, the man who maneuvers a raft or boom of timber, acres of free-floating logs held together by an encircling chain of logs down the free ride of the Grandfather. The image of the logger with pike in hand leaping from rolling log to jammed log does not apply: the Mississippi log-rafter was more a boatman than a lumberjack. Still, Henry Thane, being unable to swim and therefore taking extraordinary pains to avoid situations in which he might have to swim, was scared, and soon quit.

In the fall of 1872, at the age of twenty-two, he "heard of the railroad activity at a new town christened 'Chicot City,' some distance below Napoleon." The latter town would that same winter complete its fall into the river; Chicot City was just beginning, just aspiring to cityhood. Henry Thane took a mail boat there, and found the landing piled high with freight and cotton discharged by the new railroad and waiting for shipment by steamboat down to New Orleans. The town consisted of many cheap buildings being quickly erected, and two railroads in the process of construction. Henry hopped on one of the trains, a few flatcars between a ten-ton locomotive and a caboose, and rode twenty-eight miles into the Arkansas interior, to the end of the line, in the pine forests. Impressed by the timber all along the route, and by the budding railroad, and by the fact that Chicot City had only one large general store, he bought a corner lot there, hurried back to Memphis to settle his affairs and arrange for a stock of goods, then settled into Chicot City, built a store, and became a merchant.

This beginning, so similar in its details to that of Everard Dickinson starting out in Buffalo City, contained a big difference: Henry Thane was a driven man. It is easy to suppose that part of his motivation came from his correspondence with his college sweetheart back in Warrenton, Miss Fanny Tidswell, a native of London who loved him but hoped he would stop roaming and settle down. There survives a letter written by her father, a Warrenton businessman named Thomas Tidswell, to his son Tom informing him that Henry Thane had suddenly shown up overnight, married Fanny, and taken her back to some eight-hundred-mile-distant *terra incognita* called Chicot City.

Fanny was appalled to discover what sort of "city" Chicot turned out to be, but she settled in gamely there and bore a child, a girl. Chicot City grew very quickly to a population of a thousand, and Henry Thane's mercantile prospered, despite periodic rampages of the Grandfather. One, in 1874, caused a local depression, hard times, and general bankruptcy, and brought Henry his closest experience to drowning; another big flood, in 1876, frightened Fanny and made her homesick for Warrenton. The owners of the railroads in Chicot City were talking of moving the terminus to a different landing. On the nation's Centennial (he loved the Fourth and would eventually die on it), Henry Thane sold his store for $100 to a man who wanted to move it to a plantation and convert it to a cabin, and he took Fanny and their daughter three miles south to live in Arkansas City.

His rise thereafter was quick, unrelenting, almost fated: he would not compete with the many merchants already in Arkansas City, but turned instead to law, studying it on his own in what amounted to that day's equivalent of the quick home-study course. He passed the easy bar examination in time to set himself up as a lawyer for the railroad just as it closed its terminus at Chicot City, killing that town, and opened a new terminus in Arkansas City, booming that town.

Was it Henry Thane who suggested, as a sort of public-relations gimmick, that the town change its name to Arkopolis? This trendy name, painted in big letters on the roof of the river side of the railroad depot and warehouse, wasn't inspired by Henry's origins in Metropolis so much as it was by the same yearning for cosmopolitan elegance that finds today's insecure "Arkansans" naming their areas Metrocentre Mall and such. Nobody told Henry or whoever that Little Rock itself, the perennial center of that parvenu yearning, had already, back in 1821, tried on the name Arkopolis, but when the fad got out of hand nationally—Missourians attempted unsuccessfully to name their capital Missouropolis—gave up the high-sounding title in favor of the simpler but belittling Little Rock. The citizens of Arkansas City filed an official protest with the post office in favor of retaining their name, and "Arkopolis" was forgotten.

The same year the railroad abandoned Chicot City in favor of Arkansas City, Henry Thane (who had already gotten himself elected justice of the peace so he could be called "Judge Thane" for the rest of his life) got himself elected mayor at age twenty-eight on the promise of bringing a semblance of law and order to that wild, free "hell of a place." Before Thane's mayoralty, according to Goodspeed's description,

> there was in this county a lawless element, outlaws and ruffians, who secreted themselves in the fastnesses of the great swamps, and at times sallied forth to murder and to pillage. All the current stories of their depredations, and deeds of danger and of strife, if collected, would make a good-sized, if not useful, volume.

Thane paid Goodspeed to print that he "was the first mayor who succeeded in ridding the town of the lawless element that always infest prosperous river towns." He also wanted Goodspeed (in 1890) to note that he served as postmaster of Arkansas City "for five years under President Hayes' and President Arthur's administrations" and in 1882 was elected to the State Senate for a four-year term. In our victory year of 1886, he mounted a door-to-door campaign to be elected clerk of Desha County. There is, strangely, no mention of his dealings to take over the Desha Bank. In none of his writings about himself, in Goodspeed or in his articles, does he ever mention his banking activity, which was the principal focus of his life. Like Flem Snopes, who rose from obscurity to president of the Jefferson Bank in Faulkner's Snopes trilogy, Henry Thane may have accumulated a closetful of skeletons. Possibly the picture of himself he wanted the world to see was not the flinthearted usurer, forecloser, moneymonger, but the civic-minded official, jurist, public servant. He was literally a man of different hats: he took off the silk hat he wore to the bank, and wore a fedora to the post office, a homburg to the mayor's office, a derby to the court, and his favorite, a wide-brimmed white planter's hat, to take over a farm, buy out a timber spread, gain control of a lumber mill, receiver a store, garnishee a payroll, evict a widow, and meet the *Kate Adams* when she docked with his latest order of cigars.

The silk hat made him feel uncomfortable, but in time it was the one he wore most often: he came to control not just the Desha Bank of Arkansas City but the banks at Watson, McGehee, Dermott, Lake Village, Dumas, and Eudora—all the principal towns of both Desha and Chicot counties, which encompassed all of southeastern Arkansas. With that much financial power, he had extravagant political power, too, and his power over the "weaker sex," as he called them, was unlimited. As "Miss Fanny" approached middle age and devoted herself to her house and daughter, Henry discreetly philandered, not even needing to enforce silence with threats or bribes. All his life, or at least into his eighties, he remained not simply potent and virile but irresistible to women, and not only because of his wealth and power but also because of his endurance in the art and act of love. Here he differed from Flem Snopes, who was impotent.

The years Faulkner would have chosen to present Henry Thane were those before World War I, around 1910–14, when Thane was in his early sixties and at the height of his political, financial, and sexual powers, and Arkansas City had crested upon its boom. The population was a stable twelve hundred, excluding the floating (both literally and figuratively) population who came on excursion boats, show boats, house boats. Henry Thane outfitted luxuriously a couple of large houseboats, the freshwater equivalent of yachts, one for his own use, one as a wedding gift to his daughter, Nellie, to live on it with her husband, George Reeze, who managed Thane's sawmill. *Reeze will have to be a principal character in our Faulknerian drama. Another character will have*

to be the young Scottish physician, Vernon McCammon, whose name
sounds right out of the Yoknapatawpha saga. Dr. McCammon's beautiful
wife, Mattie, has to have a minor part, too, threatening to become major.
Other actors in the story will have to include J. L. Parker, president of
the rival Bank of Arkansas City; Sophia Furlong, proprietress of the
Commercial Hotel; and Bill Reitzammer, who runs the corner store and
newsstand. Our heroine will have to be, not Mattie McCammon,
but Stella Maynard, who is the niece of Fanny Thane, recently
deceased.

Thirty years younger than her aunt and her uncle Henry, Stella
will have come each spring or late winter from Warrenton, Missouri,
when it is still in the grips of chill, to visit Arkansas City, watch the
greening of the grass that covers the levee, and stay until the first magnolia
blooms. She alone will have to know the extent of Uncle Henry's involvement with Mattie McCammon. Henry Thane will have to have imported
the young Scotsman, fresh out of medical school, to compete with old Doc
Cotesworth P. Smith, whom Thane did not like, and Henry Thane will
have to have fallen, as any man would, for Vernon McCammon's lovely
wife. Stella will have to have a powerful crush on the young doctor, and
will have to be hoping that her uncle Henry will steal the doctor's wife
and leave him available to Stella.

J. L. Parker's bank will have to be only half as big as Henry's, but
J.L. will have to be even more ambitious than Henry once had been while
building his empire, and J.L. will have to concentrate on cotton and let
Henry have the lumber. Cotton will have to be thriving; lumber will have
to be dwindling. J.L. will have to escort Stella a couple of times to the
opera house to see the popular melodramas, Sweetest Girl in Dixie and
Cow Puncher, and he will have to be close enough to Stella to be on
the verge of learning what she knows about Henry's cuckoldry of Vernon
McCammon. The opera-house plays, trying out here before moving on
to Little Rock, always will have to have a villain played by the most
handsome, dashing actor in the company, and J.L. will always identify
with this figure. He, not Henry Thane, will have to be our villain. But
Henry Thane cannot be our full hero; that role will have to be reserved
to Vernon McCammon.

Like the Snopes saga, our Arkansas City tale will have to have three
separate narrators. There will be likable Bill Reitzammer, the grocer and

newsdealer, good-natured, witty, self-educated, shrewd, and given to long-winded philosophizing about the goings-on around him. If he reminds us of V. K. Ratliff, so much the better. Then, for a kind of counterpoint, there will have to be the narration of George Reeze, Henry's son-in-law and manager of the sawmill, crude, rough, foul-mouthed, earthy, sardonic, cynical, direct. He will have to have special reasons for hating both J. L. Parker and his father-in-law, and from earliest childhood he will have to have been the bitterest enemy of good Bill Reitzammer.

Finally, there will have to be the narration of Stella Maynard herself, in a cultivated, poetic, nearly lyrical voice, omniscient and with a wisdom tainted by her innocence and good intentions, for though she will have to love Vernon McCammon and will have to hope her uncle Henry will steal Mattie McCammon, she will have to be extremely devoted to her uncle Henry, who has always been good to her.

What will happen? Given the setting, in Arkansas City, and the time, the carefree days before World War I, and these people, these basically good but ambitious and grasping characters, anything could happen, and anything will, and always will have to: Kim on the levee imagines this story still going on, without resolution or climax, the plots thickening in a perpetual coagulation of incidents, narrative thread stretching infinitely toward a perpetual horizon.

It will not spoil her imagination of the story, or ours, to know this "outcome": Stella married Uncle Henry. Henry Thane at the age of sixty-three gave her the first of three sons; the last one was conceived when he was a ripe old sixty-nine. Having built the St. Clement's Episcopal Church (still standing, although its congregation is reduced to three) for his first wife, Miss Fanny, he now built for Miss Stella the large red brick Christian Church (now torn down after years of slow deterioration). For Miss Stella he also built the Tudor house on Front Avenue, which remained in her hands until her death on the Fourth of July in 1974, thirty-six years after his, at the age of eighty-eight. We must imagine that Stella tamed Henry during all those later years of his life, satisfied all his desires, and comforted him during—or, rather, for long after—the Great Flood of 1927, which destroyed his empire.

In his short essay, "Floods," of 1932, Henry Thane does not even mention the big one, of 1927, just as none of his writing contains mention of his bank. He mentions the formation of, but not his leading role in, the Desha Levee District in 1886, and the building of a vast system of drainage ditches. In 1917 he was the representative of Desha County in the stage legislature that voted to consolidate all the levee districts and to raise all the levees from six feet to their present height of twenty feet or more. He briefly discusses the 1922 flood, when a split in the levee, called locally a "crevasse," brought out great numbers of convicts from the state penitentiary for repairs and rescue—bringing to mind Faulkner again and his story about the 1927 flood, "Old Man," incorporated into the novel *The Wild Palms*.

The epic voyage of the "tall convict" in Faulkner's story begins when a deputy shouts, "Turn out of there! The levee went out at Mound's Landing an hour ago. Get up out of it!"

Mound Landing, Mississippi, is directly across the river from Arkansas City, Arkansas. The crevasse in the levee there was one of the worst, but it brought cheers to the anxious citizens of Arkansas City, because the breaking of a levee on one side of a river lessens the pressure against the levee on the other side. Kim remembers how Plug Eaton had explained the situation of floods on the St. Francis at Lake City: Plug's father and other men would patrol the levee with shotguns on their side of the river to keep people living on the other side of the river from sneaking over and deliberately cutting the levee to reduce the threat of flooding on their side. But that was the relatively small St. Francis River. This was the much greater Grandfather.

Ironically, the Grandfather himself did no harm to Arkansas City during the 1927 flood; the danger, and the damage, came from the Arkansas River, breaking through a large crevasse at Pendleton later in the same day when the crevasse opened at Mound Landing, and hitting Arkansas City from behind, unexpectedly. The realization that the town's peril was coming from its namesake river hit with awful force.

Water sweeping over the land from a crevasse, as it spreads for miles inland, does not, contrary to the imagination's picture of it, rush and roar and engulf everything before it in a tidal wave; it creeps and rises slowly, almost imperceptibly, yet insidiously, until, as the simple aphorism has it, in "seeking its own level," the water comes to rest against any ground higher than itself. This level, in the 1927 flood at Arkansas City, reached to the second floor of Henry Thane's bank and inundated all the one-story buildings along Front Avenue; every building within the limits of the town was at least partly submerged. There was no escape except to the levee, which became a thin, fragile island in danger of breaking from the sheer weight of the hundreds of people and animals taking refuge atop it. During the days and nights that the water remained high, it is a wonder how anyone in the refuge camp managed to sleep, save from sheer exhaustion.

Now that levee is tranquil again, and it is night. Now that levee is almost a useless anachronism, miles inland from the present peaceful snore of the Grandfather. The levee does nothing except delay the daily sunrise by a few moments, and tomorrow the sun won't appear to Kim. She has driven in search of accommodation for the night to McGehee, the county's larger town, still on arterial U.S. Highway 65. The one good motel there is filled with a group of casket salesmen en route to an undertaker's convention; she has to take a poor room in a less mentionable motel nearly hidden alongside the busy highway. All the motels along this route seem to be managed by Pakistanis who speak imperfect English. Restless in her room, Kim grabs a quick bite at a local restaurant that does not even have the "atmosphere" of Grundy's Blue Front, and she wishes she had dined there and perhaps slept in her car afterward; already "homesick" for whatever pleasure and happiness she had felt in Arkansas City, she drives back there, eleven miles, to look at it in the darkness. So few of these lost cities has she ever viewed in darkness; at night they are even more lost. But she finds this one. The expression used to describe the nocturnal evacuation of small downtowns, "They roll up the sidewalks at eight o'clock," scarcely applies to a village where every single block is bordered on every side by an ancient sidewalk that remains perpetually unrolled and unused. Grundy's Blue Front is closed; you don't find supper at a plate-lunch joint. Only one other establishment is open—Robinson's Café—and it doesn't look like the sort of place where eating is the main activity. Kim observes that most if not all of the customers are black. She parks a block farther on, at the "main" intersection of Sprague Street and De Soto Avenue, beside the outdoor basketball court where Henry Thane's bank had stood. There are no other cars parked anywhere in any direction except at Robinson's Café. She sees headlights moving up and down the top of the levee, twenty feet above her level, and, rolling down her window, she hears coming from that direction voices and the sound of car radios playing hard rock music. It is the first "noise" she has heard in Arkansas City.

Kids, she thinks, and remembers the nightly cruising of the Main Street in Beebe, Arkansas (and of what her correspondent in Brookings, South Dakota, has written about the Main Avenue there). Nowhere in any of these lost cities, not even the larger ones like Cave City or Lake City, has she seen a teen-ager, let alone watched to see how they amuse themselves at night. A lost city is an unlikely place to find the young.

A car comes by. Moving slowly, it heads for the levee, turns, climbs the levee, is gone a while, comes back, and parks across the street from her. The noise on the levee has ceased. The occupant of the car is a lone male. He gets out. He is a black man, and not young, and he holds something in his hand into which he is speaking. A tape recorder? For a moment Kim imagines that a fellow reporter is joining her. She has heard that the editor and publisher of *Ebony*, the largest weekly magazine for blacks, is a native of Arkansas City. But this man is talking into the radio phone of his automobile, which is a patrol car, the town marshal's official vehicle. Kim gets out of Zephyra, crosses the street, says hello to this man, tells him her name, tells him she's "doing a story" on Arkansas City, and asks, "Do you work for the marshal's office?"

"I am the marshal, ma'am," he says, with a kindly chuckle. "Nathaniel Hayes is the name." He pronounces it "*Nay*-thaniel." "Folks call me Nath."

"Do you mind if I get my tape recorder?"

"No, ma'am," he says. "You do that."

She fetches her tape recorder, parks it on the hood of his car, and asks, "How did you get this job?" Nath Hayes likes to talk, and he tells her the story. Same year Henry Thane died, 1938, Nath started as a part-time deputy for the sheriff's office, and worked part-time until 1951, when he was appointed a full-time deputy by legendary Sheriff Robert Moore (for whom the town's only nonsteamboat street is named). Nath worked for him for twenty-one years, until the day the sheriff died, then for Moore's widow, who replaced him for the remainder of his term as sheriff. In 1979, at the age of seventy, Nath Hayes retired from the sheriff's office—"That is, I *thought* I retired," he says, chuckling, "but after about three months of retirement, I tried a job as a security guard over at McGehee, until I heard that the town of Arkansas City had done got put out of a marshal, and I started workin here."

"What exactly do you do as marshal?" Kim asks.

"Patrol the streets, mostly," he says. "I just try the best of my ability to protect the citizens of Arkansas City. Not too much trouble. *Occasionally*"—he draws out these five syllables, pronouncing each precisely—"we have something. Things do happen. But it's not like what you'd expect in larger places. Because here everybody knows just about everybody by their first name, and we get along real good with both white and black."

Kim gestures toward the levee, where the high-school kids have quieted down. "Are they pretty well behaved?"

Nath smiles, revealing a fine set of teeth. "Yes, the young folk up on the levee there were gittin a bit loud with their music and their voices. Did you hear 'em? I just drove up there and said, 'OK, now, young folk, you're gittin a little loud, too loud, and we'd really appreciate it if you'd cut your music down.' They just said, 'OK, Mr. Hayes.' And those are the white kids, too, up on the levee. Sometimes the black kids shootin their basketballs there on the court beside your car, they'll stay a bit late and I'll get a complaint that they're gittin noisy, or maybe somebody usin a little profanity. I warn 'em and they'll say, 'OK. Sorry. We won't do it any more.' And they don't. And that's it."

"Mr. Hayes, do you remember the flood?"

"Call me Nath. Which flood? I remember a whole lot of floods, but you must be thinkin of the 1927 flood. OK. That one, I was workin for an engineer in charge of a section of the levee; we worked at this sackhouse over here, fillin sacks with dirt to sack the levee where the Mississippi was runnin over. We were takin a load of sacks down to a landing below here when we noticed the water had just started rollin in from that way, from the west, where they wasn't any Mississippi out that way. It was the Arkansas River, and we turned around and came back to town and got a phone call that the levee had broke at Pendleton, on the Arkansas. I remember this was maybe about twelve-thirty on Sunday afternoon of the twenty-fourth of April, and everybody started gittin out of their homes whatever they could to carry to the levee, right there. By nightfall the water was all over town, over our heads right here where we're standin, up over the top of that building there."

"Were a lot of houses destroyed, then?"

"It was a lot of 'em destroyed, yeah. Some of 'em were moved from their foundations and carried to the south end of town."

Five million acres of land in Arkansas were submerged. A flood gauge at Arkansas City, which had recorded progressively higher floodwaters—forty-six feet in the 1859 flood, fifty-five feet in the floods of 1912–13, and fifty-eight feet in the 1922 flood—reached the unprecedented depth of sixty feet in the 1927 flood, with some areas of level ground nineteen feet beneath the crest.

"We didn't know how high this water was goin to come over on the land side. It was up to the housetops all over town." Seventeen-year-old Nath Hayes took a truck and drove out to his mother's house to rescue her and her belongings.

"During normal times, in those days, was the Mississippi waterfront right out there against the levee?"

"Sure was!" he says, and begins walking along Front Avenue; the "front" implied that it was the waterfront. Kim walks along beside him, thinking, *I had a white cop, Plug, to show me Lake City. Now I've got a black cop, Nath, to show me Arkansas City.* Nath Hayes's memories of his little city extend much further into the past. "Arkansas City used to be right *on* the river. It was beautiful to see when the *Kate Adams* would come in with its freight, and those men that would unload it, they were called 'rousters,' and they had that rhythm in their walk, I mean, just like somebody square dance, they had that rhythm walkin up the gangplank. It was fun to just sit there and watch 'em. Oh, and we had these excursion boats, the *Island Queen*, the *S.S. President*, and the *Capital*, and people would come from all over southeast Arkansas and get on those boats and dance, and the boats would drift down the river in the moonlight for maybe two or three hours, and them dancin, and then finally about midnight it would come back here to the landing. And the showboats, yeah, the *show*boats, too! Vaudeville shows on those boats, and you could hear 'em a-comin up the river, hear them playin that . . . cally, whatever you call it, cally ump. . . ."

"Calliope," Kim says.

"Yes'm, that's it, that's right, that's the name it was called, back there in those days, I remember the first time I ever heard a calliope."

Blacks, of course, could only listen to the calliope; they could not attend the shows, or board the "floating palaces" except as porters and maids. The showboats did not have the elegant names of the excursion boats but were called things like the *Golden Rod*, the *New Sunny South*, the *Spirit of Liberty*, or simply the *New Grand Floating Palace*. The very best shows were presented by Captain French's *New Sensation* as early as the year Henry Thane moved to Arkansas City, 1876, and continuing until the year Nath Hayes was born, 1909. These dates mark the golden age of the show-boat, which was replaced in time by the nonfloating opera house, the circus with its "Wild West Show," the carnival, and the minstrel show. Except for that sound of the calliope, which later he came to associate with the street carnival's merry-go-round, Nath Hayes does not remember the showboats.

The *Kate Adams*, for whom First Avenue was renamed Kate Adams Avenue and the old river lake where the steamboat landing had been was named Kate Adams Lake, was not one boat: at least three had her name over the years. She was not a showboat or even a passenger boat as such, but a freight boat and mail boat that sometimes took on passengers, and sometimes, toward the end of her life, in the 1920s, worked overtime on weekends as an excursion boat. The third and last *Kate Adams*, built in 1898 and burned at Memphis in 1927 (before the flood), was the one that Nath Hayes remembers; she is dear to the memory of others who refer to her as the Bonnie *Kate* or the Everlovin' *Kate*.

"Now, right there," says Nath Hayes, pointing at the relic of a long, low building fronting on Front, "that shed? That was a freight house. We had a little train depot, closed down after the flood, used to sit on the side of the levee there. I worked as the station porter, cleanin it. The U.S. mail, it came by steamboat for years, then it came by train until the railroad was taken out, then it came by bus for years, now it comes by truck. The lumber mills used to ship out maybe ten or twelve carloads every day, so we had a train leave out from here every day."

Henry Thane's Saw Mill and Lumber Company, which at the height of its operations had as many as seven million board feet of lumber stacked in its yards, covered eight blocks of the waterfront southwest of where Kim and Nath are walking. All of the lumber washed away in the flood. The railroad tracks have been taken up for years, and all that remains is the tiny depot of the railroad's last years, with a fading "Railway Express Agency" sign beneath the letters "ARKANSAS CITY." Where the tracks ran now runs the fence of a horse paddock, wherein a pair of the animals, descendants of those who lost their status to the powerful locomotive, reassert their mobility in the absence of the machines.

"Here stood the confectionary," Nath says, pointing to the vacant lot where part of a white marble floor remains, a mosaic of small hexagonal tesserae spelling out the words "PALACE

CONFECTIONARY." "Mr. E. L. Sponenbarger's candy store. They had a soda fountain with old-time soda jerkers. Pool hall in the back. Men only. *White* men only. And *here*"—Nath gestures with a flourish—"still stands the hotel. Yes, ma'am, this was the hotel, upstairs. It was called the McCammon Inn. Downstairs was the funeral home."

Still stands: a large, two-story brick building, each of its floors fronted by a gallery or veranda, each supported by posts with decorative wooden-arched brackets in a kind of steamboat-Gothic style. McCammon, did he say? Yes, not Dr. Vernon, but his wife, Miss Mattie. Spending the last years of its life as a hotel, or simple inn, this place, built in our hospitable year of 1886, is not only one of the few impressive original buildings of any of these lost cities still standing, but the only one built in that particular eventful and sometimes magical year, a hundred years ago, and therefore, by the dictionary standard of being a hundred years old, an *antique*—not the only antique building in Arkansas City (some of the blacks' shanties are just as old, the opera house is nearly as old), but the only building here on the main, Front or De Soto Avenue still retaining a semblance of its former glory. Built originally as the Parker House by a Joshua Seamons, it changed hands and identities several times before Mattie McCammon took it over, or took over the upper floor for her inn, allowing the lower floor to become a funeral home. Did it bother the living patrons of the inn to sleep above the dead patrons of the funeral home?

Now a single light bulb, naked, burns within the incongruously empty-but-cluttered interior of the former mortuary. Nath Hayes explains that a man is using it for a workshop, a farmer who uses the interior to work on his farm machinery. In the weeds on the other side of the hotel/undertaker's were a group of storefronts: a furniture store, a dry-goods store, a Chinese grocery, another dry-goods store, another Chinese grocery.

"Chinese grocery?" Kim asks. She is not sure she heard Nath correctly. Yes, Nath can remember when there were no fewer than four Chinese grocery stores and a Chinese laundry, but the last of the Chinese people moved some years ago to the village

of Marked Tree, which is about halfway between Lake City and
Mound City. During the 1870s some of the larger Arkansas plantations "imported" Chinese laborers from California to work in
the cotton fields as an alternative to the "uppity nigger," who
had gained his freedom after the Civil War and would no longer
work as a slave or for slave wages. The Chinese were induced to
come to Arkansas by a monthly allowance of a half-pound of
opium per worker, but when the cost of this narcotic rose to $18
a pound the planters abandoned their use of the Chinese. Most
went back to California, but a few remained to establish stores
and laundries in southern-Arkansas towns. (This temporary "cap-
tivity" of the Chinese would find a later parallel of a sort during
World War II, when thousands of Californians of Japanese ancestry were "relocated" into concentration camps at Rohwer, a
most un-Californian landscape near Arkansas City, to be held
until the Japanese surrender. None of the Japanese stayed to
open stores in southern Arkansas.)

Marshal Hayes's short tour of Front Avenue takes Kim back
to their cars, at the main intersection, now flanked by the fire
station and basketball court on one side, and on the other side
by a large vacant lot containing a magnificent sycamore tree and
a few brickbats suggestive of a former edifice, which was indeed
there: on the second floor of the block-deep brick building was
Sophia Furlong's Commercial Hotel, rival to the McCammon
Inn, above *another* undertaker's parlor (those progressively missing from the decennial census did not *all* emigrate to California's
greener pastures), a drugstore, a variety store, and, as Nath pronounces it, a the-*ay*-ter—yes, a moving-picture establishment dating back to the first showing of *The Great Train Robbery*.

Next door to the vacant corner lot, and still surviving as a
grocery store called Red Star, is the Reitzammer building, besides
the old hotel the only two-story building remaining on Front
Avenue; for many years it housed the Reitzammer Bakery. "I
used to work at that baker shop when I was goin to school," Nath
says. "I delivered groceries with a one-horse wagon. Mr. Reitzammer would bake bread and doughnuts and cinnamon rolls. I
guess they quit bakin about the time of the flood."

Leonard "Rocky" Reitzammer, whose father, John, had immigrated from Nuremberg, Germany, in 1882 to establish (and build with handmade bricks) the Red Star Grocery and Bakery (and whose brother William was the newsdealer), ran the business throughout this century until he retired at the age of eighty-nine; he died a year later, in 1979. He and his wife, Verna, the one who was the postmaster for forty-two years, lived in an apartment upstairs over the grocery/bakery. Rocky Reitzammer was, in addition to being a baker and grocer, the town's fire chief, the town's justice of the peace (who performed most of the marriages in Arkansas City in this century), and the manager of the Kate Adams baseball team which played in a league with teams from Natchez, Vicksburg, and New Orleans on the Arkansas City diamond.

"You should talk to Miss Verna," Nath Hayes suggests.

"I've got an appointment with her in the morning," Kim says, and prepares to take her leave, but asks Nath one more question: "Is there anything you miss from Arkansas City's past?"

Nath Hayes thinks about this. Glancing at the Red Star, he says, "Yes, ma'am. If it was possible we could have one good supermarket where we could get fresh meat and fresh vegetables, that would be a great help to us. We need a good dry-goods store, too. Say my wife needs a pair of shoes, we have to go to McGehee." Nath ponders the question some more. "But most of all," he says, "what we need is a first-class restaurant."

"Have you eaten at Robinson's or the Blue Front?"

"They're OK," Nath says. "They're OK."

The next morning, bright and early, Kim decides to have breakfast at Robinson's Café. Feeling that her long talk with Nath Hayes has broken the racial barrier, she does not realize she is the first white woman ever to eat alone at Robinson's. "Alone" is the word: there are no other customers at all, no one there except a young black man who is the cook, and who is mildly surprised when she sits down at a table and asks for the breakfast menu. He points at a simple sign, chalked figures: "Dinner 3.59,

Breakfast 3.09." Kim studies it for a moment, then decides, "Well, I'll have breakfast." The young black disappears to his kitchen, is gone a very long time. She wonders what sort of breakfast he is preparing. Waffles? She studies the interior of the large room, takes an inventory of it. The metal folding chairs and odd tables have not been straightened from the night before, when black men sat around drinking beer, playing cards, talking, or whatever. There are two gumball machines with giant gumballs in their glass globes, a cigarette machine, a pinball machine, a juke box; one corner is occupied by a riding lawn mower. Empty egg cartons are stacked beside boxes of salt and boxes of grits: these provide some clue as to what might be served for breakfast. Sure enough, in time, the waiter/cook comes back to her table and asks, "How do you like your eggs fixed?"

She does not drink coffee, usually drinks diet cola even at breakfast, but apparently the only other beverage available besides coffee is beer, which she likes even less than coffee. The man takes a very long time doing the eggs or whatever. She says to herself, I can hardly believe I'm going to eat in this place. What if I get poisoned? She wonders if the café has passed the health standards. She would feel more comfortable if another customer came in, but she is there alone with the cook, who has taken enough time to have raised the chick into a chicken and forced it to lay eggs. Finally he brings a plate. It is as good a plate of eggs, bacon, biscuits, grits, and gravy as she has ever tasted, but somehow the atmosphere of Robinson's prevents her from enjoying it.

Afterward, at the Bixlers', she finds that Judy has been busy setting up a whole day's schedule of interviews for her with several people who are eager to talk about Arkansas City and who seem to have time on their hands. First, and most important, is Verna Reitzammer. She no longer lives in the apartment above the Red Star Grocery hand-built by her father-in-law, but has built her own, very contemporary, spacious brick ranch-style on the site of her family's home, in the neighborhood of the courthouse. In a vast living room filled with mementos and collectibles, few of them compote, she receives Kim with warmth, garrulity, and the gentility befitting an officer of the Desha County Historical Society, St. Clement's Episcopal Church, and the United States Post Office, which used to be located so conveniently right next to the Red Star. A black maid brings coffee.

Kim is thinking, *I wonder what she would think if I told her I just had breakfast at Robinson's.* Kim decides not to tell her. Instead she begins by asking about those forty-two years Mrs. Reitzammer worked at the post office, in one of which she was named national Postmaster of the Year. "Did you prefer being called 'postmistress'? 'Postmaster'? 'Postal manager,' or what?"

"I don't like to be called 'postmistress'!" Mrs. Reitzammer emphasizes. "I've had that argument at the postal conventions. I was a postmaster. Master of the post!" Then she asks a question: "What have you seen so far in Arkansas City?"

"Well, I started with the cemetery . . ." Kim begins.

"Cemetery?" Verna laughs. "Have you ever had any dealings with a *dead* cemetery?" She laughs again, explaining how the cemetery has been neglected, taken over entirely by the black people (her maid, Miss Pearl Seals, is more or less in charge of it), what is left of it, the flood-obscured graves, washed-away headstones. . . . But Verna Reitzammer can remember seeing it when she was only five years old and it was being fixed up, an iron fence put around it.

"Do you remember a lot from the age of five?" Kim asks.

"You know, it's hard to say whether you remember something or whether you *heard* it said so that you think you do," Mrs. Reitzammer says. But she mentions her earliest memory: of pushing her baby brother in his little buggy down the wooden sidewalks and trying to keep the wheels from going through the slats. The trees were so big and beautiful—of course, when you're small, everything looks bigger—the houses were larger then than they seem now, and people kept their yards so pretty. But the streets were so dusty and there was no stock law, so the animals roamed the streets.

"Here would come a cow down the street, and I would just be frightened to death!" she laughs. "I remember Momma sending me down to a neighbor to borrow a cup of buttermilk, and all the way home there was this cow, and I just knew it was after *me*. So I sat on a bench and cried, holding the cup of buttermilk so it wouldn't spill, and I hollered for someone to come and get me, save me from the cow!"

What does Kim think of the town so far? "I can't get over all those sidewalks," Kim says, and only after Verna laughs uproariously does Kim realize her unintentional pun.

"I can't get over them, either," Verna says. The big wide beautiful sidewalks, so much an example of good city planning along with the wide avenues, were ruined by the '27 flood, or the subsequent moving of the houses broke up the concrete. On those sidewalks—unlike those of a true city, where you may walk a sidewalk and never speak to anyone—you always speak to anyone you meet. "Even if you can't call them by name, you can find out in two minutes who they are," Verna says. "We're all one big family." Her biggest regret about retiring from the post office is that new people have moved into town whom she does not know. "I miss *that* more than anything: not knowing *everybody*." Since she doesn't drive—her eyesight isn't good enough for driving—she can't get "downtown" to the post office, which used to be such a social center when it was her domain. The mail used to come four times a day! Verna would have to be up before daylight and at the post office for the first mail, which came at six in the morning, then again at ten, at three in the afternoon, and finally, the "late-evening" mail, which came at eight. Verna closed the post office at five o'clock, but everyone would go home for supper and then return to gather and wait for the eight o'clock train, which brought the last mail. "To think that people in a small town would have to have their mail four times a day!" Verna says, shaking her head, but clearly missing those times. Customers of the post office had been known to arrive by every possible means: on foot, horse, bicycle, boat, car, horse and wagon, and once even by airplane. Verna tells a story of an airplane that deliberately landed on the levee just so its pilot could come to the post office to buy a special migratory-bird stamp.

But such excitements were rare, almost as rare as the stranger who would remark upon the presumptuousness of the place in calling itself "City." Verna quotes to Kim the song:

> It aint a town and it aint a city,
> Just a little place called Ditty Wah Ditty.

This old wheeze, popularized in a song by Phil Harris, can be traced to folklore, wherein the last stop on a mythical railroad to hell was named, as it is alternatively spelled, Didy Waw Didy. Unlike others of these lost cities, some of which are commonly called by their names with the omission of "City" (e.g., Buffalo City is called simply Buffalo), Arkansas City is always called by its full name. To call it simply "Arkansas" would be both confusing and grandiloquent.

Look magazine, the once-popular weekly now as defunct as any of these lost cities, had a regular contest for "All-Americn City," and Verna Reitzammer entered her town in the contest. "*Look* was impressed," Verna relates, "and we came home with honors, but I understand the reason we didn't get first place was simply because back then our school was not integrated." The school now, like all those in Arkansas, is integrated, and Kim has appointments to talk to both the former principal, black, and the present one, white. She does not wear a watch, and wonders if they are waiting for her.

Verna Reitzammer is one of the few living residents of these lost cities who have already been mentioned in a book: Pete Daniel's *Deep'n As It Come*, a study of the 1927 flood (Oxford University Press, 1977), a mostly oral history, quotes at length Verna Reitzammer's account of being trapped in her father's store as the floodwaters rose, of climbing on a meat block and being rescued by a boatman. She is quoted as saying, "I remember sitting up on the upstairs steps and watching my piano floating out the front door, piece by piece, one key after the other. That's the only thing I cried about in the flood." Verna admits to Kim that she (like Henry Thane) had never learned to swim until after the flood. She laments the damage caused to the two-hundred-year-old trees, cottonwood and sycamore, whose limbs were hanging down into the water. "I just imagined I was in Venice! I said to myself, 'I'll never get to Venice, so this must be the way it is!' But I'll tell you, when I did go to Venice eventually, I was disappointed—I'd have rather lived in Arkansas City!" Verna laughs. "They didn't have any pretty trees hanging in the water in Venice! Old dirty buildings and old dirty canals! All the garbage running down the streets!"

No, she would take the peace and quiet of Arkansas City over Venice any old day. A dear friend of hers once told her that there were only four sounds heard here, but four sounds that always reminded her of Arkansas City, wherever she heard them:

1. Cows mooing
2. The boats on the river blowing their whistles
3. Roosters crowing
4. The courthouse clock striking

The striking of that courthouse clock reminds Kim that she has other appointments to keep. And of the four sounds, it is the most faithful, an aural reminder, in a way, of Henry Thane, who spent $10,000 in 1899 to commission the building's design by Rome Harding. This obscure Little Rock architect was working in the Romanesque Revival popularized by Louisiana-born Henry Hobson Richardson, a genius who died young in our solemn year of 1886; by the end of the century most Richardsonian principles had become *retardataire*, although courthouses throughout the American hinterland continued to employ them. The Romanesque features of the Arkansas City courthouse have become so diluted and secondhand—the rounded arches, the square tower, the Richardsonian dormers in a steep roof—that some journalists have referred to it as "Spanish," and one book on Arkansas courthouses wrongly identifies the style as "Pseudo-French Renaissance Revival"(!). But there are still echoes of the bold Richardsonian Romanesque, forerunner of modern Brutalism, which makes a courthouse seem more a place of punishment than an institution of justice. Made of delta-clay brick whitewashed in more recent times, it and the wooden Lake City courthouse are among the few white courthouses in the state; it rises more massively than any grain elevator or cotton gin as a landmark in southeastern Arkansas, and the clock tower, with four gilded Roman-numeraled faces, is the nearest thing to a skyscraper to be found in the Arkansas delta.

Covetous of the court, larger McGehee has tried for years to steal away the seat of county justice. As Nath Hayes told Kim, "That effort to move the courthouse to McGehee has been goin on a long, long time. Started back in the early thirties. Each time they tried, we defeated 'em, but they got all the county offices, and the only thing we got left *is* the courthouse. They take that away from us, it would just leave us *blank*." All of the county officials have to commute to Arkansas City from McGehee. But every effort to relocate the courthouse, the last a referendum in 1978, has failed. Since the courthouse building could not literally be moved to McGehee, it was symbolically moved in the form of a new red brick fire-station-type eyesore called Desha Court Building, which most McGeheeans think of as the real courthouse.

The courtroom, with a pressed-tin ceiling twenty-three feet above the floor and old ceiling fans hanging over the bench, the bar, and the jury seats, is not the only auditorium remaining in Arkansas City. There is also the lodge hall of the Masons, in a white wooden building strongly suggestive of a New England town hall, except that the Masons, in their unending quest for secrecy, have in modern times boarded over with clapboards all of the windows on the ground floor. When Kim, driving around, first saw this building, she thought it might be some kind of monastery, eyeless and veiled, until she saw the sign over the door, "Riverton Lodge 296 F&AM," and the symbol of the Free & Accepted Masons. Asking Verna Reitzammer, she has learned that this was formerly the opera house, a building dating back to theatrical 1886. The floating opera on the riverfront was seasonal, docking in the autumn; *this* opera house could be used year-round for minstrels and for plays, road shows on their way to Little Rock or Memphis, and opera companies from New York staying at Sophia Furlong's hotel and doing Verdi's *Il Trovatore*. The opera house doubled as a social gathering place, with ice-cream suppers, oyster suppers, dances, and masked balls, as well as the year's main event: the annual Christmas Eve Tree, a giant holly set up on the stage and decorated with candles and strung with popcorn and cranberries in a public ceremony and gift exchange.

The second floor was also a temporary ark of refuge during the floods of 1912, 1916, and 1927. Perhaps the Masons have preserved a couple of the second-floor windows for easy access in any future flood. On the totally cloistered ground floor, a lone air conditioner sticks out from the blank wall, as if to save the claustrophobic Masons from asphyxiation. To Kim, this building, with its few windows as sparsely placed as the few buildings in town, seems to represent the present town of Arkansas City itself: shut off, bare, withdrawn.

But there is still one more auditorium in town. The opera house never held more than 250; twice that many could, but don't, sit in comfort in the new and cavernous auditorium of the Arkansas City Schools building, constructed in 1970 from designs by a Little Rock architectural firm more experienced with the metropolitan and cosmopolitan edificing of that city, and financed by the taxes paid by the Potlatch Corporation, who convert the delta timber into pulp and paperboard in a giant mill at nearby Cypress Bend. ("Potlatch," from the Chinook Indian word *pat-shatl*, "giving" or "gift," was a Northwest Pacific Coast custom whereby the host gave valuable goods to his guests or destroyed property to show that he could afford to do so; it is a highly symbolic and appropriate name for this huge industry and the lifeblood it is pouring into the community.) The school district has an average daily attendance of only 170 but, thanks to Potlatch's taxes, can afford to spend $4,000 a year per pupil, versus a statewide average of only $1,500.

Kim will interview Gene Gregory, the young white superintendent of schools, but first she wants to talk to "Professor"

J. B. (for Joseph Barry) Payne, the black former superintendent
of the old school around whose modest building the new Arkansas City Schools edifice, with its one huge, modern entry arch as
a kind of distant echo of brutal Richardsonian Romanesque, has
been built. Professor Payne was born with the century, and was
well past the mandatory retirement age for educators in 1972,
when he quietly yielded his job and his old building to the coming
of the new edifice. He remembers hauling wood to burn for heat
in his school, and then converting to coal heat and, finally, to
natural gas. Despite his honorific, more a nickname than a title
("Everybody calls me that, but I don't know why," he tells Kim),
the professor is the sort of elderly black man that Kim would
expect to see sitting on the riverbank with a cane fishing pole,
and she is not surprised to learn he always went fishing twice a
day during the school term, early in the morning before classes
and then again about sundown.

He still fishes. "I can go across that levee and catch a fish at
any time," he tells Kim. But he would rather teach than fish.
"When I was teachin I didn't leave each day until I thought I'd
accomplished *some*thing with some student." He thinks the schools
turned out a better student in those days, but that wasn't entirely
his own accomplishment: he didn't have to compete with television for their attention. Nowadays, since television, "I never
see 'em carryin a book."

Until black and white students were integrated in 1956, his
school was entirely black. From 1956 until his retirement, Professor Payne taught both black and white students, and he knows
everybody in Arkansas City except the new "Potlatch generation,"
who came after he retired.

Mr. Gregory, as everyone calls the young superintendent,
takes Kim on a tour of the sprawling educational plant potlatched
by Potlatch. He shows her sections of interior wall that were part
of Professor Payne's old school and explains how the modern
building was constructed around the old one. "Professor Payne
has given his life to this school and this town," Mr. Gregory
declares. "He's given his life to the education of black children
in the community, and he's very well respected by both white

and black. He attends every activity we have here at school. We make sure, when we have faculty dinners or whatever, that Professor Payne is invited."

Herself a teacher who has taught an average of thirty students per class, Kim is impressed to learn that Arkansas City High School has only fourteen per class. But though being the state's richest school district allows for more expenditure per pupil, Gene Gregory explains that this does not necessarily translate into higher salaries for the faculty. Faculty here remain as underpaid as faculty elsewhere in the state, which ranks next to Mississippi as the state with the worst-paid faculty in the nation.

Unlike some school buildings Kim has seen, this one is immaculate. The walls and floors are clean, and the students seem to respect the building and take care of it. The team mascots are the River Rats. (When the lighthearted sports editors of the *Arkansas Gazette* voted recently for the "Best Dozen Mascots," the Arkansas City River Rats came in first, followed by the Lake City Catfish. In fifth place were the Cave City Cavemen, beating out other towns' Alligators, Redbugs, Sandlizards, Jackrabbits, etc.) Gene Gregory explains that the River Rats have a good-natured sports rivalry with McGehee, but never so heated as the contention over the county seat. "I think the attempt to move the courthouse," he says, "has caused more of a competitive spirit than anything else."

"Out of a typical graduating class," Kim asks, "how many go to college?"

"Probably a third," he says. "We're isolated and most of our kids don't have much of a look at the outside world until they graduate. We try to do things for them, take them to the capital, Little Rock, other places on field trips. Most of them are born here, raised here, and they don't know much away from here."

Later, when Kim goes to see the Arkansas City Museum, she will wonder if any of the students ever take a field trip (they could walk) to their own museum. Blowing the dust off, and signing, the register, she discovers that she is the first visitor since the previous summer. The museum is housed in a small one-story brick building, erected in 1882, with a toothed cornice and its one floor elevated in case of floods, located at the intersection of Kate Adams and Capitol. Once it was a law office for Xenophon Overton Pindall, who practiced there before becoming governor of Arkansas for one year and eleven months in 1907–8, when the elected governor had a nervous breakdown. Ove Pindall never returned to Arkansas City except for visits after his career in Little Rock, preferring to practice criminal law there until his death. Although Kim thinks it is "neat" that Arkansas City even has a museum in the first place—none of the other lost cities has one—she is dismayed to find that the collections are a dusty hodgepodge of junk and gewgaws, an unwanted detritus of old things: Indian arrowheads, rusty guns, faded and fading photographs. Nothing is really catalogued, classified, labeled properly, or cared for. There hasn't even been an attempt to re-create the interior of the law office it once was. *Do we care so little for our past?* Kim thinks, and does not stay long. The museum is the forgotten town's forgotten attic.

She has one more appointment in Arkansas City, with an octogenarian. In a small green cottage on a lot within sight and sound of the sleek plant of the Arkansas City Schools lives Sarah Haley, born in 1899, who in the early twenties moved to town with her husband, a millworker at Henry Thane's Saw Mill and Lumber Company.

Mrs. Haley tells Kim how important that sawmill was. Half of the people in Arkansas City, both black and white, worked there. Henry Thane constructed modest mill houses for the employees, charging them $15 a month for rent and providing them with playgrounds, tennis courts, horseshoe arena, car garages, and a commissary store. Sarah Haley lived in one of these factory houses, identical to dozens of others—all destroyed in the flood,

along with the mill, the lumber, the timber, the woods, everything.

For entertainment, there was the music coming from the
river, from the *President*, a big, beautiful boat, but Sarah Haley
never boarded it: she listened to its music from the porch of her
house. She also heard the morning whistle, at 5:00 A.M., from
Henry Thane's company, waking all, for work began at 6:00. The
screaming whistle sounded again at noon and at 5:00 P.M. And
she heard the sounds the Grandfather made when he rose. Every
year there was a Water Scare. When a Water Scare came, she
started packing. But she never had to use what she had packed,
until 1927. That year it was everybody for himself, and she took
care of herself and her husband.

Mrs. Haley does not tell Kim what Kim has already managed
to figure out on her own: it was Henry Thane's relentless rapacity
for lumber, for gain, symptom of man's grasping wresting of all
the earth holds, that caused the flood. Thousands of acres of
the big woods all along the Mississippi and the Arkansas, whose
roots had quaffed the spring runoff of rains and stopped
the water before it could reach the Grandfather, were cut down
for lumber. Now there was nothing to slow, let alone stop,
the eager guzzling of the Grandfather, and, yes, his consort,
too, the Arkansas; call her the Grandmother. They both became drunk with an overdose of rain, and rampaged beyond
reason.

Did Thane know this? If he did know it, would it have stopped
him?

Mrs. Haley has one strong image remaining engraved on
her memory of the flood, which she shares with Kim: a log floating past. On the floating log were a dog, a cat, a chicken, and a
snake.

"I imagine that was a little scary for them," Mrs. Haley remarks. But no animal bothered the others. The dog, the cat, the
chicken, and the snake coexisted peaceably on their ark. Whether
or not that ark was eventually swallowed up by the Grandfather
or Grandmother, whether or not the animals perished, is im-

material: for a long moment in a time of disaster they were comrades, neighbors.

One last question to Mrs. Haley: Did you ever wish that this place would actually become a *city?*

"I like quietness," Mrs. Haley says. "The older you get, the more you like quietness."

Garland City, Arkansas

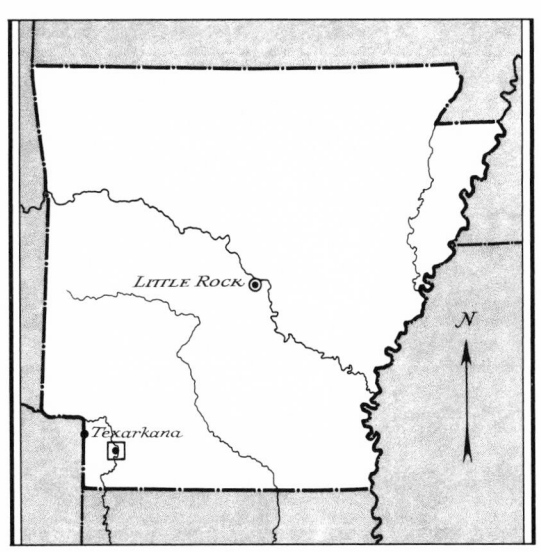

LITTLE ROCK

Texarkana

N

CITY HALL
NEW
DUMPING HOURS
TUES. 2 — 6
SAT 8 — 12
ONLY
City Hall

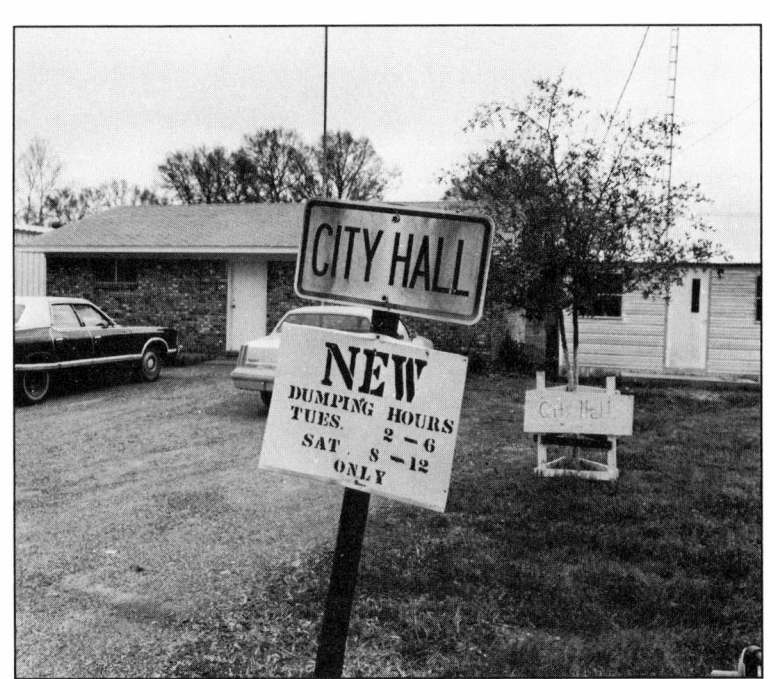

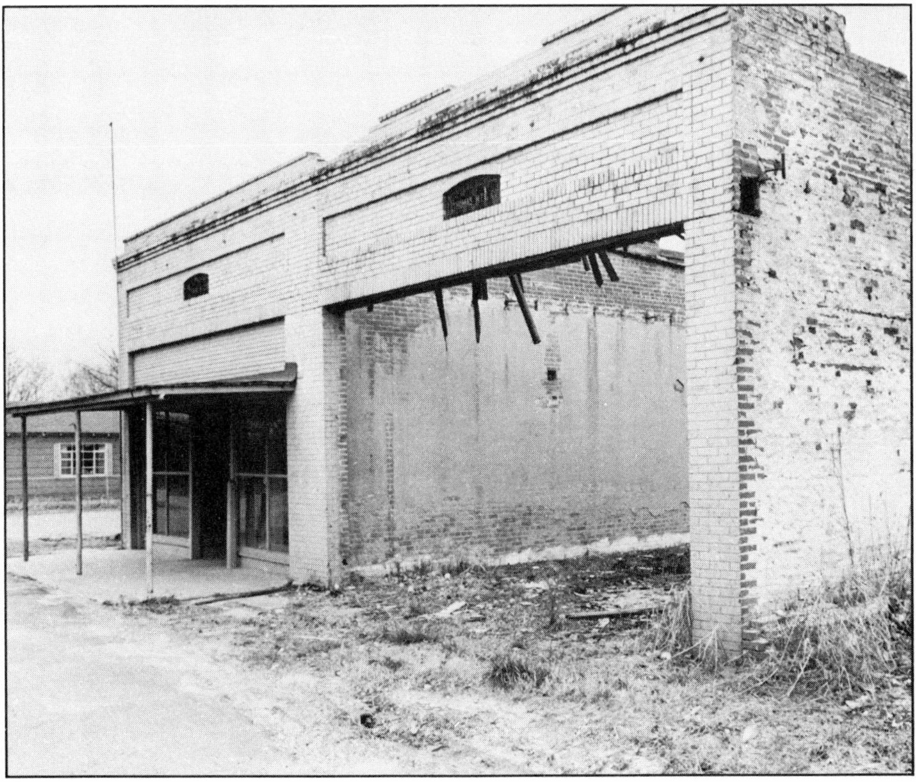

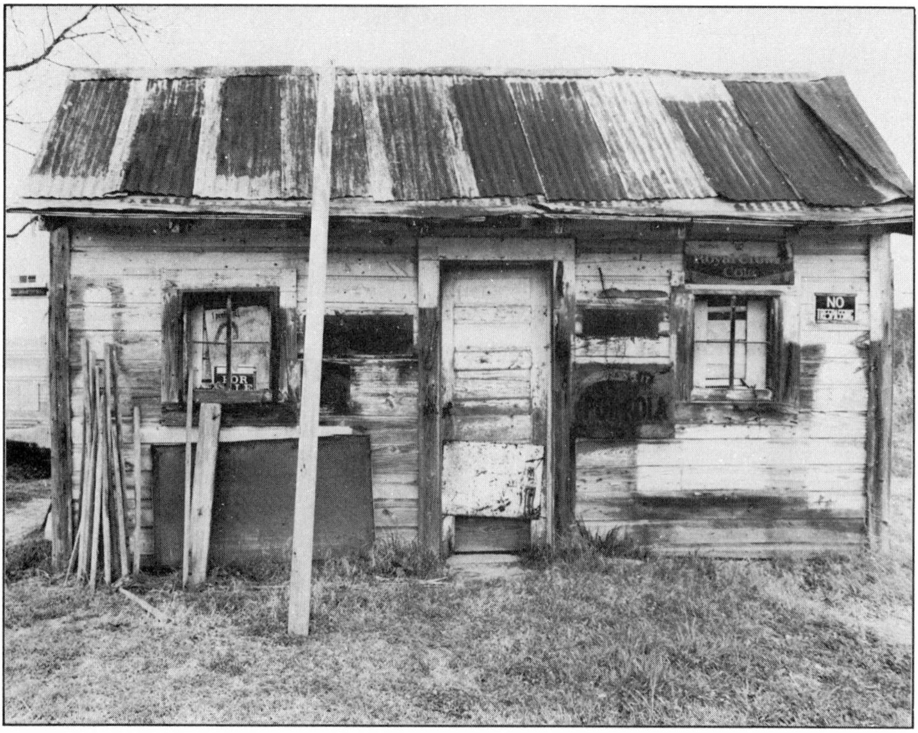
NO
FOR

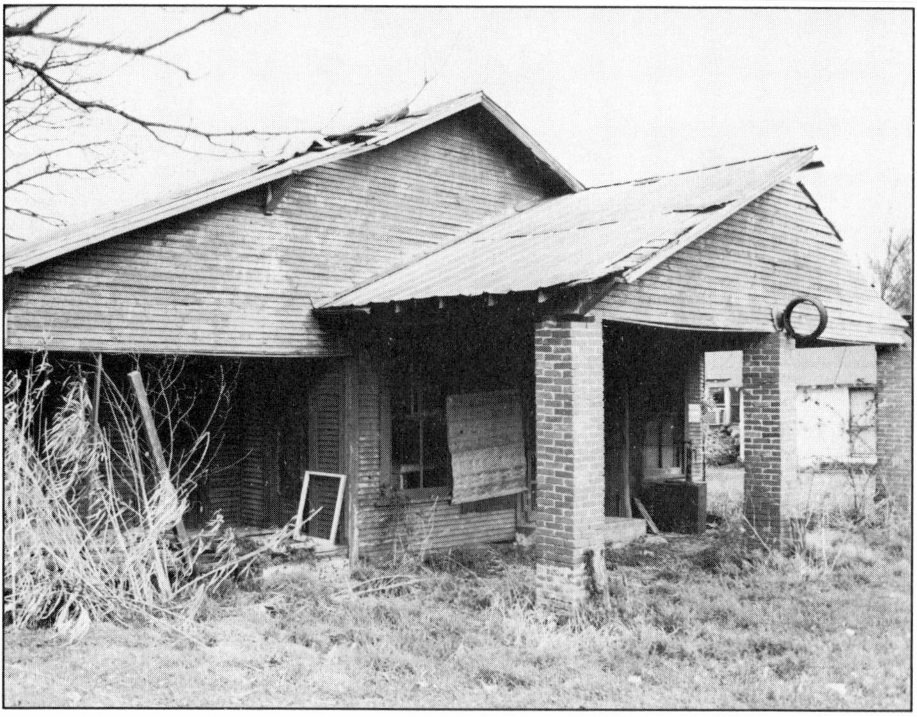

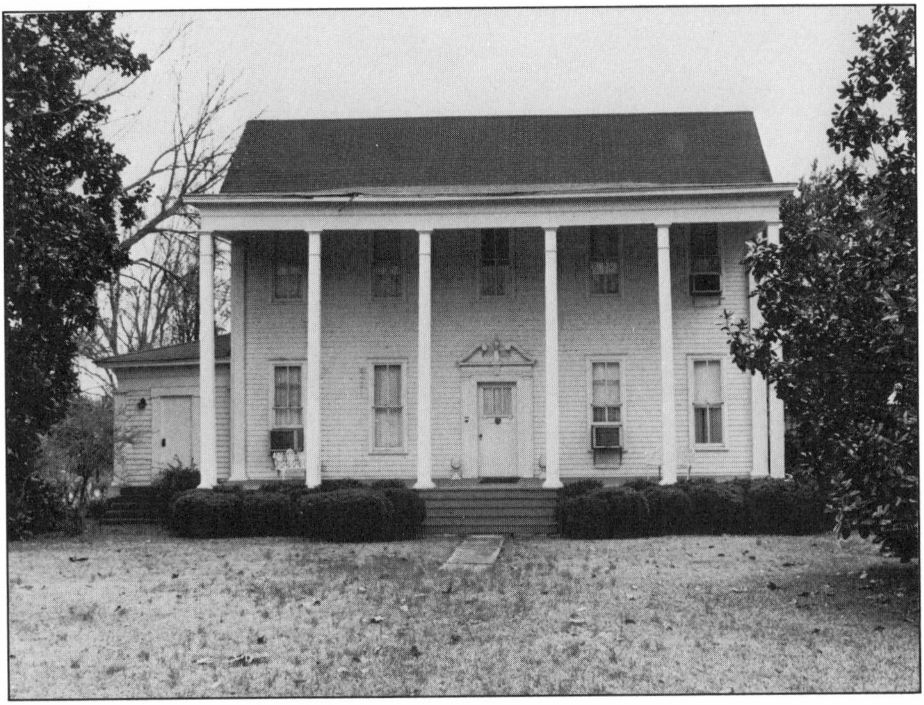

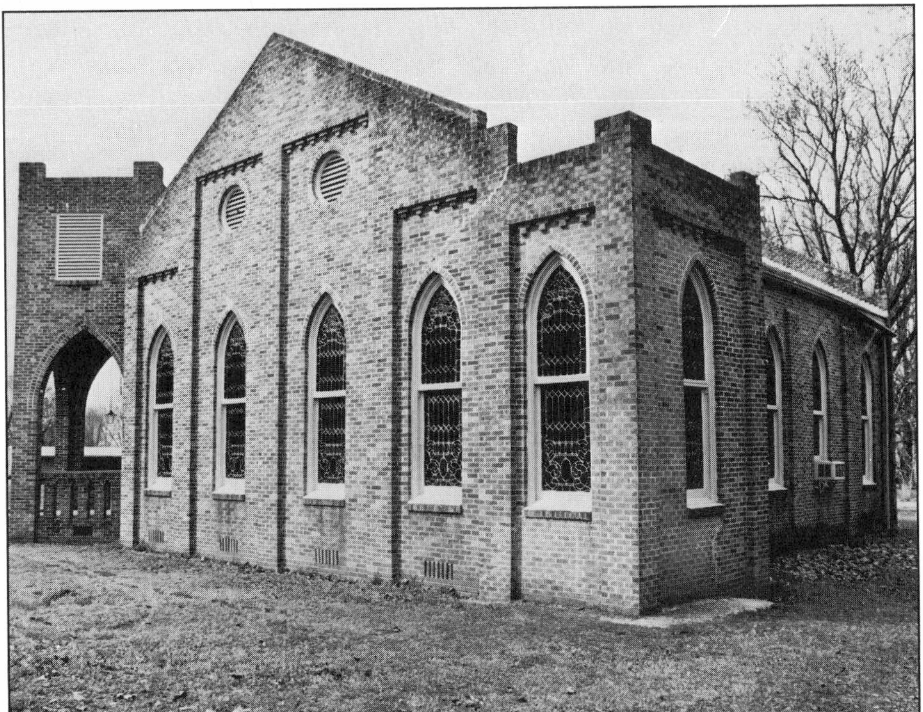

Come and sit by my side if you love me,
Do not hasten to bid me adieu,
But remember the Red River Valley
And the girl that has loved you so true.
*   —Southwestern folk song*

THERE ARE TOWNS named Garland in Alabama, Kansas, Maine, Montana, Nebraska, North Carolina, Oklahoma, Pennsylvania, Tennessee, Texas, Utah, and Wyoming, and so much of Garland, Arkansas's mail was misdirected to those places, especially before the invention of the Zip Code, that they (the post-office people?) changed the name to Garland *City*. That is just one theory. But in this place, more than our other lost cities, there is general disagreement about the name of the town, the use of "City" as part of its name. In Buffalo City there was some confusion because of the two places with the same name on opposite sides of the river. Here, there are people on opposite sides of the same table who will argue over the use of "City" in the name.

Government agencies do not agree: the U.S. Census lists it merely as Garland, the post office as Garland City. The town smokestack says "GARLAND"; the town depot, where trains do not stop any more, says "Garland City." The Arkansas Highway Department calls it Garland City but insists in parentheses, "Garland P.O." More recently the United States GNIS calls it Garland City Station and lets it go at that, but though it is more than *only* a station, it is, needless to relate, not a city, and never was.

Of our eleven lost cities, Garland is in most respects the least attractive, except insofar as wreckage itself is fascinating, squalor and desuetude have their perverse charms or at least, like romantic ruins, appeal to our passion for what is broken, flawed, failed, and gone.

Coming here was not an easy decision for Kim. She could have chosen instead more populous, less squalid Junction City, but it straddles the Louisiana state line and belongs half to that southerly state. Or she could have picked from more than half a dozen other less populous places in this same southwestern quarter of Arkansas: Bluff City, Bragg City, Capps City, Joyce City, Crain City, Kress City, Gin City (particularly intriguing because of its suggestion of booze, though the reference is merely to a cotton gin)—each of these is a bona-fide, officially named, once-aspiring *city*.

But Garland City, while lost, is within sight and sound of busy U.S. Highway 82, whereas the other places are all on state or county secondary roads, and thus it is the most accessible in the mind of Kim, who may want to get out of town fast once she has found it.

It is easy enough to dislike this part of Arkansas for the simple reason that it is closest to Texas. Parts of the six sharp corners of Arkansas poke themselves into all the regions of the heart of America: the Great Plains, the Ozark Mountains, the Midwest, the Delta, the South, and the Southwest, but southwestern Arkansas is separated from Texas only by the Red River, and Garland City is on the wrong side of that river. Confusing? Look at a map. Miller County, in which it is located (named after James Miller, the first, bumbling governor of Arkansas Territory, an 1812 soldier whose "I'll try, sir!" made the history books as a wimpish battle cry, and whose later, doddering life in the Custom House at Salem, Massachusetts, furnished the brilliant introductory of Nathaniel Hawthorne's *The Scarlet Letter*), is an oddly shaped catchall for all the southwesternmost townships of Arkansas and has the mentionable distinction of being the only county not connected by dry land to any of the others: the meandering Red River, which defines its jagged northern and eastern edges, divorces it from the rest of the state. It might as well be in Texas.

The traditional antipathy of every good Arkansawyer toward

Texas and all things Texan derives not simply from a long-standing fierce rivalry between the sports teams of the states' universities, but from a kind of paternal disdain for a wayward, boisterous prodigal son. Arkansas was the sire of Texas in the sense that Stephen Austin and Sam Houston were footloose, foolhardy Arkansawyers for a time before they pushed on into the dry lands belonging to Mexico and colonized them, establishing the Republic of Texas. (Cities in that state named after them have become real metropolises, whereas Austin, Arkansas, and Houston, Arkansas, remain mere hamlets.) Texas's passion for bigness and the concomitant braggartism and self-applause have always seemed unmannerly and arrogant to Arkansawyers, who watch and listen to the bullshit with the embarrassment and offense of a proper parent for a vaunting adolescent. Except for its oversize, a poor second now to Alaska's, Texas has nothing Arkansas lacks.

Garland City even has oil wells, a status symbol that completes its Texafication. Coming into town from the east, Kim notices the first one without knowing what it is. Beside the highway, the huge steel arm of a pump rises and falls slowly on its rotor. There is no derrick, which is what Kim would identify as an oil well, but the derrick for "New Garland City Well No. 1" did its drilling in 1951 and was removed, and the well capped with the pump, which has produced a mere 263,000 barrels since, whereas "Old Garland City Well," to the west of town, drilled in 1932, has produced a more respectable 2.25 million barrels.

There is no J. R. Ewing in Garland City; the closest thing to him is Glen Price, whom Kim will meet this afternoon. Now she passes the oil pump, passes the little New Gum Point Church, the blacks' white wooden twin-towered church, and approaches the high, arching steel-girder bridge over the Red. Costing $500,000 in the Depression year of 1931, this bridge replaced one costing $500,000 the year before, which was dynamited, possibly in a gangland bootleggers' war, in the only Event that has ever made news for Garland City. *Who blew the bridge?* is a question that Kim will find herself asking fifty-five years later as if it had happened the night before she arrived.

Below the bridge flows the fabled Red River, which begins Way Out West as the border between Oklahoma and Texas and accumulates stories, legends, songs, and lies all along its thousand-mile length into this small corner of Arkansas, then wanders on into and bisects Louisiana, who thinks she owns it or is at least glad that it is called, not the Red River *of* Texas, or the Red River *of* Oklahoma, let alone the Red River *of* Arkansas, but the Red River of Louisiana. Never mind that Louisiana has no valleys for the girl who asks the cowboy to come and sit by her side if he loves her. . . .

The flow of the Red beneath the bridge at Garland City is not a pretty stream when Kim sees it: swollen, roily, the slop and surge of entirely opaque, rusty mud. It is "red" only by the same optical illusion that tricks men into calling rivers White, or Black, or Green: not truly a shade of blood-red, rose-red, or ruby-red so much as a fecal henna, a copious diarrheal ooze. But its color is distinct from the Grandfather's. James Miller's comrade, the surgeon Joseph Paxton of neighboring Hempstead County, on the north bank of the Red before Miller County was named, put it this way: "As well might you mistake an American for a British soldier, in their respective uniforms, as the blue banks of the Mississippi for the red alluvia of Red river."

This was in *Raft of the Red River*, a long discourse written in 1828 from Dr. Paxton's clinic at Mount Prairie (upstream from Lost Prairie, where Rufus Garland would open a store in 1833), in the form of a letter to Ambrose Sevier, congressman from Arkansas Territory. It was printed by the Twentieth Congress in February 1829, when Paxton died at the age of fifty. He was convinced that Sevier, who would lead the fight for Arkansas statehood in 1836, would persuade Congress to take extraordinary means to destroy the raft, which was not a conventional floating transport at all but an enormous logjam of timber, driftwood, debris, and sand blocking the Red River for a length of a hundred miles through Louisiana and into that corner of Arkansas Territory, making navigation of the stream impossible and flood control inconceivable. It was not until 1841 that Captain Henry Shreve, whose name the river's largest port would come

to bear, managed to direct a partial opening through the block-
age, a natural phenomenon known widely as "the Great Raft of
the Red." But after fifteen years of neglect the Great Raft closed
up tighter than ever, requiring further congressional appropri-
ations, which finally opened the channel for good and reclaimed
vast acres of wasteland. (Possibly Lost Prairie, as the place where
Rufus Garland settled the future site of Garland City was known,
got its name from the fact that it was annually lost beneath the
backwaters dammed by the Great Raft.)

Dr. Paxton's letter, a discursive meditation upon the prehistoric and historic origins of the Great Raft which examines
the natural obstructions of a riverway as methodically as a pa-
thologist examines the blockages of the body's vascular system,
forwards the interesting theory that the Red River and the At-
chafalaya, another of Louisiana's internal rivers, were one and
the same until a prehistoric Great Raft separated them into two
distinct rivers.

His long essay-letter, assuming Sevier and his congressional
colleagues took the time to absorb it (or that, more likely, Sevier
read the whole thing into the *Congressional Record* during a fili-
buster), stood as an example of how governments and legislative
bodies might direct enormous amounts of energy, like a mag-
nifying glass directing the rays of the sun to burn a hole into
something, into the solution of obscure problems. This overkill
of verbiage finds a counterpart and parenthesis in modern times
in the only other printed publication concerning Garland City,
also in the form of a "letter," this one titled simply *Red River at
Garland City, Arkansas* (U.S. Government Printing Office, 1961)
but subtitled not so simply, *Letter from the Secretary of the Army
Transmitting a Letter from the Chief of Engineers, Department of the
Army, Dated March 31, 1961, Submitting a Report, Together with
Accompanying Papers and Illustrations, on a Survey of Red River at
Garland City, Ark. This Investigation Was Made in Response to an
Item in Section 203 of Public Law 86-645, Approved July 14, 1960,
Which Calls for an Immediate Study to Be Made of Emergency Bank
Protection Along Red River in the Vicinity of Garland City.*

This thick document, prefaced with letters of support from

President John F. Kennedy, Governor Orval Faubus, and the secretaries of Agriculture and the Interior, focuses all its words, and its graphs and charts, on the expenditure of less than a million dollars to control the Red River for one mile upstream from the bridges at Garland City by stabilizing the banks with "pile dikes, rock groins, board revetment, and channel excavation." The exact purpose of this work, other than the protection of the bridge approaches, is not clear.

Like all Corps of Engineer projects, which have become a joke or bugbear for environmentally conscious Arkansawyers, it was overzealous meddling and bureaucratic make-work, and did little for the town of Garland City, which actually lost a little of its population in the decade following. In contrast to most of these lost cities, Garland City has had a relatively stable population through several censuses, though "stable" may just mean "stagnant" here: the town numbered 325 in 1940, 351 in 1950, 377 in 1960 at its peak, and back down to 321 in 1970. Through annexation of outlying "suburbs" in the 1970s, the official census of 1980 doubled the population to 660, but that was not evident in the appearance of human activity in the town.

Among our lost cities, this is the only one named for a man rather than for a substance, tribe, geographic feature, state, animal, or location. But of Rufus Garland, who set up that mercantile store at Lost Prairie in 1833 and died the same year, very little is known other than the coincidence of his given name, which means "red" like the river. Much more is known about his son, Augustus Hill Garland, born the year before and only one year old when his father died and his mother moved a few miles away from the river, into Hempstead County. He is the Garland for whom Garland County (which comes next) is named, and, elsewhere in Arkansas, Garland Creek, Garland Lake, Garland Mountain, Garland Springs, Garland School, and a Garland Street in every large town.

Augustus Garland gave his name to the legal case known as *Ex parte Garland*, in which he challenged before the Supreme

Court the right of the re-United States to deny him the right to challenge the Supreme Court in matters of law because he had been on the Confederate side during the unpleasantries of 1861–65. After winning that case, he went on to become governor of Arkansas and U.S. senator from Arkansas, and, more important, the first and only Arkansawyer ever given a Cabinet post, when President Cleveland appointed him attorney general to balance his Cabinet with a Southern and Western point of view. In our judicious year of 1886, the legal affairs of the nation were handled by Attorney General Garland.

He was a legend in Washington because of his refusal to wear dress suits, a personal quirk of fashion of which he had warned President Cleveland before his appointment, and which the president condoned by the simple expedient of not inviting him to any dress functions. He also favored corncob pipes years before they became a trademark of another Arkansawyer, General Douglas MacArthur, and kept a demijohn jug of corn liquor handy until one day he simply decided that "I have had my share" and remained a teetotaler for the rest of his life. His tenure as attorney general was tarnished by a scandal involving the telephone company in those early, predivestiture days before Bell's monopoly, when he owned stock in Bell's competitor; a congressional investigation lasting for a year kept him nervous.

Returned to private life and law, Garland sought, like Peter Mankins, to watch the new century come in, but, also like Mankins, he fell short, dying in 1899.

More Garlands around the country have been named for Hamlin Garland than for (no relation) Augustus. The Son of the Middle Border who Travelled Main Roads in search of Prairie Folks discovered that rural life is not so idyllic and pastoral as it was cut out to be in the popular mind of the 1890s, and dispelled that image at the cost of exaggerating the poverty of the peasant. Rural poverty is as mythic as pastorality, and both are relative, subjective, and alien to the true city-dweller. Hamlin Garland spent too much time in Boston before returning to the Middle Border.

No one in Garland City has read Hamlin Garland, but no

one there can tell you anything about Augustus Garland, either. The place has no sense of history and knows little of its own past. There is not one local historian who can tell, let alone publish, the chronicles of the town's long, slow transformation from Lost Prairie into Garland City. Except for those two government-printed documents 130 years apart, there is no literature of Garland City. Kim will have to start from scratch, and she decides, because of her luck with the mayor at Lake City and the mayor's wife at Arkansas City, to scratch first at the mayor's door. This isn't too hard to find: separated by a vacant lot from the newish, official-looking U.S. Post Office building is a row of nonofficial but utilitarian-looking buildings, or sheds, metal and brick, that might be part of a construction site's temporary offices but are marked with an official sign on metal, "CITY HALL," and a less official echo on plywood, "City HaLL." The former lists NEW information on dumping hours, but there is no town dump in sight—unless, as a local wag suggests, it refers to "dumping on" the mayor additional problems. A large late-model automobile is parked out front.

Martha Franklin owns the car. Her salary as mayor is only $200 a month, but she gets a lot more than that moonlighting mornings as a postal-route driver for the post office, which she has done for thirty-seven years. Unlike Pat Qualls of Lake City and Judy Bixler of Arkansas City, Mrs. Franklin is no forty-three-year-old beauty; she is "getting up there in years," a matriarchal figure who does not simply govern the town but rules it, upheld by the town marshal, who just happens to be her husband.

Kim opens the door of City Hall and finds herself at once in the main meeting room, where two women, one young, the other old, are sitting at a table, painting ceramic figurines. They look up from their work as she enters.

"I'm looking for the mayor," Kim says.

"I am she," declares Martha Franklin, with a note of authority in a Southwestern drawl that is all business and no nonsense. Her dress and makeup, like her speech, are smart and neat.

When Kim had introduced herself and explained her mission, she is offered a chair and introduced to the younger woman, who is Mrs. Franklin's secretary, Peggy Mauldin, age twenty-nine, like Mrs. Franklin a native of Miller County. Her official title is "assistant mayor," but that includes a lot of things, like helping the mayor paint these figurines.

Kim finds it unusual that the ladies are engaged in such work during official hours, and she indicates a row of the compote ceramics and inquires, "Is this part of your regular duties?" Both ladies laugh, and Mrs. Franklin explains that it is just part of a fund-raising campaign. They are always doing things to raise money for the fire department. The pottery will not be sold directly, but used as prizes in Bingo games.

During her time in office Mayor Martha has seen to the installation of twenty-two fire plugs around the village, where there were none before; the training of twenty-eight firefighters; and the purchase of a $55,000 fire truck. She explains to Kim that she first got into politics, back in the late sixties, because of the town's lack of fire protection, the "extortionist rates" that fire-insurance companies were charging because Garland City's water system was so substandard. She ran for mayor with a promise to get the water system overhauled in 1970, at a time when there wasn't a single woman mayor in the state of Arkansas (today there are forty of them). She also promised to put blacks on the city council and to schedule regular council meetings. As a final fillip, she offered to install road signs marking the city limits of Garland City. "Nobody even knew where the city limits were," she tells Kim, and adds that she has extended the city limits twice during her fifteen years in office.

Although she defeated the incumbent mayor by a two-to-one margin, her first term wasn't easy. "I tell you right now," she tells Kim, "the first four years I was a mayor no one knew if I had any sense, 'cause I was working carrying the mail, working on the farm, I just worked, worked, worked, and went to church, and people must have thought, 'Now she's been elected, she'll get everything in such a mess we'll have to come in and straighten it out.' I really had to prove myself for the first four years."

She kept her promises: fire-insurance rates dropped not once but twice, the annexations doubled the population of the town, and she learned how to apply for (and receive) federal grants, which have really pumped new life into the town, helped pave the streets, install a sewer system, improve the drainage system, and rehabilitate housing, a slow process of eliminating the worst eyesores (there are many such dwellings) and sprucing up those that are worth saving.

There are a disproportionate number of the elderly in Garland City, more even than in Cave City or Lake City, and Martha Franklin, who isn't getting any younger herself, is very concerned for them. She has arranged for a van to transport them for shopping trips and health care to Texarkana, the county seat, which gets its name from its inability to decide whether it is in Texas or in Arkansas (it is about half in each).

There is also a hot-meals program for senior citizens; if Kim hangs around long enough, she will see how it works. Her interview is interrupted by two black youths who want to talk to Mrs. Franklin about their involvement in some upcoming fundraising event. While she has them in her office, Kim chats with Assistant Mayor Peggy Mauldin.

"As a young person, how do you feel about the future of Garland City?"

"I hope it continues to progress the way it's going now," Peggy says. "Mrs. Franklin has really done wonders, and I'm not saying this just because she's my boss. I've said a hundred times she ought to be on 'That's Incredible.' "

"Do you ever want to go away to a larger town?"

"Not really," Peggy says. But she thinks about the question and adds, "There used to be a lot more to entertain people here."

From the other room, Mrs. Franklin hollers to her assistant, "Why don't you get Smead to come talk to her?"

Peggy makes a quick phone call, then returns to Kim. "Mr. Franklin's gonna stop by. He's the marshal, but he does a lot of things besides just patrol. He takes care of our banking, and he makes repairs, takes care of breakdowns. We've never had a murder, at any time. He was in the hospital recently, and we had a shooting—a couple of young boys got after an older man's daughter, picking on her, and they got into a gunfight. No one was hurt, but if Mr. Franklin hadn't been in the hospital I don't think it would have happened. We don't even have a jail in town any more."

Marshal Smead Franklin comes ambling in, looking just like an elderly marshal in a Southwestern town, complete with the silver star pinned to his shirt. He removes his cowboy hat, sits down, and tells Kim he's at her service.

"What is it people like so much about you?" she asks him.

He smiles modestly. "Aw, I guess I'm just fair to everybody. I don't pick on people. The big's the big, and the little's the little, but they're all the same to me. Whether you're black, white, pink, or yellow, I just go by the book."

Smead Franklin has been the town's marshal for twenty-eight of his seventy-three years, and in all that time things have been pretty peaceful. If there's any trouble, what is it usually about? "Oh, family troubles, man and his wife, you know. Very little theft, people stealin things like batteries off of cars." Robberies? "Let me tell you, we got three whiskey stores here that handles a lot of money every day. They never been robbed. Never. I don't know the reason why, unless this place would be so hard to get away from—you're covered both ways out of town, to Lewisville east, to Texarkana west."

The Franklins themselves used to have a liquor store, along with the several other occupations that both of them had to make money to raise six children. Most liquor dealing in the county is legitimate, with very little moonshine trade out in the country, although it wasn't always that way. . . .

During the 1920s, Garland City was the liquor capital of a large area of the Southwest, home of a special amber-colored whiskey called Garland City Pride that was consumed in large quantities in Shreveport, Little Rock, Dallas, and other cities. Prohibition had nothing directly to do with it (although the author of the Eighteenth Amendment was a senator from Texarkana—the Texas side), because Arkansas had been nominally bone dry for years before Prohibition, but Prohibition boosted the economy of moonshining to the price of $15 a quart, until price wars and liquor feuds gradually whittled that cost down to $4 or $5 a gallon in the 1930s. The untold story of these liquor feuds, which, like Civil War bushwhacking and jayhawking, divided whole neighborhoods and even families, may have had something to do with the dynamiting of that bridge.

Bootlegging (the name derives from the colonial smuggler's concealment of liquor flasks in the legs of his tall boots) came to Garland City at a most opportune time: after World War I the price of cotton plunged, and the local cotton economy, already battered by a disastrous flood of the Red in 1915, collapsed, leaving farmers and their tenants impoverished. Oil had not yet been discovered here. From the time when Goodspeed described Garland City in 1890 as a mere hamlet of "two or three stores and a station," until national journalism in the 1930s investigated the gangland liquor wars here and described it as a sleepy village where "peaceful merchants keep two or three stores open for supplying fat salt pork and corn meal to the colored folk," Garland City had not changed, not grown or declined; the one hundred whites and two hundred blacks had lived and bred and died, becoming increasingly pauperized by national economic trends, until the only way a white man could feed and clothe his kids was to start a hidden distillery, and the only way a black man could feed his kids was to do the dangerous work of tending the still fires for the white man, and answering, for the white man, to any agents of the Federal Revenue who came along.

All along the Red River bottoms, among the cypress trees of the alligator-infested swamps, black men fueled the copper boilers, not with telltale smoky wood fires but with gasoline, which leaves no smoke though it is tricky to burn. From wholesale houses in Texarkana came the carloads of charred kegs (made from oak staves barreled at Henry Thane's mills on the other side of the state) to give some semblance of "aging" to the stuff, enough to turn it amber, and glass fruit jars to bottle it in. The "two or three" ever-blooming stores in Garland City did a land-office business in corn sugar and cracked corn for the mash, since corn will not grow in cotton fields.

Garland City Pride was no better or worse than any other moonshine; that is to say, it was potable, bald-faced, popskull swamproot, but it acquired its own mystique, just as Perrier is no better or worse than ordinary H_2O. Transient roughnecks of the southern Arkansas oil fields, moving on to Texas or Louisiana, carried with them many memories of blissful drunks they had tied on with the help of the Garland City booze, and motivated the demand for bootleggers to travel out of their way to acquire supplies of the stuff. Like any product whose reputation is based on mystique alone, Garland City Pride (traditionally mixed half-and-half with "Co-Cola") gave to its drinkers not only the usual euphoria or stupor achieved by any alcohol, but also a fraternal sense of he-manliness, bravado, and good-ole-boyhood (even to the rare female who tried it). Those who swore by it but had never seen the "city" of its origin began to dream up mythologized visions of the sort of special place that Garland City was, just as today Lynchburg, Tennessee, has acquired (partly through expensive advertising by Jack Daniel's Distillery) the image of the archetypal down-home country village. The few drinkers of Garland City Pride who ever actually stumbled upon the town, or slowed down enough on U.S. 82 to observe it, must have been disappointed to see nothing but those "two or three stores."

Profit breeds corruption the way tainted meat breeds flies. The "gangs" who took over Garland City and fought to dominate its liquor traffic were not your Chicago mobsters with machine guns, but local rednecks, backwoods entrepreneurs who had the power to determine who could set up a still and who could not, who could distribute the product and who could not, and were ready to enforce their decisions not with machine guns but with their own rustic weapons. The heart knows no difference between the sting of a machine-gun bullet and a buckshot pellet. No man was blasted in his barber's chair on the streets of Garland City (there were no barber's chairs), but out in the hinterland, once a month at least, some would-be distiller not authorized by the "family" would be put to death. In 1929, two farmboys were found at the bottom of a deserted well, badly decomposing, when their mother missed them after several days, and at the inquest evidence came forth that the boys had attempted to operate their own still without permission from the local ganglord. No one was convicted.

The "pride" part of the whiskey's name may have been partly a jape. Unquestionably the manufacturers took pride in their beverage, especially in contrast to the more poisonous hooch on the market, but there is something ironic or sarcastic, or both, in the concept of Garland City pride as it applies both to a corn juice and to a down-at-the-heel municipality. Pride of place is a characteristic of any sense of home, perhaps not so much pride as simple identification with the familiar, yet it has nothing to do with any effort to improve the familiar or even keep it looking presentable. Arkansas City's Front Avenue contains the derelicts of a past commercial glory, but Garland City has a Front Street that fronts not upon the Red River, but upon the railway, running, for most of its passage through the town, along the top of the levee before braving the rickety iron of the 1881 bridge across the Red. Though this Front Street was never much of a shopping district, it had a few storefronts, including a brick "block" of twin stores, illustrated here. One of these housed the old post office, behind big glass windows now vacant beneath their frail porch roof next door to the even greater emptiness of its sister, a store gutted not just of its glass front but of its whole interior. With all the signs removed, the post-office sign and whatever shop sign this store once had, the block is not just faceless but nameless. Thus it takes on the essential identification of any ruin, from a semiotic point of view: the absence of any *sign* except the overall appearance of its abandonment. Maybe someone should finish tearing it down, and maybe it is already gone even as these words are written, but it might be better for it to remain even in half-decay, bigeminally whole and lame, as a silent monument to the death of the American downtown.

Whoever did business in these twin buildings, even if only buying or selling postage stamps, watched the daily comings and goings of the trains, the jerkwater combinations of freight cars with few or no passengers, that made up the once-glorious St. Louis Southwestern Railway. This line was known all over as the "Cotton Belt," for it cut a large swath from Cairo, Illinois (not St. Louis, despite its grand name), down through most of Arkansas's cotton country and on to Waco, Texas. In modern times the "Cotton Belt" has merged with the Southern Pacific, laid off hundreds of employees, and may soon merge with the Santa Fe and lay off hundreds more. But for years before Garland was incorporated as a city in 1903, the railroad was the town's principal access to the outside world.

The year 1903, coincidentally, saw the publication of a paperback jokebook, *On a Slow Train Through Arkansaw*, by a Chicago man named Thomas W. Jackson who simply hopped on the bandwagon of a whole genre of paperbacks aimed at the amusement of train riders, who included everybody who could afford to travel in the great railroad era. A compendium of mostly stale gags and yarns, some with ancestry in the Middle Ages, none with specific relevance to Arkansas, it sold millions of copies and contributed enormously to the common image of Arkansas as a backward yokeldom where the hilarious trains stop not only once at every station but twice if the station has two doors.

People who think Arkansas is *per se* a riot of hilarity usually find that blacks, or Jews, or Poles, are intrinsically funny. Not by accident is most of the humor in *On a Slow Train Through Arkansaw* directed not at the rube Arkansawyer himself but at the stereotyped comical "darky"—indeed, the book is subtitled *Sayings of the Southern Darkies—All the Latest and Best Minstrel Jokes of the Day*, and it employs all of the racial epithets: "coon," "burrhead," "niggah," and "nigger."

Kim is surprised to notice that white people in Garland City clearly say "nigger," or at best "nigra," whereas everyone she talked to in Arkansas City said "black," or at worst "nigro." Arkansas City is distinctly Southern, with some of the South's sense of gentility and manners. Garland City is Southwestern, with Texan arrogance and rudeness.

"We don't intermingle as such," Mrs. Franklin says. "But there is no *de facto* segregation. It's just sort of a custom." The Garland City public schools, which, everyone agrees, are a complete disgrace, have been nominally desegregated as long as any other schools in the state, but there is no socializing between black and white, and many white parents have arranged to send their children to Lewisville, eight miles east, to attend the "better" schools there. In contrast to Arkansas City, the richest school district in the state, Garland City is near the bottom in school expenditures.

But Mayor Franklin is universally loved by the black people of her town, and she is one of the few whites who call them "blacks," not "niggers." "I want to tell you another thing about blacks," she tells Kim. "I found this out from my black friends. During slavery days—they didn't have baby bottles then—the white people went to church in the mornin and the black mammies nursed the white women's babies and their own babies, too, while they were gone to church. Then, in the afternoon, the blacks went to church, and so the black cooks in the house left their babies with the white women, who nursed their black cooks' babies. They switched, you see." Mrs. Franklin pauses to let this sink in. "And the blacks *still* go to church in the afternoons."

The door into the City Hall meeting room opens, and a black man carries in a stack of covered trays. "Dinnertime," Mrs. Franklin announces, explaining that the meeting room is used for a hot-lunch program for senior citizens, both black and white, who eat together.

Marshal Smead Franklin says that sometimes he joins them. "I'm a senior citizen, aint I?" He winks at Kim. A few elderly blacks appear and take their places at the long tables, from which the ceramic figurines have been removed, and the hot-lunch trays are spread out. The two or three elderly white people who enter do not sit next to the blacks but, rather, at a separate table.

A tray is placed on the table in front of Kim. Nobody has

formally invited her to join them for lunch, but it seems she is expected to. She looks at her plate: meat loaf, white beans, lettuce salad, and cornbread, almost identical to her lunch at Grundy's Blue Front in Arkansas City. She wonders if it has been treated with any geriatric vitamins or medicines.

An elderly black man seats himself directly beside Kim. His interest in her tape recorder bespeaks an eagerness to leave some record of himself in whatever form it will take, and Kim is reminded of her occasional feeling that her chance contacts seem to be ready and waiting for her. He wants to be remembered: David Adams, age ninety, used to farm a little, work a little on the Red River, now retired, except for being a proud member of Mayor Franklin's six-member city council. "I try to help the town. Anything we can do to help the town."

Kim brings up a subject of mild controversy. "Do you say 'Garland City' or just 'Garland'?"

"I says Garland, Arkansas, ma'am," David Adams declares.

From across the table, Marshal Franklin declares, "It's Garland *City*, lady. That's its name. Just like if your name was Mary Ann, I wouldn't call you Mary, I'd call you Mary Ann. Same with the 'City' part, ma'am. This is Garland *City*."

"But," says Mayor Franklin to Marshal Franklin, "the city charter, the incorporation papers made out back in 1903, has just 'Garland' on it."

"Well, but most folks say 'Garland *City*,' " the marshal reaffirms.

"Most black folks says just 'Garland,' " David Adams says.

The two men eye each other. Kim changes the subject. "As a councilman," she asks David Adams, "what improvements do you think the town needs most?"

"I'd like to see some industry come in to help the people out," Mr. Adams says. Mayor Franklin and Marshal Franklin nod their heads in agreement. That's what Garland City needs most: industry, *jobs*. It is the same story Kim has heard in Cave City, Lake City, Arkansas City: when a town has a few hundred people in it, it has to have an industry to survive. Garland City has none.

"This food is pretty good," Marshal Franklin comments.

"The food is really good," David Adams agrees. Kim looks around and, without counting heads, determines that about a dozen people, most of them black, are eating. David explains that his wife, with whom he has celebrated a golden wedding anniversary, has a bad heart, wears a pacemaker, and can't join them for lunch. Later he will take a lunch home for her. He likes the lunch program: it gives him a chance to get out of the house and see some friends. "Sometimes we sing," he says. What songs do they sing? "Oh, we just sing church songs, you know. Or one of those Elvis Presley songs."

But there is no singing today. As soon as Mr. Adams has finished eating, Kim has time to ask him just one more question before he leaves to take lunch to his wife. He is obviously in good health. Has he never worried? *Never*, he says. Never in his life has he worried. "Whatever happens, I say it happens. Worryin don't stop it. Don't change it. It happens." Then he shakes her hand. "I appreciate talking to you." He is gone.

"I tell you," Martha Franklin tells Kim, or her husband, addressing both, "the blacks have a better time than we do!" She asks Kim, "You didn't know that? Well, *they* know it! Oh, yes, they have a better time than we do!"

"What do you mean by a better time?" Kim asks.

"They just do have a better time, because, well, they can go fishin and they don't worry about their bills. They get after me for worryin and scurryin around here and workin for them, and they tell me every day I'm not goin to live long and all this stuff, because I do worry. And they don't lose things and they don't hurry. They get after me constantly about me scurryin around and hustlin and tryin to do too many jobs at once."

Kim asks the mayor and the marshal, "Is David Adams the oldest person in town?"

"*Person?*" says Mrs. Franklin. "Funny you use that word, because the oldest person in town is Corinne *Person*—that's her name." Where does she live? A stone's throw, if you threw the rock hard, from City Hall.

* * *

"Have you worried a lot?" is one of the first questions that Kim puts to Corinne Cargill Person, widow of Levin Person, a lawyer and planter, in her mansion, set back across a broad lawn on East Fifth near its end at the levee. The Garland City levee is not nearly so high as the Arkansas City levee. The "Person place," a townhouse rather than a plantation house, is one of only two mansions in town, but, unlike the other, the Price place, which Kim will visit this afternoon to interview another widow, is not authentically antebellum: its tall, slender columns and its door-way with split-ogee pediment are stock lumberyard fixtures added to make a two-story Victorian house look classical.

"I have a very easy disposition and I do not hold grudges and I do not talk bad about people," Corinne Person declares. "And I have a weak mind and a strong back." She laughs at her transposition of the adjectives. She neither looks nor sounds her age, which may or may not be older than David Adams's, though she was born on October 1 of the same year as he, 1895. "I used to think it was 1896, because . . . But you don't want this trash on there, do you?" She points at Kim's tape recorder. She is a handsome woman with dark hair, and her house is lovely. She will give Kim a tour. Did Kim notice the church right behind the house?

Yes, Kim noticed the church—"chapel" would be the word for this small red brick neo-Gothic structure. Its many pointed-arch windows are set with stained glass, not in awkward repre-sentation of lambs, saints, Christs, or Levantine landscapes, but in abstract geometric and floral motifs that, when the sun is shining in the east of a Sunday morning, bathe the pews with rainbow light. (In the fructuous year of 1886, John La Farge had revived the art of stained glass with his work *Red and White Peonies*, setting a standard for floral motifs.) The church has no steeple or tower to speak of, other than a sort of canopy over an open vestibule placed on neither the front nor the side of the edifice but upon the corner, giving the plan further Gothic asymmetrical organic freedom but also "addressing" not the Person place or any house on the other side but the open "common," if a vacant lot can be called that, in the area of the post office and city hall, if they can be called those. Although the building and the self-effacing architect are of the twentieth century, the style harks back to the English medieval parish church of the thirteenth and fourteenth centuries, "one of the most beautiful and appropriate buildings that the mind of man could conceive," as one Victorian neo-Gothicist called it. This church would look out of place anywhere in America outside of, say, tidewater Virginia. Here, surrounded by the ugly, the undistinguished, and the feebly parvenu, it seems entirely miscast, anachronistic, misplaced, and supremely lonely in a place of great loneliness.

On a bronze plaque affixed to a brick pier of the catercornered portal are the words "TO THE GLORY OF GOD AND IN LOVING MEMORY OF CHARLENE BEASLEY PERSON WHO MADE THIS CHURCH POSSIBLE." Nothing else. No date, no builders, no congregation.

"My mother-in-law, Mrs. Person, built that church for this community, and it's a community church," Corinne Person tells Kim. "Anyone, Methodist or Baptist, can preach there, although the Methodists want it to be only Methodist and the Baptists want it to be only Baptist. But she, my mother-in-law, built that church, paid for every nickel of it, and she wanted it to be a *community* church for *any* denomination."

The conflict between the Methodists and the more numerous Baptists is partly solved by letting the Methodists have it early on Sunday mornings; next comes a "mixed" Sunday School; then the Baptists get it for the 11:00 A.M. service. Blacks, of course, never enter it.

Charlene Beasley Person's son, Levin, his widow explains to Kim, "used to be called a 'planter,' but now they call them 'rancher.' " Levin's mother bought this house, which was the Murray place, and changed it into the Person place sixty-four years ago. The Murrays were an "old family" before the Persons became an "old family." There are few other "old families" in town; Kim will meet widows surviving two others, the Prices and the Phillipses, later this afternoon. The Franklins, declares Corinne, Martha and Smead Franklin, are definitely *not* "old family."

"You *must* meet Demie Price," Corinne urges Kim. "She is one of my best and oldest friends, and I love her so. But she is

ill." Corinne is anything but ill (although there are people in
town who say that she is eccentric, dotty, or nuts) and, thinking
of Demie, "who *paints*," she jumps up and begins to conduct Kim
on a tour of her house, to show her paintings of her own. "I
paint, too, or I *did*." The paintings are mostly pleasant landscapes,
no local views, not primitive, not amateur. Among the paintings
not her own there is one small painting of a girl, ornately framed,
which Kim could swear is a Renoir, or a perfect copy of a Renoir.
Corinne smiles. "That isn't *mine*. I mean, I didn't paint it. My
grandmother Harrington acquired that." Kim asks how the name
is spelled.

Every room is filled with antiques whose provenance Mrs.
Person wants to relate to Kim. She paid only $25 for this beautiful
wardrobe. That divan was the Beasleys' but this étagère was the
Harringtons'. She shows Kim a once-common musical instrument, the melodeon, a sort of small reed organ, which Kim has
never seen before.

After the tour, Kim asks her casual question about whether
the town should be called Garland City or simply Garland. Corinne Person shrugs. It is not important, she says. She doesn't
really care. Call it whatever you wish.

"Do you think there's much community spirit here?" Kim asks.

"Very little now. It used to be big, a busy little town, when
I came here as a bride. Wagons and horses and so many niggers
everywhere. And there were a lot of nice people here, too. Not
now. My sister says to me, why don't I just leave? Since Lev died,
what is keeping me here? But I can't just leave. My roots, whatever I've got, are here."

"What happened to the community spirit?"

"There were so many people here, so many wonderful white
people, and they all moved away. I tell everybody, 'There's nobody here but me and the niggers!' " Corinne laughs at herself
and says, "But I say that just to be silly."

Ira Phillips was born in 1896, a year later than Corinne Person,
but like her came to Garland City as a bride when "it was a

booming little town." Although Corinne has referred to hers as an "old family," her husband was actually just a railroad worker who later drove a school bus, and Ira lives alone in nothing approximating a mansion but a modest compote house without antiques, closer to the railroad depot that said "Garland City." "Why they put 'City' on that depot I'll never know," she tells Kim; she and most people say nothing but "Garland," which is what the post office said for years.

Kim realizes there were topics she meant to ask Corinne Person about but forgot, such as the floods and the dynamiting of the bridge. Regarding the former, Ira Phillips declares she can't remember any serious floods since the big one of 1927 (although, according to the U.S. Army Corps of Engineers hydrology records, the town was "flooded" in 1935, 1938, 1945, and two years in succession in 1957 and 1958). About the dynamiting, Ira, like just about everyone else, does not know who did it, but she remembers, laughing, "Everybody was asleep and everybody got up at the same time, I 'magine."

Though she raised five children in Garland City, they are all scattered to faraway places now. Kim asks if they ever come back to visit and what they think of Garland City these days. Ira says, "Well, we don't comment on it."

Seeming to drive in circles, Kim finds herself right back across the street from Corinne Person's mansion to locate Ira Phillips's good friend Vera Wright. A relatively young seventy, compared with the other widows, she lives alone in an attractive "permanized" house trailer, an immobile mobile home, full of potted violets. When she first came to Garland City the year after the 1927 flood, her family moved into a tenant house where the overflow's mud had to be scraped from the walls and floor.

Her late husband was born and raised in Garland City and called it that, but she has always said just "Garland," although "I don't know really what it's supposed to be. What is it on the map?" (All official state maps have it as "Garland City," but all service station maps say only "Garland.") Although she loves the town and wouldn't be happy anywhere else, "It's not the Garland I knew when my children were growing up. We had a school. It was segregated. Some people even then, if they could afford it, sent their children to Lewisville to school. Now . . . our schools are just something else again. There's nothing here for young people; they *have* to get out if they're going to do anything."

When her two sons had grown up and flown the roost, she and her husband left, too, and stayed away for seventeen years; but her husband's homesickness was incurable and he never gave up hope of returning. This they did, after he had retired. Now that he has died, Ira Phillips and Corinne Person are her only buddies. "You have to have *someone* to associate with. This is a town of widows."

Kim mentions that she has seen Corinne Person and her lovely home full of antiques. Vera Wright says, "She's like the rest of us now. She's alone. And can't get anything done. Everything falls down around us."

This is a town of widows. Demie Price, Vera Wright has told Kim, "hasn't been well for about a year," which is the information that others have given Kim, too. But she decides, as the afternoon moves on, at least to see the Price mansion, which is at the end of Price Drive, on the western end of the town, near Garland City's tiny "airport," which was mostly a private strip for the Prices' airplane. From the mansion and airstrip the Prices' plantations extend as far as the eye can see westward and southward. The mansion was built by William Wynne in 1835, a year before statehood, just two years after Rufus Garland settled the area. Except for the Albert Pike mansion (1840) in Little Rock and other antebellum houses there, it is the only authentic "Southern" "colonial" "antebellum" "Greek Revival" mansion that Kim has ever seen outside a movie theater: it might have served as a set for *Gone with the Wind*. In contrast to the parvenu frailties of the Person place, it is authentically classical, massive, and very, very Southern. It lacks only Spanish moss hanging from the live-oak trees to complete the picture.

Kim will never discover what "Demie" is short for—Demetria? Laodamia? Adamina?—or exactly how old she is, give or take fifteen years on either side of seventy, but Kim meets her and is welcomed into that "monstrous house"— the words from her notebook, later. She is perhaps too awed by the woman and the interior even to think of asking her what "Demie" is short for and how old she is. Or quite possibly she realizes very soon that she would not get correct answers if she did ask, for Demie Price, although not "ill" in the manner Kim had come to expect— she is not diseased, she is not in a wheelchair—lives at the mercy of the inventions of her lonely mind. Facts mean nothing. She tells Kim she has lived in this house for only fifteen years, but later Kim will learn that she has lived in the house for around forty-five years.

But her perceptions of Garland City are not distorted. In answer to various questions concerning her opinions of her town, she declares:

> It's a small country village. It has one good grocery store and a couple of gas stations.

> It exists, but that's about all. It has no personality.

> There's no white and black dissension. No racial problem. I think we're pretty lucky that way.

> For a little town, I guess it does pretty well. There's very little crime committed here.

There have been no burglaries, no break-ins, at the Price mansion, which is remarkable because she lives there alone. (From some distant room, Kim can hear a small dog constantly barking.) But in a town where none of the three liquor stores has ever been held up, it is not incredible.

As Corinne Person had done, Demie Price insists on a tour of the mansion. Kim leaves her tape recorder running during the tour, but Demie's voice is quite weak, rambling, trailing with nostalgia, and Kim can catch very little of it. The rooms are like a museum; they do not appear to be used, not even the large studio where Demie Price has done much of *her* painting, which has a style distinct from Corinne's but is not lifted out of ordinariness by any personal quirks or tricks. There is quite a large collection of guns, rifles, shotguns, bullets, paraphernalia: years before, Demie was a champion trapshooter.

While they are touring the house, they are abruptly joined by a man, who says, "You're Kim." He is tall, middle-aged, rugged in cowboy boots, suntanned, and well fed. Kim's first, startled thought is that he is Professor Harrigan from South Dakota, come to surprise her and join her, but before she can say "What a surprise!" he explains, "I've just been on the phone with your father." He lets that sink in for a long moment of bewilderment during which Kim wonders if Professor Harrigan has been in touch with her family in an effort to locate her. But *he* doesn't use a phone. Then *this* man wraps his arm around Demie Price and introduces himself: Glen Howard Price, age fifty, Demie's son. He explains that he sometimes does business with Micky Gunn, who had mentioned to Glen that he had heard his daughter was destined for Garland City.

Glen Price answers the questions that his mother cannot accurately handle: there are not a "few hundred" acres here on the Price plantation, but twenty-seven hundred of them, making it one of the largest plantations in this part of Arkansas, cultivated to combinations of wheat, rice, beans, and the usual cotton, which keeps on going out of fashion.

Mother and son do not agree on the name of the town: it is Garland to Demie, Garland City to Glen. He laughingly explains, "I say 'Garland City' as a habit, but I started it as a joke, 'cause to me it's really *not* a city."

Glen does not live in this house; he and his wife live elsewhere "on the farm" but would like to leave entirely and move into Texarkana, where most of his business activities center. His travels take him all over, and in places as far away as Colorado he has met people who have heard of the legendary Garland City Pride whiskey. The dynamiting of the bridge, however, had something to do with a lucrative ferry business run by a noted figure named Jess Smith. "Talk to his grandson about that," Glen urges Kim. "Jess T. Smith Johnson." He gives her directions to the house.

But before she goes off to interview Jess Johnson, she will have one other interview suggested by the Prices, one more widow, a black one. Learning that the Price house is indeed antebellum, she asks if there were slaves, and, if so, are there any descendants of those slaves still living in the area? Demie Price and Glen look at each other. Glen says to his mother, "Martha?" His mother agrees, "Yes, Martha."

Her grandmother was a slave who cooked in that mansion, Martha McGough, age eighty-three, tells Kim from her wheelchair. The small house in which she is confined is in a black neighborhood on the other side of the highway from the Price plantation. "She died before I was born, but my father told me about her."

Martha herself, a large, cheerful, laughing woman, worked for Demie Price for forty years, and before that she worked for Demie's mother-in-law. "I love her," Martha says of Demie, and explains that Demie's husband, Earl Price, died about nine years ago.

Though for three years she has been in the wheelchair and unable to work for Demie, she is strong and can still look after herself. Kim doesn't think she looks as old as eighty-three and tells her so, but Mrs. McGough protests, "Oh, I think I look *ninety-six* since I got in this chair!"

Kim casually asks. "Do you like Garland City?"

"Do I *like* it?" Martha McGough is almost indignant at being asked. "I love it. I wouldn't live nowhere else! No, ma'am! Oh, Lord! I've never made my home nowhere else but here! All these eighty-three years I've been here!"

"What's so special about Garland City?"

"Well, it's quiet. It's peaceful. You just feels free to do what you wanter do. If you wanter get out there and plant something, you just do it! I mean, you can raise anything you want

here. . . ." Does she know Mrs. Franklin? Of course she knows
Mrs. Franklin. "I love her. I hope she's mayor as long as I'm
alive. I want to tell you what I like about Garland. You don't
have no trouble out of whites. If they's anything they can do to
help you, they'll do it."

Years ago, Martha McGough knew blacks who "got rich"
helping whites make bootleg whiskey, which she calls "white lightning—never you mind nothin you hear about 'Garland City Pride.' "
She laughs. Did she remember the bridge being dynamited? "Oh,
yeah, I do; I was grown and married when that happened. No,
ma'am, I never did find out who blew it up. The only thing I
know about it is I heard the commotion of it; I heard it and I
thought it was lightning. It scared me, good lands!"

Though Martha McGough doubts that any white folks could tell
Kim anything about who blew up the bridge, Kim decides to talk
to a man who wasn't born when the dynamiting occurred but
who is the grandson of the man who, some think, decreed the
blast. As Arkansas City was largely under the control of Henry
Thane, Garland City during the 1910s and 1920s had his counterpart in Jess T. Smith, who had forty-five hundred acres under
cultivation, owned the mercantile stores in Garland City, the bank
(such as it was), the unsanctioned liquor store, the cotton gin,
and, most important for this story, the ferries across the Red,
which, before the bridge was built, were the only way that traffic
other than the railway trains could get from one end of southern
Arkansas to the other.

Jess T. Smith Johnson, born in 1948, was only seven when
his grandfather and namesake died, but he lives today in a house
Jess Smith built in 1924, across the street from Charlene Beasley
Person's church ("Corinne's mother-in-law really went broke
funding all of those churches," he tells Kim) and closest of any
house in town to the dynamited bridge. Jess T. Smith Johnson
is just finishing his supper when Kim arrives, and she realizes
she has not eaten and the afternoon is fading. He is very wel-
coming and hospitable, just short of offering her anything to eat.

He drags out the family scrapbooks and photograph albums to show Kim pictures of Jess T. Smith, who looks like an overweight version of J. R. Ewing of "Dallas." Other pictures are of Jess Smith's ferry, which Jess T. Smith Johnson remembers as being in a very decayed state and not operating when he was a youngster.

"Grandpa had one hundred head of horses, one hundred head of mules," enumerates Jess T. Smith Johnson, "and seventy-five nigger families living on the place. Just about all the niggers in Garland City are descendants of those seventy-five families of Grandpa's." He becomes reflective. "He owned quite a bit, and did quite a bit, but that era faded out, so to speak."

Kim would like to ask, "Is there any place to get supper in this town?" But instead she asks, "Did he blow up the bridge?"

"He dealt in Arkansas politics quite a bit," Jess T. Smith Johnson says. "Although he was more or less in the background, a background figure, you know. Over on the river—he had a picnic grounds over there—and he'd invite thirty-five hundred people at one time for a party. He'd take all the whiskey out of his liquor store, and he'd slaughter whole cows and goats and what have you, and he'd invite all the dignitaries, politicians, and everybody from all over, and he'd wine 'em and dine 'em for the people who wanted interests thrown their way. He was sort of the background man, in the background, you know."

"Was he in the background of the dynamiting of the bridge?"

"Now, actually, the man who ran the ferry wasn't Grandpa but Grandpa's brother, Uncle Tom Smith: Grandpa was too busy to mess with the ferry." He adds, "Of course, I wasn't around at the time, so I'm not sure. I think the bridge had been built for five or six years when they blew it up."

"Who was 'they'?"

"And of course the bridge was rebuilt completely, to what it is today. But when it blew up, it shook this house right here right off its foundation and blew out every one of these windows. We had a farmhouse *five* miles down the river, and there was shrapnel from the bridge all over the yard."

"Who . . . ?" Kim begins to try once more, but decides to

shift the subject and depart. Her stomach is threatening to growl
with hunger. "What do you like about Garland City?" she asks.

"Oh, I like the *history* of it," Jess T. Smith Johnson says. "The
schools, of course, are a disgrace, but otherwise . . ." He explains
that he sent his own children to the Lewisville schools until the
new integration laws required them to return to the Garland City
school, where they were not happy. "But it *is* a nice close-knit
community, and I'd rather raise children here than, say, Texarkana or any other larger place."

What about race relationships?

"White people and niggers have known each other's families
for years and years. There are no strangers. We watch out for
the niggers and they watch out for us. I know of no incidents
here with racial overtones."

"Well, thank you, Mr. Johnson." She stands, turning off her
tape recorder. "Could you tell me if there is any place to get
supper in town, or nearby?"

He ponders. "Well, there's Ham's. You could try Ham's."

Somehow, "Ham's" sounds to her as if it might be another
Grundy's Blue Front, but she asks for directions and he gives
them: very simple, get on 82, just around the corner, and drive
to the other end of town, less than a mile. On the right. You
could miss it, but you'll find it.

You could very easily miss Ham's Fish and Steak House if you
were not looking for it, or if you were not one of the hundreds
of loyal customers who drive miles and miles from Texas or
Louisiana just to eat there. Nobody from Garland City eats there
except the cooks and waitresses, who might be commuters. In
her travels around Garland City, Kim has driven right past Ham's
at least three times without noticing it: on her way to the Price
plantation, on her way to Martha McGough's house, and once
to view the cemetery, which is directly across the highway from
Ham's. (And which is, incidentally, the most unsightly cemetery
Kim has ever seen in all her travels or ever hopes to see again.
She did not actually go into it, because many of the graves have

gaping holes and tunnels as if large animals were burrowing into them or ghouls had given up. The headstones, some in the shape of Valentines, tilt at rakish angles and appear about to be swallowed up by the holes. Drainage ditches have been cut like open wounds to ease whatever soggy seepages plague the soil. Jungles of kudzu and wakefield crud encroach upon this plot, which, being directly behind the Price mansion, probably originated as a private burial ground for the slaves and continues as a predominantly black cemetery.)

Fortunately for her appetite, Kim has entirely forgotten having stopped to cringe at this cemetery just a few hours before. Now she locates Ham's mostly by the help of one of those Porta-signs on wheels, a kind of earthbound marquee advertising the otherwise nameless and signless edifice, a flat-roofed enlarged shack. The presence in the parking lot of several expensive cars with Texas and Louisiana plates makes Kim think at first that the facilities are being reserved by a convention of oilmen, but she soon discovers that it is a family restaurant, and she is one of the family, gathered in a down-home if not downright homely atmosphere to stuff themselves on the best fish available within a few hours' drive.

There is no menu. Steak is available, but nobody seems to be eating that. Everyone is paying the same price, $8.95, for the same successive accretion of plates: iced boiled shrimp (all you can eat), fried shrimp (ditto), crab roll (one is enough), followed by the main course: a huge steaming platter of catfish, not just *a* catfish but several catfish fillets in batter, deep-fried, and whole baby catfish and steaks cut from larger catfish. There is so much catfish on the platter that Kim wonders if she is supposed to pass it on to others, but she is alone at her table and the platter is all hers . . . if she can eat it. She cannot, being already stuffed with shrimp, not to speak (oh, never speak!) of all the accompaniments: golden-brown hush puppies, cole slaw, onions, pickles, peppers, relish, shrimp sauce, tartar sauce, butter, and lemon wedges. To wash it all down is a tumbler of iced tea that seems to keep refilling itself as if by magic.

Kim sighs. If only she had Professor Harrigan to help her

eat it all. The batter the catfish is fried in seems to be not merely
a coating but something the fish grew as part of its natural covering, and is so golden it ought to be assayed. Thinking of gold,
however, makes her think of the next city, the penultimate lost
city of her travels, Bear City, which was a gold-mining boom
town, and she is eager to get on, having finished Garland City
earlier than she had anticipated; there is so little here.

But Ham's leaves a good taste in her mouth as she drives
out of a town that has left a bad taste. She will remember Ham's
long after she has forgotten the shanties and mansions, the ruins
and the compote. Not far out of town, stopping to consult her
road map and wonder how far into the night she will have to go
before coming to a motel (Texarkana is twenty-four miles westward, closer to Texas, and she has chosen to drive back east to
Lewisville instead), she realizes that what she should have done,
although it had not occurred to her (she was too busy enjoying
the food), was interview Mr. Ham or whoever owned or managed
the restaurant. Wouldn't a restaurant owner have a lot to say
about the little lost city in which he served his food?

It is a question she will remember to ask at another restaurant, in the last of these lost places.

After a search, she finds a motel of sorts north of Lewisville, a
few miles out of town on State 29, called The Coachlight or The
Lamplighter or The Tavern Lamp or something like that. She
is so tired, and it is the humblest motel she has ever stayed in:
very plain and simple, no pictures, no decoration whatever, very
inexpensive, but reasonably clean and comfortable.

By coincidence worth mentioning here, that stretch of plain
back-country highway on which it is located, that two-narrow-
lane State 29 which runs for twenty-three miles from Lewisville
to Hope, was once *walked*, during his freshman year in college,
by Professor Harrigan. It happened like this: During his January
break he had hitchhiked from Fayetteville down to Houston,

Texas, to spend a few days with an old boyhood pal, and on his way home had decided to detour to Hope, Arkansas, to surprise an old boyhood girlfriend named Gladys. It was after sundown when a man who had given him a ride from the East Texas hill country let him out at Lewisville and offered him overnight accommodations at his home there, warning him not to hitchhike after dark on that lonely road into Hope. But Harrigan was eager to spring his surprise on Gladys, and he thanked the man and resumed hitchhiking, or trying to hitchhike, north along State 29, walking, putting his thumb in the air for each increasingly rare passing vehicle, walking onward into the cold January night, passing, without seeing it, this same humble motel where Kim is now (or maybe it did not exist in those days of the fifties). All night he walked, never getting a car to stop for him. Twenty-three miles. Cold. All the dogs at every house barked at him as he passed. It was dawn when he staggered into Hope, and although Gladys was tickled to see him, she did not fully appreciate the lengths he had gone to.

Now, as Kim is checking into The Lamp after dark, Harrigan is checking into the Hilton M. Briggs Library at South Dakota State University an armload of books he has had checked out. And, while he is at it, doing some research on garlands and on gold. Earlier this day, he has purchased for a trifle a secondhand car, a 1969 Ambassador, to replace his old faithful four-wheel-drive Blazer, whose motor block cracked in the South Dakota winter.

He cannot check out any of the new books he finds, but he can copy pages on the library's Xerox machine, and he stands feeding nickels and dimes into it, amassing an armload of pages, all kinds of information about gold, its historical significance, the mining of it, legends, the psychology of gold seeking, etc.

His last nickel he spends to copy a page from a 1948 issue of *Colorado Magazine*, an article entitled "Garland City, Railroad Terminus, 1878," a reprinted letter by Mormon colonizer John Morgan (1842–94). The Garland City of which he writes is not *our* Garland City, but one in Colorado; still, what he says might serve as an *envoi* here: "Soon Garland will be a thing of the past and only battered oyster cans, cast-off clothing, old shoes, and debris generally will mark the site of where once stood a flourishing city, with its hotels, its stores, its theatre comique, etc." All because it was losing to another town farther down the line its status as the railroad terminus. Before the pivotal year of 1886 had even begun, *that* Garland City was already a ghost town.

Kim has never conducted so many interviews in one day before and she is exhausted. She notices that the walls and ceiling of her room, a plasterboard module close beside the highway, are covered with a textured paint a shade of excremental brown suggestive of the Red River, which she does not plan to cross again. In South Dakota, it is the Big Sioux River that Harrigan will never cross again.

Bear City,
Arkansas

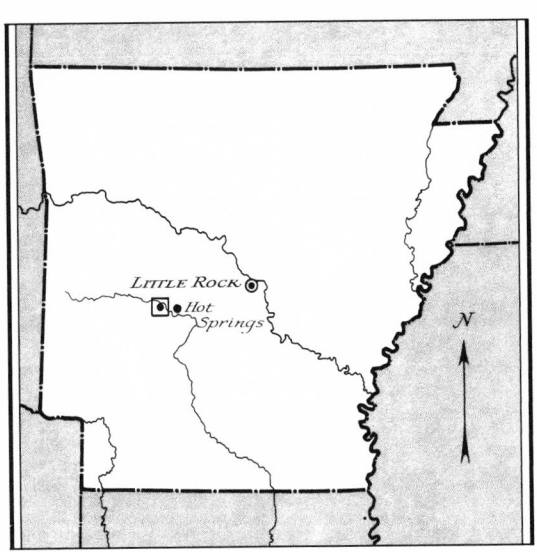

LITTLE ROCK
Hot
Springs

N

I need a place to sing, and dancing-room,
And I have made a promise to my ears
I'll sing and whistle romping with the bears.
—Roethke, "The Dance," Four for Sir John Davies,

1953

EIGHTEEN EIGHTY-SIX, that special year for hope and event, was the year when gold appeared to have been discovered in the Ouachita (pronounced "Washitaw") Mountains of western Arkansas, near a mountain called Bear and an already existing furniture-making settlement called Rouse's. The place became Bear City overnight and was to remain a city as long as the hope of gold remained, several years, and then lapse back into a furniture-making settlement, which it still is today, long after the hope of gold here or elsewhere in Arkansas has faded into an old joke.

Bears and chairs—these are our true themes, not chimerical gold. When Kim puts the two themes together, she cannot help visualizing the three bears of the tale of Goldilocks, each sitting upright in his or her chair. But by the time the first chairs were made at Bear City, there were no bears left to sit in them.

More than the mythical razorback, the bear is the animal of Arkansas, which for years, before some promotional boosters wanted its license plates adorned with "The Land of Opportunity," was known far and wide by the nickname "The Bear State." This was in no small measure due to the most celebrated anecdote ever published about the state, "The Big Bear of Arkansas," from the 1840s pen of Thomas Bangs Thorpe, and widely circulated by the *Spirit of the Times* magazine, a kind of nineteenth-century version of *Sports Illustrated*. The yarn took its title not from the animal but from the man who told it, a mysterious traveler known as the Big Bear, an Arkansas backwoodsman who, returning from New Orleans aboard a Mississippi steamboat, regales his fellow cabin passengers with the story of his hunt for a huge "unhuntable bar" (as "bear" was, and sometimes still is, pronounced). Big Bear, after many failures to catch the big bear, is surprised by it one morning while in the act of relieving himself in the woods near his house and, having his bear rifle at hand, shoots the big bear.

> Instantly the varmint wheeled, gave a yell, and *walked through the fence* like a falling tree would through a cobweb. I started after, but was tripped up by my inexpressibles, which either from habit, or the excitement of the moment, were about my heels, and before I had really gathered myself up, I heard the old varmint groaning in a thicket near by, like a thousand sinners, and by the time I reached him he was a corpse. [Thorpe's italics.]

Big Bear concluded that the eponymous animal, who had eluded all previous attempts by men and dogs to take him, had decided its time had come and permitted itself to be killed by the Big Bear.

Shortly after its publication in *Spirit of the Times*, Thorpe's story appeared on the front page of the *Arkansas Gazette*, then (1841) as now the most important newspaper in the state, and this recognition seemed to reflect the pride Arkansawyers took in belonging to "The Bear State." Even before Thorpe's story, *Spirit of the Times* had published several bear-hunting tales by the afore-mentioned C. F. M. Noland of Batesville (see p. 180), promoting the legend of the state's excess of bears.

In 1844, the young German novelist-to-be Friedrich Gerstäcker published his *Streif- und Jagdzüge durch die Vereinigten Staaten Nordamerikas*, a "travel" book that is essentially his story of exciting bear hunts in the wilderness of Arkansas. Although it would not be translated into English for another ten years, when it did appear as *Wild Sports in the Far West* (Arkansas then *was* about as far west as one could go without being in Indian territory) it gave Arkansas an international reputation as a sportsman's paradise in which the bears outnumbered people. Gerstäcker's first novel, *Die Regulatoren in Arkansas*, was published two years after his travel book, establishing his reputation as a romantic novelist of adventure in faraway places. The Arkansas "regulator" was a self-appointed lawkeeper of a breed later called "vigilante." If Peter Mankins was the first American cowboy, Gerstäcker was the first writer of "Westerns." But his fascination with outlaws and frontier justice always took a secondary position to his love of the hunt, particularly the bear hunt, in which he himself had thrilling and hazardous experiences all over Arkansas, though never in the vicinity of Bear City–to–be.

Arkansas's reputation as a shooting gallery for bears made life miserable for the animal: by the end of the nineteenth century the bear was nearly extinct. Bear hides, which sold for a dollar in the days of Gerstäcker, Thorpe, and Noland, were no longer used as carpets in every cabin. Bear oil, which once had fueled the lamps of all the settlers, gave way to kerosene, but in its day had been so plentiful that one of Arkansas's quaintly named villages, Oil Trough, on the White River near Batesville, took its name from the hollowed-out tree trunks that had been packed with huge quantities of bear oil and rafted down to New Orleans. The oil was also used for cooking, grooming the hair, and dressing leather.

The prevalence of bears in Arkansas, either in reality or imagination, is reflected in the naming of places: though there is only one town called Bear City, there are seven Bear Mountains and a Bear Head Mountain, thirteen Bear Hollows as well as a Bear Spring Hollow, a Little Bear Cave Hollow, a Bear Water Hollow, a Bear Pen Hollow, a Bear Hole Hollow, and a Bear Wallow Hollow; five Bear Bayous, two Bear Branches, four Little Bear Creeks, six Bear Sloughs, four Bear Lakes, a Big Bear Lake and a Little Bear Lake, and a Bear Pond, not to mention a Bear Brake (swamp), Bear Pen Falls, Bear Waller Spring, Little Bear Cave, Bear Spring Gap, Bear Wallow Prong, Bear Wallow Slough, and Bear Island.

In modern times the State Game and Fish Commission has attempted to restock the woods with bears, and after years of laws forbidding the shooting of any bear, a limited hunting season has been tried, with a "legal kill" averaging only thirty a year. Bears adore honey, and landowners who fear for their beehives have been illegally killing on sight any bears who wander onto their property. Poachers stuff their freezers with illicit cuts of bear carcass. The $1,000 fine for this misdemeanor rarely gets paid. If caught, some hunters claim that they shot in self-defense, but there is no verified record of a bear attacking a human in recent Arkansas history. The state's present population of bears is fewer than two thousand.

The human population of Bear City reached two thousand in 1886 but is fewer than fifty now. No bears inhabit the township or the surrounding forests, although the oldest resident, eighty-five-year-old Clarence Jewell, claims that bears have been spotted in modern times. As in Garland City and a few other lost cities, some of the residents drop the "City" and call the place simply "Bear." Indeed, on the official state highway map, Bear City appears only as "Bear." Its identity problems have been further compounded by having for most of its life been in Montgomery County, with little Mount Ida as the county seat, but being de-gerrymandered in modern times eastwardly into Garland County, of which Garland City is no part, and of which Hot Springs is the seat.

Hot Springs, the sixth-largest city in Arkansas, is perhaps the best-known city outside of the state, after Little Rock, because it contains Hot Springs National Park, which contains the famous hot springs, the federal spa, America's Baden-Baden, Aix-les-Bains, and Bath. It is a mere eleven miles east of Bear City (sixteen miles before the roads were paved). In 1541 de Soto took a month off from his mad quest for gold to rest and recuperate at these thermal waters. The springs remained the private preserve of Indians until the federal government established a reservation there in 1832, four years before Arkansas became a state. The Indians told de Soto nothing about the gold in them thar hills to the west of town, around Bear City, for the simple reason that there was no gold, then or ever. In the resort year of 1886, Hot Springs was already overcrowded with out-of-state tourists—the Elegant Eighties' equivalent of today's trendy jet set, frequenting its shoulder-to-shoulder hotels, bathhouses, saloons, and casinos—when the jammed accommodations were further strained by an influx of prospectors seeking overnight lodging and a quick dip at the Free Bath House on their way to the supposed gold fields at Bear City.

Kim's initial plan is to follow in the footsteps of these Argonauts by stopping overnight in Hot Springs en route to Bear City, or, since it is doubtful she will find any trace remaining of Bear City's three-story hotel, or even its several two- and one-story hotels, she will just establish her bivouac here in the comfort of the spa. But the annual thoroughbred-racing season at Oaklawn Park, which brings more visitors to Hot Springs during March and April than the baths, has just ended; the city has the look of still recuperating from the bettors' sojourn and the overstay of jockeys, grooms, clockers, tipsters, bookies, and hanger-on whores. The place looks tired. Bath House Row is not overworked but *déclassé*, most of its palatial dip joints now shuttered for good. The whole city has the air of a once-overconfident resort that didn't know when to stop putting up one more tacky motel, whose prices have not fallen with the popularity. Kim decides not to continue trying to decide among the dozens of them whose signs whine "Vacant" as a self-indictment of vacuity. A few of the motels follow her out of town, like beggars trying a last pitch for her notice. Surely she can find *some*thing less blatantly touristic closer to Bear City.

But as U.S. 270 carries her closer to her destination—the same highway that will later take her on to her destiny at the final lost city, called Y, where it, the highway, ends, or becomes two other roads diverging into a wood—the commercial billboards of Hot Springs give way to vernacular advertising: "Tree Dogs for Sale," "Bates' Bait Shop," "Arktiques," "Rocky's Rock Shop," "Free Crystals." As she nears the turnoff to Bear City, two miles north of the highway, even these cease, and there are no more signs, no letters anywhere, as if she had entered a private realm of illiteracy. Of all these lost cities, Bear City alone has no identifying markers, signs, mileposts, words of any character. It is a semiotic barren. The refrain *A traveler passing through will never know a town was there* does not exactly apply: there is clear evidence of once-populous habitation, a variety of buildings still scattered about, some dwellings still occupied, but no sign whatever to announce "Bear City" or to indicate "Former Post Office" or "One-Time Doctor's Office" or "Erstwhile Uncle Jep Smith's General Store," or even—and this is the important one, Kim's present objective—"Still Functioning Bump Furniture Factory." The latter could so easily be mistaken for an old unused barn, and Kim drives past it twice without realizing that it never held a cow.

She is back in the hills now. After all those days in flatland eastern and southern Arkansas, she has returned to the uplands; even if she will not quite yet catch another snatch of the Theme of the Faraway Hills, she is embraced again by highland slopes. Rising ground surrounds her, though not spectacularly: Bear City is in a little holler between knobs not more than three hundred feet higher than the village; the summit of Bear Mountain itself, 1,368 feet above sea level, is only seven hundred feet higher than the village, and not visible from it.

But the sense of *fastnesses*, both of the forest and the hills, enwraps and enraptures her. In her notebook she writes, "Bear City is like a fairy-tale town, something in a child's memory." Bear City is the coziest of all our lost towns. Snug. Forsaken by men (most of them), it is redeemed by nature, who is doing a really nice and neat job of reclaiming it, covering it over with thick up-sprouting trees and creeping vines and lush dense undergrowth, of which even the pernicious wakefield crud is not too oppressive. By comparison with other lost places she has seen, Bear City is a jungle. Nature is returning it to the condition it was in when men first found it and one of them described it: "situated in a lovely and romantic dell, surrounded by verdured mountains and skirted north and south by two crystal brooks whose dancing waters join in the east suburbs and flow onward to the Ouachita."

Those two crystal brooks, north and south, were named by
the two founders of the town, each for himself. It takes two to
make a town, and keep it. One came from North Carolina by
way of Georgia and Alabama in 1866, Wiley Rouse, stopping all
along the route to make and sell chairs. He claimed the southern
brook and called it Rouse Creek. A year later he was joined by
another man coming from Tennessee, Larkin Melson, who claimed
the northern brook and called it Melson Creek. The two brooks
meet at a triangle on the southern edge of the village and together
form Bear Creek, which flows into the Ouachita River.

Both men were primarily subsistence farmers, but Wiley Rouse
was by trade a chairmaker and Larkin Melson a surveyor and
blacksmith. Both had wives, Elizzabeth Rouse and Martha Melson, who would bear the first daughters of Bear. Before they
could plant the land, Wiley and Lark had to clear it of its virgin
hardwood timber. Lark Melson burned the trees he cut to clear
his pastures. Wiley Rouse took the red oaks he cut and carved
them into spindles and slats to make furniture, while the chairs
were seated with strips of white oak shaved into splints and woven
together. Thus began the one true "industry" that Bear City has
ever had, one that is still continuing today.

Wiley Rouse's daughter Julia somewhere found a handsome
French Canadian named Philander La Bumph, responded to his
wooing, and agreed to his proposal of marriage on condition that
he leave wherever it was she found him and come home with
her to Bear. He also left his French name, Anglicizing it to "Bump"
despite Julia's attempts to explain to him the English meanings
of "bump," as in "a bump on the head," "a bump on a log," and
the many meanings as verbs—"to kill," "to impregnate," "to dis-
charge or fire," and "to thrust the pelvis forward." No one ever
called him Philander, even if they had known it meant a loving
man, which is what he was. Nor did they call him Phil. The
mountain folk of Bear called him Phi, pronounced "fie," as in
the twenty-first letter of the Greek alphabet.

Phi Bump joined his father-in-law, Wiley Rouse, in the operation of his sawmill and furniture factory, and later, when the
town became a city filled with prospectors and stockbrokers, and

everybody was trying to get rich from the central hoax of gold, Phi went on lathing his chair parts and getting Julia to bottom them, and teaching their children how to lathe and bottom a fine, sturdy, no-nonsense Shaker-style dining chair and rocker, which Phi Bump's great-grandchildren are today still trying to escape the responsibility of having to learn how to do. It paid well in those days, 50¢ a chair. Even at $50 a chair today, it is not paying work.

The first person Kim meets in Bear City is a chairmaker. After driving around to reconnoiter the village and see that there are still traces of all the crisscrossed platted streets—First to Seventh running north, and Broadway, Main, West Main, Walnut, High, etc., running west—she pulls Zephyra up on Water Street, alongside the most picturesque of Bear City's ruins. From the board-and-battened, vine-clung "shack" shown here, the western side of it shaved away, there once rose a stepped false front that *did* bear a fine, big sign, "U.S. Post Office, Bear City, Arkansas." But this was taken down sadly over fifty years ago, on Halloween of 1933, by the last postmaster, Clarence Jewell, who lived in the wing to the right, or east, festooned with the junglish vines of kudzu and the tentative tendrils of wakefield crud. Indeed, all of the surrounding yard, where once the wagons and horses and mules stood while their owners sorted through their mail, is swallowed up by these vines. Kudzu, a Japanese vine, *Pueraria thunbergiana*, was once imported as a fast-growing succulent fodder and forage for livestock, but is so prolific and determined that it is doing a better job than any native plant in helping nature reclaim the entire Southland from man's mowings. Without the kudzu, this old post office would be just one more firetrap tumbledown derelict, but with all those climbing, creeping, snaking tendrils and twining vines, even without the lavish foliage that will appear later in the spring to turn all this gray to overwhelming green, the building becomes enchanted, and if nature is a female she is here a witch.

Though Kim gets out of the car to look, she cannot step through the thick mat of wakefield-crud creepers. The building is obviously abandoned, one side plastered with roofing tin and one window shaded by the same corrugated, rusting metal. She will not learn until later that it was the post office, and also a home for Clarence Jewell and, for thirty years before him, the dwelling of Peter Huber, a strange bachelor German who came out of nowhere to be a genuine postmaster for the town, albeit a drunken, harmonica-playing, crippled one. Even learning all about Peter Huber will not change Kim's first impression of this building as the most compelling ruin she has encountered.

Water Street is now only a dirt trail, full of mudholes, which Zephyra has waded through disgustedly in order to stop here. Once it was a busy thoroughfare that also contained the town jail, which was built into an abandoned mine entrance across the creek; Wiley Rouse's dam on his creek, where he built his original chair factory, of which no trace remains; Wiley Rouse's spring, a fountain of pure water; and several of the better homes of Bear City, only one of which, built by Clarence Jewell's mother, still stands, converted by its present occupants into a year-round semi-modern home.

Because Water Street is so rarely used, a man driving a red pickup truck spots Zephyra parked there and pulls up to investigate. Without getting out of his truck, he hails Kim.

"Lost? Could I help you find anything?"

She turns to him, a handsome blond-haired near-forty outdoor type who looks like . . . well, perhaps an assistant superintendent of a power plant, which is what he is. His words remind her of Kate Scraper's medicine men who "could tell you where to find something you'd lost."

"I want it lost," she says. "I like it lost."

He laughs. "Bill Hopkins," he says. "I can tell you anything."

"Tell me the history of Bear City."

Again he laughs. "Now, *that* I don't know. You ought to talk to Dallas Bump. Lives right there." He points at a house, or cabin, across the road. This building, with two towering ashlar stone chimneys at either end and a house-length front porch strewn with handmade chairs, rockers, and porch swing, was Lark Melson's home, begun as a one-room log cabin and expanded in 1881, before the gold rush, into a dogtrot by the addition of a second pen or "house," separated by a breezeway (the mountain man always refers to the other half of his dogtrot as "my other house," even though it shares the same roof with the room he is in). As in many dogtrots, the breezeway was boarded over in modern times to make even more interior room.

Kim knocks, then knocks again, but there is nobody home. Bill Hopkins's red pickup pulls alongside Zephyra again. "Well," he says, "I guess he must be up at his shop." He gives her directions to the shop, just up the road, on Walnut Street, formerly much more the main street than Main or West Main ever was, and he starts to conclude, "You can't miss it," but seems to think better of this and says, "You *can* miss it, because it looks just like some old barn."

Bill Hopkins explains that he works full-time at the power plant, but in his spare time, especially during the Christmas rush, he helps his friend Dallas Bump fill chair orders, and throughout the year he maintains the factory's equipment and helps Mr. Bump get his split timber. "I can't tell you the history of Bear City, but I can tell you the history of the Bumps," he says, and goes on to explain how Philander Bump passed on the skills to his son Fred, and Fred passed them on to his son Dallas, and Dallas tried to pass them on to his son, Freddie, who, however, would rather earn a lot more money working as a lineman in the construction business and doesn't have much enthusiasm for learning the ancient family trade.

With Freddie gone, Bill "takes up the slack" in the chair factory when he can.

"Maybe Dallas Bump thinks of you as a son," Kim suggests.

"In a sense," Bill admits. "That would be an honor, if he did. He's one in a million, someone you just enjoy being around. He's twenty-five years older than me, but he doesn't act like it— he treats me like an equal, makes me feel a part of it all. Go meet him. Tell him I sent you."

Again Kim thanks him, and follows his directions a couple of blocks down Walnut Street, past the site of the splendid but vanished Ozark Hotel, now Dallas Bump's cow pasture; past the equally disappeared Willingham Hotel; up to Uncle Jep Smith's

General Store, its false front removed, too, leaving the gable of
a cottage in which lives Dallas Bump's eighty-four-year-old mother,
Della Bump, and his "baby sister," sixty-five-year-old Ola Bump.
Up a rising circular driveway behind the former general store
sits the board-and-batten long shed (apparently vertical boards
rather than horizontal clapboards were favored throughout the
erection of Bear City), with wings of sloped roofs rising to join
the peaked gable of the central barn-doored chamber of the old,
incognito furniture factory. Another porch swing, surely made
here, hangs suspended from the branches of a graceful young
sycamore tree, almost like a shop sign advertising the woodcraft;
if indeed the swing was meant as such, it is the only "sign" in
town.

A lone automobile, an old bile-green Ambassador with a
headlight missing, the front fender all crumpled, and the license
plates gone, sits outside the door. All the doors of the factory
are wide open, for the afternoon is becoming very warm; Kim
removes her cotton jacket, beneath which she is wearing her
favorite T-shirt, which says "Cotton" beneath a picture of a fluffy
boll of it. Dressed thus, she steps through the big main barn door
and confronts the dark interior of the shop.

The moment is frozen, and preserved. With the blinding
sunlight behind her, her hair becomes the color of the precious
metal that men once hoped to find in this town. She stands still,
letting her eyes adjust to the dark interior. She is tall, blonde,
and blue-eyed. A man stares at her in wonder.

He is sitting on a bench in the gloom deep in the clutter of
the shop, an incredible jumble of machinery, wooden boards,
wooden spindles, wooden chips, and many years' accumulation
of sawdust thickly carpeting the whole interior. This man sits
whittling a stick with a pocketknife, and smoking a cigarette in
disregard of all the combustibles.

"Mr. Bump," she says, "Bill Hopkins told me where to find
you, and said you could tell me about Bear City. I'm Kim—"

"Yes, yes," he says. "Kim." In a very deep voice, he says her
name wonderingly, as if he were pronouncing a strange new
language. He is not simply looking steadily at her, she detects as

her eyes become adjusted to the darkness, but almost ogling her, although his eyes never leave hers to roam to other parts of her image. He certainly doesn't look sixty-six years old, or even fifty. He has large hands, capable of having made ten thousand chairs, but they are not gnarled or arthritic or scarred: they are smooth and young. His full head of long, soft hair is not exactly silvery but sort of pewter. Dressed in an old flannel shirt in a brown plaid, and blue jeans so faded that Levi Strauss himself must have hand-stitched them, he stands up, shifting his pocketknife to his left hand and using his right hand to take hers and hold it tightly. He *towers* above her, a very tall and big man. "You are lovely," he says, and the way he says it does not embarrass her at all.

"I was told you could tell me about Bear City," she says.

"Pardon?" he says, and gestures to his left ear, where there is a hearing aid. When she has repeated herself a bit more loudly or carefully, he motions for her to sit at the other end of the short bench. Strange that a chairmaker would have no chairs for sitting, only a bench; the room is filled with tossed and turned chairs and rockers in various stages of construction. "You really ought to talk to Clarence Jewell," he says. "He knows so much more than anybody else about Bear City."

"You are modest," Kim says, and, because he exudes such understanding and fellow-feeling, she confesses, "Everywhere I go, in the lost cities of Arkansas, I'm always being told, 'So-and-so could tell you more than I could,' or 'I don't really know very much,' when actually they are the most knowledgeable people in town. Are they just trying to be self-effacing or self-doubting or what? So who is this Clarence Jewell?"

He smiles at her, warmly and sympathetically, but she is not certain he has heard a word of what she has just said. At length he says, "Well, what would you like to know?"

"Wasn't there some sort of gold rush?" she asks.

"Goldfish?" he says. "You mean those in Wiley Rouse's mill-pond?"

"*Rush*," she says, shaping her lips. "There was a big boom here when people thought they had discovered gold."

"Oh," he says. "Yes," he says. Then he says, "Well." A long

moment passes, but he never takes his eyes from hers, as if he were compensating for his inability to hear her by reading her entire soul. She is not uncomfortable, and waits. Then he says, "Well, I'll tell you." And speaking in his warm, throaty bass voice, he begins to narrate, as if it were engraved upon his heart, the entire story of the great Bear City gold rush of 1886–87.

No one knows how it started. The times were ripe for rumors, just as in certain seasons flying saucers are seen: there are years when men have to see the saucers and years when they have to hunt for gold. (The Bear City fool's-gold rush coincided with an almost identical one in faraway Five Corners, Vermont, of all places.) Neither Wiley Rouse nor Larkin Melson had any interest in gold, or any expectation that their settlement would grow into a city as a result of it, and neither made any profit from the booming of the town. While both men went on living in their log cabins, Wiley kept on making chairs and Lark kept on blacksmithing but sold his cow pasture for the construction site for two hotels. Both men, as high officials of the Masonic Lodge, which they had co-founded in 1881, were careful about which of the newcomer prospectors and boomtowners they accepted for membership.

For years there had been talk of "Spanish gold" in old legends and folk tales. The Spaniards were almost stereotyped as gold-crazy; in the popular imagination every galleon was loaded with bullion, and every conquistador led a pack train of burros staggering beneath the weight of ingots, which were left buried in every conceivable cache of the Arkansas mountains. Tales of a "lost Spanish mine" and the fabled "lost Louisiana mine" opened every bear's den and rabbit hole to digging by the greedy. The Spanish reputation was not totally undeserved: de Soto ransacked Arkansas in 1541, not to Christianize the Indians, but to find gold. The same year (the same fever), Francisco Coronado, that least of the Spanish explorers, had combed the Southwest, penetrating into Kansas and Nebraska, trying to find the "seven cities of Cibola," each a reputed Fort Knox, and found only a few pueblos. You are searching for eleven lost cities of Arkansas; do you know of the Seven Lost Cities of Cibola? They were illusions, as was Bear City.

But both Montgomery County (in which Bear City was then located) and Garland County (where it is now) had honest, earned reputations for being "the mineral belt" of Arkansas. Although little gold or silver had actually been discovered, there were deposits of platinum, copper, lead, and cobalt, not to mention the humble novaculite, used by the Indians for arrowheads, by millers for grindstones, and still considered today the finest whetstone for knife sharpening, known universally as "Arkansas Stone."

In 1881 the precious-metal fever had created a miniboom at a community a few miles west of Bear City that quickly called itself Silver City, and served as a preview of what would happen at Bear City five years later, even with many of the same supporting cast of prospector, stock salesman, saloonkeeper, and newspaper editor. Silver and gold are often found together in the same ore, but silver is of course the less valuable, and while both metals were supposedly buried in huge quantities in the hills of Silver City, the boomtown got its name and its central focus from the mineral of the moon, not the sun. If you go looking for the remains of Silver City after you leave Bear, you won't find anything; much less is there than here.

Itching for something better than silver, the men of Silver City moved in three directions. At the head of the valley of the Arkansas River, near its source in the territory of Colorado, was a place called Oro City, a gold-rush boom and bust town during the 1860s that renamed itself Leadville in 1878, after the discovery of lead and silver in great quantities. In the 1880s it was one of the largest boom cities in the country, and several Silver City disappointees went there to find the real stuff. Others, their fever hiked by the news of the huge South African gold rush of 1886 and the Washington rush of the same year, changed their goals from silver to gold and headed either north, to a place in Logan County called Golden City, or east, just a few miles down the road, where it was rumored that somebody had actually discovered the lost Louisiana mine on the southern side of a hill adjoining Bear Mountain. They tore down their jerrybuilt board-and-batten shacks in Silver City, moved them to Bear Mountain, and began staking claims everywhere. Larkin Melson and Wiley Rouse, who had shared equally in the division of the creeks and the establishment of the little community, each donated 160 acres from their spreads to the establishment of the 320-acre Bear City, which was expected to reach a population of ten thousand within a year.

A man named Mr. Fulmer (his last name is *all* that is known about him) owned the claim, which he might or might not have purchased from Lark Melson's southwestern forty, up on the south slopes of the nine-hundred-foot knob called Louisiana Hill, a claim fancifully called by Mr. Fulmer (or by his "mining operations superintendent," Orson Hager) the Lost Louisiana Mine. Whether Fulmer and Hager were in collusion with other fraudulent operators, or were acting alone in the sincere belief that they had discovered a deposit of ore rich in gold, is a source of idle and almost irrelevant speculation, because soon the boom exploded all over Bear City, and other "mines" were established on every hillside and in every hollow. A man advertising himself as "Prof. R. R. Waitz, Assayer, Chemist & Metallurgist," came to town and pronounced the ore samples to be loaded with gold. An old forty-niner named Captain Billy Johnson arrived on the scene, took a quick tour, and announced, "I have seen all the mining camps in the United States and I know Arkansas has the greatest mines in the world." To prove his faith, he began constructing the handsomest residence in Bear City and buying up lots and claims. Herman Beyer, a former miner in Oro City, came from Colorado to inspect Professor Waitz's ore samples (and perhaps, since he was an old friend of Waitz's, to "salt" the samples with flecks of real Colorado gold). Charley Jacobs, who had been a mere notary public at Silver City and had failed to get rich, offered four hundred thousand shares of the C. H. Jacobs Mining Company for $10 million and found no shortage of investors from out of state.

Forty-six other mining companies, with such names as Eureka, Ozark, Accident, Nonpareil, Phoenix, and Champion, were organized and incorporated, offering more than four million shares of stock for prices in excess of $80 million. Americans rushed to own stock certificates lavishly printed on fancy paper that was worth more than any gold they claimed to represent.

Forty carpenters worked around the clock to build new structures in Bear City. The four hotels and six boardinghouses could not hope to hold the influx of people. Tent cities sprang up in every open field and along the roads. Wiley Rouse charitably posted a sign at his best bubbling spring of water: "Wiley Rouse, their owner, dedicates these springs to the public forever. June 10, 1887." A weekly newspaper, *The Bear City Times*, congratulated itself in print for all the excitement in town, and promised to become a daily momentarily (the linotype had been invented in our newsy year of 1886). By the summer of 1887, Bear City had reached its apogee.

How the new city could thrive for almost a year without any evidence of the actual mining or milling of gold is a mystery. Eventually some investors began to insist upon more proof of attempts to recapture the gold from the dirt. "Diamond Jo" Reynolds, a robber baron of the Gilded Age who had taken up permanent residence in Hot Springs after its waters had helped his rheumatism, and had brought a whole posh railroad with him, announced his intention to run his railroad onward into Bear City, *if* any gold was actually smelted there. A mining tycoon from Missouri, Colonel Moffet (his first name remains unknown), arrived in town with much fanfare (including the prearranged shooting off of sticks of dynamite in the branches of trees along his route of arrival) to build and operate a forty-ton smelter for extracting the gold from ore. Professor Waitz opened his Lixiviation Mill; "lixiviate" is an impressive word meaning simply to wash or percolate the soluble matter (water) from the metal (gold). Another "professor," A. M. Beam, discovered what he called "Beam's Electric Process" and set up a plant to extract gold from dirt by magnetism. Several "stamp" mills were built for the process of stamping the ore: pulverizing it to ready the gold for Beam's magnets or Waitz's lixiviation.

Several more months went by. The stamp mills did not stamp

any gold. Beam's Electric Process failed to magnetize any. Colonel Moffet's smelter did not produce any metal. Diamond Jo Reynolds' railroad was never built.

Thousands of investors lost their shirts. One of these out-of-state speculators (native Arkansawyers failed to invest, not because they knew of the hoax but because they were too poor), named John Benz (no known relation to Karl Benz, who in our mobile year of 1886 invented the motorcar), had plowed $1,375,000 into shares of the Ozark Mining Company. His worthless certificates were found years later hidden in the walls of an abandoned house in Bear City. Did Benz commit suicide or simply fade away in a poorhouse somewhere? In the whole history of Bear City, there is no *record* of a single suicide.

The state geologist was called in, not just to inspect the "mines" of Bear City, but to conduct a survey of all the hundreds of supposed gold mines in Montgomery and Garland counties. His report: there was some gold, silver, and other minerals in tiny quantities, but not enough to justify the costs of mining it; the mines of Bear City were virtually worthless and in some cases fraudulent; the Lost Louisiana Mine was not an old Spanish mine. The state geologist was hanged in effigy on the streets of Bear City.

Waymon Hogue's autobiographical *Back Yonder* (1932), the best nonfiction book to come out of the Ozarks, recalls a trip he made as an Ozarks backwoods boy with an older neighbor, Tom Boman, to look for employment, if not actual gold, in the boom town of Bear City. As he and his companion neared the town,

> The road was full of men going to and coming from the mines. We met many who looked disappointed and dejected. We were stopped by a man wanting a match. He was a middle-aged man, carrying a bundle tied up in a red bandana handkerchief suspended from a stick which he carried on his shoulder. Tom asked him the distance to the gold diggings.
>
> "T'ey's not any coldt," he said. "T'ey toldt you a lie—a cot tam lie. You are a tam fool if you go up t'ere!"

"Wal, mister," said Tom, "we want work. Do you thank they will give us work?"

"T'ey gif you not'ing," he said. "T'ey got no work. T'ey got no coldt. It's all a cot tam lie!" Saying this, he walked on.

After the rush, no more outsiders came into Bear City until modern times, when a few retirees, or young people like the couple who live in miner Harley Green's Victorian "mansion," came here for gold of a different sort: golden quiet, golden solitude. All of the people connected with the gold rush left town, many to try their luck at Pike's Peak in 1891 or look for the end of the rainbow elsewhere in the West. By 1892, the population of Bear City had dropped to 120, and half of those were gone by the end of the century, when, of all the operations, only the first, the Lost Louisiana Mine, remained stubbornly "in business"; a few diehards continued to insist that all that was needed was a better process for extracting gold from the ore.

Larkin Melson reclaimed his cow pasture from the gardens of the Ozark Hotel, and kept on blacksmithing. Wiley Rouse went on making chairs.

Kim has interrupted him only once, so that she could change the tape in her tape recorder. Now he concludes, with almost cosmic melancholy, " '*Auri sacra fames.*' Do you know Latin? Vergil wrote, '*Quid non mortalia cogis, auri sacra fames?*' 'To what do you not drive the hearts of men, O cursed greed for gold?' But sometimes I think the possession of gold is worse than the pursuit of it. *Non teneas aurum totum quod splendet ut aurum nec pulchrum pomum quodlibet esse bonum. . . .*"

"I'm sorry," she says. "I really don't know any Latin." She wishes she did. She wishes she could talk for hours with this man in a dead language. "Do you work all day in here? Eight hours? Ten hours?" Kim asks.

"I don't work here at all," he says.

A pickup truck pulls in between the old Ambassador and

Zephyra, and a man comes into the shop. "Sorry to keep you waiting," he says. He is an older man, past sixty, dressed in overalls and with curly white hair beneath the edges of his farmer's bill cap. He moves with authority around the shop and then sits down beside the other man, whom he does not resemble at all: he is much shorter. "Bill told me you were looking for me," he says. "I've been over to Royal on some business, and—"

She looks back and forth between the two men. "Are *you* Dallas Bump?" she asks the older, smaller man.

"That's right," he says, smiling most cordially. "Sure am. What can I do for you?"

She looks questioningly at the younger, taller man, who has talked so much to her and told her the history of the gold rush. *He* continues to look kindly and warm, but there is a twinkle in his eyes as if the two of them have a secret. Maybe they do. She addresses *him*: "Who—?"

Dallas Bump looks at him, too, and the younger man says to Dallas, "We were just wondering how many hours a day you spend in this shop."

Dallas Bump laughs modestly and says, "Not nearly as many as I ought to! Three or four hours is the most I can stand, though I can remember when I used to work ten, twelve, fourteen hours in here and think nothing of it."

"Where do you sell your chairs?" she asks.

"Mostly just people driving by," he says.

"But how do they know this is a chair factory?"

"Oh, they've heard about me, I guess," he says.

She wants to ask the younger man, "Are you just a friend of his? What were you doing in the shop?" But she can't ask that. Instead she asks Dallas Bump, "How much are you charging for chairs these days?"

"Well, rockers run anywhere from thirty-five to a hundred fifty dollars. The dining chairs will cost you fifty or sixty. Materials are just getting so expensive these days."

"The stools?" Kim indicates one of the splint-woven-seat ottomans.

"Those are twenty dollars," says Dallas Bump.

"I think I'll buy one," she says, and opens her purse.

The younger man offers, "I'll put it in your car for you." He carries the stool out to her car.

She says to Dallas Bump, giving him the twenty, "But I didn't come just to buy a stool. I wanted to ask you some questions about chairmaking and about the history of Bear City."

"You really ought to talk to Clarence Jewell about that," Dallas Bump says. "He knows a lot more than me about Bear City."

"That's what *he* says," she gestures toward the younger man, who is outside trying to figure out how to open Zephyra's hatchback. "About chairmaking, too?"

"Sure," says Dallas Bump. "Old Jewell had a much bigger factory than mine. It was a real *factory*, too, not just a shop. Had a whole bunch of people working for him. Ran a sawmill, too. Only place my dad ever worked, besides making chairs, was Jewell's sawmill."

"If you and Clarence Jewell are such rivals, why do you try to send people to him?"

"I wouldn't call us rivals. He hasn't made chairs for a long time, and he's nearly twenty years older than me. My dad always said, when you had competition it made business better—that was his theory of it. It was more friendly competition than rivalry."

Just as in the beginning, when Bear City consisted of only Wiley Rouse and Larkin Melson—not exactly loving each other but willing to help each other in a neighborly way and maybe even marry off a daughter, Tennessee Melson, to a son, Robbie Rouse (except that Robbie never asked her), yet each stubbornly determined to build Bear City from scratch, his *own* scratch— even in the end now, Dallas Bump and Clarence Jewell are the only two that make a town. The back end of Kim's car contains a pair of nylon zipper bags, red and yellow, duffel-style; a six-pack of glass bottles of Royal Crown Cola; a small plastic ice chest; two pretty dresses neatly laid flat on hangers that must be lifted so that the rectangular wooden stool can be placed under them. Ask him if they see each other often.

"Are you and Clarence good friends?" she asks Dallas Bump. "Do you see each other often?"

"Just comin to the mailbox now and again," Dallas says. "Neither one of us is great to visit, but if we need one another, we're there."

Every man secretly despises his neighbor. Though he may profess friendship, and it is a friendship durable and true, a man resents his neighbor's sharing of a close piece of earth and would rather have him at a distance, or at the great remove that comes from having him on the opposite side of a wall in a real city's close confines. A neighbor is good for competition, but the contest can become too strained if his success with his grass is greater than mine. I watch closely for the slightest flaw in his yard. He fuels a grudge out of my slightest misdeed. We warm the air between our houses with our fuming. Though I take comfort from his closeness in time of need, I shut him out of my mind whenever I can, except when my idleness festers while watching him better me. Even if I do not covet his wife, I covet his marriage to this space that ought to be all mine. We are brothers, sons of the same plot of this mother, earth, and we contend for her favor. But I am not my brother's keeper, except when he is helpless. I don't even speak to him when I can avoid it; I would rather invite into my house people from far down the road. Perhaps every man fails to love his neighbor as himself because he first must finish hating his neighbor as he finishes hating himself.

Meanwhile, if I need him, or he me, we're there.

Dallas Bump went away once, for ten years. Back in the fifties, trying to break out of the family tradition, routine, habit-pattern of chairmaking, he upped and went to Illinois. He took his wife, his son, Freddie, and "three extra kids to raise"—an adopted child and two of his wife's sister's children—enough dependents to force a man to look for more profitable work than chairmaking. Even in Illinois he could not escape wood, and worked for ten years as a carpenter. Carpenters are to chairmakers as physicians are to surgeons, lawyers to judges, Indians to chiefs, but carpenters are usually paid by the hour, not the piece.

"Weren't you homesick for Bear City?" Kim asks Dallas.

"Oh, I'd come back two or three times a year. . . ."

"You *were* homesick!"

His father, Fred Bump, kept the chairmaking business going back in Bear City. Fred, who had learned it at the age of thirteen from *his* father, Phi Bump, never did anything else. Dallas was twelve years old when Phi Bump died, and that same year Fred Bump started teaching Dallas how to make chairs, having already "employed" him for years to tend the shop's engines and keep them supplied with water for cooling, thus staying within sight of the lathes so that he could pick up the rudiments of wood turning just by sight, without verbal instruction. Fred Bump was a man of few words and less patience.

"He thought he'd tell you how to do something one time and you'd know how to do it!" Dallas says to Kim. "He'd never tell you twice." At the age of twelve, Dallas was smart enough to learn something after being told it once, but dumb enough not to understand why he *had* to work in the chair shop. "I thought he made me work just to keep me from gettin out and playin!"

(In Teutonic, "Dallas" means "playful," although Dallas does not know this. When Kim asks him where he got the name, he answers, "I don't know. I've asked my mother. My dad named me after a friend he had. I've run across a few other men with that name." The Irish, however, used "Dallas" as a shortened form of "Daedalus," from the Greek meaning "the cunning workman," and as in Stephen Dedalus. Daedalus Bump is a playful, cunning workman.)

There were (and still are) two lathes in the shop, the Big Lathe and the Little Lathe. Dallas was trained on the Little Lathe and in fact was never permitted to use the Big Lathe, which only Fred used, until after his father's death. The Big Lathe had been built by Wiley Rouse himself when he first came to Bear City in the 1860s, its wooden parts carefully crafted by hand and the metal parts poured in a Hot Springs foundry. To power the Big

Lathe, Wiley Rouse built a dam on Rouse Creek and constructed a water wheel; later the Big Lathe was run by a steam engine; today Dallas Bump uses an electric motor.

The walls of the shop are hung with dozens of wooden templates or patterns in all shapes and sizes, used for determining the exact length, thickness, and form of every conceivable chair part; most of these templates, however, hang stacked beneath an old coating of dust. "My dad could go and pick off whichever one of those he wanted, but I've never been able to learn 'em all," Dallas says; he has labeled the few he uses.

His father was angry, then simply grieved, when Dallas left Bear City for Illinois. Another Bump, Fred's brother, Guy, who had helped Phi and Fred operate the Bear City factory, moved during World War II to Oil Trough (of the bear's oil) over on the White River to be closer to the good oak timber of that part of Arkansas. The Bumps and the Jewells had just about denuded the Bear City area of its oak forests.

When rocking-chair man John F. Kennedy was elected president, the whole country went crazy for rocking chairs, and the Bump business boomed. Fred Bump renewed his efforts to persuade Dallas to come home from Illinois. Since severe winters in Illinois were beginning to get to Dallas, he was tempted. His son, Freddie, had already gladdened Grandpa Fred's heart by moving back to Bear City at the age of twenty to learn how to run the Little Lathe. When the temperature during the winter of '64 dropped to twenty-eight below in Illinois, Dallas had enough and decided to come home for good. By then Kennedy was dead and the rocker fad had faded, but the steady customers who just dropped by the shop continued dropping by, and Dallas was reasonably contented operating the Little Lathe until his father's death, in 1977, allowed him to take over the Big Lathe. Young Freddie, who had worked so well with his grandfather, did not continue working for his father, but sired three Bump sons who may or may not become the sixth-generation Bump chairmakers. The oldest is twelve, the right age for learning, and Grandpa Dallas is teaching him when he gets the chance.

"Where did your husband go?" Dallas asks Kim.

"My husband?" she says. "Oh, he moved to Little Rock, I think, last I heard of him. . . ."

He stares at her. She stares back at him. He gestures toward the door, through the open doorway, toward the place where the old Ambassador was parked but is no longer. "That man who was with you . . . ?" Dallas says. "He put your stool in your car and then he just took off."

"*With* me?" she says. "He wasn't with *me*. I thought he was with you; I mean, I thought he was a friend of yours."

Dallas smiles and shakes his head. "Never saw him before." She is looking so puzzled that he tries to reassure her. "Well, people come and they go. My door is always open. He wasn't in your car, anyhow."

She wants to protest, "But he knows the whole history of the gold rush!" She doesn't say this, however, for she is no longer in the shop; she has jumped up and rushed outside, and is looking up and down the road. Dallas follows her. It is plain that whoever this other customer was, he has departed. The old piece of junk he was driving has rolled off down the drive and gone south or north. To get off the subject, Dallas suggests to her, "Could I show you where anything is at, in this old town?"

She takes a long moment to respond to his question, to understand it, and then to think about it and answer. "Is there . . . where is the cemetery?"

"Funny you asked," he says, "because there isn't one. Never was. Most folks are buried either at Lowe Cemetery over at Mayberry, or else at Cunningham Cemetery down at New Hope." This is indeed strange. Of all our cities, Bear is the only one without any sort of cemetery, the only place where the dead— and there have been many of them, over the years—had to be taken not simply a comfortably safe distance away from the living but to different settlements some miles away. Not that there aren't suitable locations, pleasant knolls and solemn glades, for a cemetery. It is almost as if all those who had to bury their dead sensed that Bear City lacked the permanence to harbor a consecrated graveyard. Nor were there any churches in Bear City until comparatively modern times, the thirties, when two small church

houses were built. Both are temple-style but lack even the traditional belfry; one is in white wood, the other in native stone;
one Assembly of God, the other Baptist; both without resident
pastors or churchyards. "But there is *one* grave I can show you,"
Dallas offers Kim, and she accepts.

They turn northward onto Walnut Street. Kim sees the abandoned store at Third and Walnut, illustrated here, which has had
its sign removed but is left with an old rusted tin advertisement
for 7-Up Cola. "That was built back in the thirties, about the
time we started to get more of those colas around here, like RC
and Pepsi and such," Dallas says. Usually, such a store's exterior
would be plastered with the brightly colored tin signs advertising
the colas, especially the one called Coca, but also Vess, Frostie,
NuGrape, Grapette, Whistle and Botl'O; but this store's generous
fenestration left little room for the signs. This store replaced
Uncle Jep Smith's General Store, which the Bumps converted
into a home in the twenties.

Like the post office and the chair factory, the "7-Up Store"
is board-and-batten: there is something about vertical boards,
contrasted to the more traditional horizontal clapboards, that
looks more "modern" at the same time that it seems more "rustic,"
more "country." Indeed, the practice of vertical board-and-batten
was popularized throughout America by the romanticism of the
1840s (the same period in which the bears became known in
Arkansas), principally through the pattern books of Alexander
Jackson Davis and Andrew Jackson Downing. The verticality was
considered suitably "Gothic" in feeling, but because it is easier
for a carpenter to clothe an edifice with vertical boards whose
interstices do not overlap, as clapboards do, but are lazily covered
with thin strips or battens of wood, the style came to be associated
with quick, hasty construction, particularly throughout the mining camps of the West. One almost always expects the boards to
remain unpainted, as they are here. The rusticality of this "7-Up
Store" is further emphasized by the posts or columns of the
porch, young saplings of wood debarked but not shaved clean
of their stubs of branches. Nothing is more classically "vernacular" than a column in which the growth of the tree is revealed

by vestigial warty, knobby branches. Here it is just one branch, allowed to extend as far as the roof's eave: notice, the branch and the roofline imaginarily join at the same point. If the Greeks' temple frieze evolved out of a translation into stone of archaic timber architecture, if the triglyph is but a representation of the butt end of a wooden beam, if the columns themselves are only infinite refinements of old tree trunks used for posts, then we are looking here at the ancestor of a future American architectural style that will perhaps translate these pimpled poles into temple columns of steel.

Along Walnut are buildings in states of deliberate or natural demolition, and one lone gasoline pump with a sign of sorts, "DX gas, The Only One, 37 ⁹/₁₀¢ a gallon," nearly obscured by wakefield crud. On the northern edge of the village, one building stands alone, distinguished by its height, two full stories; by its paint, white; and by its style, Queen Anne Victorian: spindlework along the porch roofs, bracketed posts, fish-scale walls in the gables beneath a gable ornament, and a general cross-gable asymmetry. Compared with elaborate urban examples of the style, it is a cute country cousin, almost farmhouse in its simplicity, but it is the most elaborate house in Bear City and the "fanciest" one in this book. Built around 1890 by Harley Green, who came from Binghamton, New York, made money from the false gold boom, and then served as the Bear City justice of the peace into the twentieth century, it is still apparently occupied; Kim makes a note to come back later and try to interview the occupants. Dallas Bump remarks that the house has a reputation for being haunted; since any Victorian house, by its very size and encrustation, suggests hauntedness, even without the help of Charles Addams, it is easy to imagine ghosts in this place.

Just north of the Green home, where Walnut bends to become no longer the main thoroughfare but a county road, was the site of Colonel Moffet's smeltery, a large mill that went through the convincing motions of actually melting down the mined ores in order to separate the gold from them. As long as it lasted, it was the largest building in Bear City.

In the deep woods along the county road, Dallas stops to

lead Kim a short distance up the eastern slope of Bear Mountain to show her a pool of fresh water, a rock-lined spring that is all that remains of (according to Julia Rouse, Dallas's grandmother) the "Old Soldiers' Home," presumably a long-gone retirement boardinghouse for Civil War veterans. A snake lies sunning itself around the spring, and Kim does not bend to sample the water.

The road passes into a ravine, hollow, or "gulf"; on the other side of the road is a steep wooded hillside, full of second- and third-growth oak saplings trying to fill the spaces harvested by the Bump and Jewell timbering activities. Some of these trees, although not yet ready for another harvest, are of considerable size. (Dallas Bump, with the help of Bill Hopkins, still must "import" the wood for his chairs from lumber mills at Malvern and Poyen, fifty miles to the east.) Dallas guides Kim through this forest, up the steep slope; she can barely keep up with him on the climb.

They come to a bearing tree. Bear City *should* have a bearing tree, to give bearings: directions, location, the intersection of Sections 16 and 17, 20 and 21 in Township 2 South, Range 21 West. The bearings were inscribed and dated 1934. Near the bearing tree, all alone in the middle of the forest, is the only grave in Bear City, that of a woman named Amy Mitchell. The tombstone as such is but an irregular slab of uncut sandstone, scratched with her name and "Died September 20, 1905."

Dallas tries to tell it. This surrounding wood was once the cleared homestead of Orson Hager, who had been Mr. Fulmer's superintendent for that Lost Louisiana Mine. (Orson comes from the Latin for "bear.") Amy Mitchell had been a black slave whose owners, the Bartenschlagers, continued to employ her when they moved to Bear City years after the Civil War, to open a hotel, but abandoned her there when the gold boom died. She worked for one, then another of the remaining families of Bear City, caring for children, who were especially fond of her; everyone called her "Aunt Em." She asked if when she died she might have the right to be buried "in just one corner of my white folks' graveyard," but when she died there was general agreement that she could not be buried among whites, either at the Lowe or the

Cunningham Cemetery. The year before her death, Orson Hager had departed for California, leaving his farm to his daughter, Miss Katherine Hager, who offered this corner of her hillside for Amy Mitchell's grave.

The effort they have taken to reach this humble grave suggests to Kim that Dallas Bump considers it one of the important places of Bear City, although she doubts that he offers to show it to just anyone who buys a stool from him. She looks around at the woods, expecting to see the man she had met at Bump's shop hiding behind a tree. Back down the hill, at the pickup, she points at the county road northward and asks, "Where does this road go?"

"Used to go to the town of Cedar Glades," Dallas says. "Just goes to the lake now. Cedar Glades is underwater now."

Sport fishermen use this road to get to the Brady Mountain "Use Area," a boat launch. At the foot of Brady Mountain, which is a sister to Bear Mountain, is the Brady Mountain Lodge, a tourist accommodation with service station, restaurant, and lodgings at the end of the road, very popular in the summertime, when the traffic through Bear City, oblivious of the existence of a town there, gets heavy.

"Are they open this time of year?" Kim asks. But Dallas Bump doesn't know.

Later on, as the afternoon wanes, Kim will drive up that way to investigate. For now she has time for just an interview or two, and Dallas wants her to meet his mother and sister. When he returns to the chair factory, he takes Kim next door, the house where once Uncle Jep Smith had his general store. Dallas's sister, Ola, was only an infant when they converted the store into a house in 1920 and moved into it.

The house has no room for compote: it is filled with Ola's artwork. With particular pride, Dallas and Ola show Kim a painting of the furniture shop that Ola did five years before, in a style agelessly primitive, direct, and as rustic as any of the chairs the Bumps have turned out. Ola painted the picture for her nephew, Freddie, perhaps as an inducement of nostalgia to get him back to the chair factory, but she kept the painting when Freddie lost interest. Elsewhere in the house are dozens of dolls, in a great variety of styles, which Ola makes to sell in Hot Springs to the tourist trade. She would rather paint than make dolls, but there just isn't as much demand for her paintings. Ola walks slowly with the help of metal arm-brace canes.

The mother, Della, ranks right behind Clarence Jewell in age, the second-oldest person in Bear City; she will be eighty-five in November. Although she is a tiny woman, greatly stooped by osteoporosis and slowed in her gait, and so hard of hearing that Ola must "translate" Kim's questions for her, she is very sharp mentally and has an excellent memory.

"What did Bear City look like when you were a child?" Kim asks her, and Ola repeats it to her mother.

She remembers both Lark Melson and Wiley Rouse, her husband's grandfather, who were old men when she was a girl. There was never any rivalry between them; they were good friends who had had to work together to build the town, and grieve together as the town declined.

"When I was growin up there was a lot of houses all over," says Della. "Been tore up *now*. This here building was Uncle Jep Smith's store. I remember him so well; he knew what the kids liked. I remember a bunch of us came in here and he asked what we wanted, and I'd say we just come to show our cousin the store, and he knew we wanted candy, so he'd give us candy!"

Della remembers when Bear City had meat markets, and saloons, and big hotels, and the whole town was lighted and powered by electricity produced from the town's own dynamos, long before the coming of "rural electrification."

Next to Uncle Jep Smith, who was the most colorful character? Why, Postmaster Peter Huber, of course. "He was such a good ole fellow, and he'd help you any way he could, and he had a beautiful handwrite," Della says. "But he had arthritis so bad."

Peter Huber stands next to Peter Mankins as one of the great personalities of these lost cities, although his early life is obscured even in the imaginations of those who tell his story. His year and place of birth are not known; that the birth definitely occurred in Germany is one of the few solid facts known about him. There was a rumor that he was of noble birth, that his name was originally von Huber, that his aristocratic parents disowned him for his profligacy and drunkenness, that he fled to America when he was driven out of his ancestral castle on the Rhine. More likely is the story that he came to this country to escape being drafted into Bismarck's army during the struggle against the Poles in their critical year of 1886. According to the tellers of the tale, he was drawn to Hot Springs either because of the "cure" of the waters, which was to help his alcoholism, or because of the rumors of gold in Bear City.

There was an area of Bear City, between Walnut Street and Main Street, nicknamed "Dutch Hollow" because there lived several Germans, including "Professor" R. R. Waitz, the "chemist and metallurgist"; his old friend from Colorado, Herman Beyer; and J. D. Stufft, who operated the Bear City Meat Market. These men spoke German, and possibly Peter Huber met one or more of them in Hot Springs and was talked into joining the Bear City boom.

When the boom burst, Stufft stayed on to sell meat, but Dutch Hollow emptied out. Peter Huber had developed a fondness for his hill-folk neighbors almost equal to his acquired fondness for the alcoholic beverage they made from the distillation of mashed and soured corn. If he had come to Hot Springs for the "cure," he had not been cured, and would continue his immoderate consumption of spirits until his last years, when Clarence Jewell's beautiful wife, Elsie, would begin rationing him to a daily dose prescribed by a doctor. But despite being the "town drunk" for the forty years he lived in Bear City, until his death on October 28, 1931, he remained sober enough to handle the postmastership for thirty-three of those years.

Clarence Jewell's father, James Bruce Jewell, had rushed down to Arkansas from Wisconsin during the height of the boom, in 1886, to prospect for gold; finding none, he had married Orson Hager's daughter Effie (also from Wisconsin) and stayed on to operate a sawmill and to serve as postmaster for four of the post-boom years in the nineties, employing Peter Huber as a postal clerk. Since the post office was "busy" only a few hours of each day, Peter Huber was left with much idle time. Jim Jewell would have given him a job in his sawmill, as he gave one to Fred Bump, but he couldn't have an intoxicated man around the dangerous saw. So Peter would sit in his favorite Bump rocker at the post office and tell the children of Bear City the fictions of Jacob and Wilhelm Grimm, remembered from his own childhood. They requested repetitions of such standards as "Cinderella" and "Snow-White and the Seven Dwarfs," but Huber's own favorites, which he would endlessly reinvent, were those in which *gold* had some central part, usually introduced by the prefatory tale "The Golden Key" and including "The Gold Children," "Rumpelstiltskin," "The King of the Golden Mountain," "The Golden Goose," and "The Golden Bird." The way he told these, gold was something undesirable or sinister, a bad thing. The children were too young to remember the Bear City gold rush but too old to be fooled into believing that there was any gold actually in the ground anywhere around them.

"Sometimes, when we was kids," Dallas Bump recalls, "we'd go down there and he'd play his harmonica for us. He had this big, old, real long harmonica, it must've been over a foot long. Everything he played was old German music; we didn't know any of the tunes except from hearin him play them over and over."

Two photographs exist of Peter Huber. In one, a formal portrait in which he wears a white shirt, a lapelled vest, and a cravat nearly concealed by his long dark curly beard, he is still young and handsome, with deepset, brooding, Lincolnesque eyes, a widow's peak in his dark hair above a lofty brow, and an imperfectly humped nose like a Roman portrait bust's. He must have been at that time the best-looking man in Bear City, and a most eligible bachelor.

"Wasn't he supposed to be a priest?" Ola Bump asks her brother and mother. "When he came over here? Seems, the way I heard it, he was trained to be a Catholic priest back home in Germany, but he didn't believe in it, so his people disinherited him. We used to go down there, and he'd tell us about these things. Yes, I think he was supposed to be a priest, and he never did get married on account of that."

The other photograph shows the Bear City Post Office in the early years of this century, stepped-gable false front and roofless porch, with a lone figure in the dark doorway: a terribly humped man on crutches, barely able to stand, peering at the camera beneath a traditional felt hillman's hat. The long dark beard could be any hillman's, but it is Peter's. The man and his office: the picture speaks volumes about both.

"He was the nicest postmaster," Della Bump says. "Always helpin me. Like I never did understand all that money-order and business stuff at the P.O., and if I got it wrong he'd say so, and he'd redo it for me. I never could write good."

When Peter Huber died, of advanced rheumatoid arthritis or alcoholism, or a lot of both, Clarence Jewell, who would immediately replace him as postmaster, built his coffin, helped by master chairmaker Fred Bump. Every community in those days had one or two coffinmakers, men who had learned enough of cabinetry to volunteer their services in the making of the coffin (a "casket" was the word applied only to a "store-boughten" coffin or one purchased from a funeral home). Depending on the person's standing in the community, the coffin might be constructed of cheap, perishable pine or more sturdy oak. Peter Huber's coffin was made of polished walnut.

"How did they make the coffins?" Kim asks Dallas.

"I guess you'll have to talk to Clarence Jewell about that," he suggests.

The Bump chair in which Kim is sitting is also made of walnut, the loveliest of furniture woods, although most Bump chairs are of red oak. But, walnut or oak, the seats are always made of woven splints (sometimes called "splits") shaved by a drawknife from lengths of white oak, softer and brighter than red oak, and the weaving is always done by women (just as, in the sexual division of labor, men made the coffins but women cleaned and prepared the body for burial). Della Bump spent most of her adult life, after marrying Fred Bump when she was fifteen, weaving the seats of chairs. How long does it take to "bottom" one chair? Della got so good at it that she could do one in ten minutes. But of Julia Rouse, Wiley Rouse's daughter, she says, "My mother-in-law could beat that! She was fast at any kind of work. She just grew up with chair bottoming, and she taught me how to do it."

Kim, who remembers all too well marrying at sixteen, asks Della about her early marriage. Fred was twenty and worked in Jim Jewell's sawmill. He would ride his bike after work to visit fourteen-year-old Della, who lived two miles east of town. The visits were always carefully chaperoned by Della's aunt or grandmother, but the day he proposed he asked Della's mother for her consent. "My mother just told him that of course I had never cooked. She said to him, 'Della don't no more know how to cook than you do!' But Fred said that was all right with him." Kim remembers that her own mother, when she learned Kim had eloped, had protested, "You can't cook. I just wish I'd taught you how to cook." Della's mother persuaded her and Fred to wait until she was fifteen and Fred was twenty-one and had saved enough to buy "a few sticks of furniture" from some people (the Hagers?) who were moving to California. "I remember I went down to Peter Huber and ordered me a little cookbook through the mail. It was an Arm and Hammer Soda cookbook and I got it through the mail and read those recipes."

The Bumps show Kim around the little house that was once a general store. They all apologize, saying everything is covered with dust, although Kim isn't aware of much dust. She is shown a large framed photograph, by a professional photojournalist from Michigan, of Della at a younger age, weaving the bottom of a chair in the furniture shop; it's almost a studio portrait, except that Della looks like the last of a vanished breed of hill-folk craftswomen.

Then, as is traditional, the Bumps and Kim say good-bye several times, and make small talk, and then say good-bye several more times before she can leave.

* * *

Kim drives north out of Bear City, the way Dallas Bump had taken her. She does not stop at the "haunted" Queen Anne house, but drives on up into the hills. Several times she has to slow Zephyra to a crawl to ford small dips in the road, where gulleys of water cross the pavement. There is no sign of present or former habitation anywhere along this road until, suddenly, rounding a wooded curve at the crest of a hill, she comes in sight of the Brady Mountain Lodge and of Lake Ouachita, a sweeping expanse of crystal water ringed distantly by mountains.

She is almost surprised to find the office/restaurant open, and to learn that she can get a room for the night; she is apparently the only guest. Her room is like a very modern motel room, though with a view not of a busy highway but of an inlet and a harbor of the lake, the waters beyond, the hills beyond— a picture. For supper she chooses from the menu, not catfish again, although it is the chef's special, but steak. Her table, the only one occupied, has the best view of the lake. The absence of other customers gives the place an unearthly quiet. She feels an anxiety. After supper she strolls down the end of the road to the lake, the boat landing, and stares out across the water at the place where it covers the charming village of Cedar Glades.

She would not, at this moment, be at all surprised if a bile-green Ambassador pulled up to her, or, since it doesn't, she would not be at all surprised later, back in her room, to hear a knock at her door and open it to see the bile-green Ambassador parked beside black Zephyra and to look up at the face of the teller of the gold-rush story once again. She spends more than a few moments thinking about that man. It had been so dark in the furniture factory, and she had not seen him clearly at all. Could he, she wonders, have been Professor Harrigan himself, come from South Dakota to join her? Why, then, did he not join her? Perhaps, she realizes with a gnawing dread, he had wanted to "examine" her first, to look at her, to talk with her, to "test" her, without committing himself, and he had not liked what he saw and heard. What an awful thought. But where was he? Where had he gone?

She is almost afraid to open her door and go out searching

for the ice machine, to make herself a drink of Royal Crown, but eventually thirst forces her to it. She looks out; there are no cars anywhere, not parked in front of any of the other motel units, or in the parking lot of the office/restaurant, or across the road at the Texaco/grocery, which has closed for the night. She goes out and wanders around looking for the ice machine but cannot find one; there is none; she tries the office/restaurant, but it has closed for the night. She is alone in the ghost town of Brady Mountain. Back in her room, she tries a taste of tepid Royal Crown, but gives it up and goes to bed thirsty; she has trouble sleeping.

The ghost town of Brady Mountain repopulates itself in the morning, and after a leisurely breakfast of bacon and eggs and iced diet cola, she checks out of the lodge and drives back to Bear City. This time she stops at the big white Queen Anne house, where a young woman is working in her yard. The young woman's name is Diane Coleman, and she knows nothing about the history of the house, which she and her husband have been renting because they wanted to take the kids out to the country. The house is falling apart; she wishes the owners would fix it up. It's a shame for such a lovely old house to be so neglected, but the rent is cheap, and there is a lot of land for a big garden.

"Is it really haunted?" Kim asks.

"I've heard that rumor," Diane Coleman says, although she has met very few of the other residents of Bear City. She keeps to herself, thinks of herself as a loner, and knows nothing about the history of Bear City. "If the house is haunted," she says, "it's not *badness*."

Nor is there any sight of the green Ambassador in the village anywhere, though Kim drives up and down the still-passable streets, Walnut and Third and Water. She tells herself she is not hunting for that car, simply taking a last good look at what's left of the town before going on to her last interview, which is with Clarence Jewell. Just as she was warned, he is not easy to find. She has written down the instructions Dallas Bump gave her: if you look carefully across the road from Dallas Bump's house, triangulated across Water Street from the old post office, you will see, dipping down toward Rouse Creek, the shadow of a trail, all that remains of Plateau Street, which takes its name from the fact that once it crosses the creek it rises and then levels out for the short length of its distance to a dead end at the Jewell place. It used to lead to the Lost Louisiana Mine, the "Spanish Lode," but that way has been blocked for fifty years by Clarence Jewell's tree farm.

Fifty years ago, Clarence Jewell, atoning for his father's stripping of the forests, reseeded the cleared land west of town with thousands of pine and oak seedlings, and these trees, grown tall now, make a new forest, or the tree farm of forester Jewell, once Postmaster Jewell, once chairmaker Jewell . . . and still philosopher Jewell, iconoclast Jewell, crank Jewell.

Kim finds the trail and eases Zephyra down to Rouse Creek, where she is stopped by a rude bridge. Rude in both senses of crude and discourteous: it seems to be two widely spaced planks laid parallel across the stream, and Kim is not at all certain that the gap between the planks corresponds to the gap between Zephyra's tires. Though she is tempted to abandon Zephyra here and walk the rest of the way, she has no idea how far the rest of the way might be. So she nudges Zephyra's front wheels out onto the planks, then gets out to check that both tires are solidly on the boards, then inches the car very slowly across, expecting the bridge to give way at any moment. Safely beyond, she finds that the trail is the roughest stretch of road that Zephyra will ever have to negotiate. But before long it comes to a dead end at the house, the old Beam place, built by "Professor" Aaron Beam, he of the simulated "Beam's Electric Process" for extracting gold from ore, and one of only two houses (the other gone) built in what was called "Beam's Addition," a platting of new streets with names like Montrose, Magnolia, Vine, and Louisiana, all obliterated by Jewell's tree farm. Kim thinks it ought to be called "Beam's Subtraction."

When Zephyra pulls into the yard, Clarence Jewell is puttering in his back yard, and he comes around front to challenge

Kim's intrusion. He is a very small man, much shorter than she, dressed in old khakis and bareheaded, with little hair. Though he was born with the century, he does not look as wrinkled as other eighty-five-year-olds she has met; he is, however, quite a bit testier and more suspicious. She apologizes for disturbing him, because he is clearly disturbed. She is sorry if she has bothered him, because he is certainly bothered. "Everyone," she declares, trying to flatter him, "tells me that you know more about Bear City than any man alive!"

He shakes his head. "Not me," he says. "You ought to talk to Dallas Bump."

She laughs at the irony. "I've already talked to Dallas Bump. He thinks I should talk to you."

"What about?"

"Coffins, if nothing else," she says.

"Coffins?" he says. "You need a coffin?"

"No, but I understand you used to make them. I understand you used to make a lot of chairs. Once upon a time, you had a whole factory competing with the Bumps."

"I never competed with the Bumps," he declares. "They sold their chairs in Arkansas, and I marketed all of mine out of this state."

"Do you mind if I use this tape recorder?"

"Suit yourself." He seems to be challenging her to ask another question, but at least he is convinced she is not selling anything or peddling any religion to replace his own strange one.

"A woman reporter once referred to you as 'the Henry Ford of the Ouachitas,' " Kim says. "What did you think of that?"

"I didn't argue with her," Clarence says, and permits himself a wry grin.

"Did people call you 'C.B.'?"

"Some names worse than that come to mind," he says, and permits himself an actual chuckle. Then he invites, "Would you like to come in?"

Inside the old house's living room, adorned not with any compote but with many semiprimitive landscapes, Kim meets the artist, whom the afore-mentioned woman reporter described, in the 1950s, as "one of the most beautiful women to be seen in the state of Arkansas," and who is still, at eighty, strikingly handsome. Elsie May Heath Jewell has been married to Clarence for sixty-two years; they have six children, twenty-one grandchildren, and twenty great-grandchildren. Her landscapes, few of them done from the Bear City area, are lovingly framed in natural wood by Clarence, who has no coffins to build any more, except his own. The paintings are overwhelmed by a large quilt hanging on the wall, which Elsie explains was done by her grandmother, although the pattern is strangely modern: a *trompe l'oeil* juxtaposition of cubes that reverse their direction by optical illusion as one stares at them. The quilt is called *Tumbling Blocks*, and they do just that.

The room is furnished with Jewell-made walnut chairs, ladder-backs, and Kim is loaned one for a seat. Her host and hostess sit nearby. "People around here don't like me," Clarence Jewell declares, without elaboration, or with only some mumbled exegesis. Later, after she has left Bear City, Kim will discover to her dismay, playing back the tape, that his voice is often weak, inaudible on the recording. She thought she had positioned the machine between them with practiced care; but of all the many old-timers she has interviewed, he is the least intelligible on tape. And Elsie Jewell rarely interrupts her husband.

Besides being chairmakers, Clarence Jewell and Dallas Bump have something else in common: both went away for a while. After living at the post office for ten years, in rooms of Clarence's construction added to the shack, near the log factory of his chairmaking operation, which continued throughout the Depression and through World War II, the Jewells, like thousands of Arkansawyers after the war, went to California, and stayed there for a while; the tree farm Jewell had planted in the thirties went on growing without him. "But I despised California," Clarence says, and they, like the Bumps, kept coming back for visits at every opportunity: "I'm just an old mountain man at heart." Finally, in the late fifties, they moved back into the post office, where Clarence had stored all his books and papers, and they lived there until the Beam place became vacant.

Clarence does not show Kim his library, but he has a large one. The living room contains only one book: Nancy Mc-Donough's *Garden Sass: A Catalog of Arkansas Folkways* (1975, Coward, McCann), a wonderful compendium of the state's folklore in the tradition of the *Foxfire* books. The author's father-in-law, Russell McDonough, grew up in Bear City and told her about the famous Fourth of July celebrations held there, but Clarence Jewell does not recall Russell McDonough.

Though he has been working for many years on a history of Bear City, he tells Kim it is only about the boom years.

"What I write about, people don't want to read," he says. He presents Kim with a copy of his only published work, *The Inception and Ascension of Man* (1977, Vantage Press—vantage as in "vanity," the most profitable of the subsidy publishers), a thin book of modest size but immodest scope: it attempts to present a theory of evolution at great variance with both Darwin and the Bible. Until only fifteen thousand years ago, man, who evolved directly from ocean mollusks and is not related to the monkeys, lived in the sea, the "coffee-colored" waters, where he caught his prey and found his bearings by "echo-sounding" like the bats and dolphins. Dogs took a liking for the sea creature man and domesticated him by accepting him into the social group of dogs and by devouring his feces as a sanitation system, enabling him to leave the sea and live on land. Women were intended to do all of the work of food gathering, diving for seafood, gardening, and preparing and serving food, leaving man free to think, which is what he was intended for. Survival of the fittest? Jewell writes: "In nature the weak and the stupid are destroyed by predators; only the strongest and the most intelligent individuals survive long enough to produce offspring. With the human species, under modern civilization, the weak, the stupid, and the vicious are cared for and survive to reproduce many more of their kind." The bibliography is limited mostly to a few back issues of *National Geographic*, although it also lists Darwin, Freud, and Gibbon. The book is not the work of a naturalist who has closely observed the life around him in Bear City.

But as an iconoclast, Clarence Jewell is of a gentler breed

than Joe Weston of Cave City. He tells Kim again that most people don't approve of him or his ideas, and this has forced him to become increasingly a loner, thinker, philosopher. The Jewells relish the off-the-road isolation and quiet of the old Beam place, in contrast to their former exposure at the post office in the center of town. After Peter Huber died in 1931, Clarence Jewell was postmaster for only two years, his thirty-first and thirty-second, until the notice came from the Post Office Department that the Bear City Post Office was discontinued, and that henceforward patrons would receive their mail at the neighboring village of Royal. The closing of the post office saddened the other citizens of Bear City more than it did Clarence. He felt that Bear City was already dead and that this would allow him more time to devote to his furniture factory, which he had started the same year Peter Huber died, just as the Depression was beginning to drive more people out of Bear City. The Jewell factory was not simply a family business, like the Bump factory, but employed twelve people, who produced up to two thousand chairs a month, wholesaling for 50¢ each to markets chiefly in Texas and Oklahoma. His best workers could earn as much as $3.50 a day, fantastic wages for the Depression years in the Ouachita Mountains.

When World War II took all the able-bodied men of Bear City, Clarence Jewell closed the factory and went to work as a carpenter and craftsman for the Army and Navy Hospital in Hot Springs. He commuted from Bear City, where, in his spare time, he made coffins for the bodies of local men shipped home from the battlefields. Then came the move to California. After ultimately yielding to the homesickness that brings most far-flung Arkansawyers back eventually, he found that there was little need for his coffinmaking skills. There were few left to bury.

"I don't know how many coffins I've made in my life," Clarence tells Kim. "Not more than seventy-five or so. I never kept count."

Whenever someone died in Bear City, a member of the family would hitch his wagon and ride into Hot Springs to buy the metal handles for the coffin, and cloth, usually satin, to cover the inside and drape over the outside of the coffin. It would usually be late afternoon or night before the materials were delivered to coffinmakers Fred Bump and Clarence Jewell, who would work together throughout the night to build and finish the coffin for the burial the following day. They never even thought of asking any payment for this work. Then the coffinmakers would go to the Lowe or the Cunningham Cemetery and help dig the grave. By Ozark custom or superstition, the grave was always dug on the day of the burial; leaving an open grave overnight was considered very bad luck, and might even bring on an early death to one of the dead person's relatives.

Superstition surrounds every movement and thought of the hill folk, but never more so than in connection with death and burial. The death itself was probably the result of some carelessness on the part of someone else: a woman who washed clothes on January 1, a man who carried a hoe into his house, a woman who forgot to fasten the door one night, a woman who sneezed with food in her mouth, a woman who swept the floor after dark, anyone who transplanted a cedar tree or burned sassafras wood or peach trees in the fireplace. The death is always foretold by a sign: a falling (as opposed to a shooting) star, a dog who howls four times (or three) and then stops, a cat who licks the door, a baby's cradle rocking by itself, a rooster crowing in the doorway, or a hen crowing anywhere at any time. Hens do not crow.

While the men made the coffins, the women worked on the body: it was stripped and thoroughly cleaned. If the person had died at home, the room in which the death had occurred was thoroughly cleaned and the bed ticks burned. Usually no effort was made to embalm the corpse, just to keep it fresh until it could be buried. Coins were used to close the eyelids; the hair was washed and then brushed into the style in which the person had worn it; the best clothes, or at least the cleanest clothes, were put on; the body was cooled and placed into the coffin.

All the women in the community who had not participated in preparing the body for burial were busy at home, cooking their best recipes for the funeral dinner, the most lavish banquet that anyone would ever attend, served usually right after the funeral service.

The coffinmakers, who helped dig the grave, had to stay to watch the last shovelful of earth thrown over their handiwork: to depart before the last clod of dirt was in the grave was likely to bring death and destruction upon the family circle, but especially upon the man who had dug the grave but did not wait to see it filled.

Kim wonders: is Clarence Jewell waiting to see the grave of Bear City covered over? She remembers Stella Beavers's last words for Buffalo City: *all it lacks is throwin the dirt over it.*

"People in this neighborhood don't really like me," Clarence tells her.

"This is the third time you've told me that," she says, trying to sound polite but chiding. "Don't you and Dallas Bump get along?"

"Oh, Dallas," Clarence Jewell says. "Sure. I practically raised him." But the others, particularly the old-timers, being superstitious (which he is not), probably resented his education and his intelligence. "They just don't approve of me," he says.

Y City,
Arkansas

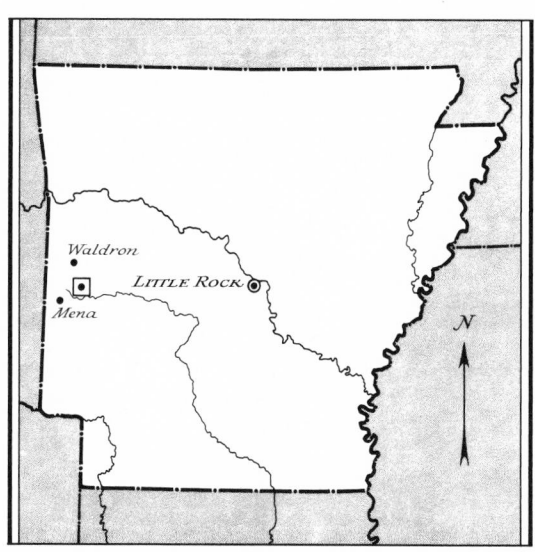

Y CITY
MOUNTAIN INN

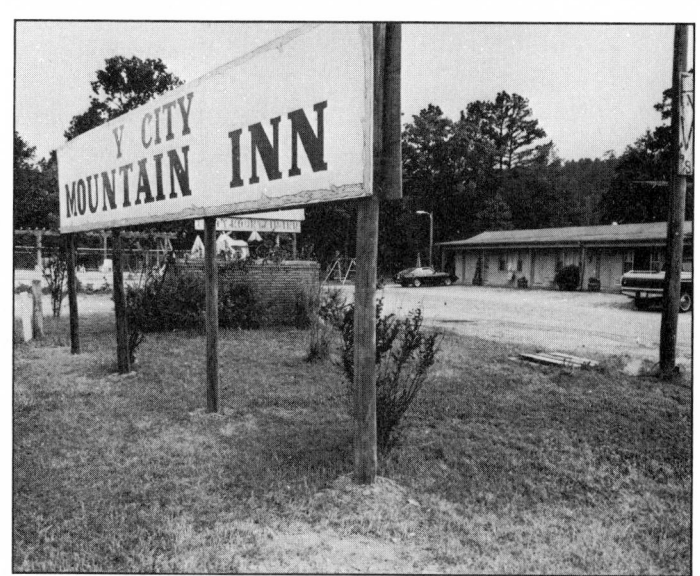

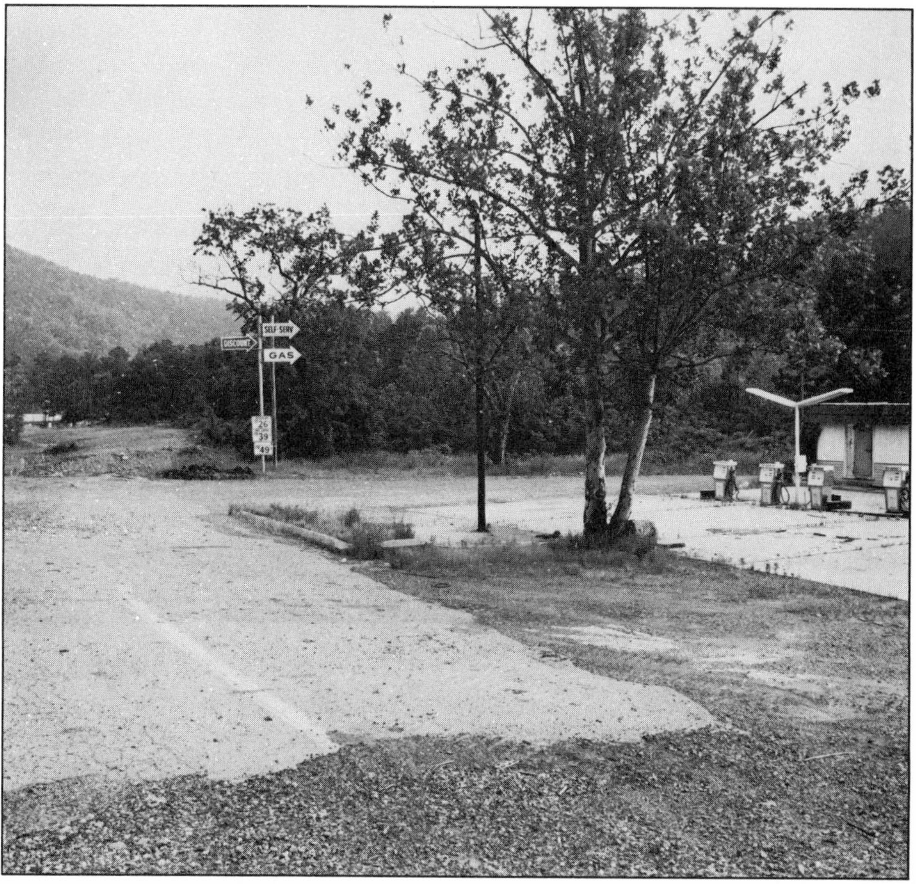
SELF SERV
GAS
26
39
49

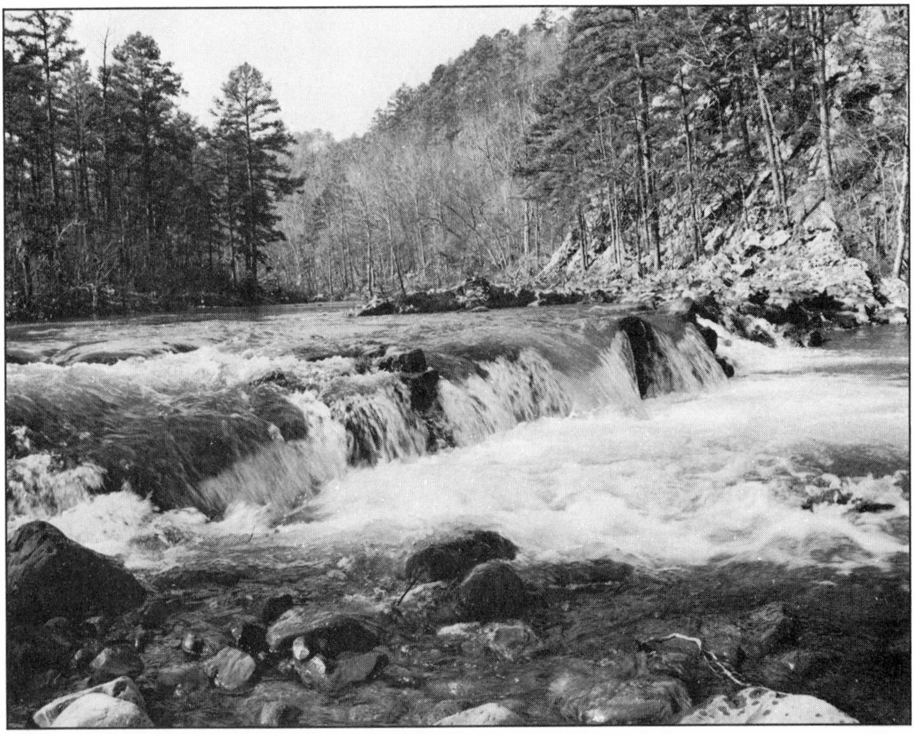

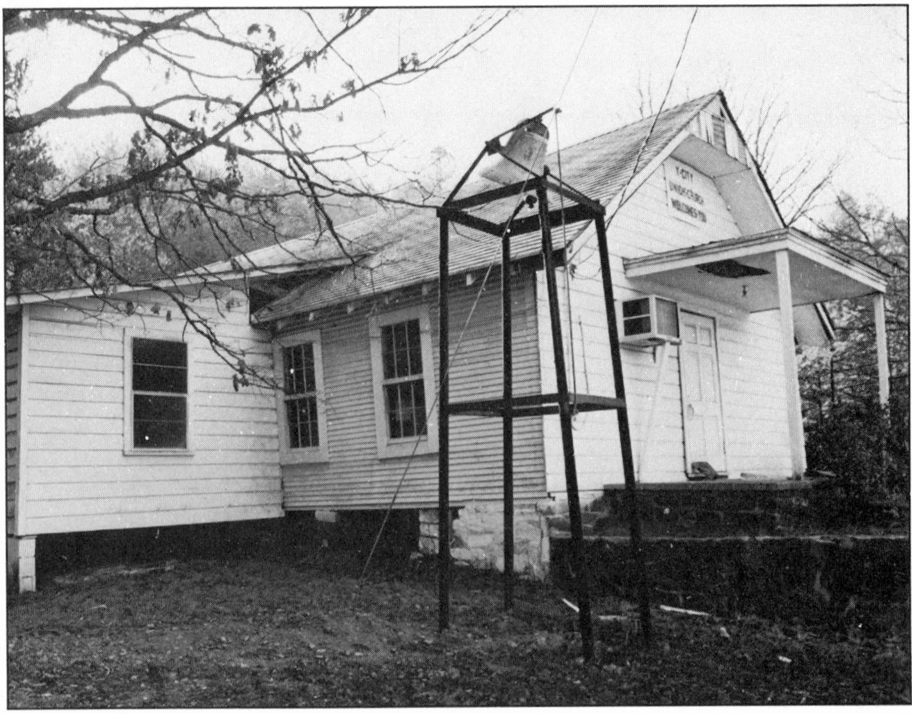

Two roads diverged in a wood, and I—
—Frost, "The Road Not Taken," 1915

SHE HAD NOT INTENDED for it to be her final town. The diverging roads lead to Pike City, Hurrah City, Process City, Golden City, Webb City, Central City, Hackett City, and Carbon City, all as lost as any of those already seen, and Kim is fully prepared to explore them all, unless Zephyra has a major breakdown. But at Y City the divergent roads seem to suggest to her a choice, not between the next possible destinations of her project so much as between continuing her journey indefinitely or bringing it to an end. Every road has a Y, and it is not even necessary to take the one less traveled by. Sometimes it is better to take neither, but to stop.

Of all these places, Y City is the only one that is not any smaller than it ever was, not a ghost of its former self, that never even aspired to become a town, let alone a city. In its history (which is long but blank), people, mostly outsiders, have suggested that, for the sake of appearance and seemliness, it ought to be spelled "Wye City," as in the lovely River Wye in Wales and England, famous for its scenic beauty, particularly where "the valley narrows into a gorge, often wooded and often overhung with great crags of mountain limestone," which precisely describes the gorge around the Y here. Why don't they spell it "Wye"? They cannot say, but somehow "Wye" is affected, cultivated, possessed of a completed sophistication out of keeping with the homeliness, earthiness, and still-in-the-process-of-completion rusticity that mark the place. It is the only Y City, or even Wye City, in all the United States. Sometimes, on some road maps, the Y is put in quotes, giving it an ironic or even a sarcastic voice, thus: "Y" City. But this may be only a self-consciousness over the fact that most cities do not identify themselves by a single letter, let alone the twenty-fifth letter of the alphabet, invented by the Romans to replace the Ionic upsilon and reinvented by highway departments everywhere to mean a splitting, forking, branching road.

Kim is all too aware of the symbolism of the divergence, and its confusing plethora of suggestions: change, deviation, abnormality, distance, eccentricity, as well as simple separation or fanning out. Wishbone and crotch, there are two semiots of the Y: hope and sex. Furcula and groin, pulley bone and privates, desire and connection. As she and Zephyra wend through the winding valleys approaching Y City this beautiful morning, she is nervous with anticipation. The longing she hears in the Theme of the Faraway Hills (which are no longer faraway but all around) is for something she is not even sure of.

A cursory glance at any road map gives one an idea of what to expect at Y City. How often does she, seeing a town on a map, visualize it, *pre*create it, often correctly. She *expects* Y City to be nothing more than a junction of two highways, perhaps with a truck stop on one side of the highway, another service station across the highway with a small restaurant attached, a couple of motels, and a scattering of houses wherein live the attendants of the gas, food, lodging. Thus, she has to stop and double-check her map when she arrives at that junction of the two highways and discovers that there is *nothing* there, nothing, that is, except a lone abandoned service station.

Deserted gasoline stations, to the ranks of which several new ones (old ones) are added every day, are fast becoming the symbol of change in America. If the derelict, cast-off town with its dead main street and its used furniture stores is ubiquitously trying to tell us something about our heedless upward mobility, the dead gas station is trying to say something about the process of the mobility itself: it matters not how we get there, the going is no longer important, arrival is everything. Time was, we pulled into a service station for "*full* service": they'd check your oil, clean your windshield, pump your gas, while you used the john or walked the dog or did whatever you liked. Now we often pump ourselves, a kind of hurried autoeroticism with the quick finish in mind, while the "attendant" attends only the cash register. We prefer to self-serve; it's a lot cheaper and quicker, like masturbation. But the self-serving multitudes are killing off the traditional service station, which is being fast replaced by the "convenience store," easy mart, quick stop, 7-Eleven, which offers cheap gas as only one of many unrelated products.

We do not even know what brand of gas was served at the Y City station: Conoco, DX, Phillips, KM? The remaining signs hopefully promise "Self-Serve" and "Discount," and the old prices are still up: 26¢ for regular, 39¢ for premium (actually the tacit dollar preceded both figures). The doors of the station are boarded over, grass and weeds grow up through the cracks in the cement, there is no sign of a vehicle anywhere (although Kim was expecting a green Ambassador), and the road itself is defunct, derelict, and discarded: a fragment of yellow center-stripe points toward a near mountain, but the hard-surface is missing beyond the "Gas" sign. We do not even know who abandoned this gas station first, the customers or the highway.

The highway is in the process of change, as all highways are. Once the junction joined the gentle curves of U.S. 270 to the wild meanders of U.S. 71, the larger but more scenic of the two roads, and here at the Y the curves were especially sharp and treacherous as they negotiated babbling Mill Creek and its gorge carved between two twelve-hundred-foot hills. The Arkansas Highway Department is devoting heavy equipment and many men to straightening out these curves, converting, as it were, the Y to a T. There is nothing romantic about a T. But the new roadwork has left the gas station off to itself, forsaken except by a clump of double sycamores, which one day will overtower the last vestiges of the last pump. Kim notices, with a start, that the sycamores are in leaf. Spring is here.

Springtime is branchtime, trillions of Y's, and she gains the branch of the road and crosses the bridge over the branch, Mill Creek, itself a branch of the Fourche la Fave (simplified by the natives into Clear Fork Creek; "Fourche" means "fork" or "Y" in French, and there are several streams, hills, and valleys in Arkansas with that name), which itself becomes a river branch flowing into the Arkansas, which branches into the Mississippi. All of these Y branches take place at different levels of the same Ouachita Mountains that contain Bear City, sixty miles southeast by east. Right around the much-straightened curve over Mill Creek, we come to a still-attended business, a modest motel, the Mountain Inn.

If Y City is the only one of these lost towns that has never dwindled from its former glory, for it had none, it is also the only one of these lost towns in which our heroine finds actual open-to-the-public accommodations for the night. Nowhere else has she found an inn in the town itself, at least not one with a vacancy, Prince Matlock's folly, The Cave Court, being all booked up. The Mountain Inn, this early in the season, has several vacancies, and Kim could take her pick, though she isn't permitted to: she is assigned to room number one, the southernmost of the units in the motel. Rooms number two and three are vacant, and remain so throughout her stay. If we look closely, as we do, we can see her entering her door. Zephyra looks happy out here in the woods, the pines, the springtime morning sunshine. Soon she will not look happy, for an uncouth green Ambassador, whom she has met briefly before, will park alongside her.

But first, before the Ambassador, who was named Bunker after an actual ambassador, gets too familiar with Zephyra, Kim will unload her things, then return to the office for a chat with the proprietress, Pat Heinen, supposedly fifty-five but looking only half that. Kim will discover that everything in Y City is actually twice as old as it appears to be; this motel has been here for almost forty years but looks much newer, possibly because of all the improvements Mr. and Mrs. Heinen have put into it. Even these piney mountains, which actually resulted from uplifts five hundred million years ago, don't appear to be any older than 250 million years. Kim is going to discover, the next time she looks in a mirror, that she appears the age she was before she married.

The windows in the motel are what is known architecturally as Chicago windows, which is appropriate, because both of the Heinens, Pat and her husband, John (who is also ostensibly fifty-five), are from Chicago; they did not, however, design this motel, and have owned it for only nine years. John Heinen emigrated from the Netherlands in 1958 and met Pat in downtown Chicago, where both worked and both hated the big-city life. They have been married almost as long as they appear to be in age. To escape from Chicago, they hit upon the idea of running a way-farers' motel in some remote spot, and began looking for one. They had heard the usual jokes and slanders about Arkansas as a hick state, but discovered on a camping trip here that it was a very beautiful and a very misunderstood state. They fell in love with Arkansas at first sight, and Arkansas returned the affection. A newspaper ad told them there was a motel for sale in the remote Ouachitas.

"Why 'City'?" Kim asks Pat, who instantly catches the word-play of the question.

"The only thing I can figure out," Pat says, "is that years ago some individual or group of individuals had a *vision* of a city growing here. Or else it was just meant as a tremendous joke, because this place is *so* remote, *so* far from being a city, and *so* lost. . . ." Pat tells Kim that whenever she returns to Chicago, or travels to any real city outside of Arkansas, and mentions the name of the place, people are immediately struck with the ring of the name, and exaggerate it, stretch it out: "Y-Y-Y City!"

Pat gives Kim the names of a few of the old-timers, natives who've lived here all their lives, and directions on how to find their houses (all of them right beside the highways—apparently nobody lives back up in the hills). But Kim is warned that she will discover Y City has no history. No one famous was born here. No battles or even skirmishes were fought here, or near here. There was never a plat map drawn for Y City, or names given to imaginative streets and avenues; the only streets were those three diverging highways and a few logging trails. Worse, there was not one single larger-than-life man or woman in the history of the place, no great personality or character or local celebrity.

All that was ever here is what is here now; it is a timeless place for wayfarers, where nothing changes or grows old. Pat tells Kim about the crossing. At one time, before it came to be known wistfully or jokingly as Y City, there was a joining of two dirt wagon-roads and a crossing of Mill Creek—a ford when the water permitted, and, when it didn't, a ferryman of sorts. This old gentleman, named Toish Miller, who lies now in Chant Cemetery, used to dwell beside the stream and had a team of mules to assist people in crossing the creek. This was before the first of the three bridges was erected (the third is being finished now).

Before the motel was built, earlier travelers could stop at Midway Park, just north of the Mountain Inn, a roadside oasis that went through several metamorphoses, from wagon camp to tent camp to tourist cabins to auto court to simply the Midway Restaurant, which it is today, a family diner. The name comes from its being exactly midway between Fayetteville, in the northwestern part of the state, and Texarkana, in the southwestern part of the state. It once advertised itself as "halfway from everywhere." Kim wonders, "Am I halfway from where I'm going?" Pat explains, "Midway Park was a rest area, a stopping place. There was always some sort of assistance here. You weren't stranded. A stopping place for travelers."

A stopping place for travelers. U.S. 71 was carved through the mountains of both the Ozarks and the Ouachitas with more thought for the scenery-seeking tourist than for the farmer, trucker, or local traveler. Farther north, as it approaches Fayetteville along the ridges of the gorgeous Boston Mountains, it is lined with abandoned rustic motels that constitute a lost city in themselves. The farther south the highway plunges into the Ouachitas, the farther apart the motels sit. The Mountain Inn is *sui generis*, the only motel for miles in any direction. Highway "service" along this stretch was limited, in the earlier days of motor travel, to the occasional farm carved into the forests that had a gasoline station built of logs and log tourist cabins, like a modern vegetable stand, right beside the road; such a spot was illuminated at night with gasoline flares, a once-common sight unknown today.

Did Pat and John Heinen have any problems adjusting to life in a mountain community? When they first came to Y City, there was a little general store at the Y, which had impressed Pat as the sort of old-timey country store she had heard about and seen pictures of; the store has now been obliterated by the highway improvements. (Right over the mountain is Pine Ridge, Arkansas, home of the "Jot 'em Down Store" made famous by radio comedians Lum and Abner.) It was the sort of store, Pat knew, to which customers went not just to make purchases but to "set and visit." Pat's first visit to the store was not long after she and John had purchased the motel.

"I went in there. The residents find out about you by some unknown means of communication—I still don't know how this happens, but it does. So everyone in the store knew who I was, but I didn't know who anyone else was. They let me go ahead and make my purchases, and no one said anything, but then one or two of them spoke to me, calling out, 'How are you doin today?' or 'Are you keepin up things at the motel?' [Imitating their voices, Pat pronounces this "*mo*-tel," with a strong accent on the first syllable.] There were four or five men and women there on the bench, just lounging around, a real general-store atmosphere, and they were intensely curious, so I just opened up and acted friendly. Then the flood started: they wanted to know everything about me."

In Chicago, Pat Heinen had been a registered nurse, and when it became known in this community that she had said she was an RN, she was called upon to do a few medical favors for the old-timers. One man with high blood pressure was given regular readings by Pat so that he could report to his doctor. Another old man she attended began referring to her as the River Nurse, and the nickname caught on.

"Why 'River Nurse'?" Kim asks.

"Probably he thought that was what 'RN' means!" Pat says. "But also because I live on the river . . ."

The river. Just out back of the Mountain Inn, Mill Creek snuggles up against the side of the craggy bluffs, and then spills over a spectacular waterfall. Did Toish Miller, or one of the Millers before him, actually operate a mill? There must have been a gristmill to give the creek its name. Later in the morning, Kim walks down the path from the back of the motel to look at the creek and especially the falls, not nearly so high as the falls she saw at Marble City (which also came from a stream named Mill Creek), but broader, as the stream is wider, and surrounded by pine trees rather than deciduous hardwoods. It is the prettiest spot, the freshest spot, she can recall ever having seen. It is a very inviting spot, *too* inviting: Kim learned from Pat Heinen that two sons of the family who previously owned the motel had drowned here, and during the time the Heinens have lived here another drowning has occurred. Downstream from the turbulent falls the creek deepens into a tranquil swimming hole that for many years was associated with Midway Park and known all over the county, and among tourists, for its aquatic felicities.

The morning is hot, but Kim did not even think of bringing her swimsuit with her. She bends and tests the water with her fingers: it is icy cold. She splashes a little of it on her face. Straightening up, she has an intuition that she is being watched. She scans the woods all around for a glimpse of eyes, but sees none . . . except a quick glimpse of what might be a brown-plaid flannel shirt behind a tree. Though she moves toward it, she loses her way among the brush and sees no further movement. So she returns her attention to the falls and the serenity of the location, a silence broken only by the gurgling of the water, enough sound to smother any noise of traffic from the highway.

Later, when she opens the door to her room, she feels that someone is inside. A sound comes from the bathroom. Kim is torn between running to the office or confronting the intruder;

her adrenalin jumps and her heart pounds. She approaches the open bathroom door. "Hello?" she says. And then repeats it.

No brown plaid appears. It is blue and white, and it is worn by a female. "Hi," the woman says, and Kim realizes that she is the chambermaid.

Chambermaid Flossie Boren is a year older than Pat and John Heinen, which would make her chronologically fifty-six, but she is slim, pretty, and full of energy, and Kim records only that she must be twice twenty-eight, her apparent age. Pat Heinen hired her seven years ago to work here, and pays her well in a community where "there's no way to make a living," but Flossie intends to quit after this season and devote more time to her own house and garden.

She will regret it, she tells Kim, because she honestly enjoys being a chambermaid. She likes to "make things look nice," and the guests of this motel are usually nice people who are pretty clean—the only ones who leave an utter mess behind are the wealthy people with expensive clothes who, Flossie guesses, "must've been used to havin people wait on 'em and pick up after 'em." The less affluent people often clean up after themselves.

Once people stay at the Mountain Inn, Flossie says, they *always* come back again. "Sometimes people leave me notes and say how they appreciated it being so clean, and how much they enjoyed their stay, and that they'll be back, oh, they'll sure to be back again sometime. That makes me feel good. Or they'll say that this motel topped anywhere else they'd ever stayed on their trip across the whole country. And that makes me feel *real* good."

Has Flossie seen a man in a brown-plaid flannel shirt? No, but if it's important, she'll keep a eye out for one.

After Flossie has replaced the Cashmere Bouquet in the bathroom, or whatever she was doing, and leaves, Kim stretches out on her queen-size bed for a while and talks alone to her tape recorder.

"You know," she tells the tape, "I think I am tired. I am now in my eleventh lost city. Eleven is a magic number for me. My first two names both begin with the eleventh letter of the alphabet. Eleven is a pair of bigeminal ones. Is *this*, just in time, my eleventh hour?"

We could explain to her that the word "eleven" comes from the Anglo-Saxon *endleofan*, meaning literally "one left"; this means one left over after counting to ten, but clearly it is also now one remaining, one last town, one left to go. But we do not explain this. We could allude to the "one left" as meaning she is in Room 1, to our left as we face the motel. But we do not. Instead, we knock on the door.

Kim hears a knock at her door. She sits up on the edge of the bed and calls out, "Who is it?," but then realizes that if it is who she thinks it is, he would not hear her asking. She wonders if Flossie locked the door on her way out. The night chain is not, of course, engaged. "Kim, girl, keep calm," she whispers to herself. The knock comes again. She would like to run to the bathroom for a quick look in the mirror and maybe a touchup or to comb her hair at least, but there isn't time. When she has moved to the door she engages the night chain, just in case it isn't who she thinks it might be. It could be one of those highway workmen who ogled her as she drove in and watched to see which room she was in. The knocking comes a third time, more insistent.

She turns the knob, releases the lock, and lets the door open as wide as the crack and chain affords.

Brown-plaid flannel shirt. Doesn't he ever wear anything else? Very tall; pewter-haired but, like everyone else around here, looking only half his age, which must be late-fortyish. Though he is in the full daylight now, he was in the half-darkness when she saw him in the Bump chair factory. In light his eyes are even kinder, and he is, of course, smiling.

She asks him, "How do you say 'Excuse me' in Latin?"

He hears her. His smile broadens. *"Excusatio non petita fit accusatio manifesta."* This means, however, not "Excuse me" but, rather, "An excuse given when unasked betrays clear guilt." And he adds, *"Kim,"* which means, "You lovely thing, you."

"You're excused," she says, "almost. Why did you meet me at Bear City without telling me who you are?"

"Pardon?" he says. She has to repeat her question until he gets it. "Well," he says. "It was too soon."

"Too soon for what?"

"May I come in?" he asks.

She removes the night chain from its catch and opens the door, floating between an impulse to hug him and a determination to keep her proper distance. As he comes into the room, she looks around for places for them to sit. She does not intend to sit on her bed. Suddenly she notices a sofa in the room. She had not seen the sofa before. The typical motel room does not have a sofa. How did it get here? "Well," she says, and gestures for him to sit at one end of it. It is not a *long* sofa, but there is more space between them as she sits than there was on the bench in the Bump shop.

He lights a cigarette and asks her after it is lighted, "Mind if I smoke?"

She puts an ashtray between them on the sofa. "You know," she remarks, "you don't look nearly as old as I expected you to."

He laughs. "Nor do you, child. Everything in Y City is only half its age."

"So you've noticed it, too? How was your trip from South Dakota?"

"Uneventful," he remarks, offhand, as if making small talk. "Boring country all the way until I reached Kansas City and got on 71, which is *this* highway." He gestures toward the road outside. "All that's worth reporting is that in Iowa I picked up a guy hitchhiking to Kansas City. Soon I had a flat tire and a couple of breakdowns, but he stayed with me and helped, because the tire tools were missing, and my old car . . ." Giving up the effort of trying to explain how decrepit Bunker is, he takes a folded-up sheet of paper out of his pocket, unfolds it. "Anyway, when we reached Kansas City he thanked me, and then he gave me *this*. He said it would be my 'emergency poem.' That's what he called it, as if it would be a necessary tool for my car, 'emergency poem.' It's called 'Degrees of Gray in Philipsburg,' and it goes:

You might come here Sunday on a whim.
Say your life broke down. The last good kiss
you had was years ago. You walk these streets
laid out by the insane, past hotels
that didn't last, bars that did, the tortured try
of local drivers to accelerate their lives.
Only churches are kept up. The jail
turned seventy this year. The only prisoner
is always in, not knowing what he's done.

The principal supporting business now
is rage. Hatred of the various grays
the mountain sends, hatred of the mill,
the Silver Bill repeal, the best liked girls
who leave each year for Butte. One good
restaurant and bars can't wipe the boredom out.
The 1907 boom, eight going silver mines,
a dance floor built on springs—
all memory resolves itself in gaze,
in panoramic green you know the cattle eat
or two stacks high above the town,
two dead kilns, the huge mill in collapse
for fifty years that won't fall finally down.

Isn't this your life? That ancient kiss
still burning out your eyes? Isn't this defeat
so accurate, the church bell simply seems
a pure announcement: ring and no one comes?
Don't empty houses ring? Are magnesium
and scorn sufficient to support a town,
not just Philipsburg, but towns
of towering blondes, good jazz and booze
the world will never let you have
until the town you came from dies inside?

Say no to yourself. The old man, twenty
when the jail was built, still laughs

although his lips collapse. Someday soon,
he says, I'll go to sleep and not wake up.
You tell him no. You're talking to yourself.
The car that brought you here still runs.
The money you buy lunch with,
no matter where it's mined, is silver
and the girl who serves your food
is slender and her red hair lights the wall.

The poet's name was Richard Hugo, and he died too suddenly
three years ago, in Montana, where he spent most of his life,
though he traveled to every little lost town he could find and
wrote poems about most of them. Philipsburg is in Montana, but
it might as well be in Arkansas, just as these lost cities of Arkansas
might just as well be anywhere in the world."

Moved by his reading of the poem, she asks, "Was the last
good kiss you had years ago?" When he does not answer, perhaps
because he hasn't heard her or doesn't know the answer, she does
not repeat her question but kisses him. Kim gives him her best
kiss. It is indeed a good kiss.

After the kiss, he can only comment, "You know, the romantic year of 1886 was the year that Rodin carved his marble
sculpture *The Kiss*."

"I think I know it," she says. "But show me."

He shows her.

Then it is her turn to present him with, or remind him of, an
emergency poem she has been carrying around. She doesn't need
to unfold it from her pocket, because she carries this poem in
her head. From her memory she recites it; it's called "Of a Lost
Town" and goes:

Of a lost town, there's little one can say.
I lived my seasons by their seasoning spell;
I knew my neighbors by their popular names,
A friend of all, and friendlier than they.

I moved among the wicked and the good,
Tried to distinguish them but seldom could.

Are towns created naturally of folks
At variance with themselves? Sure enough.
I never really lacked sufficient proof.
Myself against the self of me provokes
Itself into a Town of One. Or Few.
Or Several, but none of whom is you.

A town is but a tournament of two!
A tilt without lances, a horseless joust,
And arms at passage, arsenals unloosed!
A town is but a passage, passing through.
Death of a town is the end of the fight.
Our arms do not touch passing in perpetual night.

Lost, lost this place, as gone as I myself.
My town, those several of me who fought,
Is emptied now of all but afterthought:
An Itless town is less a man than sylph.
Yet sylphs are less ephemeral than man.
I'll be a sylvan sylphid if I can.

He must recognize the poem, because its author is himself, or the self who died too suddenly several years ago, in Vermont, where he spent most of his life, though he traveled to every little town he could find and wrote books about some of them. He is visibly moved that she knows his poem by heart from her re-readings of the novel it was in, but all he can say is "It sure is sylvan around here."

"And you've turned me into a sylphid," she says. "I'm not sure I like being so young, and I'm starving to death. Let's go see if that waitress has red hair that lights up the wall."

"My car or yours?" he says.

She drives him in Zephyra, who doesn't mind and is glad to get away from Bunker, a short distance, just around a couple of curves, to the Midway Restaurant. Their waitress, sure enough, is a slender young girl of flaming red hair, though it does not quite illuminate the wall, which is covered with multi-antlered deer heads and an elk head. Big game. Waiting for their cheeseburgers to be grilled, she asks him, "Were those deer shot in the woods around here?"

"I'm sure the management hopes that people would think so," he replies. "But, no, it's like the gold mines of Bear City being 'salted' with gold from Colorado: a lure, or bait. The owner and his wife—that's him over there at the desk—bagged those deer and elk on a hunting trip to the wilds of Colorado, had their heads stuffed and mounted, and brought them home." He smiles. "Not that we don't have deer or elk that big in Arkansas . . ."

"Listen," she says. "You know so much about everything, what do you need *me* for?" When he responds, "Pardon, I'm sorry, what did you say," she tries a paraphrase: "You know everything about the gold mines in Bear City, and I'm sure you know everything about Y City. . . ."

"There's hardly anything to know about Y City," he declares.

"Then why are we here?" she wants to know.

"We have to meet *some*where," he says. "And eleven, as you know, is a magic number."

"But if you already know so much about Y City, or all of these cities, why do you need *me?*"

"I can't hear," he reminds her. He points at the man behind the desk, the owner, and says, "When we've finished our lunch, we'll call him over and you can ask him your usual questions, and get his answers on your tape recorder. His name is Bird Vines, and he grew up at—"

"Wait," she says, and demands, "Aren't you just making up his name? What kind of name is 'Bird Vines'? Something a novelist might invent. All the names in all these towns, didn't you just fabricate them, like a novelist?"

He laughs. "Oh, *Kim*," he says. Then he suggests, "Ask *him*."

When they have finished their lunch, and the place is empty of other customers, she asks the red-haired waitress, "Could we speak to the manager?"

"Did I do y'all something wrong?" the waitress asks.

"Oh, no," she says. "We'd just like to chat with the boss."

The waitress speaks to the man, and he comes over. He was born in the neighboring community of Boles a year before Flossie Boren, and looks like a farmer, not a restaurateur. "Now, what could I do for you kids?" he asks.

"Is your name really 'Bird'?" Kim asks him.

"Yeah, it is."

"How did you get that nickname?" she asks.

"No nickname. I was named for the family doctor, Dr. Bird, who brought me into this world."

He pulls up a chair and sits down. She explains to him, "We're researching the history of Y City."

"Honey," he says, "it don't have no history."

"Well, just the people here, then. Where did you get those deer?"

"Colorado," he says.

As far back as Bird Vines can remember, it has always been called Y City. He can remember a time when the junction down there had three or four stores, but "it just all faded away." Considering what the Highway Department has been doing lately, straightening out the Y and the adjoining roads, most people may soon start calling it "Goof-up City," as far as Bird is concerned.

Why do all the pine trees around the Midway have their trunks painted white? We could tell her, but we let Bird do it: "Just for ornamental purposes. Appearance. They give it a kind of eye-catchin appeal. I haven't repainted in a couple of years, 'cause I caint get the right kind of lime to make the whitewash." But everywhere you see a white tree trunk, it indicates a park or recreation area, which the Midway used to be: there used to be a lot of picnic tables out there, which he gave away to churches for their socials, and the Midway Park Swimming Hole, no longer there, Kim has already seen the ruins of. The old tourist cabins remained here for years after they were closed, and people used to keep trying to come back to them, just as customers keep returning again and again to the Mountain Inn. Bird fetches the old ledger used for signing in for a cabin. "I would've let some of 'em keep on comin back even after it was closed, but I was scared to. These old cabins filled up with scorpions and Santa Fe's." Kim wonders what a Santa Fe is, but before she can interrupt to ask, we slip her a note card: "Santa Fe: old-time Ozark pronunciation of 'centipede.'" That year of '55, when the cabins closed, was the same year Bird opened this restaurant. From the first it has been a "hangout" restaurant, popular with regulars as well as travelers on 71, especially during the racetrack season at Oaklawn Park, and also for school buses stopping with their loads of school kids going to track meets and band meets. This used to be a Greyhound bus stop, too. Bird used to have a service station across the road, actually just a gas pump or two. Always pumped it himself, or had an attendant do it. None of this "self-serve" business.

High schools used to come here for their senior trips. The nearer high schools, at Boles, or the county seat, Waldron, used to bring their senior classes in the spring for an all-day senior trip, to use the Midway Swimming Hole and dine at the restaurant, but nowadays the kids charter buses to distant attractions, or even go on airplanes. "That's what killed this part of the country," Bird Vines believes, "bigger and better things."

Bird Vines employs twelve to fourteen people, keeping the restaurant open from 6:00 A.M. to 10:00 P.M. (8:00 P.M. on Sundays) all year round. It gets pretty slow this time of afternoon. "Y'all visit the gift shop before you go," he suggests. Everything in his gift shop is Arkansas-made, or at least American-made: some of it had to come from Missouri.

Before they leave, they do take a tour of the two large rooms, at opposite ends of the dining area, which are filled with long rows of shelves and counters and display stands covered with every conceivable Arkansas product of interest or use to the tourist trade: souvenirs, pottery, jewelry, toys, booklets, candy, crafts, gewgaws, gimcracks, whatnots, and trinkets.

Kim wonders to herself: Have I, at the end of my travels, found the *source* of all the compote in all the rooms I have seen?

She cannot find anything she wants to buy. Nor can her companion, or consort.

"Y'all come back for supper," says Bird Vines.

They will. Pat and John Heinen are building onto the Mountain Inn a little restaurant of their own, but it will not be ready to open for another month or so. Farther north up 71 are *two* more restaurants, Fred's Country Cookin' and The Rivercrest, but Kim will not discover these until she will be leaving town, and time will be changing quickly to the future tense. Ideally, whenever a story reaches the point where its ending seems inevitable it ought to downshift into the future tense, for the future tense never has any end, being always open to whatever *will* or *shall* will or shall allow. The moment at which the shifting is made need not be of great moment; it ought to be the place where there is no turning back to what has gone before, though it is coupled with a strong desire to hang onto the present lest it become faded and gone. In the future tense, lost towns are never entirely lost: they *will* always be there, waiting for someone to find them.

Kim will plan to conduct her next interview with a couple of old (old?) natives whose names will be Granville and Cordie Rogers, but she will insist that her companion, or consort, whose name will become familiarly yclept simply "Don," attempt to conduct the interview himself, just to see if he can do it, just to see, if nothing else, what it has felt like for her to conduct the eighty-odd interviews of this project. This time, she will be silent, operating the tape recorder but asking no questions. Although the one called Don will protest that there is no way he can manage to hear anybody well enough to conduct an interview, Kim will insist, "*Just once.*" She will drive Zephyra back out U.S. 270 a short distance from the Y, where the Rogers house will be sitting right beside the road, and the Rogerses will be sitting as if waiting for her right in front of their house, on the porch, a cluttered and unkempt gallery of old furniture and strange smells. Both Granville, who will look not more than half his seventy-six years, and especially Cordie, who will be ten years older than whatever age her husband is, will be using forms of oral tobacco, smokeless, and will be frequently pausing to spit, Granville off the porch, Cordie into a rusty tin can.

Don will introduce himself and Kim to the Rogerses and will say, "We'd like to ask a few questions about Y City."

"Sorry," Granville will mutter. "We aint buyin nothin today."

"Thank you," Don will say, and will sit down, uninvited, on a chair between the couple. To Mrs. Rogers he will say, "Were you born in the neighborhood?"

"She's deafer'n a post," Mr. Rogers will say. "But she aint buyin nothin today, neither."

"I do believe it might rain before long," Mrs. Rogers will say.

"How far is that from Y City?" Don will ask.

"Are you sellin hearin aids?" Granville Rogers will ask, and will point at Don's ear.

"Yes, since I was twelve years old and had meningitis," Don will say.

"That hearin-aid business is a racket just like everything else," Granville will say. "I fit her up with a hearin aid once, but it didn't do her no good. I give four hundred seventeen dollars for one of them hearin aids. Batteries go dead on ye."

Don will look helplessly at Kim and at her tape recorder, which will be running, getting it all, for whatever it will be worth. "Were you born in Y City?" he will ask Granville.

"Well, close enough. It was—"

"Did anyone ever hope that it would become a real city?" Don will ask.

"Oh, I doubt it," Granville Rogers will say, and then he will begin speaking rapidly, as if trying to finish his sentence before he's interrupted again. "There used to be stores—lots more than now—had a café down there at the fork—once they even had a laundry—and there was this old log store that—"

Don will say, "Well, Mr. Hicks . . ."

"Rogers is the name," Granville will insist.

"What?" Don will say.

"*Rogers*," Granville will say. "You called me Hick. My name is Rogers."

"Oh," Don will say. "I used to know a man named Granville Hicks. I'm just confused."

"You sure are," Granville will say, but Don will not hear him.

"Yes, there's liable to be a real hard rain tonight," Cordie will say.

Back in Zephyra, on the road, Don will become annoyed, even angry. "Why didn't you speak up?" he will demand of Kim. "Why didn't you join in and help me out?"

"They didn't really have much to tell us," she will say. "When you've been doing interviews as long as I have, you can usually tell right away if the person knows very much, or is willing to tell very much. But it could be that there simply isn't much for *any*one to tell about Y City." Kim will have on her tape recorder something else that Don will not have heard: Granville Rogers insisting that there were others who knew more about Y City than he did. What others? She will check the few names on the list Pat Heinen has given her. She will stop Zephyra when they reach the Y and will pull off the highway beside the abandoned service station and will stop. "Don," she will say, "there is a very old woman named Pearl Miner, who is so old that even at half her age she will still look old. What do you know about Pearl Miner?"

"I don't know anything about Pearl Miner," he will say. "I certainly didn't invent her name."

"The Miners are one of the oldest families in Scott County. Pearl Miner is very deaf, deafer than you are, deafer than her best friend, Cordie Rogers. I am told that Pearl and Cordie visit each other every Sunday, and just sit for hours hollering at one another, neither of them hearing anything."

"We could write down some questions for her . . ." Don will suggest.

"She is illiterate."

"Well, doesn't anybody live with her who could communicate with her for us?" he will ask.

"I am told that she lives only with her son, who is feeble-minded."

"Oh," he will say.

"And furthermore," she will say, "their yard is full of vicious dogs." She will let this sink in, adding, "*Biting* dogs." She will summarize: "Ninety-six years old, completely deaf, illiterate, idiot son, mean dogs." In all her travels, Kim has never heard of anything so formidable.

"Well? What are we waiting for?" Don will say. "Let's go!"

She will have to admire his determination. Our last group of illustrations will show the Miner home, like the Rogers home right alongside the busy highway, U.S. 71 south of Y City, but set back from it farther, in the direction of the peaked mountains. Our illustration will manage to capture the dogs—if nothing else could capture them—the lighter one guarding the entrance, standing on the steps like a defiant Cerberus, the darker one chained up in the back yard, in the distance, his head lowered like that of a bull about to charge. The picture will not capture their noise, their raucous barks, their snarling and growling and snapping. A chest-high wire fence will surround the property, preventing the lighter, free-ranging dog from attacking, although he will try his best, leaping at the fence again and again.

"Nice doggie," Don will say soothingly, extending his hand palm up toward the fence. Kim will not get out of her car. Surprisingly, in all her travels around Arkansas, she has encountered no dogs before, or at least no dogs who made themselves as obstreperously discernible as these two will be doing.

"Don't open that gate!" she will call to Don. He will not hear her, but he will have the sense not to enter the yard. Instead, he will "holler the house" in the customary fashion, calling "HELL-O?" loudly several times.

While we will be listening to the ferocious commotion of the dogs and waiting to see if our calling gets any response, this will be as good a place as any to consider the architecture of the house, which is akin to that of multitudes of rural poverty dwellings all over the country. To call it a "hovel" would be insulting, nor is it exactly a "shack," being more commodious than your average mobile home. It may seem old, and is certainly weathered, but its modernity is revealed by certain details: the board sheathing is not the older clapboard style but beveled wide boards, tongue-and-grooved; the windows are actually modified International style with metal casings rather than traditional sash windows; even the low pitch of the roof attests to its contemporaneity. For purposes of comparison and contrast, it is shown at the same angle as the Melson-Bump cabin of Bear City. Each is typical of its time; the earlier house has massive twin chimneys to contain the fireplaces, while the Miner house has but a single metal tubular flue above the woodburning heater. But both have porches, without which no rural home should be. No self-respecting dog should continue to live at a house without a porch.

Don and Kim will confer, the former observing that apparently nobody is at home, the latter pointing out that if the mother is stone deaf and the son is retarded, how could we expect them to come to the door?

"Most people," Kim will remark, "are usually waiting for me, as if they were expecting me to come for the interview."

"Maybe they are waiting for you," Don will suggest. "Only they are waiting inside the house."

But at that moment a pickup truck will come into the driveway and park behind Zephyra; a young (young?) man will get out and say, "Hi! You folks lookin for *me*?"

He could be twenty-six; therefore we have to assume that he will be fifty-two. Unshaven, or perhaps one of those men who *always* look as if they have gone three days without a shave, whether it be three or thirty days in reality, he will be small but very lively, animated and wide awake, in strange contrast to his eyelids, which will seem on the continual verge of slumber. The dogs will stop barking at their first whiff of him and start an expectant thrashing of their tails. He will open the gate.

"Do you live here?" Don will ask.

"If you aint from the Watchtower, I do," he will say, with a big smile of straight, perfect teeth. "If you're from the Watchtower, no, I live down the road somewheres else."

Don will not hear this, but will say, "We were looking for Pearl Miner."

"Maw's always home," he will say, holding the gate open for them. "Come in. But she just don't hear, at all."

Kim will be very reluctant to enter the gate, but Don will whisper to her, "Dogs won't bite you when their master is around."

"Are you sure he's their master?" Kim will whisper back, but Don will not hear that.

They will climb the porch and enter the house, whose deep living room will be crowded with all kinds of chairs and sofas, as if it were a used-furniture store. At one end, Pearl Miner will be sitting in a chair that is more like a nest, surrounded by the things she wants and needs, including a rusty coffee can into which she occasionally will spit tobacco juice. Her teeth will be browned and stained but she will not look her ninety-six years. There will be no sign of the idiot son; perhaps they keep him locked in another room.

But Alvie Miner, born October 5, 1931, is the only son here, and he is no idiot, or even feeble-minded, or anybody's fool, although his appearance and manner may have led some of his neighbors to suspect that he "isn't all there." It will be Alvie who will discourse upon the conversion of the beloved Y into a trite T, using his fingers and hands to illustrate the difference. He will tell Kim and Don that he is convinced it will become officially T City, and he will sound so persuasive that they will wonder if he has private information unknown to the other inhabitants.

Pearl Miner will sit throughout Alvie's explanation as if politely listening to something she has heard before, but it will be clear that she hears nothing. Occasionally she will look at Kim as if expecting a question. The woman will seem to understand the subject of their inquiry: the rise and fall of Y City, or, rather, the simple facts of its existence, for it has neither risen nor fallen. Occasionally she will say something about there once being some stores down at the Y, but her words will not record at all on the tape.

"She's got a real good memory," Alvie will say. "She can remember everything, and she could tell you anything there is to tell, if there was anything to tell. If she could only hear . . ."

Kim will reflect, and will later remark to Don, that Pearl Miner is like a lost town herself. She has shut down, closed up, and lives not so much in the present as in the past. Like lost towns, she is difficult to reach.

Don, whose pocket always contains small blank index cards in case somebody needs to reach him, will scribble in block letters a question that he will hand to Alvie, asking, "Could you somehow ask her this?" The card, which will be preserved, says, "DID YOU EVER HOPE THAT Y CITY WOULD BECOME A CITY?"

Alvie will read it slowly, will look at the reverse side, which is blank, then will read the obverse again. He will shake his head. "She caint read," he will say. "And I couldn't holler it to her so's she could get it. But I doubt if ever she gave that any thought." When the meeting will reach the point where neither Pearl nor Alvie will have anything further of substance to say about Y City, Alvie will show them a photograph, a framed enlargement of an old snapshot of the front of a magnificent "saddlebag" dogtrot log cabin, not unlike the Jacob Wolf house of Norfork, though more recent. "This is where I was born," he will say. He will lead them out to the front porch and point: "It was just this side of that white trailer house you can see over yonder. This old double log house sat right there."

Don will exclaim "A two-story dogtrot!" and will examine the picture carefully. Both floors are porched for their entire length, a real vernacular veranda, though the porches are enclosed with chicken wire—not to keep out the legendary Ozark mosquitoes of giant size, but to keep small children, of whom Alvie is one, from falling off. The logs are not hewn and dovetailed at the corners, merely overlapped with saddle notches, indicating the less permanent, or more impatient, form of construction. Don will insist upon taking a photograph of this pic-

ture. Alvie Miner will laugh uproariously, finding it very funny
that a photograph is being taken of a photograph, but he will
obligingly hold it close to the camera, very still and steady.

Kim will explain, "We are going to do a book." *There*, she
will admit to herself, *I have said it: we* WILL *do a book.*

"That'll be amazin," Alvie Miner will exclaim, opening his
heavy-lidded eyes wide. "It'll be very amazin, ma'am. A book
come out on Y City! That'll be a real seller! Everybody'll buy it!"

"Think so?" Kim will ask.

"Yeah, boy, I'm tellin ye!" Alvie will insist. "It'll be amazin
how they'll all buy that book, and they'll say, 'Boy, I bought me
a book here on Y City. *Y City!*' " He will shake his head at the
wonder of it, and then will apologize: "I wish I could give you
more information than I did, but there's just not much. If you
ever come back this way, maybe I can help you another way. I'll
be glad to help you any way and any time."

"Thank you so much," she will say.

Alvie, who will have figured out that Professor Harrigan
doesn't hear an awful lot better than his mother, will say to Kim
in parting, "And you take care of *him*."

"I will," she will say, and will mean it.

As they are driving back to the motel, Don will remark, "You
know, we should have asked them what those dogs' names are."

There will not be much more to tell. That evening, they will go
once more to the Midway, for supper. What they order, and what
they eat, will not be recorded, or even observed; presumably it
will have been edible, even tasty, at least nourishing. They will
be so absorbed in each other that all they will notice—and it's a
wonder they will notice that—is that the lights will briefly go out
following a loud crack of thunder. Through the big windows of
the Midway, in the early darkness, they will see Cordie Rogers's
prediction come delugingly true.

"Did I leave my car windows down?" Kim will wonder aloud.

"I'll get them," Don will say, and rush outside.

"Wait!" Kim will call after him, too late.

He will be thoroughly drenched in the few leaping steps from the door of the Midway to the door of Zephyra, will jump inside, and will discover that there are no handles to crank to raise the windows; instead there are switches that activate the power windows, but these switches will not function unless the ignition key is turned on. After fumbling with the switches on both doors for some time, he will climb out into the downpour and rush back to the Midway, where Kim will be waiting in the shelter of the doorway, holding out the car keys to him; he will take them and go out into the rain a third time, and, after finding the right key to turn the ignition to activate the window raisers, a fourth time. He will return to their table looking as if he had walked through Mill Creek Falls. His brown-plaid flannel shirt, she will be happy to decide, will have to be replaced, changed out of, very soon. They will skip dessert.

Back at the Mountain Inn, Don will sound sheepish: "I haven't even taken time to check into my room yet."

"You have a *room?*" she will ask.

"Number two," he will say.

"*Reserved?*" she will ask. He will nod. "Well," she will say. She will think. Until this moment, she will not have given any thought to such contingencies. Then she will say, "Later you can check in. Right now, you'd better use my room to change into some dry clothes. You *do* have another shirt, I hope?"

He will have another shirt. Three or four, in fact. She will pick out the best one, more urban than a flannel plaid, more springtimey, too, more in harmony with the pewter hair.

"Do you have a necktie?" she will ask, smiling.

"For what?" he will say.

"You could dress up and go to the desk and say to Pat Heinen, 'Now, where is this Y City?' " He will not get it. She will ask, "Do you know Pat Heinen?"

"Only by mail," he will say.

"You've accomplished a lot by mail," she will observe.

"Mail can make miracles," he will say. "Mail made me meet you."

Has he already told her that in the magic year of 1886, Rodin

made a sculpture . . . Yes, he will already have told her that, but
she will kiss him again, or he her, she isn't sure which. Has he
told her that in the passionate year of 1886 Victor Herbert came
to America? He will be almost sure that she has never even heard
of Victor Herbert, or of "Kiss Me Again," although she will have
heard of "Ah, Sweet Mystery of Life," which he will not be able
to hum for her, but the themes of which will replace the Theme
of the Faraway Hills as background music for the rest of this
enchanted evening.

Of all the endless subjects they will cover in the course of
their marathon conversation this evening, with the sound of the
rain growing and swelling and fading then growing again, only
a small amount will be relevant to the subject of this book. They
will, of course, talk too rapidly and too much, trying to tell each
other their entire life stories, filling in the details they have neglected in their great correspondence. When, sometime in the
stormy night, it will dawn on Kim that she will never be able to
tell her story in one evening, and that, besides, there will be other
evenings, many other evenings, she will give up the attempt.

These are my streets, she will say. *And here are the names I meant
for them to have. Only this one was my boulevard, and it led from here
to there; those several were my avenues, running from there to here. Each
of these blocks was intended to have an alley, for access, for garbage,
and for cats. On this corner would have stood my city hall, across from
my opera house, or symphony. There would be my small park, or plaza,
a pleasance for pigeons and balloons filled with helium. On this row of
benches sit my ancestors, going way back, and talking of times that once
were as if they are happening this afternoon. They will happen this
afternoon, and tomorrow's newspaper, published in this little building
here, will make each of them, however trifling, have dignity and meaning
and historical significance. Oh, and here we would have seen my post
office in all its glory, where letters are never lost, and stamps cost only
11¢ forever and never go up, and the postmistress is the best storyteller
in the city, whenever anyone asks her. Because she will have read the
backs of postcards. Catty-cornered from the post office is my little café,
where people sit to read their mail—the laughingest place in town, because
the mail is always funny. If the contents of a letter, or even a piece of*

junk mail, are particularly amusing, the recipient will say, "Hey, every-
body, get a load of this," and will read it aloud, and everyone will share
in the comedy. The city tour bus will pause at the door of this café, and
the tour guide will attempt to explain the significance of all the laughter
to the curious but solemn passengers. The tour bus also stops here, *at*
my city's monument, and here, at my architectural wonder, and over
there, at my day-care center, and there, at my hospital, and here, beside
my lagoon, where the passengers can step down to feed the fishes and the
swans, and talk to the lovers. The last stop of the tour bus is my Palace
of Best Memories, where each passenger is required to express onto per-
manent tape a narrative of the sweetest episode of his or her life. None
of the passengers will consent to leave town when the tour is finished,
for they will have discovered that none of the residents of the town will
ever leave it, because it is the best place they have ever lived. But if you
must leave, this area you pass through on your way out of town is not
the zoo but my wildlife refuge, which no one is permitted to enter. Beyond
the refuge is the Y.

Will he be hearing all of this? He will raise one hand, first
a fist but then, with the little finger raised and the thumb splayed,
making two horns. "This is a *Y*," he will say. "In sign language
this is the way you make a *Y*." With his other hand he will lift
her hand, close his fingers over hers to make a fist, raise her little
finger, spread her thumb. "That's it: *Y*, which also stands for
'you.' What else does *Y* stand for? It stands for yellow, which was
the prevailing color of Peter Mankins's dreams and of the disappointed dreams of the rushers to Bear City. Yellow became
the color of Sulphur City, and of your hair, now and at the time
you were there. Listen, Kim: there isn't really any sulphur in
Sulphur City, or not enough to amount to much. There are no
Cherokees in Cherokee City, except Kate Scraper, who lives far
out of town. There is no real marble in Marble City, only limestone. No buffalo in Buffalo City, no lake in Lake City, you couldn't
find the mound in Mound City, no 'Arkansas' in Arkansas
City, no garlands in Garland City, no bears in Bear City. But
now . . ." He will hold up the sign language hand of the *Y* again.
"There is the *Y* of 'you' in Y City, and that is all that I"—he will
wiggle the little finger forming half the *Y*—"this is I, or *i*, and

you are all that I have been searching for. Watch." He will lower the little finger, raise his index finger, so that with the splayed thumb it forms the letter *L*: "This is *L*, for 'love.' Raise it in the middle of the *Y* and you have three letters conjoined: *I* and *L* and *Y*: 'I love you.' "

She will form her fingers like so, too.

"Do you know," he will say, almost conspiratorially, as if sharing with her an important secret, "that the Y in the road does not signify the splitting or divergence of a road into two separate paths? No, rather, it means the coming together of two separate paths into a common road. You just have to look at it the other way around."

"I hadn't thought of that," she will say. She will think about it, and then it will be she who will suggest, "Let's come together."

When Flossie Boren will knock to make up the room, they will both be still asleep, and Flossie will go away. Word will have spread quickly through the tiny community that there is a girl at the motel who is trying to discover the life of the place, and that there is a man who appears to be traveling with her and performs magic, such as making everything appear to be only half its actual age, and Flossie will open room number two and discover that it is not occupied, although a green Ambassador is falling apart right outside the door, and she will put two and two together. She will spread this gossip elsewhere along the grapevine, so that when Don and Kim will appear at the Midway yet again, for breakfast, the waitresses and the cook, too, will whisper among themselves. Perhaps all of them will be hoping that the girl and the man will interview them next, but there is only one person remaining in this town, in this book, who will be interviewed.

When the eggs and the bacon will be placed before them, Kim will ask Don, "Well, what comes after *Y*?"

"Pardon?" he, adjusting his hearing aid to the new day, will say.

"What comes after *Y*?" she will repeat.

"Z," he will say. He will smile and elaborate "Z, as in Ze-phyra."

"I meant, where do I go next?"

"And I meant, you go in Zephyra. Wherever you want to go."

"There are no more lost cities?"

"Oh, there are lost cities everywhere. But when we finish Y City, we are done with this book."

"*When* we finish Y City?" she will ask. "Aren't we finished yet?"

"Not quite. You haven't seen the cemetery, and you haven't talked to Susie Rogers."

She will sigh. "If I have to be shown one more photograph of some old lady's grandchildren . . ." She will sigh again. "If I have to stand at one more door spending fifteen minutes just saying good-bye . . ."

"This will be different, I promise," he will promise.

On the way to Susie Rogers (she is a sister-in-law of Granville Rogers), Don and Kim will stop to photograph the only church in Y city, which is not a church any more and is scarcely used, except during elections, once in two or four years, when it becomes a polling place for the community. Pat Heinen had told Kim, "Last time I stood at the pulpit and filled out my ballot, I felt as if I have become a part of the place." The sign in the pediment says: "Y-CITY UNION CHURCH WELCOMES YOU." The white building was donated to the community by a wealthy person whose name no one can recall, and was intended, like the Garland City church, to be nondenominational; there, however, the similarity ends. In style this last church in the book might be compared with the first church in the book, that in Sulphur City: both have the bared rafter ends of the 1930s "Craftsman" style, both have six-over-six windows, and both are of white wood. But the Y City church is true gable-end temple form (although a much later addition spoils the symmetry) and is thus a country cousin of the white churches at Cherokee City and Marble City, without the belfry. Possibly because the unusually large bell needs support stronger than that afforded by a wooden belfry, it is mounted not on the roof but on a sturdy metal frame planted in the churchyard. Its rare ringing can be heard for miles. The air conditioner protruding from the bare front wall recalls the Masonic lodge of Arkansas City and, like that lodge's unit, seems to be a nose on a face, admitting oxygen.

The little-used white building stands "just this side of" (as they express directions hereabouts) Susie Rogers's house, which is on the opposite side of the highway. Otto Rogers, who was one of twin older brothers of Granville, built this modest but "modern" house thirty-four years ago, when almost all of the houses and buildings of Y City were still made of logs, and planted it square in the middle of the broadest "valley," or wide hollow, of the town. Two years ago, Otto Rogers died suddenly of a heart attack, and Susie Rogers, in her own words, "went to pieces"; in the words of her neighbors, she hasn't been the same since.

Don and Kim will find her yard protected by dogs, too, but these are not ill-mannered mongrels like those they encountered at the Miner house; rather, they are a pair of ginger-colored registered Doberman pinschers, who are excellent sentries, performing their duties with the efficient authority of Pinkerton guards. Don and Kim will feel that they are not being set upon by hooligan curs but politely interrogated by uniformed police.

Susie Rogers will come out into her yard, and the police will become silent. Two months later, Kim will play back her tape to verify the facts, and, sure enough, Susie Rogers's year of birth is 1909, but she will not look anything like that. The tape will also verify that she has had twelve children.

"I like to be friendly, but I don't like to be pushed," Susie Rogers will greet them. "You have a free right to your beliefs, but I have a free right to mine, and I don't buy none of that Jehovah's Witness stuff."

"We aren't Jehovah's Witnesses," Kim will insist.

"What are your dogs' names?" Don will ask.

"This one is Gretchen, and this one is Zack," Susie will say.

To Kim, Don will say, "Z is for Zack." This will be on tape. Then, to Susie, he will say, "We aren't selling anything. And you *were* expecting us, weren't you?"

"Please come in," Susie will invite, and, sure enough, the compote clutter of her house will look as if it has been hastily tidied up, if not dusted, in expectation of visitors. "I'm a bachelor woman now," she will say, by way of apology for the unkempt interior: clothes are neatly folded but stacked in piles on a sofa and chairs; there are no lamps, just a naked bulb hanging from the ceiling; a clothes line across the ceiling is hung with overdue bills and letters attached with clothes pins; six goldfish swim in a small bowl, and one small parrot shrieks in its cage. The wall contains three pictures of Jesus in compote attitudes and a reproduction of an unknown picture that is the most thoroughly compote art that either Kim or Don has encountered: in blue and purple pastels, a big eighteen-wheel tractor-trailer is barreling down a wet highway in the night, in the worst storm imaginable, above the imprinted title *Jesus Saviour Pilot Me*.

The only buildings in Y City when Susie McCullar was growing up were the gristmill (which did not grind flour but only cornmeal), a little general store, and the post office, which was not called "Y City" but "Chant," after an early family. Susie attended a little school up on the hill where Midway Park is now, which had an enrollment just large enough "for the boys and girls to play a game of baseball," using a stick for a bat and "a ole wore-out sock for a ball."

Her grandfather Robert Shaddon was a country doctor, or at least he practiced medicine without benefit of medical school, carried a black bag, "rode a horse, and doctored all around," delivering babies, dispensing his own medicine and drugs from an office at the gristmill. Doc Shaddon's first wife was Susie's grandmother, but he married eight more times after her. *Eight?* Yes, and his last wife, taken when he was seventy-five years old, was Susie's best friend and playmate, a girl fourteen years old. "Me and her kept on playin together even after they was married." They fashioned dolls out of "a strip of cloth wrapped around a corncob."

Susie herself married at fourteen, "but we didn't make a go of it." After marrying Otto Rogers when she was nineteen, she settled into a hard life of raising twelve children and trying to make ends meet during the Depression years. "These hills, I tell ye, you don't know how many steps I've took in these mountains and hills, a-scroungin for my family." She scrounged for wild fruit, picking huckleberries, muscadines, and blueberries, which she sold. The fruit had to be canned first, put up in jars; she "set up till midnight cannin, then struck out the next day to pick some more."

Her father, G. B. McCullar ("Now, honey, I caint begin to tell you when or where he was borned"), had predicted Y City would become a *city*. Her father liked to tell how things had been, in contrast to how they would become: *his* father had driven oxen and made a nickel box of matches last a whole year. "They didn't have nothin but wood heat to keep warm and for cookin," Susie will say, with wonder; she has bottled gas to run her space heater. But this is a relatively recent convenience, and her life has been hard. "You see, we didn't live out of a paper sack from a store. If we didn't have it, we didn't have it, and we did without it. But I aint the only one. That's the way everbody was here, back then." Susie's frown will go away, and she will smile. "But it's been a good life. Seems like we were happier back when we didn't have nothin than when we did."

"It's beautiful around here . . ." Kim will say, as if the beauty of the natural setting might have compensated for the harshness of the way of life.

"I went out to California once, to visit," Susie will say, and she will fetch a framed photograph, blow the dust off it, and present it for Kim and Don to admire. It will be the last photograph of grandchildren that Kim will ever be required to look at. But it will be different, as Don had promised: not just somebody's anonymous, sweet-faced adolescents, but a quartet of strikingly handsome young people, the son and three beautiful daughters of Susie Rogers's California son, whom she hardly ever sees any more. Kim will wonder if these beautiful kids have ever visited the Arkansas of their roots. Susie will declare, "There was only one thing I liked about California, and that was the flowers. The rest I hated, the mad rush, the mad rush of the people."

Also, as Don will have promised, the good-byes will be long but different. Of all the people Kim has interviewed, Susie Rogers will strike her as the one most in tune with her natural surroundings, almost a part of the landscape, and the best personification of the community in which she lives. Susie is very lonely, still grieving daily for her dead spouse, and somewhat bewildered that her own body and mind are beginning to fail her.

In the yard, moving slowly toward Zephyra, they will go on talking. Susie will say she wishes she could be of more help, but there just isn't much to tell about Y City. Don will comment on what a beautiful pair of Dobermans she has, and what a nice beginning of a garden. Kim will assure Susie that she has been of more help than anyone else in town.

Susie will smile and say, "I want to believe that years later on you'll still think about me."

Nowhere near the Rogers house, or the white union church, or the junction itself, but north, beyond the Midway, north toward home, is Chant Lane, off 71 to the east, and Chant Cemetery. The name Chant Lane sounds more like what one would find in England, whence all these families came. The place is enchanted. Of all the cemeteries Kim has seen, this one, the last, will seem to her the most beautiful. The hills around it, the morning sunlight, the verdant trees now in springtime's full leaf (as a penultimate gesture of magic, Don will cause every twig of wakefield crud to vanish from the grounds). Kim and Don will spend several minutes wandering among these graves while Zephyra and Bunker wait tail to head beside the highway, pointed north, their ultimate direction. Some of the headstones are primitive home-fashioned markers: slabs of poured cement embedded with brightly colored marbles, children's agates, forming names and legends. One headstone has the deceased's favorite bent briar pipe, without which he was never seen, embedded in the cement. Some of the women's names reflect the originality of hill-folk christening: Arria, Othelana, Icevinda. The family names, too, are unusual:

Tephentaylor, for instance. But here are the graves of those whose living kin we will have met: Rogers, Miner, Shaddon, McCullar.

Otto Rogers's grave is still bare of grass, as if only recently filled in. Kim will wonder how often Susie comes here. (Susie had told her, "I drove a car since I was fourteen, but when Otto died I was afraid to take hold of a steering wheel.") Kim will hear again Susie's parting words, and she will speak them aloud to Don: "I want to believe that years later on you'll still think about me."

And he, as if to prove that he will not have been deaf to everything that Susie said, will repeat to Kim the words Susie spoke that seem to him the best motto for any town that aspires to be a city and doesn't make it, or any person who aspires to greatness and fails: "Seems like we were happier back when we didn't have nothin than when we did."

And then the magician will perform his last act of magic: from all around in this lovely Chant Cemetery will come the voices of every last one of us chanting the refrain of that good old Ozarks funeral hymn:

> Farther along we'll know all about it,
> Farther along we'll understand why;
> Cheer up, my sister, live in the sunshine,
> We'll understand it, all by and by.

Epilogue and Acknowledgments

> *Cities, like men, are embodiments of the past and mirages of unfulfilled dreams.*
> —*Sibyl Moholy-Nagy,* Matrix of Man, *1968*

IN THE DROUGHT YEAR of 1886, when creeks and springs were drying up all over Arkansas, a man dug a well. In a broad valley of the Ouachita Mountains south of Booneville, less than forty miles north of Y City, he was digging a well on his farm when he excavated some stones with yellowish flecks in them. He sent a sample to Little Rock to be assayed. Within days, his meadow held a hotel, several stores, and a post office, called "Golden City." The events and excitement occurring at Bear City happened simultaneously here (and at faraway Five Corners, Vermont, and undoubtedly several other remote spots all over the globe). Sooner than the Bear City boom fizzled out, the Golden City hopes and eager anticipations died abruptly: it was revealed that the man's son had "salted" the stones with gold dust from Colorado. Strangely, the new town was not abandoned; it continued as a small but active community for many years. Although the village was finally deserted in modern times, it still appears on maps as Golden City. Kim and Don will stop by. Not to research the place, not to interview anyone (there is no one to interview), not even to photograph it (except for a faded sign pointing toward it), but just out of curiosity and because it won't really be out of their way, on their journey to where they are going.

They will not stay long. Leaving Zephyra parked in Booneville (the roads to Golden City are all dirt and rough), they will ride in Bunker, whose already defective exhaust system will be submitted to further dents, twists, and snaps. They will find a couple of empty houses, not of architectural interest. There is a defunct brick schoolhouse, not really old. The cemetery is small and unremarkable. "Well," Kim will say. She will reflect that Golden City was worth the detour for the sake of helping her "taper off" from her travels and her search. She will not have to "quit cold turkey" but will be able to remember Golden City as a sort of mildly interesting place, worth a visit but not of more than forty-five minutes' duration.

All of the rest of their lives, which will be spent together, Kim and Don will never pass up a chance to take a look at a lost city. Kim will suggest, "Why don't we put at the end of the book a list of all the places called 'City' in America?" And Don will think that is an excellent idea, and they will do it. Long as the list will be, it will be confined only to the cities of America, and they will come to realize, and to see, that the surface of the earth is covered with towns that wanted to be cities.

Their first objective will be to find a real city, not one called "City," to provide for a while a few advantages: the city's visual pleasures of orderliness (squared blocks, kept lawns, trimmed hedges); the city's conveniences (supermarkets, garbage pickup, newspaper delivery); and the city's advantages (good libraries, bookstores, newsstands). It will also be nice if the city's square has an 1886 building that once held the doctor's office (upstairs) of Don's grandfather, and also the state university that is his alma mater. And a few old friends who will help them settle.

All blurred will be the line between story, which will have no end but only epilogue, and acknowledgment, which will give not simply credit but perpetual thanks to those who will have helped make the book possible.

Kim and Don will be indebted, most of all, in gratefulness and love, to those of whom this record is made, the good Arkansawyers who people these pages, whose names are rendered large in the text. They will need no further mention (but one of them shall have it).

One of the first things Kim and Don will do, after settling temporarily into an old house in the historic district of Fayetteville, will be to apply for assistance from the Arkansas Endowment for the Humanities. Jane Browning, its director, will inform them that they have received a grant, and Sharon Reel, the assistant director, will handle all the phone calls to Kim and letters to Don concerning the application for and administration of not only the grant, but also a subsequent pair of "minigrants."

In order to have applied for the grants, they will need to have a sponsoring organization, and the Ozark Institute, which later will become a lost city itself, will sponsor them, through its director, Edward A. Jeffords, and its assistant director, Barry Weaver.

It will not hurt that both Jeffords and Weaver will be very old friends of Don's, the latter his college roommate. Both will also serve on an advisory committee for the project.

The advisory committee for the purpose of the Arkansas Endowment for the Humanities grant will also consist of several professors at the University of Arkansas: Walter Brown, Ernie Deane, James J. Hudson, Marvin Kay, Cyrus Sutherland, and Elliott West; two professors at the University of Missouri, Rolla, who are old friends and advocates of Don's: Michael Patrick and Larry Vonalt; and three Fayetteville friends: Ellen Shipley of Special Collections at the university library, Peter Tooker, and Robert Besom, director of the Shiloh Museum of Springdale, which will become the project's sponsoring organization when the Ozark Institute follows Edd Jeffords into limbo (or Waco). Tom Dillard, director of the Department of Arkansas Natural and Cultural Heritage, will also agree to serve on the advisory committee.

Anne Courtemanche-Ellis of Newton County will greatly encourage the project in its inception and early stages.

Those at the University of Arkansas library who will also help in the research will include John Harrison, the director, and

Larry Perry, Steve Chism, and Debby Cochran; Michael Dabri-
shus, director of Special Collections, and his staff, especially Ethel
Simpson and the afore-mentioned Ellen Shipley, who will assist
Don and Kim in many ways other than mere research.

Bryan Gammill, their landlord and friend during those months
in the historic district, will lend Don his Canon AE-1 camera,
with which most of the photographs in this book will be taken.
They will be developed and printed at Fayetteville's The Camera
Shop by Thomas E. Tiller and David Schick.

In October, on a gorgeous Saturday, the Messrs. Gammill,
Weaver, Besom, Tooker, and a few others on the above list will
look odd, attired in their conceptions of the dress of the old-time
Ozarker, attending a special Ozark wedding, officiated by Justice
of the Peace Steve Anderson, an old friend, and featuring a
backyard pig roast, or *cochon de lait*, whose chef will be the father
of the bride, Micky Gunn, assisted by his wife, Jacque. Speakers
at the nuptials of Don and Kim will include the afore-mentioned
Professor Mike Patrick, Professor Mike Luster representing the
deceased Vance Randolph, and Professor Donna Darden of the
University's sociology department, who will also, throughout
the length of this project, provide many other kindnesses too
numerous to catalogue.

People who do not read acknowledgments will miss the real
climax of this story, buried in the above paragraph.

Once the tedious transcription of all her interviews is accomplished, Kim will be able to resume the correspondence she has
carried on since childhood with her pen pal, Jane Bowers of
Wisconsin, whose long letters will contain countless observations
of interest to this story of lost cities. From faraway New Zealand will come a wedding gift from an old pen pal of Don's,
Martin Lawrence, who will send David McGill's *Ghost Towns of
New Zealand* (1983, Reed), a down-under counterpart of this
volume.

Other people outside of Arkansas will hear about and encourage this project: Don's former editor, Llewellyn Howland
III; his friends John Irving, Doug Wood, and Linda Hughes, a
third member of the "Rolla triumvirate." Martin Moreman of

Kentucky will send a crucial newspaper clipping from a Lexington paper about a professor finding lost towns in that state.

In Arkansas, Don and Kim will have contact by mail or in person with individuals who will help with the particular cities. *Sulphur City:* Geneva Price Brashears, Harold and Charles Cate, Alan Clack, Hildy Crawford, Mrs. Louallen Fine, Ouida Harkreader, Lloyd McConnell, Dave McKee, Austin and Carrie Reed, and Marie Wofford. *Cherokee City:* Fannie and Lloyd Baxley, Kathryn Clausen, Janiece Elder, Maurice Loux, E. Alan Long, Mickel McClish, Dott B. Rumsey, Maggie Smith, and Mr. and Mrs. George Wolfe. *Marble City:* Mrs. Thomas J. Bardin, J. E. Dunlap, Jr., Tollie Ervin, Joy M. Geisler, Mrs. H. K. McCaleb, V. N. "Bud" Phillips, Gene Raney, Irby E. Russell, Mrs. Frank P. Russell, and James Villines. *Buffalo City:* Phyllis Hanson, Alyce Marbury, Alice and Joe Misic, Margaret Ross, and Lyle Wood, as well as the "Mountain Home triumvirate" of Sue Brown, Sonny Garrett, and Rick Rankin. *Cave City:* Debra Allen, Anna Lee Carreiro, W. K. McNeil, Mr. and Mrs. Charles Matlock, Caruth S. Moore, Craig Ogilvie, Eugene Street, and Sherry Watson. *Lake City:* strangely, no one other than Hershel L. "Plug" Eaton, who will have given such a long interview and who will write several letters to Don and Kim. *Mound City:* Maridine Sievers, of Memphis. *Arkansas City:* Marjorie Buckley, Edgar Gannaway, Etta Montgomery, Connie Nations, and Michael Rice. *Garland City:* Linda Callahan and Mary Medearis. *Bear City:* Margaret Arnold, Inez E. Cline, Bill Curle, and Bob Lancaster.

Among the Arkansas lost cities that Don and Kim will not be able to include, and the people who will have been waiting to help, will be: Bluff City, Jerry McKelvy; Carbon City, Otto Schmalz; Central City, Vernon H. Carter, Sr.; Dodd City, Pam McIntyre and R. D. Owen; Forrest City, Ree Routon; Gin City, Wade Cryer, Elliott Gildon, and F. J. Schweitzer III; Golden City, Patricia Curry and Vernia Lovett; Hackett City, Dr. Robert R. Harriage, Mrs. I. J. Robinson, and Mrs. Bill Terrell; and Kress City, Frances Chamberlain McJunkins. Nancy L. Arn of the El Dorado library and Mrs. Sam B. Allen of the Fort Smith Historical Society will also help.

Helen Wolff, a genius at topiary in the garden of words, will become the editor for this work.

Finally but rather primarily, the Author, who will have to exclude from responsibility for the opinions expressed herein his colleague, collaborator, and wife, will want most fervently to dedicate the entire project:

To Kim

Appendix: The Cities, Found and Lost, of America

(Larger cities are in boldface type. An asterisk identifies places currently without population.)

ALABAMA

Alabama City
Alexander City
*Bluff City
Bull City
Central City
Choctaw City
Clay City
Coal City
Cobb City
Columbus City
Daisey City
Eady City
Falls City
Flint City
Ford City
Frisco City
Garden City
Gate City

Glen City
Hobson City
Hooper City
Industrial City
Iron City
Liberty City
Mason City
Midland City
Morgan City
Muck City
Nitrate City
Park City
Pell City
Phenix City
Pinkney City
Plant City
Pratt City
Rainbow City
Reece City
Rock City (2)

Rossland City
Sardis City
Scant City
Scott City
Tarrant City
Vulcan City
White City (2)
Zion City
Zip City

ALASKA

*Copper City
*Dall City
*Golden City
*King City
*Railroad City
Tin City

ARIZONA

Arizona City
Black Canyon City
*Bradshaw City
Bullhead City
Circle City
Colorado City
Huachuca City
Joseph City
Lake Havasu City
*Meteor City
Midland City
Sun City
Tuba City

ARKANSAS

Arkansas City
Bear City
*Bell City
Bluff City
Bragg City
Buffalo City
*Capps City
Carbon City
Cave City
Central City
Cherokee City
College City
*Crain City
Diamond City
*Dodd City
*Dodge City
*Dumas City
Forrest City

Garland City
Gin City
*Golden City
*Joyce City
Junction City
*Kress City
Lake City
Marble City
*Mound City
*Pace City
Pike City
Pine City
Process City
Rose City
Star City
Stark City
Sulphur City
Webb City
Y City

CALIFORNIA

Amador City
Barber City
Big Bear City
*Brandy City
Butte City
*Butte City (ruins)
Cactus City
California City
Canyon City
*Canyon City (site)
*Carmen City
Castro City
Cathedral City
*Cave City

Century City
*Chloride City
College City
*Copper City
Crescent City
Culver City
Daly City
Date City
Douglas City
Ford City
*Garden City
Grover City
Hamilton City
Harbor City
Highway City
Holy City
*Iowa City
Junction City
Kern City
Kettleman City
King City
Lake City
*Lake City (2)
*Lost City
Marin City
Midway City
Mill City
*Mokelumne City
*Montgomery City
Motor City
National City
Nevada City
*Oil City
*Oregon City
Palm City
Panorama City
*Pine City

Plaster City
*Prairie City
Project City
*Queen City
Raisin City
Redwood City
*Rock City
Russell City
*San Joaquin City
*Shake City
Sierra City
Silver City
Spicer City
*Star City
Stirling City
Studio City
Suisun City
Summit City
*Summit City
Sun City
Tahoe City
*Telegraph City
Temple City
Tyee City
Union City (2)
*Universal City
University City
Verdugo City
*White Mountain
  City
*White Rock City
Yuba City

COLORADO

*American City
*Apache City

Canon City
*Capitol City
Central City
Colorado City
Commerce City
Garden City
*Garland City
*Holy Cross City
*Iron City
*Kerper City
Lake City
*Lulu City
Orchard City
*Park City
Plateau City
Spar City
*Spook City
Stone City
Sugar City
*Sunset City
*White River City

CONNECTICUT

*Gay City
Jewett City
Little City
*Lower City
*Mansfield City
Union City

DELAWARE

Delaware City
Spruance City

DISTRICT OF COLUMBIA

Ivy City

FLORIDA

Aladdin City
*Amelia City
*Bay City
Bean City
Cameron City
Carol City
*Central City
Cooper City
Crescent City
Cross City
Dade City
*Deem City
De Soto City
Everglades City
Floral City
Florida City
*Forest City
*Frog City
*Galt City
Garden City
*Garden City
Greenacres City
Grove City
Gulf City
Haines City
*Hall City
*Harbeson City
Highland City
Indian River City

Intercession City
Kerr City
Lake City
Leisure City
Lemon City
Little Lake City
*Miles City
Mission City
Mullis City
Myakka City
Ocean City
Orange City
Palm City
Panama City
Plant City
Polk City
St. James City
*Steele City
Sun City
*Thomas City
White City
*White City
Ybor City

GEORGIA

Anderson City
Bibb City
Chatham City
*Cole City
Garden City
Harris City
Hill City
Iron City
Junction City
Lake City

Liberty City
Lumber City
Mountain City
Park City
Peachtree City
*Pebble City
Pecan City
Ray City
Sale City
Silver City
*Tate City
Turner City
Twin City
Union City
*White City (2)

HAWAII

*Hauola City
Lanai City
Makakilo City
Pearl City

IDAHO

*Artesian City
Atomic City
Butte City
*Caribou City
Elk City
Falls City
Garden City
Hill City
Idaho City
*Keenan City

Magic City
Malad City
*Moose City
*Ruby City
*Sawtooth City
Silver City
Sugar City
*Thunder City

ILLINOIS

Bay City
Bayle City
Beeecher City
Belle Prairie City
Bluff City
*Bluff City
Calumet City
Central City (2)
*Clarke City
Clay City
Coal City
*Cora City
Crescent City
Dallas City
Dalton City
Deering City
*Degoigne City
Diamond City
*Droit City
*Emerson City
Fairmont City
Farmer City
Forest City
Future City
Gibson City

Granite City
Grove City
Hanna City
Hervey City
Hunt City
Illinois City
*Jefferson City (2)
Johnston City
Junction City
Lake City
Leisure City
*Logan City
Mason City
*Mid City
Midland City
Miller City
Monroe City
Mound City
National City
*New City
Norris City
Park City
*Parker City
Pearl City
*Pickle City
Piper City
*Poplar City
Prairie City
Rapids City
Rend City
Rock City
*Schram City
*Scott City
Shale City
Standard City
*Star City
Steel City

Texas City
*Valley City
Wayne City
West City (2)
White City (2)
Yates City

INDIANA

Baugh City
Beaver City
Boundary City
Burns City
Cambridge City
Clay City (2)
Coal City
Columbia City
Forest City
Fountain City
Garden City
Gas City
Gimco City
Grant City
*Harris City
Hartford City
*Island City
Jay City
Lincoln City
Michigan City
Mineral City
Miner City
Monroe City
Oakland City
Parker City
Prairie City
Richland City

Rome City
Saline City
Scott City
Star City
Switz City
Tell City
Valley City

IOWA

Albert City
Barnes City
Cedar City
Central City
Charles City
Columbus City
Dakota City
Davis City
Decatur City
Dow City
*Eagle City
Forest City
Garden City
Gilmore City
Grant City
Iowa City
La Porte City
Lake City
*Lime City
Mason City
May City
Orange City
*Pacific City
Polk City
Prairie City
Promise City

Rockwell City
Sac City
Sea City
Shannon City
Silver City
Sioux City
Stone City
Story City
*Walnut City
Webster City

KANSAS

Arkansas City
Bain City
Baldwin City
Bird City
Bluff City
Bush City
Cawker City
Dodge City
Elk City
*Forest City
Garden City
Hill City
Junction City
Kansas City
Lake City
*Maple City
Mound City
Ness City
Osage City
Page City
Park City
Scott City
Strong City

Sun City
White City

KENTUCKY

Allen City
*Anderson City
Bell City
*Bell City
Birk City
Bluff City
Calvert City
Cave City
Central City
*Cimota City
Clay City
Cumberland City
Elkhorn City
Future City
*Gold City
Grange City
*Island City
*Jewel City
Junction City
*Lake City
Lee City
*Lost City
Lynn City
*Mining City
*Oil City
Park City
Shelby City
*Silver City
Sublimity City
Tri City
Union City

*Union City
West Future City
*White City (2)
Whitley City

LOUISIANA

Alluvial City
Bell City
Bossier City
Bridge City
Garden City
Intracoastal City
Junction City
McClane City
Morgan City
Oil City
Ouachita City
Weber City
Zion City

MAINE

*Forest City
Lake City
*New City
*Old City
Slab City
*Slab City (2)
*Sprague City

MARYLAND

Chesapeake City
Cottage City

Ellicott City
Maryland City
North Ocean City
Ocean City
Pocomoke City
Saint Marys City
West Ocean City

MASSACHUSETTS

Attleborough
   City
Charlton City
Ludlow City
Montague City
Old City
White City

MICHIGAN

Barton City
Bay City
Beal City
Boyne City
Brown City
Carson City
Cass City
Cement City
Copper City
Filer City
Foster City
Garden City
Gibbs City
Gould City
Grind Stone City

Howard City
Huron City
Imlay City
Kent City
Lake City
Mackinaw City
Maple City
Marine City
Mass City
Minden City
National City
Nessen City
Oil City
Pearll City
Rapid City
Reed City
Rogers City
Rose City
Sherman City
Silver City
*Star City
Summit City
Tawas City
*Tent City
Traverse City
Union City
White City
*White City

MINNESOTA

Alma City
Big Bend City
Cannon City
Center City
Chippewa City

Chisago City
Clara City
Forest City
Garden City
Grove City
Hill City
Holmes City
*Ilgen City
Lake City
Minnesota City
Murphy City
Pine City
Rose City
Rush City

MISSISSIPPI

Calhoun City
Delta City
Garden City
*Junction City
Lake City (2)
Michigan City
Minter City
Mississippi City
Morgan City
Mound City (2)
Oil City
Silver City
Yazoo City

MISSOURI

Appleton City
Avenue City

Bates City
Bell City
Benton City
Boulder City
Bragg City
Cedar City
*Cement City
Central City
*Champion City
Circle City
Clark City
Clifton City
Crystal City
*Farmers City
Flamm City
Ford City
Forest City
Garden City
Gilman City
Golden City
Grant City
Green City
Gunn City
Hayward City
*Hedge City
*Hill City
*Island City
Jefferson City
Johnson City
Kansas City
King City
Kingdom City
Knox City
Kohl City
Lake City
Lowry City
*Main City

Martin City
Mineral City
Missouri City
Monroe City
Montgomery City
Mound City
Neck City
North Kansas City
*Oil City
Osage City
*Page City
Phelps City
Pierce City
Pine City
Platte City
Prairie City
Queen City
Quick City
Saline City
Schell City
Scott City
South West City
Spring City
Star City
Stark City
Stotts City
*Sue City
Summit City
Tiff City
Union City
University City
Valley City
Virgil City
Webb City
White City
*White City

Wilson City
Wright City

MONTANA

*Blackfoot City
*Cabin City
Cooke City
*Copper City
*Diamond City
Gallup City
Jefferson City
Martin City
*Montana City
Miles City
Park City
*Park City
*Reynolds City
*Silver City
Virginia City
*Wall City
*White City
*Whites City

NEBRASKA

Beaver City
Central City
Dakota City
David City
Elk City
Falls City
Loup City
Mason City
Nebraska City

*Nim City
Pawnee City
Republican City
Rising City
South Sioux City
Steele City

NEVADA

Boulder City
Carson City
*Humboldt City
Lane City
*Metallic City
Mill City
Mountain City
New Washoe City
Silver City
*Spring City
Virginia City
Washoe City

NEW
HAMPSHIRE

Cornish City
Quaker City
Slab City
*Squag City

NEW JERSEY

Atlantic City
Centre City

Corbin City
Egg Harbor City
Garden City
*Gigantic City
Gloucester City
Holiday City
Jersey City
Margate City
McKee City
Neptune City
Ocean City
Roosevelt City
Sea Isle City
Surf City
Union City
Ventnor City
West Atlantic City

NEW MEXICO

Air Base City
Cotton City
*Estes City
Hillburn City
Humble City
Jones City
*Las Vegas City
*Navajo City
Oil City
*Sacramento City
Silver City
*Virginia City
*Weber City
Whites City

NEW YORK

Air City
Border City
Button City
Cottage City
*Forest City
Garden City
Grant City
Groton City
Johnson City
*Little Rock City
Long Island City
Model City
New City
New York City
Old City
Perry City
Pine City
Rock City (2)
*Rock City
Rock Falls City
Slab City (3)
White City

NORTH
CAROLINA

*Bay City
Bessemer City
Bryson City
Buffalo City
Cove City
Elizabeth City
Elm City
Forest City

Fort Raleigh City
James City
Morehead City
Oak City
Rebel City
*Ruby City
Siler City
Silver City
*Soul City
Surf City
Tabor City
*Thermal City
Tin City

NORTH
DAKOTA

Grace City
North Valley City
Pick City
Tower City
Valley City
Watford City
Willow City

OHIO

Beach City
Burton City
Cream City
Crown City
Dexter City
Eagle City
Garden City
Grove City

Jerry City
Jones City
Junction City
Lime City
Limestone City
Lore City
*Marl City
Miller City
Mineral City
Murray City
Ohio City
Plain City
Pleasant City
Quaker City
Tipp City
Tremont City
Union City
Valley City

OKLAHOMA

*Beer City
Boise City
*Burke City
Cox City
Custer City
Del City
Dill City
*Douglas City
Eagle City
Elk City
Elmore City
*Empire City
Garden City
*Gas City
Harden City

*Indian City
Kaw City
Little City
*Lost City
Marble City
Midwest City
*Oil City (2)
Oklahoma City
Ponca City
Pruitt City
Ratliff City
*Reno City
Silver City
Spelter City
Strong City
Union City
Webb City
Wright City

OREGON

Bay City
Cabell City
Canyon City
Columbia City
Cutler City
Elk City
Falls City
Island City
Junction City
*Kansas City
Lincoln City
*Malheur City
Mill City
*Opal City
Oregon City

Pacific City
Pelican City
*Pine City
Power City
Prairie City
Shale City
*Silver Falls City
Tri City
*Vanport City
White City
Willamette City

PENNSYLVANIA

Arnold City
Blain City
Broad Top City
Cambria City
Central City (2)
Cherry City
Coal City
Custer City
Dallas City
Derrick City
Dickson City
Duff City
Elk City
Evans City
Fairmont City
Fayette City
Ford City (2)
Forest City
Garden City (2)
Glade City
Glass City
Gowen City

Grant City
Greece City
Grier City
Grove City
Harrison City
*Hill City
Homer City
Horton City
Houston City
*Iron City
James City
Jamison City
Karns City
Lake City (2)
Lumber City (2)
Mahanoy City
Marble City
Mill City
Oil City (2)
Pine City
*Pithole City
Quaker City
Queen City
Russell City
Sawyer City
Spindley City
Spring City
Steel City
Tower City
Trade City
Turkey City
Union City
*Wallace City
Weber City
West Ford City
Westmoreland
    City

Wick City
Windy City

RHODE ISLAND

Garden City
*Rice City

SOUTH CAROLINA

Garden City
Johnson City
Lake City

SOUTH DAKOTA

Big Stone City
*Canyon City
Central City
Claire City
*Crook City
Garden City
Hill City
*Hub City
*Junction City
Lake City
Mound City
North Sioux City
Prairie City
Rapid City
Silver City
Trail City

TENNESSEE

Ashland City
*Beechnut City
Block City
Bluff City
Cumberland City
Fountain City
Goat City
Iron City
Jefferson City
Johnson City
*Kansas City
Lake City
Lenoir City
Lupton City
Marble City
Maury City
Middle City
Morrison City
Mountain City
North Johnson
  City
Oak City
*Obey City
Owl City
*Owl City
Park City
Pearl City
Proctor City
Rayon City
Richard City
Rock City (2)
*Sal City
*Silver City
Spring City
Summer City

Tennessee City
Tracy City
Union City
Webber City
White City
Windy City

TEXAS

*Abell City
Airport City
*Angel City
Archer City
*Arkansas City
Arthur City
Bay City
*Beach City
Bowers City
Bridge City
*Burns City
*Cain City
*Caney City
Canyon City
Center City
*Chavez City
*Citrus City
Clarksville City
Close City
*Coffee City (2)
Colorado City
Coy City
Crystal City
*Custer City
Dell City
Denver City
Dodd City

Electric City
Falls City
*Foard City
*Frankel City
Garden City
*Glaze City
Gun Barrel City
Haltom City
*Hay City
*Hill City
Horizon City
*Hynds City
Jacinto City
Johnson City
Karnes City
Knox City
Lackland City
Lane City
League City
Liberty City
*Lime City
Magic City
Mirando City
Missouri City
Monroe City
*Mound City
*Mountain City
*Nelson City
*Oil City
Ore City
*Pearl City
*Pope City
*Provident City
Queen City
Rio Grande City
*Rose City
Royse City

Scharbauer City
*Schwab City
*Silver City (4)
*Sinclair City
Sterling City
*Stone City
Sullivan City
*Tee Pee City
Texas City
*Todd City
Twin City
Universal City
Victory City
Warren City
*White City (2)
*Willow City
Wolfe City
Wright City

UTAH

Bear River City
Brigham City
Cedar City
*Christmas City
East Carbon City
Garden City
Heber City
*Mound City
Oak City
Park City
Plain City
Salt Lake City
Sandy City
*Shenendoah City
*Silver City

Spring City
*Valley City

VERMONT

Goose City
Old City

VIRGINIA

Bluff City
Chase City
Dale City
*Franklin City
Garden City (2)
Gate City
*Pike City
Royal City
Spring City
Stephens City
*Virginia City
Viscose City
Weber City (2)

WASHINGTON

Basin City
Bay City
Benton City
*Clay City
*Copper City
Coulee City
*Diamond City
Electric City

Elmer City
Fall City (2)
*Fall City
Garden City
*Gould City
Grays Harbor City
Junction City
Lake City (2)
*Mineral City
Mock City
Moxee City
*Oil City
Navy Yard City
North City
Ocean City
Pine City
*Pinkney City
Royal City
*Skagit City
Wiley City

WEST VIRGINIA

Blackberry City
Coal City
*Crown City
Cub City
Dupont City
Elk City
Hartford City
Kanawha City
Lost City
Mineral City
Paden City
Raymond City
Star City

Sulphur City
Union City
Wyoming City

WISCONSIN

Bay City
Bloom City
Buffalo City
Coral City
Cuba City
Falls City

Fountain City
Genoa City
Glenwood City
Hager City
Hub City
Jersey City
Junction City
Oil City
Plum City
Sauk City
Slab City
Sweetheart City
Tunnel City
*White City

WYOMING

Atlantic City
*Bald Mountain
   City
*Clay City
 Jeffrey City
*Lee City
*Oil City
 South Pass City

BOOKS BY DONALD HARINGTON
AVAILABLE FROM HARCOURT BRACE & COMPANY
IN HARVEST PAPERBACK EDITIONS

The Architecture of the Arkansas Ozarks:
A Novel

The Cherry Pit

The Choiring of the Trees

Let Us Build Us a City

Lightning Bug

Some Other Place. The Right Place.